OCTAVIA, DAUGHTER OF GOD

BY THE SAME AUTHOR

Miracles in Enlightenment England

OCTAVIA, DAUGHTER OF GOD

The Story of a Female Messiah and her Followers

Jane Shaw

for Celeste

with every good wish.

[signature]

September 25th 2011.

Yale

UNIVERSITY
PRESS

New Haven and London

First published in the United States in 2011 by Yale University Press.
First published in Great Britain in 2011 by Jonathan Cape.

Yale University Press books may be purchased in quantity for educational, business,
or promotional use. For information, please e-mail sales.press@yale.edu (U.S. office)
or sales@yaleup.co.uk (U.K. office).

Printed in the United States of America

Library of Congress Control Number: 2011929586
ISBN 978-0-300-17615-5 (hardcover: alk. paper)

A catalogue record for this book is available from the British Library.

This paper meets the requirements of ANSI/NISO Z39.48-1992 (Permanence of Paper).

10 9 8 7 6 5 4 3 2 1

For Sarah Ogilvie

Contents

Preface

I first visited the Panacea Society in 2001, in the shadow of the millennium. It was drizzling with rain as I drove down the street of respectable, middle-class late-Victorian villas, to the Panacea headquarters at number 14 Albany Road, Bedford, a market town in the centre of England. I parked and rang the doorbell with a keen sense of anticipation, but what I found inside exceeded all my expectations and would – it turned out – absorb much of my life for the rest of the decade.

The Panacea Society had been founded in 1919 by Mabel Barltrop, a vicar's widow, renamed Octavia by her followers who believed her to be the daughter of God, a messiah who could lead them to immortal life on this earth. At its height in the 1920s and '30s, the Society had seventy resident members who lived in those very same Victorian villas – the community houses – that I had just driven past. They worshipped, ate, lived and worked together in joyful expectation of the Lord's coming and their never dying. They also had hundreds of corresponding members around Britain and in many other parts of the world: the USA, Canada, France, Australia and New Zealand. Their healing ministry, begun in 1923, had in the last eighty years reached out to over 130,000 people around the world. I had read about the Society in the papers because they had held an auction of their treasures that summer. I hadn't been able to attend the auction but, as both an historian and an Anglican priest, my fascination with the Society lingered. Such millenarian communities were rare in the twentieth century, and more commonly associated with America rather than England. I wrote to them, and received a charming reply inviting me to visit.

I was greeted by two of the last surviving members. Mrs Ruth Klein, the Chairwoman of the Society, an upright and well-dressed woman with pearls and neatly waved grey hair, probably in her late sixties, welcomed me. As I stepped into the hallway, I saw three pictures on the wall that gave me a hint of the affiliations and interests of this group. There was Mabel Barltrop, the community leader and messiah figure, in sepia tones: a dignified woman in profile, with beads and fur around her neck and tortoiseshell combs in her swept-up hair. Alongside her was a posed photograph of the present Queen of England and Prince Philip, from 1977, marking the Queen's silver jubilee. And finally, William Blake's extraordinary painting of the twenty-four elders worshipping God in the Book of Revelation, the final book of the Bible that promises the Apocalypse and the Second Coming of Christ. It was a heady mix. Mrs Klein gave me tea in a bone-china cup and delicate biscuits on a plate as she and another elderly member, John Coghill, quizzed me on my beliefs and asked me whether I believed in the Second Coming. Both he and Mrs Klein were adjusting to the fact that the millennium had passed without the return of both Jesus and their own messiah, Octavia. But this was a community that lived by signs and sought evidence of the end times, and they looked optimistically to the future.

As I looked round, it felt as if I had stepped into a time capsule. The headquarters were modernised, but they were crammed full of Edwardian and Arts and Crafts furniture. The Society's books were everywhere. As I looked at the recent auction catalogues, I realised that I had just missed seeing a period piece intact. In two other huge houses owned by the Society, just behind the headquarters where we were meeting, the furniture, china, silver, jewellery and clothing had been undisturbed for decades. They had left everything untouched as members died, believing that those members would need their possessions when they returned at the Second Coming of Christ and Octavia. Why had they sold them at all? The Charity Commissioners (with clearly not an historian among them) had told them that, as a charity, they must 'liqui-date' their wealth so that it could be used for charitable purposes.

Mrs Klein and Mr Coghill sent me on my way with some of the Society's published books as well as their home-grown organic vegeta-bles and fruit. I did not know then that they believed their garden was the original Garden of Eden and the apples I was eating might have some very particular significance. Back home, I read their several-volume history by one of the members, Rachel Fox. I learned about their origins in the Great War; their building of the community – the

New Jerusalem in England – and their understanding of God as feminine as well as masculine. I read about the women who did everything in the Society, from public speaking to translating Octavia's writings into multiple languages to presiding at the Eucharist, and most especially about the earliest members, Octavia's apostles, who were suffragettes and vicars' wives and sisters and daughters, Victorian gentlewomen of decidedly middle-class background. I even had a dream in which Rachel Fox delivered a female baby to my doorstep in Oxford and entrusted me with its care. These women of the 1920s and '30s had entered my psyche definitively and I knew I wanted to write about them.

I went back to visit twice more that autumn. They let me stroll through their gardens and pick my own apples from their trees, and dig up rhubarb from their allotment. In due course they took me into other buildings. There were the two great houses empty now of their furniture and goods; the beautiful Arts and Crafts chapel; the printing press with its great store of books – thousands of volumes which, Mr Coghill told me, would be 'called for' one day; and, at last, Octavia's house. There, Octavia's bed was left just the way it was the day she died, with the calendar set to 15 October 1934 – she died on the morning of the 16th. There, I saw her furniture, her pictures and photographs, her china, her books, the mementoes of her life, all preserved and regularly dusted.

In January 2002, on my third visit, I plucked up the courage to ask Ruth Klein and John Coghill if I could write their story. I didn't know what their reaction would be. They smiled and Mr Coghill said, 'We've been waiting for someone to do that. We think you've been sent by God.' They took me out to lunch to celebrate and, over a plate of poached salmon, Mr Coghill marvelled at how God had spoken directly to Octavia for eighteen years. Later I realised that just as I had been wooing them, in the hope that they would let me research their unusual story, so they had been wooing me – to tell their story for them.

At that point, all I had seen were the Society's published books: Octavia's published prophecies which were known as the Scripts, some of their pamphlets, copies of *The Panacea* magazine, and Rachel Fox's volumes on the Society. But I soon walked into another world. I was taken into other rooms on every floor of the headquarters. In every chest of drawers, bookcase, trunk and wardrobe there were letters, diaries, papers, meeting minutes, records of rituals and liturgies, written confessions and photographs. It was all uncatalogued. Here was a perfect archive, such as most historians never experience or see in their lives. It was an historian's dream. One Oxford colleague called it my own Dead Sea Scrolls.

The archival record of their activities and beliefs is phenomenal: they threw out nothing. They wrote endlessly to each other, about theology and much more. They documented their activities in home movies and hundreds of photographs. They wrote their candid confessions – and didn't always burn them. They kept their accounts impeccably. They ran an international healing ministry and documented with precision the ailments and cures of the tens of thousands who participated in it. Octavia kept every scribble she ever wrote, and many of the followers kept detailed diaries. All of this remains in Albany Road, a remarkable treasure trove of material from which to write the full story of this unusual community whose mostly female members came to believe in 1919 that a fifty-three-year-old vicar's widow was the daughter of God. With the help of the administrator of the Society and my research assistants, the archive was gradually catalogued. It was the first time that anyone outside the Society had ever had access to it. We never knew what we might find as we opened brown envelopes, untied the string on brown paper parcels or looked inside ordinary-looking exercise books.

As I read their diaries and letters I had an eerie, almost uncanny, sense of the responsibility of my task. Octavia had written to one of her followers in 1919, urging her to address her more formally in letters as 'Dear Mrs Barltrop' despite their affection for each other because 'You see, we may write letters which will one day be used.'[1] Octavia always had an eye to posterity, explaining at a staff meeting one day in 1931, 'how necessary it was, in public work, to have Histories of everything' in case 'anyone came to look into the affairs of the Society.'[2] I realised that I was that person. But I also learned that Octavia could not bear to throw anything out; she was afraid of parting with letters, of letting books go out of the house, as her followers commented. This accounted for the extraordinary wealth of sources, but it also gave me a problem. What was I to *do* with all this material? And how would I write about it? Was I primarily writing a biography of Octavia herself? I rejected that because the point of Mabel Barltrop's life as Octavia was the community she built. How then was I to write about the community? And how would Octavia, the charismatic and autocratic leader, fit into that? Her life was the most important of them all, but it could not dominate the book. The resources were so rich that I wanted to convey a sense of who the members were and what documentation they left about themselves, and thus give a glimpse into various facets of life in the interwar years in Britain and its Empire, as illustrated in the diaries and letters in the archive. But this opened up the possibility of writing about tens or even hundreds of people.

As I read more and more, I began to allow the forms and rhythms of the community's life to drive the narrative. I found myself writing a life or biography of the community itself, not a group biography. In a closed and inward-looking community, such as the Panacea Society, it is the group's dynamics, the gossip, the activities and foibles of individuals, that are the endless source of fascination and preoccupation *within* the group. I was reminded of this when a friend who has done fieldwork in the Antarctic talked about the oddness of being there for months at a time: it was not so much the extreme temperatures or the extraordinary landscape or even the fact that there is nobody really old or really young there that held people spellbound, but rather the intense relations within a small and inward-focused research group, the result of being thrown together in an isolated place.

This was the case in the Panacea Society: largely (though not wholly) separated from the outside world – diaries record trips into town to the 'talking pictures' and bicycle rides into the country – the members became consumed with what was going on inside the community. This preoccupation with each other is generally the case in closed communities (think of the tiresomely introspective conversations between participants in the *Big Brother* television series), but something very particular was happening in the community life of the Panacea Society. The dynamics between members were not just the result of their circumstances; they were the very essence of their lives, given profound theological significance. How members interacted with each other was seen as the path to achieving perfection and thus immortality. Put simply, how members dealt with each other determined whether they would live for ever or not. This was because the aim of Panacea community life was to prepare for immortal life. To do this, one had to change one's whole character: 'the things that nobody troubled about, but which make it difficult to live peaceably with some people, are the things that must be altered, for they are worse than sins, because they make other people sin.' This religious practice was called Overcoming. Frequent confessions and self-examination were central to its practice. Living with others you found difficult was also part of the training to become immortal. Community houses were sometimes rearranged so that people who disliked each other were forced to live together. As one surviving member explained: 'We were all put together in the houses with someone we rubbed up against. This way our faults and failings would show themselves and they had to be fought against.'[3] The irony of this is that the more a person tries to erase their faults, the more those faults are highlighted. This dynamic drove the Society, and it is the dynamic that drives the story told in this book, a history or biography of the members' shared life.

What these dynamics also reveal is the making of a religion, its shift from a charismatic and rather free-form network to an institution with rituals, rules, and the requirement of obedience. There is the rise of the charismatic leader: Mabel Barltrop, named as not only a prophet but also the daughter of God, and in that capacity known as Octavia. There are the squabbles among the disciples, the jostling for power, the jealousies. Just as the male disciples following Jesus wanted to know which of them he would favour, so the women gathered around Octavia competed for her attention. And the women were acutely aware of this. Rachel Fox wrote, as the Society was being formed, to another follower: 'Now if you recall the disciples, they were (probably) always fussing as to whether Tom, Dick & Harry were doing their right share of the work, and each, doubtless, had their right share of the work, & each, doubtless, had their favourites & their antipathies, and the Lord had hard work to harness them as a team to His plough.'[4] There is the formation of the community, charmingly loose at the beginning but soon beset by rules. And then there is the question of how order was to be kept, of how this growing body of people living cheek by jowl in their cluster of Edwardian villas – all trying to become perfect and therefore immortal – would be managed. Obedience to the religious rules and strict adherence to the religious practices was the answer. But who would enforce this? As the community grew, Octavia found it increasingly difficult to be priest, preacher, writer and spiritual director to so many while also trying to keep order. In 1923, four years into the Society's history, a rather ordinary member of the group named Emily Goodwin emerged as the one who would police and manage this flock. The Society's new theology of God, in which God was both Father and Mother, enabled this, for Mrs Goodwin claimed that she ✓ spoke as the voice or 'Instrument' of the Divine Mother. Octavia and her followers believed her. Mrs Goodwin, in her guise as the Divine Mother, prescribed what could and could not be done by members, rather like Paul who made so many of the rules in early Christianity. While Mrs Goodwin enforced the rules, Octavia could get on with what she was really good at: writing, leading worship, spreading God's word, drawing in new members, offering spiritual advice.

Like all inward-looking religious communities, the Panaceans faced the question of how much to conform to the world. The earliest Christians, clustered in small groups and house churches when facing persecution in the Roman Empire, addressed the question all the time. Paul wrote in his letter to the Christians in Rome in the first century: 'Do not be conformed to this world but be transformed by the renewing of your minds' (Romans 12:2). The Panaceans faced an additional challenge because they had to negotiate this tension at a time of rapid social change. Like the rest of their contemporaries, they were attempting to come to grips with the influence of modernity – motor cars, air travel, cosmetics, the decline of the aristocratic order and the rise of trade unions, fewer domestic servants, ribbons of suburban housing, ocean liners, the wireless, an ever expanding consumerism, the gramophone, jazz and big bands, the talking pictures, modernist art and novels, psychoanalysis and psychology, and reliable birth control. All of this and much more represented the dizzying speed with which change was happening, creating both excitement and dislocation across society. How were the Panaceans to conform or not to this? And how far was their lack of adaptation, their nostalgic looking back, part of their appeal to people who wanted certainty and some kind of still point after the dislocation of the Great War? And yet how, in other ways, did they represent modernity themselves, with the opportunities they offered to women, their startling theology and their eclectic mixture of beliefs?

At the heart of many of the controversies, dramas and breaks in their shared life was sex, that most vexed subject. For the Panaceans, as for some of the earliest Christians in the first and second centuries, sex was the 'switching point' with the world. If they could take sex out of their lives, then they would be less sullied by the world. The Panaceans believed that the celibate life was best, and it was prescribed for the inner circle of resident members; in cultivating perfection, they believed they were going back to the state that Adam and Eve enjoyed in Eden before the Fall. But resident members messily fell in love with each other. Their desires became entwined with old jealousies. New members came to live in the community and caused consternation with their sexual activities when they thought they were above the Society's rules. Many of the Panaceans struggled with how to remain chaste. Non-resident married members faced all the usual problems of marriage in a society whose attitudes to sex were fast being challenged, with the advent of reliable birth control, the falling away of chaperones for young women in the wake of the war, and the cultivation of more companionate marriage. And they wanted to know what their distinctive Panacean religion would have them do in response to all of this. The vast correspondence about sex and so many other subjects – economic hardship in the Depression, the use of the newly marketed cosmetics, religious experiences, domestic violence, books and articles of the day, to name just a few – gives us a glimpse into the ordinary problems that people faced, the questions they asked in the face of rapid change and the ways in which they tried to make meaning in their lives.

The Panaceans' shared life therefore reveals not only an extraordinary testament to faith, but also a slice of social history, a sketch of the preoccupations and concerns of middle-class society in the interwar years in microcosm. The members of this community asked the same questions that their contemporaries did about politics, religion and society, but happened to come up with infinitely more unusual answers: questions about the state of the world in the wake of the Great War, the role of women, how society should be governed and ordered as popular democracy increased, what was to be done about the economic crisis of the late 1920s, and where to find the proper locus for faith when, it was felt, the Established Church had so badly failed the country, especially during the war. They watched the opposing forces of Fascism and Communism squaring up and they became increasingly motivated to try and defeat what they – along with many other political conservatives in Britain – regarded as the Bolshevik menace. They despaired about the gradually declining influence of the British Empire, and participated in Buy British campaigns to try and boost the British and imperial economies. They shared the grief of their contemporaries: Panacean women had lost sons fighting in the trenches, and several of the men who joined the Society had been emotionally scarred by the war. This is the story of a group's attempt to find an answer to the pressing questions of their day, and of what they endured and did to work for a better world where there would be no more tears and suffering.

Historians differ on what life was like in Britain during the interwar years. Some (most recently Martin Pugh) argue that it was not as dismal as often portrayed: the advent of the motor car, the talking pictures, a boom in housing, low prices for consumers, and more opportunities for holidays and travel, balanced out the gloominess of the General Strike, mass unemployment, class divisions and poverty.[5] We might say that it all depended on where and who you were. The Panaceans were decidedly middle-class, living in a comfortable middle-class market town. Only a few members owned motor cars, but all enjoyed the convenience of the newly popular canned foods and visits to the cinema. In daily living, their class meant that they could enjoy the material wealth of these years though their natural frugality, combined with their belief that they should save their financial resources for the day when Christ returned, meant that community life was not lavish. Indeed, their *attitudes* were closer to those sketched by historians such as Richard Overy who has recently described the interwar years as 'the morbid age'. He argues that many people had a sense of civilisation in peril, a fear of decline and collapse: not just in the 1930s, as the possibility of a second great war seemed hauntingly likely, but in the 1920s too, in the wake of the calamities of the war and as new ideas and technologies were made widely available through increased mass communication. Overy's doomsayers were the eugenicists, socialists, peace activists and psychoanalysts. He argues that far from being marginal intellectuals, these people formed 'networks of anxiety', and that pessimism was contagious.[6] The Panacea Society can be seen as one such 'network of anxiety': at one level a small heterodox religious group, and at another level a striking symptom and hugely evocative symbol of the age. Its members –

mostly middle aged – had one foot in the values of Victorian England and another in the advent of modernity. Most of the founding members were born in the 1860s, so they had grown up with Darwin but they adhered to traditional views about the age of the earth and the Creation story. They were both strikingly conservative and radical at one and the same time. They appealed to people's fears and anxiety while offering them assurance and certain belief, and they made use of print culture, rallies, meetings and the press to spread their message. Just as much as the idealistic socialists of the day (whom they deeply opposed), they had a sense that their mission could save the world.

We know the end point of their story: that they failed in this – though the surviving members would simply remind me that Jesus has not come *yet*. Looking at their history from this end it appears as one of decline and failure, but the point of this book is to enter at the moments of hope, to understand what it was they were trying to do and why. One surviving member said to me that in 1946 she bought a new winter coat, and thought she would never need to buy another one because the Lord would come. This book seeks to enter imaginatively into that moment in 1946 when Gladys Powell walked out of the shop with her new winter coat, and all the other myriad moments of hope recorded so dutifully in the Panacea members' diaries and letters, to tell the story of a group of people who wanted to live for ever.

The book begins with several chapters about the origins of the Society, and Mabel Barltrop features centrally here: I refer to her as Mabel before 1919 and Octavia after 1919. Part II, the central section of the book, tells the story of the community's life in the 1920s and early 1930s. Its name from its foundation in 1919 until it became a charity in 1926 was the Community of the Holy Ghost. But for ease of reference, I call it by its post-1926 name throughout: the Panacea Society. Part III looks at the ways in which the Society interacted with the world, focusing especially on their political ideas and their (often one-sided) interactions with the Church of England.

I

Octavia

I

Seeking

On Valentine's Day 1919, a former suffragette and vicar's daughter named Ellen Oliver declared that she had received a divine 'revelation', which was confirmed, in the days and weeks that followed, by a group of middle-class Englishwomen who had gathered themselves around Mabel Barltrop. The revelation was that Mrs Barltrop was the daughter of God, a female messiah. On the basis of that divine message, many of these women gave up their homes, old friends, and even family connections, and went to live in Bedford, to build a community there: the New Jerusalem, the kingdom of heaven on earth, the place where they believed they would achieve immortality. How did Mabel Barltrop, an ordinary Church of England vicar's widow, come to believe that she was the daughter of God and that she could lead a community that would bring her followers to everlasting life on earth? How did she transform herself from a largely self-taught but well-read woman who had always relied on her intellectual understanding of theology to someone who trusted what she came to believe were direct inspirations and messages from God, now directing her life and the lives of others towards such radical ends?

This story has many beginnings. We could start, as a conventional biography might, with the earthly birth of Mabel Andrews in 1866, a middle-class girl born into a family with literary connections and the usual Church of England attachments and sensibilities of the time, who married a young curate named Arthur Barltrop, had four children and was widowed when she was just forty. Or we could root the story in her eventual dissatisfaction and disillusionment with the Church of England, as an intelligent woman in middle age who felt dismissed by its patriarchal structures and alienated by its theology. Then the story would begin with Mabel Barltrop's religious awakening in September 1914, when she picked up and read a blue leaflet about Joanna Southcott, a prophet writing in late eighteenth- and early

nineteenth-century England who provided her with a radically alternative vision of Christianity in which woman has a large part to play.

But if we start the narrative with Joanna Southcott, we could say
that the whole story really began a hundred years before Mabel's religious awakening, in 1814. This was when Joanna Southcott, a domestic
servant from Devon with little formal education, claimed that she would
give birth to 'Shiloh', a messiah figure. By then, Southcott had moved
to London and had at least 10,000 followers. Her latest claim was the
talk of all of London. Southcott died at the end of 1814, without having
given birth to a physical baby, much to the satisfaction of the nay-
sayers. Many of her followers believed, however, that a spiritual child
had been born and immediately taken up into heaven; they therefore
awaited the incarnation of that child. For the circle of women who
had gathered around Mabel in 1919, this was the story of Mabel's spiritual birth, for they believed that she was that child, Shiloh, the daughter
of God.

Why was another messiah figure needed? Had Jesus not died to save
humankind? According to Mabel Barltrop, that Saviour was not enough
because suffering still existed on earth. The problem was this: despite
Jesus' death on the Cross, sin still existed in the world. A further saviour
was needed to enable the salvation not just of the soul – with rewards
in heaven – but also of the body, with rewards here and now, on earth.
Original sin had to be overcome completely, and humanity needed to
be returned to its pre-Fall state. We could then begin the story at the
very beginning of the beginning in the Christian tradition, with the sin
of Eve in the Garden of Eden, a garden which Mabel Barltrop and her
followers came to believe – extraordinarily – was their very garden in
Bedford. If woman was responsible for the Fall, then only woman could
achieve the ultimate redemption. Original sin could only be completely
overcome in the original garden, the New Jerusalem founded by a new
female redeemer. This is who Mabel Barltrop came to believe she was,
and this is why those otherwise conventional middle-class women came
to Bedford to gather around her: to bring an end to sin; to follow the
new female messiah figure; and to prepare themselves for immortality.

We shall begin the story on 9 September 1914, when Mabel Barltrop, a
forty-eight-year-old woman who was short and stout but nevertheless
handsome and well-dressed and always wore a veiled hat when walking

out, went to her local library, as she had done every week since she had been a teenager, to borrow some books, for she loved poetry, novels and essays as well as theology. A female library assistant came up to her and said, 'Very few ladies read really good books; you are one of the few who search these shelves, so I think you are the best person to whom I can give this',[1] and she handed Mrs Barltrop a small blue leaflet. It told the story of Joanna Southcott. Mabel was convinced that she had come across something very wonderful, and took it to her best friend Kate Firth, a practical Yorkshirewoman who lived near her in Bedford. They sent away for further books, which were advertised in the leaflet. Mabel read them 'like a famished creature' and immediately knew that she was now going to be 'taught of God'.[2]

What led Mabel Barltrop to see Southcott's theology as the path to the truth? She had been a very dutiful vicar's wife, teaching Sunday school in her husband's parishes; keenly participating in the recently founded Mothers' Union; visiting the poor. But her husband had given up his ministry early because of illness, and had died of a brain tumour in 1906. Left with four children to raise by herself, she attempted to earn a living as a freelance literary critic and editor, her income supplemented by financial help from her Aunt Fanny (who lived with her), and her husband Arthur's family. While much of her energy was absorbed by the practical difficulties of widowhood, her questions about the Church did not recede. She had always been a seeker, hoping for reassurance that she was really saved. An early letter that Arthur had written to her, most probably when they were engaged, suggests that she had always struggled with her faith and he had tried to reassure her. He wrote, 'When you feel farthest from God then perhaps you are nearest. If one always felt a sublime pleasure in worship and contemplation where would be the exercise for faith?'[3]

Although Mabel *felt* her agonies about faith, to the extent that they led to two nervous breakdowns and two residential stays in mental hospitals, she had always tried to work out those problems *intellectually*. She was well read in the Christian tradition for a woman of her time, studying the latest in theology in her search for answers to the ultimate questions. After her husband's death, this quest intensified: it became increasingly clear to her that this was not simply a problem to be solved by her mind. She began to have the first of the visions that characterised her early years as a prophet, and she also developed what she called 'a most trying form of illness – a dread of being in church!' She found that she could not overcome a terrible feeling of anxiety as she approached the altar, and so she stopped receiving Communion, simply kneeling throughout the service. She later wrote, 'Throughout this time I was constantly depressed by the apparently useless efforts I made to obtain what is called "assurance". I left no stone unturned.' She continued to go to church several times a week, and made 'exhaustive and careful confessions'.[4] She tested all parts of the Church of England (Low, Broad and High – the last of these being where she felt most naturally at home), and even thought of converting to Roman Catholicism. She placed a great deal of emphasis on the sacraments (especially Communion and Confession) and dismissed the Protestant Nonconformist churches, where the sacraments were less important than preaching, even though her paternal grandfather Edward Andrews had been a celebrated Nonconformist minister.

Mabel's concern was that the Church of England taught that the kingdom of heaven is at hand but did nothing about it. It taught the salvation of the soul but not of the body. It promised the wiping away of pain, illness and tears – but only in heaven where, as she put it, those things do not exist anyway. She wanted these things – so often relegated to a future heavenly life – on earth. She complained that in the season of Advent, that month before Christmas in the church calendar, most preachers simply used their sermons to prepare for Christmas. This did not satisfy Mabel, for whom the Second Coming of Christ was an imminent event. Much to her disappointment and disapproval, there was no attempt in the usual Church of England vicar's Advent sermons 'to prepare for the actual prophecies of the Second Coming'.[5]

Mabel wanted hope for a brighter future, and Southcott's writings gave it to her with their clear promise of Christ's Second Coming. Southcott taught that there is a 6,000-year period of man's reign on earth, at the end of which the millennium will come. Mabel calculated that those 6,000 years were almost at an end, and therefore Christ's Second Coming was imminent. This filled her with expectation and excitement. For what was distinctive about Southcott's views was the idea that the millennial state to which Christians look forward is to be on *earth*. The saints will not be taken away before Christ comes and establishes his rule (quite the opposite of what happens in the *Left Behind* books and films, which have been so popular in the USA in the last few decades, where the saved are taken up to heaven in an instant, leaving a pile of clothes or a half-finished task to the bemusement of their families and friends). According to Southcott, the saints or the saved will remain on earth; they will be protected from God's judgment, free to enjoy God's kingdom of peace and justice here.

Mabel found this idea of God's kingdom and the end of suffering *on earth* deeply appealing. Suffering and loss had been a constant theme in her life, and her own suffering utterly preoccupied her. Her father had died when she was just nine years old. Two years later, her beloved older brother had left for South Africa, seeking relief from consumption in a warmer climate, and he had stayed there to make his fortune, as many young men did in the Empire at the time. She never saw him again, for he died after falling from a horse in South Africa in 1891, the same year that her mother, an invalid who suffered badly from rheumatism, also died. Her husband, Arthur, had become ill only seven years into their marriage, and after a decade of uncertainty, anxiety and suffering, he died in Holloway Sanatorium on 22 November 1906. Aged just forty, Mabel had been in the local mental hospital, the Three Counties Asylum in Stotfold, Bedfordshire, at the time of his death, diagnosed with melancholia, the 'exciting cause' of which was 'Domestic worry'. In short, she was completely unable to cope with an ill husband and four children, though after Arthur's death she rallied and managed to return home.[6] And then in 1914, World War I began, with all its attendant carnage.

Despite Mabel's dutiful attendance at church from a very young age, her involvement in church societies and philanthropic activities, and her exemplary life as a curate's wife, she felt that the Church had given her no satisfactory answer as to why all the people she was closest to, except her Aunt Fanny (who partly raised her) and her own children, suffered and were taken from her when they were still relatively young, and before she was forty years old. Such family loss was not uncommon in the late nineteenth and early twentieth centuries, and Victorian culture made much of death, with elaborate funeral rites, precise mourning rituals and vast gravestones. But those rites were of no comfort to Mabel, and they would soon prove utterly inadequate to a whole generation in the face of the overwhelming loss and grief of the war.

Mabel Barltrop was sick of mourning and widow's weeds, invalids and illness. She wanted to bypass death, to eradicate it. She wanted to find a way of living on earth without pain, suffering and death. That possibility is what she found in the Book of Revelation and Southcott's prophecies. Her husband had preached on the subject, and this gave her another clue to the theological way forward: 'I recall a remarkable sermon of his, somewhat on these lines, in which he said something to the effect that we have never found the right gate out of the Revelation which will take us back to Genesis before the Fall.'[7] If the extraordinary promises of Christ's coming were to be fulfilled, if there was to be the cessation of pain and death, then they must return to the very start of things, to Genesis, the first book of the Bible, and to the life of Adam and Eve before the Fall. In her formation of the community in Bedford, Mabel's aim was to get back to that 'Church in Eden'. Later, when the Panacea Society had been in existence for several years, she wrote: 'we have found the gate which led us there'.[8] However, after reading Southcott's writings in 1914, she did not forge her own way forward immediately. She tried the path of the Church of England first.

Joanna Southcott had not only published a number of her prophecies, she had also sealed up several of them in a large wooden box in the early nineteenth century, leaving instructions that this box was to be opened in a time of grave national danger by twenty-four bishops of the Church of England. The bishops represented the twenty-four elders sitting around God's throne in chapter 4 of the Book of Revelation. When Mabel read Southcott's published prophecies and biblical interpretations, her first instinct was an enthusiastic desire to tell the clergy of the Church of England about them and ask the bishops to open the box. She firmly believed that after the opening of Southcott's Box of Prophecies, England would become the new Israel and the biblical promises would come true. Despite her disillusionment with the Church, she still regarded it as capable of listening and thought the bishops would willingly open Southcott's box. She expended all her energy on writing to bishops and many of the clergy with 'the joyous news of the imminent approach of the King'.[9]

Mabel was not the only woman interested in Southcott at this time. There already existed a campaign to get Joanna Southcott's Box of Prophecies opened. There had been a revival of interest in Southcott in the early part of the century, largely promoted by Alice Seymour, owner and headmistress of a private girls' school, Headlands College, in Plymouth in Devon. Beginning in 1907, Seymour had republished, or in some cases published for the first time from manuscripts she held, Southcott's work as a series of 'Express Leaflets'. Seymour also published in 1909 a two-volume work about Southcott, *The Express*, which attracted considerable attention. The *Daily News* called it the book of the week and, according to Seymour, the *Daily Mail* was interested enough to send a journalist to talk to her. Following that, Seymour republished all of Southcott's sixty-five originally published books. These books and pamphlets were distributed through networks of Southcottian believers and at meetings in the 'commodious houses' of London social hostesses as well as more ordinary tea parties and speaker events. They extended far beyond Britain and were even mailed out to Australia, Canada, New Zealand and the USA. A woman and young man in San Diego, California, for example, reprinted all the books and an edition of *The Express* and travelled a thousand miles in their car making the cause known. Interest in Southcott caught on through networking, hard work and word of mouth.[10]

Who were the Southcottians? They form a vital backdrop to the story of Mabel Barltrop and her Society, and therefore merit a brief diversion. Mabel was inspired by Southcott's writings, and by the writings of other prophets who came after Southcott and developed her ideas. But it was not only the writings that were important. The Panaceans drew heavily, especially in the early days, on existing groups and networks of the various different sorts of Southcottians for the membership of their own community. Indeed, Mabel's aim was to unite all the Southcottian groups under the Panacea umbrella; though she drew many in, she never succeeded in achieving this goal.

After Joanna Southcott's death in 1814, some of her followers fell away disillusioned, while many continued to believe but split into various groups.[11] By the beginning of the twentieth century, there existed several Southcottian groups. These groups, taken together, are often referred to as The Visitation. First, there were the 'old' Southcottians, those who had never given up their faith in Southcott's original vision and were still awaiting the coming of Shiloh. These believers had kept the faith alive during the time of despondency and disappointment just after Southcott's death in 1814, and had passed their devotion and faith down the line, in particular through several prominent families: the Jowetts, the Foleys, the Jones family and others. Their sole interest was in Southcott and her theology and they had a special concern that her Box of Sealed Prophecies was kept safe and in the possession of a Southcottian believer at all times. They were not, however, activists about getting the bishops to open the Box, believing rather that the bishops would seek them out when the time was right. They awaited the physical coming of Shiloh, aware that one of Southcott's last commands in the summer before her death was 'No more meetings till Shiloh comes.'

Southcott had never tried or wanted to start a church. She had published her prophecies and acquired a following. She had instructed her followers to worship in the Church of England (after her own brief and rather unsuccessful flirtation with the Methodists). She had Church of England priests amongst her followers and she wanted Church of England bishops to test the truth of her writings. Her ministry was carried out largely through print. People *read* Southcott's writings (and the Bible), individually or together in small groups. Worship together as Southcottians was not necessarily central to their faith, though there were Southcottian chapels in parts of England. Networking through the distribution of printed literature was their central evangelistic activity; sharing literature and discussing it their primary communal activity. The Southcottians therefore formed a fairly loose movement, and usually worshipped in their local parish church. Southcottians might be sitting in the pew next to you in church, and you would not know.

However, some followers did not remain content with Southcott's writings alone. New prophets sprang up: they produced more prophecies and gathered followers around them, some more successfully than others, splintering off from the 'old' Southcottians but still forming fairly loose groupings.[12] Yet others had a more ambitious vision. They wanted more than reading networks: they wanted to live out their prophecies, enact them in purpose-built ideal communities. The most influential of these new prophets were John Wroe, who in the 1820s set up a group called the Christian Israelites in Ashton-under-Lyne near the newly growing industrial city of Manchester, and James Jezreel who set up the New and Latter House of Israel, commonly known as the Jezreelites, with headquarters in Gillingham, Kent, in the 1870s, a group which in the early twentieth century still held Sunday services and midweek Bible studies at 'Israel's Hall' on the Camden Road in north-west London. Both of these men extended their tentacles abroad, and made the Southcottian movement international. John Wroe visited Australia several times, and it is there that the Christian Israelites still

thrive today in churches in Sydney, Newcastle and Melbourne. James
Jezreel went to America, which he toured on several occasions, and
where offshoots of his group also continue to exist, most notably in
Benton Harbor, Michigan, in the Israelite House of David, founded ˅
by Mary and Benjamin Purnell in 1904.[13] This group later split after
Benjamin Purnell's death and Mary Purnell set up Mary's City of
David. Like squabbling siblings, these various groups and communities, all stemming from Southcott's teachings, kept tabs on each other
but often bitterly disagreed about their understanding of scripture, the
interpretation of Southcott's writings and the role of new prophecies
and how they should be lived out.

When Mabel read the blue leaflet in 1914, these different groups
still existed, while Alice Seymour's publications of Southcott's work
in the first and second decades of the twentieth century were gener-
ating new interest in her prophecies. Seymour was astute in targeting
her literature. She sent it to priests, rabbis and to middle-class women
like herself. The result was a wave of new believers, often disillusioned
in some way or another with the Church of England but longing for
a faith that held meaning and excitement.

Many of these new Southcottian believers were women. Those who
were attracted to other vogue-ish movements of the early twentieth
century – vegetarianism, heterodox religious and philosophical groups
such as Theosophy, Higher Thought and Spiritualism, women's suffrage
activism – might also be attracted to Southcott's writings. Indeed it
was possible to be a Southcottian and all of those other things at once.
The women who formed new Southcottian networks were middle class
and self-taught; they held meetings in their drawing rooms, passed
books around to each other and engaged in correspondence about
Southcott's ideas. It is no surprise that women were particularly
attracted to Southcott's writings, for Southcott gave women a distinctive role in the redemption of the world, teaching that if Eve had been
the original cause of the Fall, only Woman could be the final redeemer.
Consequently, almost all versions of Southcottianism gave women
active roles in the leadership and running of the movement. This new
interest in Southcottianism dovetailed with the women's suffragette
and suffragist movements, which were regarded by Southcottians as
fertile ground for potential converts. Through female suffrage networks,
Seymour's leaflets were passed around. Ellen Oliver, later to be the

first identifier of Mabel Barltrop as Shiloh, and a founding member of the Panacea Society, was given the blue leaflet about Southcott by an elderly man as she left a women's suffrage meeting in 1914. In turn, she circulated Southcott material through her own networks. Alice Jones, who would also become a central member of the Panacea Society, learned about Southcott in the early summer of 1915 when she was secretary for the Church League for Women's Suffrage and received that same blue leaflet about Southcott, sent by Ellen Oliver to the secretaries of all the societies she was interested in.[14]

The war gave further impetus to the Southcottian revival. Many of the new followers thought that this was the time of 'national trial and tribulation', and a campaign to get the bishops to open Southcott's Box was initiated. After the early patriotic jingoism, the horrors of the war became increasingly apparent as the months went by, leading many people to seek an answer as to why the war had happened, and a solution as to how it might be brought to an end. In this atmosphere, the promises of Southcott's Box of Prophecies seemed to many as good as anything else. The Southcottians began a publicity campaign. The old Southcottian families were nervous about the zeal of the new converts and the publicity they generated in their campaign to get the Box opened. This did not stop Miss Seymour and others from working tirelessly towards that end. There was increasing interest in the press too. On 11 February 1915, the *Daily Mail* carried an article about the Box, describing it as 'A deal box weighing with contents 156 lb. Measuring 2' 11" long, 1' 7" wide, 1' 7" deep, containing the sealed prophecies of the late Mrs Joanna Southcott related to the Second Coming of Christ'.

A central task was to get bishops interested. In the summer of 1915, Rachel Fox, a wealthy Quaker with spiritualist interests (the same Rachel Fox who later helped found the Panacea Society and wrote its history), who had been given Southcott's writings by a friend two years earlier, and her cousin Lady Portsmouth (Beatrice Pease), managed to secure a meeting with the Archbishop of Canterbury, Randall Davidson, largely because he knew and liked Lady Portsmouth. The fifteen-minute meeting had mixed results. The Archbishop would not sanction the opening of the Box by the episcopate because that would give the impression that he was endorsing any writings it might contain, but he did think the Box worth opening, even though he knew nothing about Southcott and her claims to divine inspiration. To Rachel Fox, and in a formal memo of the meeting, which he filed away in his papers, he spoke warmly of Rachel Fox's books which he had been reading; privately, in a letter to Lady Portsmouth, he admitted that he had not been impressed by the writings.[15] It is surprising that he took time in a very busy schedule to read the 'collection of "automatic" writings & psychic experiences about the War' that Mrs Fox had selected for him.[16] Rachel and Lady Portsmouth later went on to meet Bishop Boyd-Carpenter, whom they thought would be especially interested in the opening of the Box because he was a member of the Society for Psychical Research, that late-nineteenth-century foundation which sought to investigate scientifically any aspect of the paranormal. Randall Davidson, a meticulous and fussy man, wrote to Bishop Boyd-Carpenter, asking him how his meeting with the ladies had gone, stating firmly: 'we must not be dragged into a matter which may easily have its humorous side'.[17] His own dry humour came out when he wrote to Lady Portsmouth after their meeting, highlighting the absurdity of the situation as he saw it: 'You and Mrs Fox assure me that there exists somewhere in Devonshire (you do not tell me where), under the custody of a gentleman whose name I do not know, a certain box, which, it is believed, contains documents placed in it 100 years ago by Joanna Southcott.'[18]

So, when Mabel Barltrop wrote to the bishops asking them to open the Box, the issue was already live. When she wrote to the Archbishop of Canterbury in April 1915 with the news that 'God has a New Revelation awaiting us and that until the Church of England rises to the occasion & investigates the writings of Joanna Southcott, *misery* will go on', he was in the middle of a correspondence that had been dragging on for some months with Lady Portsmouth, to try and arrange the meeting he would have with her and Rachel Fox in June, and he had also received letters about Southcott from Alice Seymour, Rachel Fox and a South African spiritualist named Helen Shepstone who was about to become important to Mabel's story.[19]

Mabel, however, remained oblivious to the activities of any others. The blue leaflet that she read about Southcott in October 1914 was a Seymour publication, and the books she subsequently acquired and read were likewise obtained from Miss Seymour. The Panacea Society would later draw members from many of the Southcottian groups. But for the moment, in the autumn of 1914 and the spring of 1915, Mabel was not in contact with any of these groups or aware of their activism. She was single-minded in her focus, and solo in her activities. This was not untypical of her character. Despite her dread of going to church and the anxiety which that caused her during these years, and despite the fact that she suffered far more nervousness and illness in the next year or so, she always remained convinced of the absolute truth of *her* way forward. In October 1914, she felt she was on the threshold of the answers to her quest. She later wrote: 'I quite understood that I was about to receive definite instruction direct from God.'[20] This single-mindedness was also one of the reasons why she and Alice Seymour clashed: both wished to be head of their own kingdom; neither wished to collaborate in any serious way with the other.

Mabel's letter-writing campaign to the bishops met with no success. Every day in the post she received a thick stack of polite but dismissive responses. This shocked her. Only one clergyman engaged in correspondence with her: a High Church Anglican priest named Bernard Hardy.[21] He had become her spiritual adviser in 1910 when he was on the staff of her parish church, St Paul's in Bedford, and she had gone to healing prayer meetings that he had run.[22] He later moved to work in the nearby city of St Albans but he remained an important spiritual figure to her for several years. His initial responses to her letters were cautious. She wrote to him soon after reading the blue leaflet in the autumn of 1914, and he replied: 'I have read your letter over, and again very carefully. Part I can follow, and part is beyond my understanding. And, to be candid, part I do not like.' First of all he distanced himself from Southcott's prophecies. He had no desire, he wrote, 'to peer into the future, or to receive revelations of things about to be, or to know more than is already known by the faithful'. However, he was willing to offer continued pastoral support and spiritual direction if Mabel definitely felt it was the will of God that she should understand 'more of the hidden Mysteries of ancient prophecy than others have understood'. If also, in obedience to God's will, she felt that she should tell him what she received, he declared himself willing, 'in obedience, too, to receive, and to do my best to profit of the teaching'. Finally, he stated that he could not, however, regard as from God 'any revelation which contradicts in any measure the Official teaching of the . . . Church'.[23]

Mabel – an indefatigable writer all her life, from whom words poured, day and night – bombarded him with letters and information. His replies remained careful, caring and yet cautious but, by early

1915, he clearly felt it necessary to draw a firm boundary. On 9 January he wrote, 'I feel quite clear that I am not meant to go further with Joanna Southcott's prophecies.' His own vocation lay on a quite different path, but he thanked her for the labour she had put into sharing Southcott's ideas with him.[24]

Hardy's hope was that his former parishioner would remain within the Church. 'If you are continuing your studies of these matters, may you be kept faithfully folded in the Holy Church. I think you will, but some of her [Southcott's] ignorances are rather alarming. She so often misunderstands the Church – apparently.'[25] For Mabel, this was (at least in retrospect) a deeply significant turning point. She gives a rather different version of events in her memoir of these years, *Brushes with the Bishops*:

> In the case of the clergyman with whom I was corresponding on the new light that was dawning – he felt it to be his duty to consult his Director, with the result that he wrote by the next post to say that he had been forbidden by his Director to enter further into these matters, and he returned to me, in a sealed packet, which I have never opened, the entire correspondence. Thus was my sole outlet choked, and in the next chapter I will relate the consequences.[26]

Early on in my research I found this packet of letters, still sealed, in a cabinet in the Panacea headquarters at the end of a long day of research. The experience of opening up these letters, which I had known to be sealed for so long, in the evening dusk, was rather chilling, especially as I now knew what came next in Mabel's life.

The 'consequences' that Mabel described were a breakdown when she had become exhausted and weakened after receiving no positive response to her many letters to bishops and other clergy. As she put it several years later, 'I began to feel that I could not stand much more if the clergy did not rise to these marvellous teachings, as I saw that we could not be saved, as a country, unless the Bishops searched into the "sealed writings" given in 1792–1814 for the express purpose of helping England in the war which was foretold.'[27] The strain of rejection and disappointment was too much. She admitted herself into a mental hospital in Northampton, and remained there for a year and a half: from April 1915 to October 1916.

2

Listening to God

Mabel Barltrop admitted herself to St Andrew's Hospital in Northampton as a voluntary boarder on 29 April 1915.[1] As she later related the episode, she travelled with a relative to the hospital, believing it was a place where she could experience a 'rest cure', a common treatment at the time for women who were 'nervous'.

> When we arrived at the place my relative who was with me, seeing the large gates said to the chauffeur: 'Don't go in there; this lady is going to a house near here, but not to the mental hospital!' We drove round and round the place, but could find no other entrance, and my friends wanted me to return with them. But I insisted on going in to make enquiries about the 'rest' house. The doctor came forward and was told that I had come by my own request for rest and for nerve treatment. He said: 'Many ladies come here as voluntary boarders', and from further conversation everything seemed to be satisfactory . . . Having decided to remain, I said good-bye to my relative and followed a nurse through a very handsomely furnished corridor.

But on entering, everything changed: the 'handsome corridor' turned into an infirmary 'where obviously insane persons were wandering aimlessly about. One came up and made hideous snatchings at me; others surrounded me with curiousity.' She remonstrated that she had not come to the infirmary part of the hospital; but the nurse made it plain that everyone stayed there for three days on their arrival. She was given a compulsory bath, had her clothes and other belongings taken away from her, and was put in a room next to a padded cell 'in which, as far as I can remember, there was a naked lunatic'.[2]

This idea that she went to a lunatic asylum *by mistake* was central to her narrative of events. She wrote, 'Know, good people of England, if you have never known it before, that thousands of persons who are merely nervous are, by being sent among lunatics, driven too far over the border ever to be reclaimed.' Mabel was reiterating the late-nine-teenth-century division between illness caused by 'nerves' and 'nervous collapse', which was particularly attributed to women of the middle and upper classes, and 'lunacy' or 'insanity' which tended to be asso-ciated with the working classes of both sexes. She was worried about middle-class women like herself who had experienced some kind of 'nervous breakdown' and found themselves being treated with 'lunatics' – which was to say, with people below their class – with the conse-quence that they became actually insane. Mabel's concern here tells us as much about her attitude to class as about her understanding of mental illness.[3]

While in St Andrew's, Mabel embarked on a new campaign: to make the dreadful conditions of lunatic asylums known, and to tell the stories of the many gentlewomen who were mistakenly trapped in there. 'In a very short time I had gathered impressions which I knew must be made public.'[4] She began new letter-writing campaigns: one to the Lunacy Commissioners,[5] and another to the bishops – this time to them in their capacity as shepherds of the lost sheep, who would help the distressed gentlewoman mistakenly locked up with the insane. After her husband Arthur had died, Mabel had worked as a freelance editor, helping authors with their books, and she noted that she had in that capacity worked with an eminent psychologist who had studied under Freud in Vienna. The knowledge she had gleaned about Freud from this encounter led to her assertion that the 'doctors of England are so behind the times in regard to nervous and mental disorders that they are no longer of any account what-ever'. She therefore suggested to her correspondents that a Royal Commission be set in motion, to investigate the conditions of lunatic asylums, and that any bill brought before Parliament should include the following points. First, it should recognise the need to prevent the admission of neurotic persons or persons suffering from nervous break-downs into lunatic asylums; that practice was causing them to lose their reason and become incurably unfit for the resumption of a normal life. Secondly, nerve hospitals should be built where people could receive psycho-therapeutic treatment in extreme cases, or suitable care and rest in mild cases. And thirdly, psycho-therapeutic methods should be adopted in the treatment of 'actual lunatics'.[6]

A century later, and many advances in the treatment of mental illness later, we can see that her suggestions were sensible and far-reaching. In fact, St Andrew's prided itself on being innovative, with the installation of telephones in the 1880s, an electrical generator in 1898, and motor transport in 1890, and it adopted occupational therapy in the 1920s, a few years after Mabel Barltrop left.

The condition of lunatic asylums and their inmates was a constant preoccupation in late-Victorian and early-twentieth-century Britain, not least because the nineteenth century had seen the building of large numbers of sanatoriums and asylums. Mabel's concerns were therefore very much 'of the day', but not surprisingly, in 1915, as a woman writing from inside an asylum, she received no replies. What is striking here is Mabel's construction of herself as 'sent' to the hospital 'as a Commissioner – a spiritual one'. She wrote that the other patients regarded her as such, saying to her: 'You are not a patient, why have you come here?' and 'You have come here to help us, you know you have.' Retrospectively, she described her time at St Andrew's as her 'work' in a 'new-found capacity'.[7]

Mabel's medical records from the hospital tell a different story. They reveal that she was only a voluntary boarder for two months of her time there: from 29 April to 3 June, and then again from 5 June to 24 June. Voluntary boarders could admit themselves at any time, without any medical certificates, and could leave at any time by giving twenty-four hours' notice. But Mabel was admitted to the hospital in a different capacity on 24 June: she was sectioned, the petitioner being Mrs Lennie Bull, her late husband's sister, who lived in Bedford. This marked the beginning of a running battle between the two women, even though they had been good friends when they were young. Lennie deeply disapproved of Mabel's heterodox religious interests, and taking a legal step to keep her in the mental hospital was just the first of a number of aggressive moves she made towards Mabel with regard to her religion and its effect on her family's life. The 1890 Lunacy Act had tightened up the procedure for the reception of patients into asylums. In non-urgent cases it was necessary to have a petition, statement, and two medical certificates, all of which had to be presented to a County Court judge, magistrate or specially appointed Justice of the Peace, in order for the person to be admitted to an asylum. In urgent cases, regarded as being for the patient's welfare or public safety, a person could be admitted to an asylum with an urgency order signed by husband, wife or near relative (the petitioner), a statement of particulars and just one medical certificate, provided by a medical doctor who had seen the patient within two days of writing the certificate. This was easy for Lennie Bull – the petitioner – to arrange, as the medical doctor at St Andrew's could provide the certificate.

The 1890 Lunacy Act had come about in part because of a famous case that showed the relationship between heterodox religious activity and the confinement of women in lunatic asylums. In 1884, Mrs Georgina Weldon successfully sued Dr L. Forbes Winslow for attempting to examine her and have her confined in an asylum at her husband's request. Georgina Weldon was a spiritualist and it was on those grounds that her husband and Dr L. Forbes Winslow had tried to have her committed to an asylum. The sectioning of women for religious reasons by families in the late nineteenth century was not unusual. Numerous husbands, fathers and brothers had their independent-minded wives, daughters and sisters forcibly admitted into lunatic asylums when those women were empowered by heterodox religious activities. Women involved in spiritualism were especially targeted because a number of medical doctors, specialising in neuropsychology and psychiatry, argued that spiritualism was a cause of mental illness and that the medium's trance was a form of hysteria (to which women were thought to be particularly vulnerable). Dr Forbes Winslow, the keeper of two private asylums in Hammersmith, had published *Spiritualist Madness* in 1877, in which he had argued that spiritualism – which had grown hugely in popularity since it had been introduced into England in the 1850s – was the principal cause of the recent increase in insanity.[8]

Historians have argued that this threat to heterodox religious women had died down by the end of the 1880s,[9] but the cases of both Mabel Barltrop and a woman she met in the hospital suggest that it still existed well into the early twentieth century. In early 1916, Mabel befriended a spiritualist medium in St Andrew's, Minnie Oppenheim, who was sectioned by her brother, the popular writer E. Phillips Oppenheim, for many years.[10] We therefore have to view Mabel's 'sectioning' in a wider context: it happened to many women liberated by their involvement in the new religions that emerged and blossomed in the nineteenth century and attracted bright women frustrated by conventional Christianity and its reinforcement of the subjugation of women.

Nevertheless, Mabel was suffering from some form of mental illness. Her case notes make this clear, though they need to be read with care, precisely because women, especially women with unusual religious interests, were still regarded as particularly susceptible to nervous disorders and even madness. Her diagnosis upon admission in 1915 was melancholia – defined in the *New Oxford Dictionary* (later the *Oxford English Dictionary*) in 1890 as 'A functional mental disease, characterised by gloomy thoughtfulness, ill-grounded fears, and general depression of mind'; and the cause cited was the 'Change of Life': she was forty-nine years old. On admission, she was described as 'depressed and restless'. The report continued: 'she says she has lost control of herself and there is no knowing what she might do . . . She has an obsession to do injury to others: she says she feels sure she would harm her son (for whom she has a great affection) should he come to see her.' There are echoes here of the medical records from the time she spent in the Three Counties Asylum in 1906 when she was also diagnosed with melancholia. Back then, she was brought from a nursing home with bloodshot eyes, caused by 'the effort to strangle herself, and not by any direct injury [to the eye]'. The admission notes for her 1906 confinement also recorded that she believed 'she has lost all control of her nerves – that her body and limbs seem to be full of movement – that her brain is too active'.[11] In both 1906 and 1915, after an initial period of fear that she might harm herself or others, she settled into a period of depression. The medical records for the months of July, August and September 1915 describe her as depressed, unstable, agitated, liable to relapse, at times requiring constant supervision, but no longer wishing to harm herself or others.

The case notes also reveal that there was a strong religious element to whatever ailed her. On 26 June 1915: 'She has delusions and believes she is possessed by a devil'; 16 July: 'She has peculiar delusions that she is worked upon by unseen agencies'; 24 July: 'She believes she has committed unpardonable sins and that God is against her.' Again, there were echoes of the medical notes from her stay in the Three Counties Asylum. When she was admitted in April 1906, it was recorded: 'She says she is not fit to live as she has . . . committed the unpardonable sin – which she explains as preaching religion to people and not practising it oneself.' And later in her 1906 stay, the more grandiose claim: 'Has become greatly agitated and depressed, says she is the cause of all the misery in the world.'[12] Towards the end of 1915, still in St Andrew's, Mabel wrote to her best friend in Bedford, Kate Firth:

The fact is that mine is so sad and dreadful [a] case, that you will be quite right in thinking it is unbelievable but it remains a fact that I cannot regain myself. I have lost myself. I am without a character which is of any value and you and Miss Seymour must go on and on and leave me out in the black darkness.

It was now that she had a crisis about her reliance on her intellectual abilities, and this crisis would shape how she went about her religious mission subsequently. She wrote in that same November letter to Kate Firth – with a consciousness of her own charisma – that her intellectualism and 'unfortunate power of making friends and attracting people' deceived them and herself. She was not, she said, deceiving anyone knowingly, but felt that she had been a fraud: 'I was self-deceived by my own cleverness if you can understand.' This left her feeling that she was 'empty now of goodness, of God . . . how can I live each day out in this torture with no aim, no ideal to reach to, no hope for time or eternity. You see it is physical anguish and must eventually show itself. I am living a lie here trying to pretend in order just to get through a day at a time.'[13]

She also reached rock bottom physically, becoming ill in December with a cold that was neglected and by January had turned to pleurisy and bronchitis, and then emphysema. She recovered from her physical illness at the end of January 1916, and although by March she was described as 'interfering and difficult with the other patients', she was also reported as having 'quietened down . . . and now has parole of the grounds'. By spring 1916, she was clearly on the road to recovery, or at least to rediscovering herself and her mission, for it was in February that she wrote to the Archbishops of Canterbury and York about the state of the mental hospitals.

By May 1916, she was back to her usual high level of activity, and her case notes remarked: 'Patient has been getting strange in her manner for some time and has now started writing letters to the King as appended. She imagines she has a special mission to perform. She apparently imagines she has had a special revelation from God telling her why the War was caused and the way to stop it.' By June, a different doctor than the one who had been writing her notes thus far, recorded: 'Patient writes a considerable amount of nonsense. Her delusions are of such a nature that they warp her judgment of almost everything. She believes that she has been specially chosen by God to improve mankind etc.' He also remarked on her ability to attract other people to herself and her ideas, an ability which would prove so important in the setting up and building of her community in Bedford: 'She exhibits a most surprising ingenuity for "catching up" people when they converse with her.' In early September, the same doctor was noting that Mabel was 'greatly interested in the writings of Joanna Southcott and writes to various people on this subject. She looks for comfort in a morbid eccentric religionism. Is more contented but stirs up trouble among other patients.'[14]

How are we to approach Mabel Barltrop's mental illness? This is a vital question, not least because we have to understand *her* complex attitude towards it. She clearly revised the story of her voluntary admission and subsequent sectioning in 1915 to make it more palatable to her followers and anyone else who might read her book – and possibly to herself: being sectioned by her sister-in-law must have been humiliating. She had to believe that she was 'sent' to the lunatic asylum for a spiritual task, that she was not like so many of the others in there. But her case notes indicate that she was depressed and unstable from June 1915 to February 1916, and it was only in 1916 that she took up that 'spiritual task' and began to write to bishops and others about the conditions of the asylum, and subsequently revived her interest in Southcott's prophecies. Furthermore, in her account of this time, *Brushes with the Bishops*, she did not mention that she had been admitted to a lunatic asylum on a previous occasion with the same diagnosis.

Both the Three Counties Asylum and St Andrew's Hospital case notes suggest that she *did* suffer from some form of mental illness for much of her life. This ran in her family: her daughter Dilys, in later years, suffered the most, and her son Adrian had a melancholic streak, as his daughter revealed to me. Mabel herself continued to suffer from 'nervous attacks' for the rest of her life and possibly from some form of what we would call obsessive compulsive disorder. Peter Rasmussen, who was one of several followers living in her house and therefore one of the intimate circle of friends in the community that witnessed her state of health on a daily basis, relates an episode that suggests this. In his 1925 diary, he wrote that Octavia's inhibitions were getting worse. She had to leave a piece of everything that she ate, and there had to be a certain amount left in the glass, cup or bottle when she had a drink. He wrote of the escalation of this: she used only to leave one piece of bread and butter, or a little bit; then she started to leave two '& now for some time she has to leave three & last night she began to leave four pieces [of] bread & butter'. Octavia laughed it off and said it was no joke 'but a most wonderful working of God', whereas Peter recognised it for what it was, writing: 'I have no strength to fight this nerves attack.'[15] It is revealing that Rasmussen, one of the most devoted of her followers, understood this behaviour in terms of a nervous attack (in our language, a psychological disorder) rather than accepting Mabel's interpretation that it was a message from God.

In the Panacea Society's beliefs, Mabel's continued mental illness was imbued with a theological purpose. Her 'sufferings', as they were called in all her subsequent writings and the publications of the Society, were regarded by Mabel and her followers as necessary for the work she was doing on earth as the divine daughter, and this was nothing less than the redemption of the body, so that the chosen might have immortality. Just as Jesus had suffered on the Cross for the salvation of the soul, so it was believed the daughter must suffer in her mind for the redemption of the body. This meant that there was always a great preoccupation with Mabel's sufferings in the Panacea Society. In their personal diaries or in letters to each other, some of Mabel's closest followers tracked her state of mind every day and regularly noted that she was 'depressed' or in 'agonies of mind', usually several times a week. They came to believe that because she suffered for them, their own chance of immortality was linked to what she endured. This had the odd effect of making everything – everyone's behaviour, everything members did – all about Mabel. If someone did something wrong, then it was Mabel who was thought to suffer: the person's own complex feelings were rarely if ever taken into account. This speaks to a strongly narcissistic streak in Mabel's personality.

Mabel was ambivalent about her mental illness: she hated it, was in some ways embarrassed about it, and yet made a sort of peace with it by coming to explain it as vital to the God-given work she believed she was doing. This is not so unusual. From a modern Western perspective – and Mabel's case notes bear this out – any diagnosis of mental illness in a person who has distinctive religious ideas, especially those as unusual as Mabel's, is likely to lead to the dismissal of their ideas as delusions. Without letting go of any of the reasonable scepticism we might have about her ideas, it may be helpful to understand that in many cultures, melancholy – and that was her diagnosis – is seen to make people particularly *fit or gifted* for religious leadership. Anthropologists have observed in a variety of indigenous cultures, such as the Australian Aboriginal and Alaskan Inuit societies, that melancholics are likely to be installed as shamans, prophets or priestesses.[16]

Mabel resolved the dilemma presented by her illness by interpreting it theologically. She also understood her time in the asylum in 1915–16 to be a vital part of God's purpose for her: 'I was driven by the Spirit into this wilderness,' she wrote to Kate Firth while still in the asylum. 'That determination of mine to come to St Andrews' was vital, she believed, if she was to participate 'in this great Drama'.[17] It was in the asylum that she had her intellectual crisis, and came to believe that she might be given knowledge in other ways, allowing the visionary and the prophetic to emerge as central to her relationship with God and her mission.

New religions or new offshoots of existing religions often claim additional direct inspiration from God as authority for their innovations, and these messages often become the new scriptures of the group. The nineteenth century was full of such texts: Joseph Smith's *Book of Mormon*, Mary Baker Eddy's *Science and Health*, Madame Blavatsky's *Isis Unveiled*. Mabel Barltrop came to claim such direct divine inspiration as the authority for all that she was teaching and doing, and the messages she believed she received from God formed her community's 'scriptures', published as *The Writings of the Holy Ghost*. It was in St Andrew's Hospital, floundering and frustrated, but sure of a divine purpose for herself and convinced of the truth of Southcott's writings, that she began to make the shift from a purely intellectual understanding of faith, which she believed had failed her, to one guided by divine inspiration.

As Mabel began to recover in the spring of 1916, she remembered the occasional messages she had for some years received – as she believed – from God, and she started to ponder how she might receive further divine messages. The person who came to her aid was Minnie Oppenheim, the spiritualist medium who was in the asylum with her, and saw a chance for her languishing mediumship to be put to use once again after years of inactivity and boredom in lunatic asylums. On 1 June 1916, the anniversary of her wedding day, when she had been in St Andrew's for nearly a year, Mabel received a message from her husband, who had been dead for nearly ten years, via Minnie Oppenheim who 'received' or channelled it in poetic form. It was a message of reassurance to a grieving widow, an encouragement to Mabel to go on with what she believed was her divine mission, and a confirmation of her theological belief that death will cease. The last stanza read:

> Weep ye not, my wife, so precious,
> Thy dear husband now is near,
> Hushed to every sign of sorrow,
> Sanctify thy every fear.
> There's no death, take thou this message,
> Forward with thy work sublime
> God shall aid thee, Love shall shield thee,
> 'Neath the Canopy divine.[18]

Mabel was thrilled to receive the message: 'I can only say that I had a period of immense joy and delight, and for some days was in a state of vision. I cannot recapture it, but I have ever since had quite a different view of life and of death owing to my husband's efforts for me, which is more precious to me than anything I possess, except the Lord's own direct Messages.'[19] She kept a copy of that poem in her bible for the rest of her life. It confirmed her path. She was on the road to a new form of theology based on direct messages from God. Minnie Oppenheim continued to 'channel' messages that she believed were for Mabel, especially from Joanna Southcott. Mabel also began tentatively to trust her own 'light', her own states of vision. Her belief was that 'the Lord will add His Wisdom to no man's wisdom, neither to that of the early fathers nor to that of later divines, nay, not even to that of the contributors to *Lux Mundi* or *Foundations* [two influential Anglican publications of the late nineteenth and early twentieth centuries].' So, she wrote, 'it is obviously necessary to empty the mind before the Lord in order to start afresh'.[20] She did not learn how to do this in a disciplined way for some time. She was still searching for a way to 'hear' and trust what she believed to be direct inspiration from God.

The problem with such 'direct inspiration' is, of course, one of knowledge. How do we know or how can we test what is true and what is not true? Or to put the question in the sort of theological language that Mabel herself would have used: what is of the spirit and what is of the devil? Once she began to receive such messages, Mabel naturally wrote to her best friend Kate Firth about them, but neither Kate nor Alice Seymour were open to either Minnie Oppenheim's messages or Mabel's own increasing sense of their importance. Mabel wrote to Kate: 'You and Miss Seymour are very stupid indeed about asylums. They are chock full of extremely gifted people and I say if God chooses to bring Joanna out of a Lunatic Asylum you can't stop it.'[21] And a day later, 'You can be so buried in the "letter" as to be oblivious of his living voice & spirit.'[22] When she sent the poem from her husband to Kate and Miss Seymour, they rejected it. 'It is really "killing" if you and Miss Seymour are going to be like the Bishops and are going to ascribe the good & beautiful things I send you to Satan!'[23] A little later she wrote, 'my own view is that you & I & Miss Seymour *must* humble ourselves before God and admit our unwillingness to accept a childishly worded *message* which was full of *Glory unspeakable*, else we are no better, not so good, as the Bishops'.[24] It was at exactly this time in May and June that the doctors recorded in her case notes: 'She imagines she has a special mission to perform. She apparently imagines she has had a special Revelation from God telling her how the War was caused and the way to stop it.'[25] The doctors' answer was to put her in the infirmary, 'back under observation', in solitary confinement. But Mabel still had letter-writing privileges and her answer was to find other help with the messages and visions that she believed came from God.

On 4 August 1916, Mabel wrote to Rachel Fox for the first time: 'I badly need a person who has "Vision" . . . I wonder if I could confide in you. Will you write to me and tell me if you have either spiritual sight or hearing, or if you believe in either or both?' She was related to Rachel Fox by marriage, through her first cousin, Blanche, who was married to Rachel's husband's brother. That alone would not have led her to seek help from a distant relative by marriage, whom she had never met, especially when her own family was, as she put it, 'so vexed with me for taking up with these things'. Other reasons prompted Mabel to write to her. Mabel had heard that Rachel had spoken on Southcott in Steinway Hall in London and had seen the Archbishop of Canterbury about the Box.[26]

Rachel Fox, by long family lineage a Quaker, was always trying to get people interested in Southcott and she gave talks on the subject not only in London but also in the garden room at Wodehouse Place, her elegant home in Falmouth. Rachel was also a believer in psychic phenomena, a practitioner of spiritualism ever since the death of her son, Barnard, at prep school in 1894, when he was just ten years old: she believed that he was one of her spirit guides. Widely read in authors such as William James, she engaged in the practice of automatic writing. Her grandson, David Laity, remembers her getting up in the middle of the night to write her books; asked about her writing, she would say that she did not know where it was coming from.[27] Rachel Fox even wrote books of biblical criticism through automatic writing. She began her first book, *Rays of the Dawn: Fresh Teaching on New Testament Problems*, in the usual way by intellectual effort, and the first section took about a year. Then in April 1911, as she was writing about the Epistle to the Hebrews, 'suddenly and spontaneously the power of "inspirational" writing' was given to her. 'Thoughts not my own poured through my mind as I held the pen, and even the pen became the force of an instrument of an exterior force, and wrote the teachings of another. I always knew what I was writing, but not what was going to be written, until the words came to my pen.'[28] Through this rapid process of automatic writing, she finished the second half of the book in record time – just three or four months. After she had received the letter from Mabel, she sent her this book, written by divine inspiration, and the correspondence began. Ever in search of a sympathetic ear, Mabel bombarded Rachel with letters, just as she had bombarded Bernard Hardy with her correspondence, though this time she got a more sympathetic response. Rachel recorded in her diary that she had received 'such an outpouring' of long letters from Mabel about her past and her present, about her brain fever and how she 'had begged to be taken to St Andrew's Mental Home – in order to rest and recover' and 'been put into the *insane* ward & kept there thro' an operation for months.' Rachel commented that 'It was evidently a highly improper way of helping to cure an overwrought brain & it seemed to me a miracle that she had not quite collapsed.' Of her new friend's intellectual and spiritual capacities, she noted: 'Her letters showed great ability & much education, intuition & knowledge of many scriptural things.'[29] She wrote to her cousin, Beatrice Pease, of her 'energetic new friend's demands' but said that she had 'now considerably checked the output and now that she feels she is understood . . . in as disagreeable way as possible, she is happy'.[30]

When Mabel wrote to her in August 1916, Rachel was already engaged in an intense correspondence with another woman who was interested in Southcott's prophecies, a South African named Helen Shepstone, widow of the colonial administrator from Pietermaritzburg, Theophilus ('Offy') Shepstone,[31] and a spiritualist who believed that she received frequent messages about the Second Coming of Christ from St Andrew and other spirit guides. Rachel Fox and Helen Shepstone had begun corresponding in April 1913, when Helen had first read Rachel's books. Rachel then introduced her to Southcott's work, to which Helen's response was: 'I believe that miracles of past ages are to be repeated in this age, and even more marvellous ones, and you and I will be instruments for the manifestation of God's power.'[32] Helen received 'wonderful communications' about the 'spirit man child that is to be born' and this she connected to Southcott's Shiloh.[33] Armed with this sense that they had very special vocations, which is one of the peculiar elements of this whole story – that the women who read Southcott fervently believed that *they* were the ones to whom exceptional spiritual things that she had prophesied would happen – the two of them pondered Southcott's life and prophecies. In particular, they wondered when and where and to whom Shiloh might be born. In December 1915, Helen had written to Rachel that she believed the time would soon be ripe and that the Spirit-conceived child would 'be sent into the world through a chosen Woman. Who? She must be living now.'[34]

They believed that it must be one of them (despite the fact that they were beyond childbearing age). At first they decided it would be Rachel, and then at the end of 1915, Helen was 'absolutely commanded' to write: 'our belief that you were to be the chosen woman to bear and to bring forth the Holy Child is an error'. Rather, it was she, Helen, 'so unworthy', that had 'been destined from the beginning of things, to be the chosen vessel of this great marvel'.[35]

A sense of special vocation, 'chosenness' and utter dedication permeates the correspondence between Helen and Rachel. They were both completely sure that they were on the right track, and yet they also had a sense that they were entering the unknown. Helen wrote, 'A great angel is with me as I write, sending intense power into my left hand', and then a few paragraphs later came the cry, 'Oh Rachel, God knows how blindly I grope.' They both, too, had a strong sense that they were reliving biblical truths, a second time around. Rachel even believed that she had received a message from God saying that they were like the Virgin Mary and her cousin Elizabeth: 'You are even as the two women of the Incarnation story, and you must share one another's holy secrets.'

It was to the mystery of the messiah-child Shiloh that Rachel Fox and Helen Shepstone were seeking an answer when Mabel Barltrop entered the correspondence in August 1916. The letters between these three women convey a sense of their being on the verge of discovering the meaning of that mystery – for them, the ultimate mystery – in which they were engaged. But how would they know if and when they discovered the answer? And by what authority? Rachel and Helen were receiving what they believed to be direct messages from God and other spirit guides almost every day, and Mabel was herself trying to glean that direct divine inspiration through her own attempts or via Minnie Oppenheim's messages. Not surprisingly, this caused conflicts between them and it was Mabel who quickly emerged as the strongest character in their correspondence, insisting that her way forward was the right one. Only a few weeks after she had written to Rachel asking her for help, when both Rachel and Helen were warning her to take things slowly, even to forget her ideas or 'lay them at the feet of the Master' and remember that God's 'work will be accomplished in His time,' Mabel wrote, rather fiercely, to Rachel:

I am so sorry that I cannot accept your warnings. I can take no advice
on anything to do with my visitation and how to carry it out. If I had
not made one straight line in this manner for myself, I should never
have accomplished anything. I regard advice *when it is opposed to my
vision* as being from the the devil! [my italics][36]

This echoed something she had written to Kate Firth earlier in the
year: 'Faithfulness to my vision has been my key note. I followed the
gleam to the best of my ability.'[37] Rachel Fox grasped very quickly
Mabel's force of character and her potential leadership, writing in late
August to Beatrice Pease, who was sceptical about Mabel Barltrop and
wanted to stay out of her way, 'I don't wonder you don't want to be
caught in her stream, but yet I believe she is to be the prime agitator
of our group.' Rachel, ever sensitive and perceptive, had a sense of
how much Mabel's agenda was about to take over her own life, and
she confided in her cousin: 'Of course I see by higher powers we
were not *meant* to know of each other till my book was done. I doubt
if it could have been done under MB's waterfall of letters and excite-
ments.'[38] Mabel, less compassionate and more easily frustrated by what
she perceived as the foolishness of others, declared of Rachel and
Helen that the mystery was 'completely misunderstood by them
both'.[39] Rachel and Helen saw Mabel's determination and tenacity
differently, as Rachel recorded in her diary for 1916, with a frankness
that did not make it into the history that she later wrote of the origins
of the Panacea Society:

There was such an extraordinary mixture of probable and improbable
things in this writing coming thro' a lady considered to be insane or
she would not have been there, that Beatrice, I and Mrs Shepstone felt
that we could not trust or countenance them – I read them all to please
Mrs B & to advise her. Mrs S. when about to type them (unread) felt
herself forbidden to do so.

Rachel wrote of the 'tug of war' that went on in their correspondence. But she and Helen were clear that it was their priority to get
Mabel away from the influences in St Andrew's, which they believed
were causing 'a false and spurious excitement with which MB's brain
could not cope'.[40]

Even though she had her disagreements with Helen Shepstone, Mabel regarded her as a significant figure, from whom she received several important divine messages at a time when she was still unsure about her own capacity to hear God's directly given word accurately. In the first of these messages, on 15 September 1916, Helen reported that the Lord said of Mabel: 'she shall depart from that place of sorrow where she hath learnt and suffered and shall enter into peace, till I call her again. Thou perchance shall help her. Hear thou my Word and send it unto My weary one.' During her last few weeks in St Andrew's, Helen's messages sustained Mabel and gave her directions: that she should go home, that she would be healed and sheltered, and that she herself should listen for God: 'I speak to her own heart, bid her listen in the stillness.'[41]

3

The Daughter of God

Mabel Barltrop was discharged from the mental hospital on 25 October 1916 and went back to her home in Bedford.[1] It was the middle of the war and her three sons were away fighting in it. Her daughter, Dilys, now aged eighteen, looked after by her Great-Aunt Fanny, and by her Aunt Lennie who lived just around the corner, was ready to resume family life with her mother. There was a household to be attended to. And yet Mabel's priority was picking up the threads of the search and solving the mystery of Shiloh. Rachel Fox wrote in her diary that once Mabel got back home, 'with ups and downs entering yet more correspondence, she has been holding on & trying to obey our advice to rest & drop all agitations for Joanna.'[2] This was wishful thinking on Rachel's part. Mabel was very busy indeed, absolutely single-minded about pursuing her path: this ultimately made her the leader that she became. She had been promised by the messages from Helen Shepstone that God would speak to her directly, and so she began to train herself 'to carry out the Lord's command to listen for His voice'.[3] To do this she wanted to master the practice of automatic writing.

Minnie Oppenheim, Rachel Fox and Helen Shepstone all practised automatic or inspirational writing. This was a technique familiar to anyone involved in spiritualism, as all three women were, and it was influential in the broader culture. The poet W. B. Yeats, who had been introduced to it by his wife on their honeymoon, relied on it for inspiration and was keen to prove the authenticity of his spirit guides.[4] Scientists in the Society for Psychical Research argued that supernatural phenomena were caused by the 'subliminal self' and regarded automatic writing as a kind of complex telepathic communication.[5] Many – whether Christian believers or not – nevertheless continued to see it as guidance of the hand by spirits or the Spirit or God. The ability to 'tune in' was something of an art and the practice of automatic writing was not always easy to master. The image of the newly popular wireless was frequently used in the 1910s and 1920s in the notion of the 'radio mind'.[6] As Rachel Fox put it, 'The wireless calls are so many that it takes time and training to recognise the one which is purely for us.'[7]

Mabel had experimented with automatic writing in St Andrew's Hospital in August 1916 – about the time she had begun corresponding with Rachel – when she 'went to the table and gave up my will. My hand rushed about quite foolishly; any way, *it went*, and I took down the message with incredible speed.'[8] Now she wanted to perfect the method. She 'began to make a practice of waiting before the Lord, with my book and pencil, at twelve and at three, and in a month or so I had quite a small volume of sweet, gentle teachings in prose and in verse'. Thus, she wrote, 'I found I was being trained to be a scribe of the Lord, for the purpose of presenting to the Church, the Truth of His imminent Coming and of the methods whereby it will be brought about.'[9] In October 1917, a year after she had returned home to Bedford, she received 'the first important writing', a message for the bishops, which she posted off to all forty diocesan bishops immediately. This message promised a new Gospel, 'the Good News of a coming redemption of the *Body*', and chastised the bishops for ridiculing ongoing prophecy and revelations, and especially for ignoring Southcott and her spiritual children 'who desire the sincere milk which can only come from woman'.[10]

Both Rachel Fox and Helen Shepstone had questions about Mabel as an 'inspirational writer'. In November 1917, Rachel wrote 'that her latest writings are too "wordy", too much about her own feelings and conditions, to have been purely received'. Helen was suspicious of 'the denunciatory words and the commanding tone' and worried that Mabel was 'carried away by her own mind and her zeal too often, yet she is yielding herself more and more and is certainly to be one of His instruments, and it seems we are meant to be united'.[11] Mabel was upset by these criticisms but not swayed from her course. Her response was to take an oath to the Lord with Kate Firth, as Joanna Southcott had, swearing to be led only by God's voice.[12] In this, she was always concerned to be entirely obedient to what she sincerely believed was God's voice. Like many a female prophet before her, she described herself as an 'empty vessel', receiving only the Lord's word.[13] She gradually perfected her technique and once the community was up and running in 1919, beginning on 28 June that year she received the 'scripts' daily, disciplining herself to sit down every day at 5.30 p.m. to take down the message from God, and then going straight to evening prayer where she read that message or script along with passages from the Old and New Testaments.

Mabel was also gathering more people into her fold. At the beginning of 1918, she opened an office in her dining room for collecting the names of believers. She took on a secretary, and Kate Firth acted as treasurer of their initial funds of £115. They began a list of names. Mabel wrote to Rachel: 'Every person I know is down. Will you tell me all you know?'[14] The circle of women was widening, as Mabel began to correspond with others interested in Southcott.

Of all Mabel's new correspondents, the most significant was Ellen Oliver, who first wrote to Mabel in January 1918 when she had become disillusioned with Alice Seymour's way of doing things. A person of sweet and trusting disposition, Ellen quickly transferred her loyalty from Miss Seymour to Mabel. Their correspondence throughout 1918 illustrates Mabel's constant quest to find an answer to the divine mystery into which she too now had become drawn. Ellen was someone with whom Mabel felt comfortable and who took her entirely seriously. When Ellen had written a letter to friends about all that was happening in Bedford, Mabel wrote to her: 'Here *for the first time* I see my own case put by another & it is a *great* experience.'[15] Ellen did not question Mabel's ideas or divine messages as both Rachel and Kate did. She engaged with Mabel, offering her ideas, reading anything and everything that Mabel suggested, and in turn offering her own ideas and books for Mabel to read, but never doubting that Mabel was ultimately right. Ellen's unswerving devotion made some of the other women – such as Rachel Fox – rather suspicious of her: 'I rather fight shy of Miss Oliver,' Rachel wrote to Gertrude Hill, a vicar's wife who was another member of the growing group of correspondents and a visitor to Bedford from time to time.[16]

One strange feature of the correspondence between these women is that their preoccupation with their religious hopes was so great that they barely mentioned the war, despite the fact that both Mabel and Kate had sons fighting in the trenches. Occasionally it intruded. On 23 April 1917, Mabel's oldest son Eric was killed in battle in France, shot down while flying a plane. She was upset, but discussed it very little in her letters. In September 1918, Helen Shepstone was drowned when the ship, the *Galway Castle*, taking her back to South Africa was torpedoed just off Plymouth and sunk. In retrospect, Mabel invested great significance in Helen Shepstone's messages to her. She wrote to Ellen Oliver, a few days after Helen had drowned: 'I have had a great grief. The wonderful woman whom the Lord used to convey to me the messages on which so much hangs was drowned in Galway Castle!' She and Helen had, in fact, never met. Typically, Mabel made the tragedy relate back to herself. 'Indeed it is more to me than any of her relatives. It is as if the Word which was as honey to my taste can never come again. Only God Himself & our Blessed Lord know what I mean & feel.' Aware that she had still not perfected her own capacity to receive God's word, she wrote: 'You see my own word does not help me, but from her to me it was the perfection of Truth & of knowledge.'[17]

The women were not only awaiting the incarnation of Shiloh, but were also on the lookout for new prophets. Mabel and Ellen had been discussing for some time, in their letters, who the next prophet in the Southcottian Visitation might be. Until she came into contact with Ellen, Mabel had been reading only Southcott's work, but inspired by Ellen she read the writings of the other nineteenth-century prophets, and wrote a short book explaining the significance of each of them and summarising their beliefs, *Keys to the Whole Body of Truth for the Whole Body of Believers*. There had been six major prophets (writing between 1790 and 1885) thus far: Richard Brothers, Joanna Southcott, George Turner, William Shaw, John Wroe and James Jezreel. Ellen, of course, thought Mabel was prophet number seven, but in January this honour was now bestowed posthumously on Helen Shepstone.[18]

Family life also intruded, and occasionally we get glimpses of Mabel juggling home life with the religious mission that was being run out of her dining room. In January 1919, she wrote to Ellen: 'I have my second son Ivan home, so I am living a curious life, all mixed up!! Scripts & Gramophone & men coming in but the Gramophone we have is glorious. Ivan has perfect taste in music & we have Schumann & Liszt & so on. I feel I have to do everything just like other people.'[19] It was good preparation for her life when the Society had formed.

Throughout all of this, Mabel remained focused on the key questions and tasks. She wanted Southcott's Box of Prophecies to be opened, so she kept up the pressure on the bishops, writing to them frequently. She wanted to solve the puzzle of Shiloh, and she read scripture and the earlier Southcottian prophets for clues. She wanted the growing community to expand, to gather in those who were inter- ested and sympathetic, winning them over to her cause. To this end, she was writing books. Most of all – believing her destiny to be of the utmost importance – she wanted to know who she was and, in the midst of a growing chorus of voices and interpretations, being steadfast about this was essential.

As the circle grew, so did the number of ideas and messages 'received' from God. All the women believed that God was communicating with them directly. They believed that all they had to do was sit down with a piece of paper to receive the message via inspirational writing or inter- pret their dreams correctly. The letters between the members of the growing group reveal an increasing sense of competition, as well as plenty of gossip about each other – who was in, and who was out. Mabel wanted to count Alice Seymour 'out'; Rachel thought she should still be considered 'in'. Mabel's efficient secretary, Jessie Johnson, in whom Mabel had had such faith initially, turned out to have too many ideas of her own. When Mabel had first met Miss Johnson in December 1917, she had been impressed by her knowledge of the millennium, not least because Miss Johnson had reached so many of the same conclusions as Mabel herself, and she had been won over if astounded by Miss Johnson's gift of speaking in tongues. Kate Firth wrote, after meeting Miss Johnson, 'Then she suddenly began to "speak with tongues"; it was amazing. I kept quiet and did not allow myself to be nervous(!) . . . please try and picture M.B., when she heard "tongues" in her simple "villa"!'[20] Mabel wrote of her great efficiency as a secretary, 'she reminds you of the Living Creatures in Ezekiel, who as soon as they heard the Word of the Lord ran like lightning to perform it, only folding their wings to hear a new Message'.[21] But such enthusiasm meant that Miss Johnson had her own grand schemes, and the other women were not impressed by her 'Plan of the Lord' – her vision that when Christ came again the world would be turned into a beautiful park studded with jewels, divided into ten-mile-square sections. By August 1918, after just a few months in the post, she was gone, her lasting legacy to the Society the notion that 'Bedford is the place of God's glory',[22] an idea that would be developed by the Panaceans in the years to come.

As Miss Johnson was packing her bags, Mabel realised the humour of the situation. There were too many people making too many suggestions about the way forward. She wrote to Rachel, 'It is really getting quite funny now. We have all got muddled up. I am laughing heartily.' And she reported that Gertrude Hill was even trying to work 'at the thing from Theosophy'.[23] Gertrude Hill in turn wrote to Rachel Fox that she was puzzled as to why Mabel made it a sort of point of conscience that they should all seek to find out *who* she was, though she supposed it was because 'she seeks this relief from her suffering, for she is, as she says, very very weary, poor dear'. But Mabel was clearly the leader amongst them, a fact that Gertrude acknowledged even as she questioned it: 'I feel we have been following our leader too much out of a kind of curiosity.'[24] Here were the arguments and power plays that are inherent in the making of any religion. Here were the nascent disciples already squabbling. Throughout, Mabel remained resolute and, in early 1919, she was rewarded.

On 14 February 1919 Ellen Oliver came to the belief that Mabel Barltrop was the spiritual child of Southcott made incarnate. As she finished reading *The Flying Roll* by the nineteenth-century Southcottian prophet James Jezreel one evening, she was immediately struck with the thought that Mabel was Shiloh. Jezreel had written that 'Unto Shiloh shall the ingathering be' – and it was Mabel who, from her dining table in Bedford, was gathering them all in. Surely, then, she was Shiloh? In one fell swoop this neatly revealed both the identity of Shiloh and the identity of Mabel, the twin mysteries over which the women had been puzzling. Ellen did not write immediately to Mabel herself, but to Kate Firth about her 'wonderful and *tremendous* thought'. Full of excitement, she told Kate: 'No wonder M.B. has a look of Joanna for she is Joanna's Spiritual Child – Shiloh!' She presumed that Kate must have seen the same thing: 'And *you have* felt this tremendous secret & been weighed down by it?! How wonderful & glorious is this ending? . . . I hardly dare put it to myself last night but this morning it seems all so clear! Do write quickly for I dearly want *your word* that this is so.'[25]

Kate did write back quickly, but not with the enthusiasm or certainty for which Ellen had hoped. 'Your suggestion re: "Shiloh" is very striking & provides much food for thought, but at present I feel quite unable to give a clear & decided opinion on the idea which has come to you that M.B. may be "Shiloh". I have always been very "foggy" in regard to "Shiloh" & have never yet been at all satisfied with any solution either read or given to me by others & always feel there is some great mystery yet to be revealed.' Furthermore, Kate raised an additional stumbling block. Mabel was a *woman* – could she be Shiloh? 'Is Shiloh feminine?' asked Kate. 'I have always imagined S. to be masculine, but as we are ignorant creatures & really know *nothing* it is more than likely that I am mistaken.' And as the one who so often had to deal with Mabel when she was overwrought and suffering – showing manifestations of her nervous illness – Kate added a further dampener to Ellen's enthusiasm: 'I am sure of one thing viz: that for the present we must keep this idea *entirely to ourselves* & not even give MB a hint.' Kate, already envious of Mabel's leading role, presented this as protecting Mabel, though she must have known that Mabel would have loved the possibility of being named Shiloh. Kate went on:

> She has more than enough problems to work out at present & this suggestion might complicate her ideas & interfere with her present work. The fact remains that she is a *very* remarkable person & time alone will prove her *special* part in this great plan of Redemption. She may possibly be the first woman chosen to be Immortal through the cleansing of her blood by her process of her *suffering*, for her sufferings are certainly greater & quite different to other people's.[26]

Ellen, undeterred, wrote back immediately to make her case once again. She drew upon scripture, Mabel's own writings, and even numerology – prevalent at the time and always popular in the Society – to support her new belief. Her persuasive abilities won the day. Kate gave in to the idea, writing to Ellen: 'I note all you say about "Shiloh" & feel that you are being given much light on the matter. It appears more than likely that she may prove to be the "Shiloh" the spiritual child (daughter) of Christ & Joanna, whose manifestation is due *this year*.'[27] Kate's hesitancy about naming Mabel as Shiloh was a symptom of her jealousy of Mabel, a jealousy that simmered until 1926, when it fully emerged.

The fact that Mabel herself – apart from Ellen's suggestion – came to believe that she was Shiloh was a turning point. It was one reason why Kate came round to the idea. As Kate wrote to Ellen: '*Her* attention has also been drawn to the fact which goes to verify the impression.'[28] Mabel had received a teaching from the Lord telling her she was Shiloh:

> Behold I am with thee always, I am knit unto thee, My Child. Dost thou know who thou art, even My Child sown into the womb of thy Mother Joanna, and caught away unto the heavenly places until I found a body likely to suffer, into which, after sufferings great and terrible, My Child Shiloh should enter and dwell there. Didst thou not come into the work one hundred years after thy Mother's death?[29]

This last phrase was an allusion to the fact that Mabel had started to read Southcott in 1914, exactly a hundred years after the death of Southcott. Mabel thus wrote to Ellen: 'Shiloh died to childhood in 1914 when I got the Blue Leaflet & took the whole in at a sweep.'[30] In affirming her identity as Shiloh, she declared both her authority and her humility in one short phrase, writing to Ellen: 'My one prayer I can assure you is that I may never deceive or be deceived.'[31]

While Ellen was bursting with enthusiasm and Kate was trying to suppress her envy, Rachel Fox was wrestling with how far she could go with all this. In March, Mabel was writing to Ellen that Rachel Fox and Gertrude Hill 'are totally "in"'. In fact, Rachel was not at all sure how much she wanted to be 'in'. She was wary of Mabel's overwhelming personality, shrewdly perceptive about what all this might mean for her own life, having often been on the receiving end of Mabel's imperious statements in the three years she had known her. In the small hours when she pondered the matter, 'sometimes I really wished I could see a way to get out of it. For I had an intense shrinking from what I can only call "the unknown quantity" in Octavia's [Mabel's] personality which I felt without being able to give a form to it.'[32] Finally, Rachel felt herself forced to consider whether Mabel would fit the missing place. 'Was it possible that the great enigma rested in her person? Was she being energised by Shiloh as Spirit? I asked myself was Shiloh – no longer the little "child" of prophecy – now ministering to her soul and body?'[33]

Rachel wrote candidly in her diary for 1919 of Mabel: 'I found I was called to support her in her arduous tasks and spiritual adventures. She is a born leader & yet I have to use my spiritual discernment &

act like both a stimulant & a check, lest her ardour should carry her onto too fast an advance.' While Ellen Oliver wrote entirely upbeat letters to her various interested correspondents, expressing her wonder and admiration at how lovely it all was, Rachel expressed, at least privately in her diary, how difficult the path might be: 'I know we are heading [into] what is a dangerous and new way but God has given us wonderful signs and seems to be going before us – none of us would have chosen this path or discovered it intellectually, it has been revealed to us spiritually as a group, & only the sense that sheer obedience is required in order that we may not lose something of vital importance to the world keeps us on this path.'[34]

Despite the private reservations of some, Mabel was now regarded as Shiloh, a female messiah figure, by her small band of followers. She also had a name change. Rachel Fox was the first to use the name 'Octavia' in a little book she wrote in May 1919, called *The Voice of the Seventh Angel*. She later said that she chose the name casually, but once Helen Shepstone had been named as the seventh prophet, it made sense that Mabel should be the eighth, bringing the lineage of prophets to completion in an 'octave'. In religious terms, the number eight is regarded as one of perfection and completion. By October of that year, Mabel was wondering exactly what name she should use and decided that she should retain 'Octavia' as it was already in Rachel Fox's writings, and 'to avoid unnecessary confusion and to keep the EIGHTH development as a concise whole'.[35]

With Octavia in place as the daughter of God, the community's theology put woman at the centre of things. The women were attracted to Southcott's idea that because Woman had caused the Fall, only Woman could bring about the millennium and the period of peace and justice which it heralded.[36] Octavia took Southcott's theology a step further, influenced by the earlier prophets Wroe and Jezreel. She believed that because Christ's death on the Cross, his atoning for sin, had saved only people's *souls*, another redeemer was required, one who would redeem the *body*, and this redeemer was to be female. Even before she was herself recognised as this further redeemer, Shiloh, Mabel had written to Rachel Fox: 'The manifestation of Shiloh will be feminine – the Bride will be Shiloh. I could write pages on this. If you want another Man except Jesus, well, frankly, I do not.'[37]

The reconfiguring of the doctrine of God, once Octavia was recognised as Shiloh, the divine daughter, meant that gender took on a new meaning in the Godhead. The community now came to believe in a fourfold or foursquare (rather than threefold or Trinitarian) Godhead. In orthodox Christianity, God is Father, Son (Christ) and the Holy Spirit (of indeterminate gender). In the community's new theology, the Godhead was now Divine Mother (the Holy Spirit) and Father (God the creator), Divine Daughter (Octavia) and Son (Jesus). Now, as they prepared to build the New Jerusalem on earth, only Woman could take them back to that original state of humanity, and restore the Garden of Eden. Because of Eve's sin, wrote Octavia, 'the immortal Feminine Spirit was removed from overshadowing God's creation, hence our sad condition'. Christians believe the Holy Spirit to be at work in the world all the time. Octavia was claiming that the Holy Spirit – for her the Eternal Feminine Spirit – had withdrawn from the world, which is why the world was in such a mess. As she wrote: 'we are as babes without a mother, hence our forlorn condition, hence our need to seek for the Holy Spirit, as for a gift'.[38] Only now was the Holy Spirit returning to the world through her and her followers. A few years later, she and her followers would make a bold claim about the return of the Divine Mother in their midst. For the moment, the Holy Spirit was manifesting itself through divine inspiration, in the new prophecies and revelations that Octavia was receiving daily in her Scripts.

All of this meant that God the Father had to take a back seat. Octavia wrote that 'The fatherhood of God has, so to speak, done all that fatherhood can do, and the joy of those who live through the coming seven thousand years, will be the joy of children whose mother, long withdrawn, returns to do for them what only a mother can do.'[39] Or as Rachel put it, 'We have all lived on the Gospel of the Fatherhood of God, now has come the day when the Gospel of the Motherhood, treasured in the prophecies of Isaiah [Isaiah 66: 13] have been revealed to woman.'[40] This meant throwing over the old theological order: 'We have been carrying on man's ideas of religion and have lost sight of God's religion which is, to restore man to what he fell from and to obliterate death. This is the only true religion, and it began in the Garden of Eden, and will finish there.'[41]

In this distinctive theology, there was a sense of the need for gender balance, a restoration of the female (which had been for so long missing) in the cosmos. This 'feminine' aspect of God had been withdrawn and now needed not just to be reinstated, but to become predominant. This was not a merely theoretical formulation. It had practical repercussions for the women who joined the community. It was women who would usher in the millennium. Octavia described her followers as 'English churchwomen, who were gentlewomen of mid-Victorian upbringing'.[42] She commented on the humorous side of this when she tried to explain to over-enthusiastic American visitors that these women were indeed in charge of ushering in the kingdom of heaven on earth, and all their practical common sense was needed for that task. She wrote to Rachel: 'The simple facts are, that God requires a few sensible, matter-of-fact women to take on the housekeeping on earth, and to begin to give their orders by word of mouth and on His behalf, until the defeat of Satan and the Divine Jurisdiction begins.'[43] She believed that women had the distinctive gifts of mothering and housekeeping that were required in the preparations for the Second Coming of Christ.

Octavia conceptualised women and men as distinctly different, a view rooted in her Victorian upbringing. The attributes she ascribed to each were thoroughly grounded in nineteenth-century presuppositions about what women and men were. Women were not, Octavia thought, reasonable creatures. 'As to REASON, you cannot bring REASON into the woman's movement. The charm of a woman is her "sweet unreasonableness!"' But 'God knows the comparative values of reason as against *intuition*.' And this was why, she believed, 'He has chosen woman to finish the whole thing for the very *reason* that she does *not reason*.' She then went on, paradoxically, to demonstrate her own logical ability: 'Reason only comes from the verb *ratio*, I think. Well, *thinking* is a very dangerous thing, and in spiritual realms it easily becomes the sin of self-communing. *Mens* or mind, men's mind, implies a man, and man *thinks*. Now for aught we know the trouble lies here.'[44]

Octavia's idea came partly from her belief that her own intellect had tripped her up, but her argument was also like that of some suffragists, who campaigned for women to get the vote on the grounds that women's moral and emotional superiority was necessary in the messy, masculine world of politics. They wanted to introduce what they saw as women's distinctive morality, fostered in the home, into the public sphere; many saw it as the only 'salvation' for a deeply troubled world. In Octavia's theology, women and men were essentially different and complementary, and now women's 'natural' capacities and gifts were required for the full redemption of the world, because they had taken second place for so long. She thought women had always been as she envisioned, and she compared herself to Eve. 'Eve and I are exactly alike; she was pleased to have her children and did her best for them. The difference between her and me is only the difference of the THINGS with which she was surrounded; where she probably made her "apron" with a thorn, my baby's robe was made with a needle!'[45]

Octavia's ideas about gender stemmed from a largely conservative upbringing. Her uncle by marriage and godfather was Coventry Patmore, the nineteenth-century Roman Catholic poet who had given the Victorian ideal of mothering and housekeeping femininity a label, 'the angel in the house,' in his long poem of that name. His wife, Octavia's Aunt Emily (her father's sister), was the model for this nineteenth-century domestic goddess. As a teenager Mabel had encountered ideas of women's university education and women's suffrage through her older and highly accomplished feminist cousins, in particular Eliza Orme, the first woman to practise as a barrister in England. But Mabel remained genuinely conservative on the subject and never embraced women's suffrage. Visiting the Orme cousins when she was nineteen, she attended a talk that Eliza gave on votes for women, but wrote to Arthur, then her fiancé: 'I am not at all likely dear to become a "strong-minded female", so don't be afraid as, so far, all their arguments have failed to convince me, of course all here are in favour of it.'[46] By the time she was the fifty-three-year-old leader of a religious community in 1919, she had become a very 'strong-minded female', but she was still against women's suffrage and she played to Victorian ideas of 'femininity' to exercise her authority.

Whatever the ideological sources of Octavia's ideas, the practical outcome of her theology was that women did almost everything in the community, and the women who joined her were thirsting to do so. On entry into the community, they had to list their gifts, and these ranged from gardening to language skills, from flower arranging to typing to public speaking. The women wrote and translated pamphlets and books, spoke at meetings, took minutes, sent out mailings, organised worship and – most importantly – were responsible for bringing in new members. Octavia attracted many women who wanted a greater role than conventional society – and especially conventional religion – allowed them. The community was, as the 1920 rules declared, 'founded for the purpose of gathering Israel'. This gave the women an immense sense of responsibility, and there was a strong feeling that they were chosen; that they were chosen because they were women; and as the 'chosen' they would be protected. This was repeatedly conveyed in the daily scripts that Octavia received. In these the group of gathered women were described as 'ye chosen Women [who] shall be endued with powers'.[47] The women also believed that they had been chosen because men (especially churchmen) had failed. The appeal of this heterodox community to these earliest female members is therefore not surprising. As the 'chosen' they had responsibility and were kept busy; they functioned like priests or ministers; and they had a theology of sexual difference in which they found themselves, as women, reflected in a way that was impossible in traditional Trinitarian theology. All of this contrasted dramatically with any role they would have been given in 'orthodox' Protestantism, especially the Church of England, which was the church of all the earliest members, except the Quaker Rachel Fox.

Women could do very little in the Church of England. There had been some deaconesses since the late nineteenth century, doing 'women's work' with the poor and sick of a parish, but laywomen could do almost nothing: they could neither preach nor read in church. Nor could they take any official part in the decision-making in their parish church because they could not be on the parish council. There was a movement for the ordination of women in the Church of England in the 1920s, led by Maude Royden, but none of those who joined Octavia's community had any relationship to it. The Nonconformist churches were a few steps ahead, but it was several years until they ordained the first women, and those few women struggled to be accepted.

Several of the inner circle of Octavia's community had fought for women's rights in the suffrage movement. This they proudly acknowledged despite Octavia's hostility to the cause. Ellen Oliver had been incarcerated in Holloway Gaol for her suffragette activities, and had been involved not only with the tamer suffragists, but also with the radical Women's Social and Political Union (WSPU), the group led by the Pankhursts. She also shared that other feminist concern, developed by groups in the Church of England such as the White Cross League, of women's sexual health and purity. Her friend Alice Jones had been involved with the more sedate Church League for Women's Suffrage (with which Maude Royden had been much associated). Gertrude Searson, one of the founding members of the Society, had worked with Millicent Fawcett, suffragist and leader of the constitutional (non-violent) women's suffrage movement, who believed that women had distinctive gifts and insights to offer and campaigned for votes for women on those grounds. Ellen wrote to Octavia, soon after naming her Shiloh: 'Of course Shiloh is a woman . . . I love it all and wish it could have been published in our suffrage papers years ago – but then we would have thought Shiloh a man.'[48] Ellen thought that campaigners for female suffrage were ripe for conversion and suggested that they should advertise the community's publications in *The Common Cause*, the weekly female suffrage paper associated with Mrs Fawcett's suffrage group (the NUWSS), 'for it is taken in and read by numbers of thinking women'.[49]

In emphasising the 'feminine' aspect of God, Octavia was not unusual for her day. Other heterodox religious groups made the 'feminine' prominent in their theology and they too attracted suffragettes and suffragists. Feminist politics were intertwined with feminist spirituality in Theosophy, for example, and in the lives of prominent individuals. Charlotte Despard, the president of the Women's Freedom League, which broke away from the WSPU in 1907, believed in the coming of Christ and awaited the return of 'the Divine Mother-Spirit of Love'. Eva Gore-Booth, who was active in the NUWSS in Manchester, was a mystical poet, playwright and Theosophist, who wanted to erase sexual difference, for, if the new age were to be ushered in, the duality of sex had to be given up. Dora Marsden, the founder of the feminist journal, *The Freewoman* (1911), and a radical suffragette, went on to develop a highly individualistic form of spirituality, equating a person's (especially a woman's) freedom with immortality.[50] Like Mabel before her, she fell into deep melancholia when no one took much notice of her ideas; Dora Marsden languished in the Crichton Royal Hospital in Dumfries from 1935 until her death in 1960.[51] Emmeline Pethick-Lawrence, former treasurer of the WSPU, preached at the all-woman Church of the New Ideal in Manchester which seems to have existed from 1916 to the early 1920s.[52] All of these women believed that the movement for women's suffrage was a spiritual crusade as much as a political struggle.

Members such as Ellen Oliver and Gertrude Hill came with ideas they had drawn from elsewhere, which they brought forward as corroborating evidence that the new community's belief in a female saviour was correct. Ellen read the work of a range of feminists, including Frances Swiney, whom she discussed in her letters to Octavia, taking from Swiney's 1905 book, *The Awakening of Women*, the idea that within Judaism, the Divine Wisdom is always spoken of as female: 'perhaps it is not generally known that the mother-essence is worshipped in the daily service in the synagogues'.[53] Frances Swiney was president of the Cheltenham branch of the NUWSS, and the author of a series of books which argued for the superiority of women in evolutionary terms, saw motherhood as divinely important, and argued for women's suffrage on the grounds that men's baser passions and instincts would thereby be brought under control.[54] Ellen's reading of Swiney's evolutionary theories seems to have influenced Octavia: in the letter in which she acknowledged to Ellen that she was Shiloh, she also expounded the idea that woman's evolutionary superiority meant that through the female Shiloh (herself) the elect of the human race would achieve immortality.[55]

Some members turned to earlier writers who had emphasised the possibility of a female figure in the future of Christianity. Rachel Fox became interested in the sixteenth-century French writer, Guillaume Postel, and in 1919 wrote a pamphlet on him. She made notes about his writings in her diary: 'Mankind's redemption could not be completed until the Divine Spirit had incarnated in Woman as well as in Man. That if there was a second Adam – Jesus – to reverse the sin of man, there must be a second Eve – who must suffer for the sins of woman.' This would increase God's glory 'more than had He conquered by the stronger sex'. Rachel took the line, as Octavia did, that it would be woman's 'natural' passivity that would in the end give her strength and superiority. God would give woman 'a voice & wisdom which none could resist, & power over every assault of the evil one, bringing to naught the wisdom of this world . . . because she was willing to be the humblest she should be the most exalted & so on.'[56]

In seeking the 'feminine' aspect of God, the community that was gathering around Octavia was not therefore unusual in the context of early-twentieth-century England, though its particular combination of beliefs and the tightly knit character of the group were distinctive. At the centre of their community life and theology was the woman who had been invested with 'a voice and wisdom' which women like the Quaker Rachel Fox, suffragette Ellen Oliver, best friend Kate Firth and vicar's wife Gertrude Hill, believed that 'none could resist'. Who was this woman who they claimed would be the most exalted, the long-expected Shiloh, the daughter of God? Who was Mabel?

4

Who was Mabel?

In describing her followers as 'English churchwomen, who were gentle-women of mid-Victorian upbringing', Octavia was also describing herself. She was born in 1866 into a middle-class family, and her youth and early adulthood were typical of girls of her class and time. She was educated, but not in an academically distinguished school, and she did not go to university. Church and philanthropy formed the core of her social life. The British Empire, at its height in the late nine-teenth century, impinged on her family life when her only sibling went to work and live in South Africa. As already discussed, loss made an impact on her psyche early in life. To these bare facts we might add one further important feature: Mabel read voraciously and had a literary family background which was not the milieu of her own child-hood, but which she recalled with pride and affection.

Mabel was born in Peckham, a growing town south of London, to Katherine Ann Buxton and Augustus Andrews who were then aged thirty-six and thirty-seven respectively, on 11 January 1866, seven years after their first child, Charles. Augustus's profession was listed on his marriage certificate as banker's clerk but he had religious and literary connections of which Mabel later made much. He was the son of Elizabeth Honor Symons and Edward Andrews, a well-known Congregationalist preacher based in south London, who had taught classics and religion to the thirteen-year-old John Ruskin. Augustus's older sister Eliza ran a famous literary salon in the mid-nineteenth century that attracted the major writers and artists of the day; another sister Emily married the poet Coventry Patmore. Katherine and Augustus's little branch of the family was rather more ordinary. Charles and Mabel were their only children, and by the mid-1870s the family unit in England was reduced to two: Mabel and her mother.

When Mabel was nine years old, her father died. This was a turning point in her young life, the first in a long line of losses of those closest to her, losses that would mark the first forty years of her life and profoundly affect how she saw the world. The death of Augustus Andrews left Mabel, Charles and their mother to work out the practicalities of how to live without a steady income, even though Elizabeth, Katherine's mother, had left Katherine her shares in the National Freehold Land Society and in the Oude and Rohilkund Railway (in India) to the value of £1,070. While other branches of the family were wealthy and well connected, Mabel and her mother and brother were the poor relations, and they had little contact with the well-off branches of Augustus's family for many years. Katherine too was ill – she suffered from rheumatism, and was eventually barely able to walk – and Charles got consumption: they both needed money for medical treatment. And Mabel had to be educated.

With the death of her father, there entered into Mabel's life the family member who had the most enduring influence on her for many decades: her Aunt Fanny. Katherine Andrews decided to join forces with her childless sister, Fanny Waldron, whose own husband, Thomas, had died just six months before Augustus. Katherine sold their furniture and her husband's books, and the family went to live in Fanny's house in Croydon, then the largest town in Surrey and growing;[1] with good railway links, it too was fast becoming a suburb of London. Estimating their wealth at the time, Octavia later wrote that they had 'hardly more than £400 per annum'. This may not have seemed like very much money to her, writing in the mid-1920s, but if the figure was even remotely accurate, it made the family very comfortably middle class in the 1870s and 1880s, when £150 was regarded as a safely middle-class income.[2] And Fanny was relatively wealthy: she owned her own house, and inherited stocks and shares amounting to just over £1,000 from her mother, as well as £2,294 from her husband.[3]

The move to live with Aunt Fanny coincided with Mabel's move to a new school: 'Mabel went to Miss Thurton's School,'[4] as Aunt Fanny noted in her diary. Mabel was not educated at one of the new girls' high schools, which were being founded in the 1870s and 1880s and had an excellent reputation, but at a smaller, private girls' school where she received a good all-round education, which included music and painting but did not demand much of her academically. In short, she received the kind of education deemed suitable for a middle-class girl whose expected role in life was marriage. She enjoyed school, writing later that 'School memories are redolent of fun and mischief, and of naughtiness of the type of the heroines in the *Girl's Own Paper* of that period',[5] and at the beginning of a new academic year she noted in her diary: 'Commenced school again. Very glad.'[6]

The move to Aunt Fanny's house meant that church became the centre of Mabel's social life and activities. Religion had always been a vital part of Mabel's life, even though her father – in reaction against his father's evangelical religion – had been an agnostic.[7] Fanny was Low Church Anglican, closer to the evangelical end of the scale; when the famous American evangelists, Moody and Sankey, came to town in April 1875 Fanny went to hear them. By contrast, Katherine was attracted to the music and ritual of High Church Anglicanism. Aunt Fanny's practical piety and her mother's love of Anglo-Catholic ritual shaped the daily and weekly rhythm of Mabel's worshipping life.

On Sunday mornings the Low Church won out, as Mabel dutifully attended Christ Church with her aunt, where they had a family pew, afterwards noting in her diary who had preached and what she thought of the sermon. A new curate invited comment: 'New curate. (Plain very.) Nice I think', as did new hymn books which were described as 'very ridiculous' – suggesting that her later resistance to the Church of England's new Prayer Book (of 1927–28) had long roots.[8] Christ Church was her parish: it is where she was, along with her peers at school, confirmed in her faith at the age of fifteen and where, in her early twenties, she taught Sunday School, helped with the Sunday School summer treats, and became involved in Temperance Movement activities.

Mabel's mother, however, who loved music and poetry and made witty remarks, went to the Anglo-Catholic church near to their house, St Saviour's. Looking back, Octavia described her mother as sanguine; she may have appeared so in contrast with her more fervent evangelical relations, but by the second half of the nineteenth century, evangelicalism as a social and political force was waning in its influence. The repercussions of the Oxford Movement of the 1830s were now having their effect in a revival of Catholic or 'High Church' sensibilities in some quarters of the Church of England. The neo-Gothic churches that were built included every sort of decoration that had for so long been absent from English churches, from crucifixes and candles to statues of saints. Frequent masses accompanied by choral or organ music and 'smells and bells' reassured the worshipper that anyone could be a member of the body of Christ simply by receiving the sacrament, the very body and blood of Christ himself. This was the form of worship that Mabel's mother and her brother Charles preferred, and for which Mabel herself began to acquire a taste. She often went with her mother to evensong, 'enjoying the music, but very critical of all the appointments which I considered to be "Romish",[9] and to special occasions such as a confirmation by the Archbishop of Canterbury, Edward White Benson, in 1885.[10] Despite her disapproval of 'Romish' tendencies, when she was with her Low Church relatives Mabel attempted to be very High Church, dressing in black on Good Friday. The result was that Mabel grew up with what she later described as 'a curious combination of a love of High Church ceremonial and a belief in Low Church principles'.[11]

Fanny's Low Church principles governed family life. Fanny was an abiding presence and more than any other adult the prevailing influence in the young Mabel's life after her father's death. In Mabel's diaries, which she kept in her late teenage years and early twenties before she married, Fanny was often discussed while Mabel's mother remained a shadowy figure, an invalid whose ventures into town with Mabel, or simply downstairs, were rare events. The house they all lived in was now very much 'Auntie's' house. Visits to the theatre and picture galleries waned; the prevailing activity of this household was the conventional occupation of pious middle- and upper-class Victorian women: philanthropy. Her aunt engaged in good works for the poor, visiting about ninety houses twice a week with milk puddings and beef tea. This made its mark on Mabel even though as a child she was not allowed to go with her aunt. 'I was never allowed to penetrate into the depths of —— Street, but though only a name, it is redolent of trials and sufferings, cobwebs and dirt unspeakable.'[12] Nevertheless, she participated in other philanthropic activities, especially working parties, at which one lady read Charles Dickens's David Copperfield while the others worked on shirts or other garments for the poor or to sell at church bazaars. At the end of each year, Mabel would list in her diary all the bazaar work she had made that year – the number of wool petticoats, mats, iron-holders and so on – obviously proud of the quantity. When she was a young woman, she had her own 'District' – a section of the parish with a set number of households – for visiting. She usually went one afternoon a week and would note those who were ill, the new babies, the new people to visit. All this youthful philanthropic activity is interesting in the light of Octavia's later rejection of charity as a form of temporary relief that did not help the world.

Mabel's other passion was reading. Her diaries are full of trips to the local library, and as a young woman she made lists of the books she was reading. In October 1884, when she was eighteen, her reading included novels by Charles Kingsley, George Eliot, Charlotte Brontë and William Thackeray, as well as essays by John Ruskin and a life of Oliver Cromwell. In October 1885, she read Macaulay's *Essays* and Samuel Smiles's *Self Help*. In 1886, she read more Eliot, Kingsley, Smiles, Ruskin and Thackeray, as well as works by Goethe, Robert Browning, Charles Dickens, Anthony Trollope and Rider Haggard, various collections of sermons and Darwin's *On the Origin of Species*. She also noted that in November she read rubbish! Sometimes, she made a comment on the books she was reading: she did not like Thackeray as much as Dickens, for example, because 'all characters have certain sameness, love of aristocracy, too much introduced, nearly every character is boasting of the grand people they know'.[13] In the spring of 1887, she took a university extension class on Shakespeare. Trips to the local library; extension classes; careful notes about the enjoyment or not of a book, and why: these are the hallmarks of the keen autodidact who does not have the luxury of a university degree or a family library.

Despite her pious aunt and invalid mother, despite the death of her father and absence of her much-loved brother, home life for Mabel seems to have been happy. Her mother and aunt left her very much to her own devices, and she spent much of her time sitting in a tree in the garden, even eating tea there sometimes with a friend.[14] Her brother Charles evoked the warmth of the close-knit family he had left behind in a letter he wrote in March 1877, from the ship out to South Africa, where he was heading for a new life in Natal: 'My Sundays at home are a source of regretful longing, for after the week's work I did enjoy my holiday . . . One's thoughts naturally revert more to the home you have left behind on Sunday.'[15]

Mabel's upbringing and education had prepared her for marriage. She left school at the age of eighteen. Later that year, in the autumn of 1884, she became engaged to the twenty-seven-year-old Arthur Barltrop whom she had first met in the summer of 1883 when she was a seventeen-year-old schoolgirl on holiday with her family in the seaside town of St Leonard's, on the south coast of England. The son of an Essex blacksmith, Arthur spent 1881 to 1883 as a schoolmaster at St John's Leatherhead, a school for boys that gave free education to the sons of poor clergymen. When Arthur first met Mabel, he was just about to begin reading for holy orders.

Because Mabel was young, her mother only gave her permission on the condition that marriage was not to be considered for a while. Long engagements were not unusual in the late nineteenth century – indeed, were recommended by marriage manuals – when couples did not know each other very well, and that was certainly true of Mabel and Arthur in 1884. So they spent five betrothed years getting to know each other, while Arthur trained for ordination and began his work as a deacon and then a priest in the Church.

Mabel's diaries for the years 1885–89 have survived, and while these are only small pocket diaries, often with just a short entry for each day, they give a picture of Mabel's life at this time, and of her developing relationship with Arthur. Daily life revolved around home and friends, church and related events, and Arthur's letters and visits. She played the piano, sang and read; she wrote letters; she saw female friends of her own age, and went for walks, played cards, attended lectures and played tennis with them; she painted and sewed, sometimes for days at a time. When her mother was well enough to come downstairs, she would read out loud to Mabel as she engaged in these tasks. She also spent a good deal of time with older friends of her mother and Aunt Fanny, many of them church friends and acquaintances of the family who would call for tea. Occasionally she made a wry comment about these visits: 'Mrs Bolter called in evening, regular old chatter-box but a trifle more interesting than usual.' Increasingly she helped in the running of the household: and as the new year dawned in 1888, she noted 'Began housekeeping at £1, 10s. a week.' She also explained duties to the maid, spring-cleaned, tidied her mother's room, worked in the garden, and painted the garden shed. Illnesses were carefully noted and even a visit to the dentist when she wrote, 'Two teeth extracted. Quite enjoyed it.'[16]

All of this day-to-day activity was punctuated with frequent visits from and to Arthur, and a remarkable degree of intimacy between them for the time – though she occasionally noted in her diary that when Arthur came to stay, she slept at the neighbour's house – as well as occasional visits to his or her relatives. She would always go to the railway station to meet Arthur, writing in her diary, 'To meet my boy. So very glad.' His departures were sad occasions, and she would get up to take him to the station, often at 5.30 or six in the morning, even though she was not an early riser and wrote in her diary that she resolved to become one. She never did, always preferring night-times to mornings. The days when Arthur left were 'wretched', full of missing him and longing, but he would often surprise her with a return visit, sometimes the very next day. When he left to go to his first curacy, after he had been ordained deacon in 1887, she wrote, 'So busy packing and oh so wretched. Cried dreadfully and at dinner too. To St Pancras and then "Goodbye" for how long (oh darling).' She woke up the next day 'so miserable. District. Everything so dull and cold.'[17]

They were two people in love who wished to be with each other as much as possible. One Sunday evening, when the others went out to church, 'Arthur and I stayed at home, too happy, confessions.' When Arthur visited her for the new year in 1887, they skated all day – 'Lovely, never enjoyed a day so much' – and when the ice and frost broke up they went walking on the muddy path and 'Arthur carried me over it, such fun. Home rather late.' They went bicycling or tricycling together: 'such a delicious tricycle ride. Got on at Norwood, tandem. All through Bromley, ever so far', but the next day 'so stiff. Arthur not well so stayed with him.' Another time they went for a picnic on the Downs, taking sandwiches and wine. Surprisingly, these expeditions were rarely chaperoned and Mabel's exuberance in Arthur's company is obvious even in the shortest of diary entries. This is not to say that they did not argue, and Mabel would note in her diary when she got angry with Arthur and the remorse she felt afterwards: 'I was so cross and am ever so sorry now.'[18]

During their long engagement, Mabel got to know Arthur's relatives, especially his sister Helena, known as Lennie, who was six years older than her. They were close as young women, but grew apart in a dramatic way later in life after Lennie had Mabel 'sectioned' in St Andrew's in 1915. But, back in the mid-1880s, Mabel and Lennie were friends, especially after Lennie's first husband died at the age of just twenty-eight, leaving Lennie with their two-week-old daughter, Rita. Mabel would help with the baby when Lennie came to stay, and it was Lennie, along with Aunt Fanny, who helped Mabel get ready for her wedding and new home in 1889. There were also visits to and from Mabel's own relatives, though Charles remained in South Africa, never to visit England again, despite Mabel asking him to come over for her wedding.

It was when she was nineteen that Mabel came into contact with her father's wealthier relatives, the Ormes. She went to stay with Eliza, her father's oldest sister, and her husband Charles, a brewer and distiller, and their children, for the first time in January 1885, planning to go only for a few days but at their insistence staying for two weeks. On meeting 'Aunt Charles' for the first time in January 1885, Mabel wrote to Arthur that Eliza was 'a dear old lady, very intellectual, one to whom it is a pleasure to talk, for she has met in her time hundreds of celebrities; she was Carlyle's favourite and Ruskin's confidante, and it is so nice to hear her talk about these'.[19]

The Ormes' home was in Regent's Park, London, on Avenue Road (the street on which Madame Blavatsky of the Theosophical Society owned a house) where they had held regular salons on Thursdays to which the great literary and artistic figures of the mid-nineteenth century came: the Pre-Raphaelites and various poets, Ralph Waldo Emerson on his visits to England, Herbert Spencer, and Horatio and Matilda, the children of Alfred, Lord Tennyson.[20] By the time Mabel entered the world of the Ormes, the great salon days were over, but the Orme children were all accomplished, and in their careers and marriages they continued the intellectual connections of their parents.[21]

Three of the Orme children were unmarried and lived at home. Charles, their younger son, became a friend and correspondent of Mabel; after their initial meeting, they often exchanged letters about literary matters and family gossip, and saw each other quite regularly. Beatrice – 'Bix' – was the cousin to whom Mabel became closest: they walked in Kew Gardens and talked about Arthur and all the things that young women talk about with each other. Most impressive to Mabel was her cousin Eliza – 'Sili' – who was thirty-six when Mabel met her and 'a darling, if ever a person were to be worshipped it is she . . . I am so proud of being her cousin', as she wrote to Arthur. The younger Eliza Orme was a formidable woman, being the first female barrister in England, a social activist, frequent newspaper columnist and keenly involved in Liberal politics. In 1871, she went to University College,

London, where she studied Law and Political Economy and won first prize in Roman law and the Hume Scholarship in Jurisprudence, but as the university did not yet grant degrees to women, she did not receive her law degree until 1888; she went to Lincoln's Inn in 1873 to read in the chambers of Savill Vaizey but because she was a woman she was not admitted to the Bar. She then went on to run a law practice with a series of female partners doing commissioned work for male solicitors.[22] Mabel wrote to Arthur, 'She has become a barrister . . . and she has become so to prove that women are fully as capable as men to act in that capacity. But she is compelled by law only to take half fees, and is not even allowed the use of the Libraries for the use of those in the legal profession. She has to buy for herself all the expensive books, one set cost £40, the other day. You cannot fail to like and admire her. I think hers a lovely character, always doing something for somebody.'

Through Sili, Mabel entered a world of intellectual women (and men) unlike any she had encountered in Croydon. While visiting in 1885, she attended a meeting of a debating society that Sili convened monthly at her home. Mabel wrote of it to Arthur, 'Some of the people are celebrities. I had the honour of being introduced to the future Head-Mistress of Girton College. She is jolly.'[23] She also went to a talk that Sili gave on apparitions (which did not frighten her as she had expected it would), and another lecture by Sili, in Hackney, on women's suffrage.

The Ormes were great supporters of women's education and women's suffrage, and were politically Liberal. This was quite in contrast with Mabel and Arthur who were staunch Conservatives. Mabel noted in her diary in 1886 that she had attended a Conservative meeting before an election, and how delighted she and Arthur felt at the victory of a Conservative candidate in Croydon.[24] Mabel sent a newspaper editorial that Sili had written, but knew that Arthur would disapprove of its liberal message (and he did). Mabel was proud of her intellectual and well-connected relatives, but she remained something of an outsider, admiring and rather star-struck. She wrote to Arthur that Sili had offered her a ticket for the Private View at the Royal Academy: 'I can scarcely believe it, she gets these things from all sorts of people. You must come too, we should see all the celebrities of the day there. Of course one does not go to see the pictures on that day but the people.'[25]

This literary and intellectual family opened up worlds to Mabel that she did not know, but she did not walk into them, at least not permanently. The Ormes and their friends remained 'celebrities' of whom she could boast. One clue here is her autograph book: well into her thirties and forties she collected autographs, either by deliberately acquiring the signatures of famous men (no women) of the day or by saving letters to her from people she admired or thought important (bishops, prominent clergy, John Ruskin and Coventry Patmore). The autograph book was important to her: in her forties, when she was a widow and had been ill, she wrote a detailed account of what each of her children should have should she die, and what provision she had made for them. The autograph book was significant enough to be mentioned and was to go to her daughter. The fact is that a person who collects autographs is not someone who belongs to the world of those whose autographs are deemed valuable. Mabel was never fully a part of the social and intellectual milieu of her illustrious and well-connected relatives.

By the time Mabel met the Ormes and began to enter their world on a regular basis, whether she yearned for anything else or not, her path was already set: she was engaged to Arthur, a man who had not gone to university but who would be a respectable and hard-working priest. Her literary education, which was important to her, was gained through her own reading efforts, rather than formally at university. She was a middle-class, Victorian young woman who was not yet questioning her role in life, but was certainly delighted and a little overawed by her new-found, rather grander relatives.

Nevertheless, a sign of her characteristic steely independence emerges in a letter written to Arthur towards the end of her first visit to the Orme household, when she wrote that she was 'tired of being petted and made a deal of'. Clearly, the practical and forthright qualities for which, as Octavia, leader of her community, she was well known, began to reveal themselves early on. There is even a peevish tone here, as if – for all her being impressed by them – she does not wish to betray her own origins, achievements or sensibilities. She wrote that she was tired of being flattered by the many relatives who visited the Ormes in order to see her and then passed an opinion on her to her Aunt Eliza. 'It is nothing to me what *they* think. I have not words in which to express my detestation of hollow compliments,' she wrote crossly. She showed a loyalty to her own little family unit, saying that it was no credit to these visiting family members who had had nothing to do with her upbringing that she had been well educated, and she wished they would tell her what her faults were, because she could then at least correct them. She finished up the letter to Arthur mischievously: 'I feel such a naughty girl, you don't know what a wicked temper I am in, I have ruffled my hair all up so that it almost stands on end. I suppose it is natural that they should all be interested in me, as they have never seen me and scarcely heard of me before.'[26]

Arthur had become Mabel's closest confidant; the one with whom she shared all her ideas and feelings, and – despite these family intellectual connections – it was through Arthur that her ideas, especially her theological views, now came to be shaped more distinctly. But what was informing Arthur's theology?

Soon after Arthur and Mabel met, Arthur began his training for ordination at Chichester Theological College, which was High Church. Founded in 1840, it was one of the new Anglican theological colleges designed to enable lower- and middle-class men, who could not afford to take a degree, to become priests. Previously, men had simply taken their degree at Cambridge or Oxford and been ordained, often into the fellowship they held at one of the colleges. For many priests, this was still the way they became ordained. But the new theological colleges were part of the wider reform of the Church of England in the nineteenth century. They attempted to educate a man theologically and train him for ordination, not simply give him a general education in the humanities. They were also designed to provide the Church of England with more priests, for it became clear in the second half of the century, as the population grew and cities developed, that there was a shortage of Church of England priests.[27] Priests had always been gentlemen, often gentry, but now men like Arthur, from the middle and lower-middle classes could join the clerical ranks.

When Arthur arrived at Chichester, the college was flourishing under the guidance of the principal, Canon W. Awdry, having recovered from a slump in the 1850s and '60s. The college had just one building, with a lecture room and a library, and students rented their own lodgings. The ordinands attended the cathedral daily, for morning prayer and evensong. Occasionally, in the evening there might be a lecture by the Principal. As one student from Arthur's generation later reminisced, 'There was little supervision – a simple code of rules, of course, but we were on our honour.'[28] What Arthur learned at Chichester was largely guided by a recently designed national Church of England theological examination, to be taken by non-university men. This broadened the curriculum in the theological colleges, counteracting the narrow partisanship that existed in some of them and ensured that all ordinands (wherever they were training) covered the same area of study: Old Testament, New Testament, Ecclesiastical History and Latin; the Creeds, the Thirty-Nine Articles and the Prayer Book. Mabel noted carefully in her diary when Arthur set off for Nottingham in 1887 to take his first set of exams, that she saw him off at the station and felt 'great anxiety' for him; but a few days later, she was able to write 'Passed!!!' He took two more sets of exams after he was ordained deacon and before he became a priest, again anxiously noted in Mabel's diary but she was able to write in her diary in November 1888 'A. passed A1' and again in December, 'A. has passed well.'

What Mabel learned theologically was also guided by that examination curriculum, for she took a great interest in Arthur's studies, reading (she later reported) Church History, Butler's *Analogy*, Flint's *Theism* and many other of his books. A surviving notebook from this period includes her careful and detailed notes about the saints and martyrs from the first to the twelfth century. She began to acquire a theological education informally, reading everything that her fiancé read. It was during this period of her betrothal that Mabel's acute engagement with the Christian tradition and with all that was up to date in theology began; when she later developed her own distinctive theology, she knew the history and texts of orthodox Christianity better than most women and many men.

Arthur was ordained as a deacon on 18 September 1887 by the Bishop of Southwell, just two days after he had learned that he had passed his examinations. Mabel did not attend his ordination but marked it in her diary, 'My darling boy's ordination. May God bless him.' He came to stay the following day and she wrote, 'So happy and proud . . . He looks such a darling' – presumably she thought he looked good in his new clerical collar. He spent his first few months of ordained ministry as a curate at Brampton in Derbyshire, but this did not work out, so nine months later he went to a second curacy at Slinfold in the Chichester diocese. Mabel visited him there and thought the church lovely and the people dear. On 23 December, Mabel went to see 'my dear boy ordained priest'. (In the Church of England, before being ordained as priests, curates spent up to a year as deacons first, as they still do.) But Slinfold was not the place for Arthur either. At the end of her diary for 1888, Mabel wrote, 'So the old year goes, there have been a few trials (Brampton & Slinfold) but much to be thankful for.' The year 1889 opened with Arthur making preparations to move to another curacy, this time at St Mary's, Dover. Getting established in a church was important if Mabel and Arthur were to be married. Mabel wrote in her diary in the new year, 'Letter from Arthur, all going fairly well at Dover I think, and the air is doing him good. Must not set my heart on Dover, "only if it be really good for us".' She went to visit him and was relieved that her 'dear boy was looking so much better for the change at Dover. Good news but nothing certain of course . . . Dover is a lovely place he says, and the church splendid.' By the beginning of February, she was finally able to write in her diary, 'Glorious news about Dover quite settled. So glad and thankful. May it prove the greatest blessing to us both.'

They could now plan their wedding, but only a week after the good news of Dover being settled, Mabel felt herself unsure: 'Arthur and I talked over wedding and came to no satisfactory arrangements. Me X.' Now that marriage was a reality, Mabel almost immediately began to have doubts about disrupting the family unit she knew so well: she was 'very troubled about leaving home and Auntie', and on Arthur's next visit she made him sit down with herself and Aunt Fanny to discuss the possibility of Fanny coming to Dover to live with them. He agreed. The move also included Mabel's mother, although she did not merit a mention in Mabel's diary entry.

Finally a date, 1 June 1889, and a church, the Chapel Royal Savoy, in London, were set; and the Revd Henry White was to marry them. They were to have a meal afterwards at the Gaiety Restaurant on the Strand in London, with a menu of soup, chicken, lamb and ice cream with fruit. Mabel began her preparations for married life, furiously making bed linen, tablecloths and other household necessities on her newly acquired sewing machine though it often seemed to go wrong

– 'tiresome thing'. It was Aunt Fanny, not Mabel's mother, who helped her with all the practical matters. In early April, Arthur, Fanny and Mabel went to Dover together to find a house and it was Aunt Fanny and Lennie who, in the month before the wedding, went with Mabel to London to the Army and Navy Store to buy kitchen utensils, knives and dinner services. Finally, at the end of May, Mabel and Arthur were together in Croydon and had great fun looking at their presents and reading the 'scores of letters' wishing them well. When Arthur left on Friday, 31 May, Mabel found it a trying day, 'the last in my dear little house'. She found the goodbyes difficult – to her neighbours, the people in her District – and 'very trying for my darling Auntie and me but let us trust it will lead to greater happiness'. 'And so,' she wrote that night before going to sleep, on the eve of her long-anticipated wedding, 'goodbye to Mabel Andrews.'[29]

In Dover, Mabel took on the duties of a curate's wife, continuing to do the kind of 'good works' that her Aunt Fanny had encouraged her in and becoming an active member of the Mothers' Union. Arthur was a conscientious Anglican priest: a caring pastor and hard-working man; a High Churchman who was not a 'ritualist', and therefore not fussy about liturgy. Mabel later described him as a careful chooser of hymns, and scrupulously careful with the parish's money. Reading between the lines he was neither an exciting nor a charismatic priest, but he was sensible and reliable, and he was beloved by his parishioners. When he left St Mary's, Dover in 1894, the Band of Hope (a teetotal society for young people) in that parish gave him a chair that still remains in Mabel's sitting room in 12 Albany Road, Bedford. He was a profoundly loyal churchman, who believed that the Church of England was 'the spiritual mother of the state', as he told his congregation in one sermon that survives. 'Our national religion is bound up with our national bliss.'[30]

In their married life, Arthur and Mabel continued to pursue their mutual interest in theology. There was a clerical society in Dover, which they both attended. When Arthur 'had to write a paper it was generally provocative of a good discussion, as he was an accurate thinker, very practical and conscientious'.[31] Mabel continued to read the theological books of the day, often as soon as they were published. In a bible that Arthur gave her soon after they were married, she wrote careful notes on the nature of all the books along the lines of the biblical criticism of the day. These marginalia represent the conscientious note-taking of a theologically enthusiastic young curate's wife, given access, unusually for a woman, to a whole library of up-to-date theological books and biblical criticism. On the inside page, before the contents page, she summed up the Old Testament:

> The Pentateuch appeals to man's conscience.
> The Historical Books appeal to man's intellect.
> The Poetical Books appeal to man's heart.
> The Prophetical Books open out to him the future.

And at the beginning of each of the individual books and letters of the New Testament she wrote a sentence which encapsulated its key theme.[32]

But Mabel's time was soon to be taken up with children rather than theological societies. Four were born in fairly rapid succession. Eric Arthur was born on 3 March 1890, just over a year after Arthur and Mabel had married. Ivan Charles came two years later on 28 March 1892, Adrian Bazeley on 18 September 1897, and Dilys Mabel on 28 September 1898. There were to be no more children, though Mabel's case notes from the lunatic asylum in 1915 give a hint that Arthur wanted more, while Mabel did not. Arthur loved children, and his daughter Dilys had affectionate memories of him all her life, even though he died when she was only eight. He was always encouraging children – both his own and those in the parishes he served – to get involved in activities, and modelled this in pursuing his own hobbies in gardening, woodwork, cricket, football and bookbinding.

After leaving Dover, the Barltrops moved to two more churches: to Maidstone in 1894 and Croydon in 1898. In each case, Arthur was still the curate, doing the hard work of the parish without a significant salary to compensate, and without the status of being vicar or rector. This is perhaps not surprising, given that he was not a 'university man'. In 1896, Arthur became ill. He remained at the church in Croydon, but struggled. In December 1902, he took a leave of absence for three months and went to South Africa, leaving Mabel to look after the four children. The Bishop of Dover wrote to Mabel the day before Arthur left, saying that he hoped the sea voyage would restore her husband's health and strength. They did not know that what ailed him was a brain tumour, and a sea voyage and sunnier climate would make no difference. Arthur was back in Croydon the next year, where they were living again with Aunt Fanny in her old house which she had retained, and looking for another job, but with no success. There were letters to and from bishops, in which job prospects for Arthur were discussed; but these prospects came to nothing. These were lean and difficult years. The sources dry up and the details are scanty, but at some point the family moved to Bedford because the schools there were so good (and affordable), and to be near to Arthur's sister Lennie, who had by now remarried. Her new husband was Thomas Bull who owned a jeweller's store in Bedford, and they lived in a large house on the Embankment by the river, just around the corner from 12 Albany Road. Mabel and Arthur made sure their children were educated well. Eric and Adrian went to St John's Leatherhead, the school where Arthur had once taught, which offered scholarships to sons of Church of England clergy. Ivan attended the local Bedford school; Eric and Ivan went to Queens' College, Cambridge. Dilys went to one of the local girls' schools in Bedford and secretarial college.

In 1906, Arthur died. Mabel's years as a widow looking after four children were punctuated with prayer meetings, which she attended with her friend Kate Firth; regular churchgoing at St Paul's Church, a High Anglican church in Bedford; and her work as an editor. Aunt Fanny lived with the family, as she had done since Mabel and Arthur had married, sustaining them and providing crucial financial support. The family photographs from this period, with Mabel looking tired and drawn, contrast with the youthful, exuberant, smiling Mabel who holds up Eric, her first-born, for all to see. It was that tired, drawn and church-sick Mabel who read Southcott's little blue booklet with such joy in 1914.

In 1924, as Octavia, Mabel wrote a short book about her early years, for private circulation within her community. She gave it to her followers as a Christmas gift, with strict instructions that it was for their eyes only, though a copy of it was sent to the British Library in 1940, six years after her death, so presumably one of her followers thought that her story deserved a more public airing. The purpose of the book was to explain how a woman with an ordinary upbringing and family life came to be 'Shiloh' and already by that time had a following of hundreds worldwide. In the selection of each fact or detail, as she told the story of the younger Mabel, the older Octavia asked: 'Does that emphasise the extreme naturalness of a life engineered by God for the performance of a most strange act?'[33] Many people write a memoir when they get to later middle age – Octavia was fifty-eight – and at that stage they shape their youth with hindsight, missing a detail here or there, reinterpreting an episode or event, seeing a particular person through a golden haze. All of this is part of any person's story as they try to explain how they got from there to here. So as Octavia pondered what constituted the extreme naturalness of her life, she was also necessarily shaping the facts of that life. What did she want her followers to know and think about her?

First and foremost, Octavia gave herself a worthy, earthly lineage, highlighting her more exalted family connections, especially the literary environment of the Ormes' household. She wrote that as a child she 'was regaled with personal reminiscences of Thackeray, Tennyson, Carlyle, Garibaldi, George Eliot, Coventry Patmore, Ruskin, Woolner, Millais, the pre-Raphaelites and so on.'[34] She portrayed herself at her Aunt Eliza's house, sitting 'on certain chairs in the drawing room – which were in years gone by, the particular favourites of one or another of these great men and women'. This conjures up a winning picture of a child bouncing from chair to chair; and as we remember Mabel's awe of celebrity, that image rings true. But as her diaries and letters of the late 1880s testify, none of this happened in her childhood; she did not know the Ormes until she was nineteen. The older Octavia embedded herself in this culture at a much earlier age. Why?

Octavia's family literary connections were central to her understanding of her identity. She considered herself a *literary* person. All of her life she prided herself on the fact that she could write clearly and well; it is a curiously self-referential, recurring theme in all of her writing and, not surprisingly, she mentions it in her autobiography. From an early age, she reports, she had a capacity 'to say what I wanted to say in suitable words'. She remarks that 'Facility in language and writing was the legacy handed from father to son from generations' – with the implication that she is part of that family line.[35] In 1912, she thought her third son, Adrian, might train for ordination, for which she wished to send him to Oxford (as it turned out he never did this);

wishing to earn some additional income for this purpose, she set herself up as a freelance editor who could edit a text or help people write their books and articles more clearly. Later, when the community in Bedford had been formed, she wrote almost all of its literature, using a variety of literary forms – pamphlets, more substantial theological works, a monthly magazine, even novels and children's books – in order to reach and appeal to a variety of readers. What she implies, in her autobiography, is that the literary milieu of her family rubbed off on her. This was not insignificant, especially for a girl. In a world in which women were generally less well educated than men, such literary connections as Octavia possessed (albeit indirectly) gave her social and cultural capital, a sense of social standing and even authority.

Octavia also had a sharply honed sense of social status – 'to live a normal life according to one's station is a public duty'[36] – so there was no shortage of pride, even snobbery, in embracing this part of her lineage. Nowhere did she mention her father's employment as a bank clerk; instead, she painted a picture of a leisured man of letters who engaged in philanthropy. In describing her own family life with Arthur, she portrayed their child-rearing practices in line with solidly middle-class, late-Victorian attitudes. The children had a nurse and they were never 'all over the place', for 'among other advantages the simple discipline of the stated time for their visits downstairs and ours upstairs, was valuable when the severe rules of school-life began'. And nostalgia for a lost era, a golden age of manners (which were such an important feature of Panacea life), floats through her memoir. 'I was very glad indeed that it was my lot to bring up my children during the late sunset of old-fashioned ways and manners . . . It is common to put down all our troubles to the war itself, but I recall many signs that decadence had set in before that.'[37]

As Octavia looked back, she was fashioning herself and the facts of her life to fit the person she wanted to be in the eyes of her followers, and as this memoir was written five years into the Panacea community's life, and ten years after she had first read Southcott's writings, she was also suggesting that God had fashioned both herself and the ordinary facts of her life for a very extraordinary purpose. She made a virtue out of her rather mediocre education, remarking: 'it is best for a woman – certainly it was for me – to be Jack-of-all-trades, though she may be master of none'[38]. Her education explains her wide reading and ultimately the eclectic nature of her religious beliefs, and we see the same magpie-like attitude to knowledge amongst many of her female followers, similarly educated. One of the surviving members of the community, when I arrived there, confirmed this, saying that Octavia read anything and everything, and took what she regarded as good or true from each book.[39] Nevertheless, she described her school as a well-known college in the south of England, perhaps with the hope that the reader might think it socially, if not academically, good.

Her memoirs evoke the varied nature of her religious upbringing: her grandfather's evangelical Congregationalism; her father's agnosticism; the Presbyterianism of her Scottish relatives; the High Church Anglicanism of her mother and brother, and the Low Church Anglicanism of her Aunt Fanny. She related that she even had a near brush with Roman Catholicism when, after her father's death, Coventy Patmore – who had converted to Roman Catholicism in 1864 after his first wife Emily died, and whose godchild Mabel 'believed' she was – asked her mother whether he could educate Mabel in a Roman Catholic establishment. Her mother declined.[40] The only aspects of Christianity that Mabel said that she had not learned about in childhood were the heterodox, sectarian religious groups that were growing and developing in that period. Looking back she found it strange that she had not: 'Considering what an omnivorous reader I was, it is curious that, until about ten years ago, neither Theosophy, Spiritualism nor Occultism crossed my path, and that even among my large number of relatives and acquaintances, I was never introduced to any of these subjects.' Looking back, we might consider it strange too, given that popular spiritualism, in the form of parlour seances, was at its height in the 1870s and 1880s. Once she did investigate these heterodox groups their 'useful' aspects were also woven into the beliefs and practices of the community in Bedford, just as their overall belief systems were repudiated.

When Mabel had her midlife spiritual crisis, all of the religious elements she had encountered in her life thus far combined to make her utterly confused about God, and what *her* relationship with God was. But this crisis too was redeemed in hindsight. These elements ultimately combined to help her, as a 'Jack-of-all-trades', to build her own new faith. As the older Octavia presents it, the young Mabel was left pretty much to her own intellectual and spiritual devices to find her path through a range of options that just about covered the nineteenth-century Christian gamut. She summed it up: 'As I look back, I can see that I learned by these very circumstances to be an independent thinker, and, that I had ample opportunity of hearing all sides, made the independent thinking of richer value. God's way of doing all His works in the midst, not at the end of a long line, is in evidence once more.'[41] The older Octavia believed that the strong arm of Providence (what others might call destiny) was at work in the young Mabel's life.

In the retelling of her life, coincidences – what Freud called the 'uncanny' – were also important: they influenced the life of the community and, Octavia believed, her own young life. Her place of birth – Peckham Rye, where William Blake had had, in the late eighteenth century, a vision of angels in a tree – was of significance not just because she, like Blake, was a prophet and writer but also because, by 1924, the community in Bedford had taken the words of Blake's 'Jerusalem' to heart, believing that they were building Jerusalem in England's green and pleasant land. Her brother Charles's place of residence, Pietermaritzburg, in South Africa was the town where Helen Shepstone had lived. Charles Barltrop's greatest friend there was an archdeacon, who was the very same man to whom Helen Shepstone confided her 'revelatory' papers about the Southcott mystery before she left for England in 1915, 'little dreaming that the subject of the revelation was the sister of his own intimate friend'. But Charles had died by the time Mabel had any connection with Helen Shepstone.

Death and loss were central themes for Octavia as she looked back, with her most acutely felt grief reserved for her father and brother, distant figures from many decades earlier whose portraits she now painted in the most idealistic of terms. Her father was 'utterly kind'; 'servants adored his benevolence'; and there were many stories 'of his graciousness and consideration for all who came in contact with him'. He was 'nearly always engaged in reading and writing. He was very delicate and highly strung, and seems to have destroyed a book he was writing, because it did not come up to his ideal.' Her brother, Charles, 'had a wonderful charm and was greatly beloved everywhere he went'. And as a fifty-eight-year-old woman she still felt that loss keenly: 'It was always a perplexity to me as a girl, knowing that I could have appreciated and understood my Father and Brother, and that I literally should have basked in the sunshine of their brilliance and charm, why I was deprived of both and knew but little of them except hearsay?'[42] This question she never answered in her memoir. Just as her father's book was never to be completed, so these were relationships never to be had, and no amount of providential explanation could take that away. God's 'engineering' was never applied to this ordinary tale of grief. No amount of virtue could be made out of this loss – unless, of course, one could beat death altogether. And we can read, just as her followers could and would have done, of the loss that had shadowed her youth with the knowledge that she was, in the Panacea community, training her disciples to overcome death, to live for ever.

Her theological preoccupations with life after death manifest themselves in the memoir. The older Octavia recalled the younger Mabel being worried that her father had gone to hell because he did not believe in God, and that her mother would go there if she did not reform and become more sober-minded. Her grandfather's preaching on predestination – that all people are predestined to go to hell or heaven by God with no account of the goodness (or otherwise) of their life on earth – had caused her father to reject the Church and caused Mabel untold anxiety. She tried to square the unkind notion of predestination with her father's generous nature and good works, 'so my poor little mind, which was of a Puritanical make, but which could detect the value of kindness, was constantly weighing up the pros and cons as to whether there was a "chance" for this man, who had the "kind heart" . . . but who unhappily was wanting in the "simple faith".' Up to the age of twenty she feared he had gone to hell and then she read a book which changed her mind: Frederic Farrar's *Eternal Hope,* a series of five sermons on the afterlife preached by Farrar in 1877 at Westminster Abbey where he was a canon.

The older Octavia commented with real sympathy for the younger Mabel's anxieties: 'Oh, the sufferings of poor souls brought up in man's teachings about God! Mercifully, we shall not have much more of it!'[43] Her followers understood that allusion: they were part of a community that believed they were being taught directly by God and they hoped to beat death. It is to those followers that we now turn.

II

The Community

5

The Female Apostles

In early 1919, before she was even named as Shiloh, Mabel began to dream of forming a community. She wrote to Ellen Oliver, 'Wouldn't a Hostel – a "Land of Goshen" be lovely! Really devoted "believers" could take up nice houses in Bedford which is a most lovely place & is going up by leaps & bounds. Selfridges is coming [&] has taken a huge block in High St & Vickers-Maxim are coming.' Her vision was that all the believers would live together, having common meals and conversation, but their own rooms. 'Who knows but in all the coming social troubles we may do something like this!!'[1] Perhaps she is the only Messiah figure in history to name Selfridges as a selling point to her followers.

Mabel Baltrop realised her dream: she formed in Bedford a distinctive, predominantly female community of which she, as Octavia, was head. In a self-conscious paralleling with the actions of Jesus, she appointed twelve female apostles. Whilst men began to join from 1920 onwards, the society remained largely female. The creation of this community, in which women did everything, was by all standards an impressive achievement and it appealed to women who were serious about religion but seriously disillusioned by the churches in which they were allowed no meaningful roles. When they came to visit Octavia, 'they felt warmed and comforted to such an extent that a kind of spiritual home-sickness would affect them when they had to leave her' and so 'they gathered around her one by one, just as the early disciples, desiring to be in His immediate vicinity, gathered round Jesus'.[2] This was not just an experience of the dissonance that always exists between what the Gospel promises and what the Church was – felt by so many Christians, orthodox and heterodox at all times in the history of Christianity – though it was in part that, but also a longing for something much more, which they found in Albany Road, Bedford.

In 1919, when it was still an all-female community, the apostles became 'brides of Christ' just as Roman Catholic or Anglican nuns might. In April, Octavia felt that she must put aside her earthly husband, who had now been dead for nearly fifteen years, for it seemed plain to her that 'Thy Maker is Thy Husband'. She wrote poignantly to Ellen Oliver about how she did this:

> I looked at my Earthly Husband's ring & then at his photographs in my bedroom. Well I had long ago cast out of *this* room all *Books* containing men's teachings & somehow I felt those pictures *must also go* – two photographs & a brooch with a photograph & the picture of the memorial put up to him in S. Augustine's Church (it has crossed palms). It was a real trial. I wept because I thought it would hurt his feelings – you can understand – but I felt it had to be & I felt 'I have had so much to bear I must surely be able to bear this' – so I gathered them all together after praying he might be made to *understand* (he was *very* sensitive) & took them into the little study. Then I came back & took my rings off & *washed* them, pouring water over them.[3]

Most of the earliest members were single, middle-aged women, confirmed spinsters and widows (though not war widows), rather than young women whose chances of marriage had been largely dashed by the war. Most were in their fifties and sixties in 1919: Gertrude Searson was fifty-one years old, Alice Jones sixty, Kate and Bess Hodgkinson fifty-nine and sixty-two respectively, Winna Green was one of the youngest at forty-six, while her sister Hilda was fifty-seven. They belonged to that generation of women born in the 1860s and 1870s, of whom 44 per cent had never married. They came to make a new home in Bedford, and as they gathered there they took a marriage oath to the Lord, as four of them did on 7 June: 'I . . . take Thee, O God my Maker, to be my Wedded Husband, and I claim vengeance over Satan, as a wife claims vengeance over her husband's murderer.'[4]

A few – notably Rachel Fox and Gertrude Hill – were married and therefore unable to come and live in the community, but this did not stop them taking the oath. Gertrude Hill wrote to Octavia that back at the vicarage where she lived with her clergyman husband, she had 'joined the group in spirit' and held 'my own little marriage service alone in my small sanctum, (my private book room) . . . the act became, as I went along, a very real thing, and I feel His nearness in a new way.'[5] Rachel Fox followed suit in July. The ceremony affected how Gertrude Hill experienced her marriage and a few months later she wrote to Mabel of her husband: 'Yes the Lord knows I love him (& how beautiful are my Lord's words about him & me) – but I am conscious that my conjugal love is dying into a maternal love, it is quite different to what it was.'[6] The women believed, from a message 'received' by Kate Firth, that through this marriage ceremony the coming of the Lord would be hastened and they would achieve immortality: 'for "behold the Bridegroom cometh" and ye shall no longer be called "Forsaken" nor your land (bodies) "desolate" but ye shall possess the land (body) which is called "Immortal"'.[7]

The women began to worship together whenever they gathered in Bedford. Initially, these gatherings were informal, developing out of the daily activities – meeting for tea, musical evenings, social evenings, shared meals – of those who were resident in Bedford: Octavia, and sometimes her twenty-year-old daughter Dilys; Kate Firth and sometimes her adult son Geoffrey, an accountant, as well as her sister, Henrietta Leach; and Gertrude Searson. In May, they organised what Gertrude Searson called in her diary a 'conference' at which she, Octavia, Kate Firth and Henrietta Leach met for two days to pray and discuss the place of Octavia in their mission. They also viewed all the presents that Octavia had received from her admiring followers. Ellen, in particular, constantly adoring, was always sending gifts to her: a rose-coloured silk jacket and handbag on Valentine's Day; a four-pronged silver fork; handkerchiefs; a bracelet; a ring; a shawl made of black Spanish lace; a pair of jet black earrings; a gold brooch in the shape of a nail; a bowl. Later, the community would set up a treasury in one of the large community houses, so that the gifts and treasures could be on permanent display.

The women were in and out of each other's houses several times a day, and from June 1919, when Octavia's messages from the Lord began to arrive on a daily basis, they would gather in the evening to read and discuss that day's script. In that same month of June, Octavia and Kate Firth were bidden by the Lord to 'watch' for ten days in the 'Upper Room', a room prepared as a small chapel upstairs in Octavia's house. Gertrude Searson and Ellen Oliver joined them in a sacramental feast and at the end they declared that the seventh church (that is, the Church of Laodicea in chapter 3 of the Book of Revelation, whose members are exhorted to listen for the Lord knocking at the door and let him in) had thus been initiated with four members according to prophecy. Here was just one more example, of many, of Octavia and her followers believing that they were enacting the biblical prophecies, chosen to live them out.

It was on this occasion, at the end of their 'Watch', that Octavia celebrated the Eucharist for the first time, with bread and water (rather than wine). One can only imagine the reaction of these women, some ninety years ago, hungry to see themselves made in the image and likeness of God, when Octavia stood as a priest at the altar that Whit Monday 1919, the day after Pentecost, in the 'Upper Room' of her house. Octavia celebrated the Eucharist in her own distinctive way – which strikes us now as rather home-made but endearing – wearing a handkerchief draped on her head which Alice Jones had embroidered with Mabel's initials, a dove and an olive branch, and sent as a gift the previous day, and a Liberty scarf arranged as a cloak or sort of chasuble. Gertrude Searson marked in her diary 'Most wonderful day!!' and wrote, 'Took our first Communion in The Upper Room – Shiloh as minister.'[8] Ellen Oliver wrote to friends who would soon join the community that Octavia 'gave the bread with the words in the prayer book – but we each said the words "May I drink deep into the spirit of Christ and may his blood cleanse me from all sin" before drinking the water', and noted that Octavia was 'wonderfully calm and collected as if born to it'.[9] Rachel, who was not at that service but was present at so many in the future, also compared Octavia to a priest: 'She seemed to know exactly how each ceremony had to be done as if she were born to the Priesthood, & yet born to serve us all.'[10] For some rituals, such as the sealing of the apostles in 1919, the ceremony in which they pledged themselves as members of the community, Mabel even wore a priest's stole, on that occasion a red one.[11] Presumably she had kept her husband's stoles and was now pressing them into service.

Further 'Watches' – periods of silence – were ordered and observed from time to time, and the Eucharist was celebrated by Octavia once a week, usually on a Thursday, but the regular daily religious service was Evening Prayer, based on the Anglican Book of Common Prayer, but with an additional reading: namely, the message or 'script' which Octavia received each afternoon at 5.30 p.m. These 'scripts' were gathered together as the Writings of the Holy Ghost, of which there were sixteen volumes. Rachel Fox conjures up the atmosphere: 'we had the daily service in the "upper room", often crowded to over-flowing, and like famished creatures we picked up and fed on the new interpretations of scripture which were flashed before us in the daily Script. Far from being elementary, these Meetings might have been compared to an advanced class on theology.'[12]

Throughout 1919, Octavia was busy appointing twelve female apostles. Ellen Oliver wrote to a friend whom she was trying to attract to the community, 'The standard of the Lord is unfurled and HE has chosen 12 women who are watching & praying and listening! Women this time, for the disciples all forsook Him & fled – pray God we stand firm.'[13] By October, Octavia had appointed ten of her twelve apostles, and wrote to tell them that they were each a gate leading into the Temple of the New Jerusalem. Each of the twelve apostles was to be responsible for gathering in one-twelfth (or one tribe of 12,000) of the final number of 144,000 who were saved, the number mentioned in the Book of Revelation.

Octavia also believed that each apostle must be from a different sign of the zodiac. Influenced by a visit from a Mr Young, a member of the New and Latter House of Israel, she had come up with the idea that the 12,000 of each of the twelve tribes were each persons whose characteristics were governed by the influence of the zodiac, and therefore each of the twelve apostles would have been born under a different sign. As she went through her list of the women who were to be her first apostles, she found to her delight that they covered a range of astrological signs. Interest in astrology had been growing amongst the middle classes in the late nineteenth and early twentieth centuries, taken up especially by some Theosophists who regarded it as a science and set out to modernise ancient systems of astrology, integrating popular astrology with esoteric occultism. Astrology gener-ally, and the zodiac and its meanings in particular, came to hold a certain fascination for those who were interested in esoteric and heterodox religion, as well as psychology. Jung, for example, consid-ered that zodiacal horoscopes supported his theory of archetypal/ original patterns of behaviour.[14] So the astrological ingredients of Octavia's decision-making were not, in her own context, as odd as they might seem at first glance.

In a conscious imitation of a ritual performed by Jesus for his male apostles, Octavia washed her female apostles' feet at the beginning of the new year, 1920, following the Lord's command received in a script: 'Thus my daughters, shall ye enter the New Year of man with washen feet, and ye shall travel along the path which leadeth unto life, nor shall ye fall out by the way, for I shall impose My Spirit upon all who gather in this place, and Satan shall come against a wall, upon which he shall break himself and his.'[15]

Who were some of Octavia's first apostles? The very first were those women who had begun the Society with her and already lived in Bedford. Prominent among these was Kate – always Kate, never recorded as Katherine – Firth (Virgo), who was described by Rachel Fox, when she first met her in 1916, as 'a good looking lady (45) medium height – outspoken – strongish Northern dialect – comfortable villa house'.[16] She was close to Octavia's age[17] and she was Octavia's best friend, but her background was more materially comfortable and she brought financial resources to the Society (which Octavia lacked) early on in its history. The daughter of a solicitor, educated at boarding school,[18] she married a stocks and shares broker, Harry Firth, when she was twenty-eight and he thirty-three, and they had a son two years later, Geoffrey.[19] They settled into life in middle-class Dewsbury in Yorkshire, with bank managers and mill owners for neighbours, and the requisite two servants.[20] In the spring of 1905, Harry Firth died, leaving Kate a widow, not yet forty, with a nine-year-old son.[21] By 1911 she had moved to Bedford – perhaps for the schools, which were a draw for middle-class parents in this period – and was living in a prototypical suburban villa, 36 Bushmead Avenue. This was just a few hundred yards from 12 Albany Road, where Mabel Barltrop, another widow, with sons close to Geoffrey in age, lived in another suburban villa. Their paths crossed, they went to the same church and the same prayer group, shared their religious experiences and beliefs with one another and became close friends.

Kate's older sister, Henrietta Leach (Libra), was also a founding apostle. She was fifty-eight when the Society began. She too had come to live in Bedford after being widowed,[22] though whether before or after Kate is not clear, but she was certainly living there by 1917. She too came from a financially comfortable background, having been married to an oil and insurance agent, Thomas Leach.[23] For a time she lived in her own Bedford villa on De Parys Avenue, just a mile away from her sister, but by 1923 she was living with Kate in Bushmead Avenue. She also provided financial help for the Society, but finance was an issue of tension between Kate and Hettie: Octavia described this as Satan's way of trying to destroy their relationship. Hettie remarried in 1923 and, ill by this time, spent the last two years of her life visiting seaside resorts and spas for treatment. Hettie was never as involved with the Society as Kate was; brought in through her sister, her commitment gradually fell away through ill health, travel and the distraction of a new husband. Because Hettie's involvement declined with time, and Kate dramatically left the Society, the Society has no identified photographs of either of them.

Gertrude Searson (Capricorn) had first met Mabel in 1914, through her aunt who lived on the same road. She was two years younger than Mabel and discovered that they had a shared interest in British Israelism, which had gained ground as a movement in the nineteenth century and propounded the idea that people of Western Europe are directly descended from the ten tribes of Israel and the British royal family from King David. British Israelite ideas had some influence on Panacea politics (as we shall see in Chapter 12). When Gertrude went to visit her, Mabel had just read Southcott and was full of enthusiasm for the writings, an enthusiasm that she passed on to Gertrude. Gertrude had been married to a doctor, 'a bad man' whom she had had to leave after 'years of misery', and she finally came to live in Bedford at the beginning of 1919, from Barnes in south-west London, to look after her ageing relatives.[24] As they lived on Albany Road, this gave Gertrude a close connection to the community as it was forming, and she became an invaluable early companion to Octavia, doing her shopping, writing her letters and running her errands. Octavia described her as 'so comforting, so equal'.[25] A surviving photograph shows her to be slim and elegant, expensively dressed in fur-trimmed coat and gloves. Gertrude's diary for 1919 records the daily progress of the nascent community, the ins and outs of the potential members, and the almost daily battle that Octavia had with fear and depression – which went hand in hand with her enormous energy and hope.

Of the others who had been involved from the beginning, but did not live in Bedford in 1919, the most important was Ellen Oliver (Cancer), the identifier of Mabel as Shiloh. A small, gentle woman, she was deeply spiritual, ardent in her beliefs – whether in women's suffrage or the completion of Southcott's prophecies in Octavia – and passionate in her loyalty and devotion to Octavia. In photographs, she looks earnest, and slightly delicate. She was spinsterly in her sensibilities, bundling herself up in flannel, anxious about the menopause, but she did not wear corsets, which was a sign of being a 'new woman' in the late nineteenth and early twentieth centuries. When she went to the doctor about her menopausal symptoms in the summer of 1919, she was advised to wear a corset, something she did not relish, and it was the more conventional Kate Firth who wrote to her: 'I can well understand that you will find corsets a great trial until you get used to them but they are a great support & I cannot imagine how anyone can exist without them.'[26]

Gertrude Hill (Aquarius), the wife of a clergyman in the Midlands, first became acquainted with Mabel in 1914 through an article she had written in the Mothers' Union magazine. She wrote to Mabel, who invited her to visit and introduced her to the writings of Southcott. She was quiet and a good listener, and Kate Firth described her as 'a fine woman, so cultured & clever'.[27] Ellen highlighted that she was '70 years of age – tall & thin and she bicycles!'[28] Surviving photographs of her at the Society show her milking a cow, reminding us that vicars' wives were often called to help the household be self-sufficient.

These first female members in turn brought in others they knew: Ellen brought in sisters, Kate and Bessie Hodgkinson (Scorpio and Leo), and Alice Jones (Pisces). Kate and Bessie first visited the community in July 1919, but had been receiving the scripts and other news of events there for some time from Ellen Oliver, as had Alice Jones. Kate Hodgkinson, writing to Mabel, described herself and her sister as very ordinary people who did their own household work and did not keep a servant. Even in the post-war era, having at least one servant was a sign of being properly middle class, but in the 1920s the shortage of young women willing to enter domestic service meant that this was decreasingly the case. Before meeting Mabel, they had got to know her through reading her *Brushes with the Bishops*, and were so impressed by it that they put advertisements for it in their local newspaper, the *Worthing Gazette* (Worthing was the south-coast town in Sussex where they lived) as well as the *Yorkshire Post* and *Lincolnshire Herald*. This was how things were done in the early days when there was little money and things were being run out of Octavia's sitting room: ad hoc and informally, and paid for by the donations of the first members. A photograph of Kate Hodgkinson shows a tall, large-boned woman, with a slight dishevelment about her. Octavia later complained, in her typically frank way, that Kate wore ugly hats.

The only photograph that survives of Alice Jones shows her playing the King of Hearts in the Society's production of *Alice in Wonderland*. She is a stout, solid woman, with a serious expression and small round glasses. She was sixty-one in 1920 when she came to live in the Society, a spinster who had spent her life doing philanthropy, working at the clothing depot for Belgian refugees in her town. Alice was the Society's best speaker, selected to get on a box and speak at Hyde Park Corner, and attend various church congresses to hand out leaflets to recalcitrant clergymen. Rachel Fox wrote: 'Difficult visitors who persist in teasing on doctrinal subjects are always handed over to her.'[29] She also knew German and was able to serve as Octavia's 'foreign secretary'.[30]

Hilda and Winna Green (Aries and Virgo) knew both Mabel and Kate early on, having been in a prayer and healing circle with them, run by Bernard Hardy, the priest from St Paul's to whom Mabel had first written when she discovered Southcott. They had moved to Bedford (from the nearby county of Suffolk where their father had been Rector of Sudbury and an honorary canon of Ely Cathedral) in 1902 after their parents had died, bringing with them their old nurse Mary Gilbert, and lived at 14 Clarendon Street, north of the town centre. Mabel had introduced them to the teachings of Southcott when she had first read them. During Mabel's time in St Andrew's Hospital and the early organisation of the group after Mabel had returned home, Hilda watched from the sidelines, but remained interested in developments and joined in 1919, closely followed by her sister Winna. Ellen Oliver was Mabel's first secretary, but after Ellen's death in 1921, Hilda did the bulk of the secretarial work in the Society. Rachel Fox commented: 'as she sits at her desk in her office, one feels that she is truly like a wireless operator, in touch with the whole world'. In fact she exercised an enormous amount of power, reading and (after consultation with Octavia) responding to all the correspondence that came into the Society. This meant that she knew everyone's secrets – but she was deeply discreet. Winna was soon organising the publishing concerns of the Society which 'with no business training, she runs as capably as a London firm could run it', commented Rachel.[31] Hilda and Winna not only brought their old nurse, Mary Gilbert, into the Society, but also, early on, their sister Mildred and her husband William Hollingworth who had been to the early prayer circle a few times. William was a printer who worked briefly for Alice Seymour at the end of the war; when they came to Bedford, he was put in charge of the Society's printing press. Mildred was a nurse and became head of the healing department when that development was introduced to the Society in 1923. This meant that all three sisters, Hilda, Winnie and Mildred, held prominent positions in running the Society.

Those who were not resident would come up and spend a few days in Bedford every few weeks, but some soon began to want more. Ellen Oliver wrote to a friend in June 1919, before she had gone to live there permanently, 'I have just had a week at Bedford & feel as if I have been "on the mountain top"! . . . I am a bit dazed at my return to earth!'[32] The first community house was 5 Albany Road, across the road from Mabel, bought by the Hodgkinson sisters, Kate and Bessie, in early 1920; several other women went to live there, including Ellen Oliver and Alice Jones. Others bought their own houses in streets nearby. Yet others lived with or stayed for periods with Octavia in her house, at 12 Albany Road, which also served as the community's head-quarters until further houses were bought. Those who came to live in Bedford initially were all women without ties and most of them were also women of some means. Those who were married and had homes and family lives that they were obliged to maintain elsewhere, such as Rachel Fox, travelled to Bedford regularly, however long and uncomfortable the train ride. In Rachel Fox's case, she made the long journey to Bedford, in the centre of England, from Cornwall, at the very south-western tip of England, frequently without complaint.

Most of these women were members of the Church of England, and many were related in some way to a clergyman. Octavia was the widow of a clergyman, Gertrude Hill the wife of one. Alice Jones, Hilda and Winna Green were all the daughters of clergymen, Alice also had a brother who was a clergyman, and Ellen Oliver was the granddaughter of one. But they were all frustrated by the Church. All had come into contact with Southcott's writings in the 1910s, and had seen there the 'fulfilment' of promises they had learned about, but which had not been realised, in the Church of England. As Rachel Fox characterised them: 'The first comers from the various towns in England, except myself and one other were members of the Church of England, and all alike were dissatisfied with the provender offered them by that Church. "Divine discontent" was writ large upon their lives. They had suffered tortures in the Church because they felt the Services and Sacraments did not alter the inward tendencies.' Once they became involved with Octavia and her circle, 'they had a curious inability to discuss seriously any other subject with their old friends in the Church and in society'.[33] The community in Bedford was not unusual in attracting women who were closely involved with the Church of England, but had found it wanting because it gave them so few opportunities to express their spirituality. Unorthodox religious groups of the late nineteenth and early twentieth centuries were full of frustrated vicar's wives like Mabel Barltrop herself; Annie Besant, who became such an influential Theosophist after she left her Church of England clergyman husband; Anna Kingsford, a doctor and Christian mystic who dabbled in both Theosophy and spiritualism, and a number of women prominent in spiritualist circles, such as Louisa Lowe, who left their Anglican clergy husbands.[34]

Gertrude Hill was one prominent member who always straddled the two worlds of the Church of England and the Bedford community. Her husband Arthur was rector of East Bridgford in the Midlands, where he had been since 1898, and where she was entrenched in life as a country vicar's wife. But she had always been on her own spiritual quest, and wrote a little book, *The Story of a Soul's Awakening*, published in 1917, describing how she received spiritual insight on the Bible and Prayer Book from reading Southcott's prophecies. She dedicated the book 'to my husband, in gratitude for what his life has done for mine. Although divergent in views yet one in aim, I claim his soul as the one and only possible counterpart of my own.' However, for Gertrude, living in the two worlds of her husband's parish and the Bedford community was not always easy. She missed the occasion when Octavia first celebrated the Eucharist, in June 1919, but received an account of it from Gertrude Searson, which described the event as the institution of the seventh church in the Book of Revelation. She read that letter before going to church for the early morning communion service one Sunday later that month and was forcibly struck by the contrast between her old church and her new community. 'When my husband and I entered we found an *empty church* not one communicant had come – only myself – quite unconsciously the tears came to my eyes. This was our day of our Dedication Festival – our Thanksgiving for the political peace, and here was a *dead church*, no response. The thing had never happened before. Well I took it as significant. "The Seventh Church" was in my heart all the time – the true the Living Church, & there was I, representing one externally, and the other spiritually.' This made her feel her mission strongly: 'I was there presenting to the Lord, the Church of His Desire.'[35]

Gertrude Hill tried to get her husband interested in the teachings of the Bedford community, and even brought him for a visit early on in the Society's development, in October 1919. She wrote to Octavia, 'you don't know, and yet you do know, what it was to me to see him sitting in *your* room talking to *you*!!' Arthur Hill was made uncomfortable by the whole experience: 'my husband both before and during his visit, was strangely irritable, he simply persecuted me digging at me with stinging darts – but I knew where all this came from, & they slid off like proverbial water off a duck's back'. Afterwards, she reported, 'He has been very much more calm, & he has been very thoughtful. I don't talk about any of those things dear to my heart. I am leaving my husband simply trustingly in God's hands.'[36] Perhaps he was simply relieved that the people she was mixing with in Bedford were not entirely weird. Kate Firth wrote to her, 'You would understand M.B.'s wisdom in picking up the threads of the old life & keeping the conversation to safe topics, as she felt it was necessary for him to see, for your sake, that she was perfectly normal & not a "freak" of any kind. We were very charmed by him & hope he will no longer look upon us with suspicion.'[37] Gertrude hoped for more than relief on Arthur's part; she cherished the belief that her husband would have a Pauline conversion and that he would be 'for the Work in some ways & probably some great way'. But it was not to be. A couple of weeks later, Gertrude had tempered her expectations, simply hoping that his resistance to her involvement with the group would have lessened. She wrote to Octavia, 'He has said very little about his visit to Bedford. He has scarcely spoken of it but I fancy when next I express a wish to go to you all he will object less. Perhaps not at all.'[38]

Gertrude thus learned that she had to negotiate the two worlds, and tried to carve out for herself a role, describing herself as a bridge between the worlds because she could represent the public, the ordinary people, who did not always grasp the spiritual wisdom that Octavia was offering them. She wrote to Octavia that there had been 'a certain slowness of comprehension which (I know dear yes I *know*

it) has disappointed you, when I have read any one of your new books
... I have been conscious of being held back from full participation
in their *message*'. She continued, 'being a Bridge, I have partaken of
the density of mind of the public for whom you write – I have longed
for something more explanatory more down to their level of spiritual
comprehension.' Gertrude was really trying to address the question
that vexed Octavia, and which obsesses so many religious leaders: why
don't people respond to my preaching and teaching? Why might they
not want this redemption that I offer them? Gertrude's question was:
how could she help people to respond to Octavia? 'I can see, – as it
were – two Cities, one material & gross, at one end of the Bridge and
another City full of Light at the other end of the Bridge and I know
the people ought to walk over from our city to the other & I want
to help yes I *want* to do this – so very much.'³⁹

The single women who came to live in Bedford were often liberated from family obligations, for they were dutiful women who were
used to fulfilling the domestic expectations of middle-class spinsterhood and widowhood. Many of them had spent time looking after
sick aunts and elderly relatives. Some continued to do so. Octavia
looked after her bedridden Aunt Fanny, even as she set up the Society,
nursing her, and often having to get up in the middle of the night to
care for her. Ellen Oliver was longing to move to Bedford throughout
1919 but was delayed because of having to keep an eye on an old aunt
who lived near her in Brighton. Conversely, when Gertrude Searson's
aunt, who lived two doors away from Octavia, fell off her bicycle and
needed her niece's help, this gave Gertrude the excuse to come and
live in Bedford, though the women commented to each other that
Gertrude's uncle was very trying.⁴⁰ Others – such as Alice Jones, who
had been very tried with aunts – were freed from such duties when
they came to live in the community. The Society was liberating for
spinsters, giving positive meaning to their unmarried status. Ellen
Oliver wrote that Joanna Southcott represented the typology of
'spinsterhood, the old maid!! The drudge? Despised by the world, but
glorified and accepted by the Lord and chosen as *The* incorruptible
Bride.' Ellen wrote: 'to me this is very wonderful and *glorious!*'⁴¹

When these women came to Bedford, they remained conscientious
about their domestic obligations, and those who owned community
houses still had to run them. They had the same preoccupations that

other middle-class women of their era had: the difficulties of running a household with one servant with whom they often had awkward relationships. Ellen wrote of Mary, her servant: 'She has been very trying to me, poor old soul, she is in great pain & speaks as she feels & I get hurt: the devil trys [sic] us dreadfully – now we have a leak in the hot-water pipe & the back kitchen has dripping going on day & night & I have the prospect of a heavy bill & Mary of no kitchen etc etc.'[42] Their letters were therefore shot through with domestic details, even when they were discussing high-minded theological concepts, such as the fact that they might just have the daughter of God living in their midst. When Ellen Oliver wrote her second letter to Kate Firth, in February 1919, confirming her theory that Mabel was Shiloh, a letter full of complex theology, she ended by saying: 'I am so sorry about your burst pipe and that you have a cold.'[43] When Ellen received a letter from Mabel, at the end of that month, confirming her identity as Shiloh, a turning-point document in the community's story, the letter closed with a note that she had received some very nice bed-socks from Kate and Bessie Hodgkinson.

The theology of the Society always had a rather domestic feel to it: ideas about God and what was happening in their midst were repeatedly refracted through a domestic lens. The Panaceans took up household and domestic images that are a key part of the Bible – though often missed – with alacrity. Signs and symbols that were closest to hand were used to make sense of Southcottian prophecies and Octavia's mission. Ellen wrote to Mabel in late 1918: 'sweeping the house diligently you are the broom stirring up the dust of the ages which choke the Bps!!'[44] And after she had identified Mabel as Shiloh she wrote: 'Shiloh is the Branch (or Broom) that will sweep evil away!'[45] The broom was a household object to which they gave particular meaning, and Octavia used the broom in her house to sweep away the devil ritualistically. When Gertrude Searson called in to see how Octavia was one day, as she did most mornings, she found herself being the witness in front of whom Octavia believed she had to switch the broom eight times. It was a significant enough event and household object for Gertrude to write in her diary with heavy underlining: 'Saw broom for the first time.' Octavia's role as the maternal figure at the head of the community was interpreted in terms of the cosily familial and domestic by Ellen Oliver when she identified Octavia as

'"The Mother" type of all that is best in modern English Homes – and then your having 3 sons and one daughter – surely that means something? Yes, the "Mother" had to have a type on earth to hold the key for the whole – *three in one*! Bride, wife and mother!'[46]

Domestic objects, clothing and household items were all invested with significance, and more often than not were seen as signs of the Society's future direction or a member's personal calling. This should not surprise us. An interest in rethinking gender relations, whether in the heavenly realm or on earth, or both, was not necessarily divorced from an interest in the home in early-twentieth-century England. The house had become, in the nineteenth century, increasingly associated with women, and by the end of that century an expression of the middle-class woman's personality. In the wake of legislation passed in 1882, which gave all married women property rights, the right to make a home was a feminist cause. Home decoration could even become entwined with female suffrage. Millicent Fawcett's sister, Agnes, was a deeply committed suffragist like her sister – and an interior decorator who went into business with her cousin Rhoda, another keen suffragist. Through house decoration they hoped to earn money and promote votes for women. Mrs Emmeline Pankhurst, the more radical suffragette who founded the WSPU, opened several shops in Manchester and London to sell furniture and home decorations.[47] Certainly, the Panacea women took great pride in their homes and how they were decorated, as photographs from the period show, and as the catalogues for the Society's auction of their goods, in 2001, confirm. One former Theosophist who joined the Panacea Society in 1924, Frances Wright, had made a name for herself as a designer of beautiful teapots with silver casings, sold in the best department stores in London.

Members of the Panacea Society were mostly autodidacts who also believed in divine inspiration. This contributed to the unusual and sometimes eccentric nature of the community's beliefs. Many of them had been to the schools for girls that were springing up all over England in the mid-late nineteenth century, but few of them had been to university. This limited formal education when combined with their eager desire to find spiritual meaning and revelatory truths in everything meant that they had an eclectic and sometimes indiscriminate attitude to reading and knowledge. They regarded as true anything that struck them as interesting and meaningful. Ellen Oliver thought that Mabel was the eighth Southcottian prophet because the name Barltrop had eight letters in it. Four was regarded as an auspicious number, and thus the 'foursquare' Godhead was regarded as correct. They had orthodox Christian precedents for such numerology: the second-century church father Irenaeus thought it was right to have four gospels because there were four winds. Octavia often turned for confirmation of her ideas to the texts of the ancient world, both Jewish and Christian, where visions, dreams and numerology held more significance than a post-Enlightenment, rational approach to Christianity allowed. In November 1920 she came across the ancient Jewish text, the *Book of Jubilees*, which purported to contain secret knowledge revealed to Moses while he was on Mount Sinai for forty days and forty nights. There she found the idea that Jacob's sons were born under different signs of the zodiac, representing different characters, and this led her to believe that the male apostles of Jesus also represented the twelve signs, and affirmed her own ordering of her apostles in this way. She also found confirmation of many of the Society's ideas in the *Book of Jubilees'* apocalyptic vision: that the kingdom of heaven would be grad-ually realised on earth, and the physical and ethical transformation of human beings would lead to a new heaven and new earth in which sin and pain would disappear and human beings would enjoy a blessed immortality. When she read *Pistis Sophia*, a mid second- or early third-century Gnostic Christian text full of dreams and visions, which had been translated into English by the theosophist G.R.S. Mead in 1896, she found it helpful because it was 'the story of the woman fighting her way through the hosts of darkness'.[48] She marked up her copy with dates from her own life and the life of the community next to passages where there seemed to be parallel occurrences.

All of this was quite typical of the Society's approach to knowl-edge: they had ideas, or believed they had received particular ideas in messages or scripts from the Lord, and then looked for confirmation of them in signs, symbols, dreams, visions and other texts. Rachel Fox's volumes about the Society are full of such confirmatory inci-dents, often trivial, but all deemed to show the women that they were on the right path. One day, they all went upstairs to look out of Octavia's window to see that the shape of a Victoria or Maltese Cross had appeared in a lilac tree. One member had tied a ribbon in the centre of the 'cross'. After the women had spent the day talking about it, they interpreted the image in the light of a dream that Joanna Southcott had related in her book *The Strange Effects of Faith*, of seeing a tree tied with ribbons, which she had regarded as 'for victors who won the Tree of Life'.[49] If the women heard knocks but found no one at the door, they assumed it was the Lord. Gertrude Searson recorded in her diary that MB heard a knock at 6 a.m. (summertime), 5 a.m. God's time, but no one was there so 'she knew it must be the Lord'.[50] The Society's records are crammed full of such incidents: any event or object could be given significance, and members must have been busily on the lookout for signs and symbols every minute of the day. They were waiting for something – the Lord's Coming – and therefore everything came to be imbued with potential significance. As John Coghill, one of the last members of the Society, put it to me: 'What I'm waiting for is the Conclusion, the Second Coming. It's a very big thing if you think about it.'[51]

These early years saw both the consolidation of the Society's theology and ideas, and determination of the community's structure and preoccupations, shaping how this group of people would grow together and interact with each other in the future. Nowhere was this more obvious than in the dynamics between the members and, most especially, in their relationships with Octavia. For Octavia stood at the centre of all things, and how each member related to her was of vital importance to them. She was the daughter of God, their mother, their Queen, their leader. Most were extremely devoted to her. When Annie, Octavia's servant, went on holiday in August 1919, Gertrude Searson went to stay in the house with Octavia and recorded in her diary: 'G.S. came to stay at No. 12. Great joy of G.S.!!' Notes and gifts from Octavia were treasured: 'The sweetest of notes from MB on my breakfast table. What a loving tender one she is,' wrote Gertrude in her diary.[52] Ellen was utterly enthralled with Octavia, even giving up her beloved Persian cats when she moved to Bedford because Octavia ruled that no pets were to be allowed in the community.[53] Octavia appreciated such wholehearted support for she was happier with those who were devoted than with those whom she regarded as possible rivals and with whom there were intermittent tensions in the life of the community. For the fact was that any one of the women in this early circle could have emerged as Shiloh, and Octavia must have been aware of that.

Rachel Fox was the most obvious contender for the leadership, a published author who had the connections and money that Octavia did not have. She lived in two beautiful houses in Cornwall; she came from the wealthy Quaker elite; she was from the family that began Barclays Bank and she married into the Cornwall branch of the Fox family that ran a lucrative international shipping business out of Falmouth. Rachel never made a bid for power, but Octavia was threatened by Rachel's perceptions of her, and we have seen that she often regarded Rachel's messages from the Lord as inaccurate. She confided to Ellen that she found Rachel 'bewildering and disappointing some days', that 'Mrs Fox does not "realise" me' and 'To be frank, R Fox is easily the cleverest woman in any society . . . [but] she has not got this "Vision" . . . She does not "see" my work either – not as you & KF & G Hill do. She will have to be led into it gently, very gently.'[54] Yet clearly Octavia needed Rachel's support and wanted confirmation from her of the rightness of what she was doing. In short, she had an ambivalent attitude towards her, and used her power to needle her. In advising Rachel on what character traits she needed to overcome in the quest for perfection and immortality, Octavia focused on what Rachel was best at: writing and her intellectual gifts. She wrote to Rachel in 1922, 'You must now get a more personal religion – that is your lack.'[55] Octavia cast doubt on Rachel's interpretations of the Society's teachings. John Coghill related to me that he used to go painting with Rachel Fox in the countryside around Bedford in the late 1930s, and she was 'a lovely person' but he had been warned not to believe anything she said.[56] Moreover, Rachel was not named one of the twelve apostles in 1919; she had to wait until 1921 when one of the original apostles left before being invited to join that inner circle.

Rachel reacted to all of this with her characteristic goodwill: 'Octavia and I are well aware of the great interest which attaches, among our readers, to the history of what I may call the "Intellectual Combat" which raged for years between us – in which I always got the worst of it, yet never did I lay down my arms . . . but I want to state here, that never on any occasion have we ever quarrelled.' This was probably because Rachel accepted Octavia's 'strictures . . . with gratitude'.[57] And yet, while recognising Octavia's probable jealousy of Rachel, Octavia's spiritual insight and sense of humour are obvious in this 'stricture', which she sent to Rachel:

You are *par excellence* a prophet and a teacher, and you need now to attend to your own innermost shrine which has nothing to do with the world, and which exists, and would exist, if only you and God existed. Forget exegesis and books and odd people for a time. Many teachers lack this sacredness of the inner sanctuary, they teach but do not learn! They are like people who have a shop and no home life and no comforts. They always want to sell their wares and get into the habit of being willing to jump up whenever the shop bell rings. Very nice of them but it tends to make them restless on all occasions. You are getting like a commercial traveller – you even carry your books and your Scripts to an evening party – *I* saw you hiding your attaché-case in the hall the last time you came to one of ours![58]

Rachel's accepting attitude to Octavia's criticism and her full and busy family life in Cornwall meant that she never emerged centre stage in the Society, and she certainly never precipitated a crisis in the community's shared life (in which she did not live until she was widowed in the mid-1930s). But she was an important and constant figure in the Society from its origins until her death in 1939, and she wrote the four volumes of the Society's history. Rachel remained devoted and loyal.

It was Kate Firth who turned out to be the real contender for the leadership, and her jealousy of Octavia simmered away until 1926 when she left the community. Not that this jealousy was always revealed at the time. In her first letter to Ellen in 1918 Mabel (not yet named Octavia) wrote, 'Mrs Firth and I are so much one.'[59] Kate wrote cheerfully to Ellen: 'Mrs Barltrop is a *wonderful* person & the *greatest* factor in this great work and revelation. She is *brilliantly* clever, but so sweet & *humble*; it is no wonder that God is using her for *special* purposes & I am proud to be her chosen & most intimate friend.'[60] But that was written before Ellen had identified Mabel as Shiloh. Kate's response to Ellen's letter making that identification had not been positive. There was an 'edge', on both sides of the relationship. Once Octavia came to trust Ellen, she confided in her: 'oh my dear sometimes dear K tries me!!! Bless her she is either so zealous that I am positively shoved nearly on my face – positively not sure whether she won't arrive at the goal first – and then later is all the other way'.[61] The imagery was appropriate: Kate *did* want to beat Octavia to the finishing line. A written confession by Alice Jones made it clear that Kate was jealous of Octavia's pre-eminent role. Early on in the Society's history, Kate used Alice's 'crush' on her to try and oust Octavia or at least take some of the authority for herself. Alice later confessed both her 'sensual affection' for Kate and her unwitting participation in Kate's attempt to diminish Octavia's position. Kate wanted more of a role in the Society, especially in prayer and worship, and got Alice to suggest to Octavia that she should have this. Octavia did not take to the idea. In turn, Alice's devotion and attentions to Kate – she helped her with typing and gave her little gifts – caused jealousy and hostility amongst the other female members, which Kate stirred up.[62]

This incident highlights the emotional dynamics of the community, the intimacies and jealousies that shaped members' daily interactions in an introspective, highly charged atmosphere. It also raises the question of how much these women were emotionally and physically attracted to each other, and how much their religious activity was the working-out of those attractions in a community which taught the advantages of celibacy. In the case of Alice Jones, we know from other confessions that before joining the Society she had had sexual relationships with women, including a vicar's wife. Alice's attraction to Kate Firth stirred up a hornet's nest of jealousies amongst the women who were living with her at 5 Albany Road, and Kate artfully used Alice's attraction (which she did not reciprocate, as far as we know) to try and gain her own benefits from it. In many other cases, the evidence is much less clear. Did Octavia hesitate to receive gifts from Ellen because Ellen had something of a crush on her? We do not know. When Octavia wrote to Ellen, 'dear GS [Gertrude Searson] does love you so, you are just *right* together',[63] what did she mean? In a community where intimacies were shared, as they were here, and at a time when sexual identities were less precisely defined than they are in our own culture, it is hard to 'name' the affections between these women, but there is no doubt that the dynamics and life of the community were affected by the intensity that comes from living cheek by jowl with others, day in, day out.

As we have seen, this early group of female members was of a particular generation. Crucially, for the culture of the community, the majority of residential members were not – as we might at first expect – that generation of spinsters left husband-less by World War I. As a result of the war, women vastly outnumbered men: the census of 1921 revealed that there were one and three-quarter million more women than men. In the war 700,000 British soldiers died, and over a million and a half were wounded. In terms of marriage prospects, this affected a much younger generation than that which was attracted to the Panacea Society. Nevertheless, the spinster, who had been much maligned in Victorian times, was now an unavoidable feature of society, and women had to strike out on their own. Women had worked during the war and kept the country's economy going; but the men who returned from war presumed they would have the best jobs. Many (middle-class) single women had to go out to work to survive, but they were expected to do jobs that did not compete with men, working as part of a typing pool, living in lodging houses and women's clubs, eating in tearooms.[64] In the Panacea Society, women did the important jobs. They ran the Society like clockwork. When they typed, they typed for the New Jerusalem, not for a mean-spirited male boss. And they did all this within the security of an ordered community, living by the conventions and etiquette of the pre-war age with which they were comfortable. In that sense, they had the best of both worlds; one foot in the past and one foot in the future.

For the first few years of the Society's history, there were very few younger resident members. Aside from Mabel's daughter Dilys, who was a resident member by default, the most prominent of the younger generation were the Gillett sisters who joined the Society in 1921, and moved to Bedford in 1923 when Evelyn, the younger, was just twenty-seven, and Muriel, her older sister, thirty-four. They were even young enough to have a brother still at boarding school. When the Society optimistically designated 16 March 1923, 'Young people's morning' it only applied to Dilys, Muriel and Evelyn. The Gillett sisters, like the older female members of the Society, had been tied to home by a demanding relative, in this case their ill mother whose spine injury impeded her mobility. Muriel had stayed at home as carer to their mother and adopted a quasi-parental stance towards Evelyn who, as a result fled the nest, living away from home, so that on the occasions she returned it was rather awkward, and 'home life was more or less a thing of the past & I went my own way trying to push through life's jungle'.[65] Muriel, for her part, was resentful of the role she had felt obliged to take in the household and the demands her mother had made on her. Moving to the Panacea Society therefore represented breaking away from an oppressive home life for Muriel, and from the absence of a settled home life for Evelyn; for each of them, setting up house together in a new location meant both independence and security, especially when their mother, who had initially shared their belief in Octavia and the community, became disillusioned with it and renounced her membership.

The Gilletts were described to me by one surviving member, who had worked as a servant in the community, as 'rich, tall, elegant, well-dressed'.[66] They were some of the wealthiest members of the community, coming from a Quaker banking family that had established a country bank in Oxfordshire in the 1820s. When they joined the Society in 1921, their father John Padbury Gillett had recently died and left each of them a considerable sum of money, the Gillett bank having been sold to Barclays at the end of the war.[67] They bought a large house two streets away from Mabel, at 19 Rothsay Road in Bedford, and set up an elegant home where they entertained many visitors on behalf of the Society. Muriel Gillett was one of the few women in the Panacea Society to have received a university education. Having been to a Quaker girls' boarding school, Polam Hall, she went on to Westfield College, Hampstead, a women's college established in 1882 (on the Oxbridge model).

The other somewhat younger member of the Society who joined in the early days was Peter Rasmussen, a Danish Australian who was forty-four years old when he arrived in 1920. He was a Southcottian based in Sydney who had been distributing Alice Seymour's pamphlets and books around Australia after being introduced to Southcott's ideas by a street preacher in Sydney in 1911. He first wrote to the Society in August 1919 and, sensing his loneliness and isolation, Ellen Oliver drew him in, while Octavia wrote to him: 'do feel we are your friends and let us be thankful for the "post".'[68] The post was soon not enough. By October, Peter had decided to move to Bedford and in August 1920 he arrived in England. Octavia immediately sensed something special about this slight, sensitive man who showed up on their doorstep desperate for companionship and eager to offer practical support and help in any way he could. She initiated him in just the way she had initiated the female apostles, by washing his feet, after 'a clear call to perform for you the act which I performed for the other apostles and I desire to do it in all humility'.[69] He became her right-hand man, devoted in every way, ever present. Octavia recognised the worth of this and explained it theologically, writing to him, 'how marvellous that one of the Lord's own sex is chosen to encourage the Woman on the Lord's behalf. This is to bring Adam's sin right'.[70] Octavia's dependence on Peter could cause jealousies. Hilda Green, for example, confessed that she was 'often annoyed' with him as she 'felt he was greatly favoured by Octavia'.[71]

A member who would later hold great significance and wield enormous power also joined in 1920, just a month before Peter. This was Emily Goodwin, a sixty-three-year-old working-class widow from Surrey with five grown children. She had been introduced to Jezreel's writings, The Flying Roll, in the late 1880s, and had from time to time worshipped at the New and Latter House chapel with the followers of Jezreel, though she never joined them. After reading Jezreel, she was expecting the arrival of Shiloh and believed it would be a woman. She later claimed that she used to say to herself: 'That woman is walking the earth and I may even have passed her in the street!'[72] When she first visited the Society to be sealed in July 1920, she was sitting in a room with several other women, waiting for the ceremony to begin, and scanned it anxiously for the female Messiah whom she so desperately wanted to meet. When Octavia entered the room she knew instantly that this was the woman for whom she had so patiently been waiting. Emily Goodwin's devotion was unswerving, and she yearned to move to Bedford, like so many before and after her, declaring to Octavia: 'I am longing for the time to come when I can fly as it were home. I feel like a bird caged up, waiting for my freedom.'[73] As she put it to Ellen Oliver, 'what a lot there is in the word home, it seems something more endearing than the churches of today, in fact you can go in and out of them & feel one by yourself quite alone'.[74] But she did not have the resources of some of the other resident members, and so the question arose as to how she would support herself in Bedford. A few months after joining, she heard of the increasing frailty of Octavia's Aunt Fanny: Octavia had been up four nights in a row nursing her and could not cope with that demand while running her growing community. Never one to miss an opportunity – though she presented as a retiring and quiet person – Emily wrote to suggest that she might come and work as resident nurse, and would even be willing to share Aunt Fanny's room in the Barltrop household at 12 Albany Road. Octavia was delighted. Emily moved there at the beginning of February 1921 and remained there until her death, aged eighty-six, in 1943.

Rachel Fox commented that Emily Goodwin's introduction to the Society was perfectly ordinary, and her presence largely unnoticed at first – Octavia did not talk with her much in the first six months except on matters to do with the care of Aunt Fanny – which was perhaps surprising given that she would later come to be so central to its life, though one of the first things she did, Rachel noted, 'was to fall upstairs when carrying a huge ewer of water, thus most unwillingly baptising the whole house!'[75] In retrospect, we can see that Emily Goodwin may simply have been biding her time until another opportunity arose for advancement. An early letter addressed to 'Octavia (Mother)' indicates how important the notion of divine motherhood was to her already. 'I do thank God,' she wrote, 'for giving me the understanding to know what the name of Mother, or the Motherhood, means to me, it is the very essence of Life, even in the mortal woman, but to know . . . that the Lord has called me to be near & live under the same roof as my Heavenly Mother, I cannot thank him enough.'[76] At that time, in 1920, she was referring to Octavia as the Heavenly Mother. Three years later, she would, extraordinarily, take that title herself as the Instrument of the Divine Mother.

Octavia's relationship to her followers – and theirs to her – changed over this crucial period as her identity was revealed and the community expanded. Early on as the circle of women gathered, when she was still ordinary Mabel, she advocated an egalitarian form of community. 'The "follow my leader" business does not come into this affair at all. It never will. It is a WHEEL, not a long *line* that we are upon.'[77] She reiterated this image of the wheel in letters she wrote to each of the women in the autumn of 1918: 'We are in the Circumference of a Wheel. We are not just following a leader. We are agreed in the centre on the one great point, but *each* has *her own* narrow lane of light to walk in & her own work, hence we must begin at once to learn to listen for our own impressions and follow them in our own way accepting any merely technical help but rejecting *advice* as anathema.'[78] Several of these early members of the community believed that they received messages and visions, and several practised automatic writing. For a while, they enjoyed the freedom to engage in this. Gertrude Hill frequently wrote out her dreams and sent them to Mabel in the belief that they were relevant. She also described how she received knowledge of God's will. 'What God gives me to know I *see*. I don't *hear* –

(I believe you *hear* what he tells you). To me it all comes a like a scene, striking on a screen – with a sense of the right proportion or relation of every part, to every other part of what is reflected on the screen.'[79] Bessie Hodgkinson practised automatic writing and received messages about Mabel, as did Kate Firth and Rachel Fox. Most importantly, all of these women received messages confirming Ellen Oliver's great revelation that Mabel was Shiloh, and as the residential community was forming, in 1919, several of the women received confirmatory messages about what they were doing. Gradually, the importance of others' messages receded, and Octavia's scripts became the focus of attention. The year 1920 marked a transition, when Octavia was still relying on Rachel Fox's messages for confirmation of her own scripts, but was beginning to exercise a more autocratic form of leadership. She wrote to Rachel in February 1920, a year after she had been identified as Shiloh: 'Your affair is merely to write your Messages as being from the Spirit and to post them, and ours to receive or reject. You are not required to *understand*; in fact you can't understand . . . Frankly *we don't want your views about anything in this matter*. I am sworn to cease from human teachings and reasoning, so what is the use my dear Rachel, of sending me either?'[80]

As the community grew, it changed from its early, more egalitarian structure to an increasingly hierarchical community. As an ordinance in the 1920 community rules put it: members 'will subject themselves completely unto the Head Administrator of the Kingdom, who will be led by the Holy Ghost and through the Writings of the Holy Ghost, to adminstrate [*sic*] for their welfare in time and in eternity.'[81] The casual and informal style that marked its opening years gave way to greater organisation and numerous rules. As the number of members increased, the women had less informal access to Octavia herself. They were now to be willing workers rather than co-leaders on a wheel with each following their own path. They were now to follow Octavia's path. As Rachel Fox commented: 'It may be well to point out that an Organiser does not want originality in her workers, perseverance in carrying out ideas, and absolute loyalty to directions alone are needed, and in this work an utter indifference to the amount of labour required, in order to put the ideas into practice, is a requisite.'[82]

There was a paradox in Octavia's exercise of power, a paradox often found in those who claim inspiration for their leadership in prophecies or other forms of divine revelation. She wrote that she was not a pontiff, but an empty vessel, an image commonly used by prophets who regard themselves as speaking only God's word, untainted by their own thoughts and impressions and prejudices. In fact she acted both as a pontiff and as an empty vessel and it was the latter which gave her the power to be the former precisely because she could say: 'God told me so.' Her definition of a prophet as one who is 'an automatic receiver of a direct Divine Message, stated in a sequence of words which he must set down precisely as he heard them' reinforced this.[83] She worried about whether she was leading people astray, but her genuine spiritual authority enabled her to give many people clear and good advice about their lives. She always knew when she was about to give people such advice because she felt 'a curious "stiffening" of her whole being' that made her conscious that there were only two ways forward for the person with whom she was meeting or corresponding and it was her duty to clinch matters. At that point, she faced the situation and rapped out a statement 'which, like the firing of a maxim gun, leaves no room for further argument'.[84] In her counsel to others it is apparent that she had a down-to-earth spirituality, an extremely direct approach and real gifts which – in another time – might have been channelled into the ordained ministry in the mainstream of the Church.

There were many other paradoxes in Octavia's character. She could be autocratic, deeply sure of her own way being the right way, and at other times she could be awake for much of the night, worried about the way forward. She was described (by a cousin) as 'a charming, attractive woman, very brilliant, witty' but with an 'excitable nature'.[85] She was charismatic, attractive to those who met her, and she set a lot of time aside each day to meet visitors and members who required advice. But she could also be strict with visitors and members alike, and emotionally removed from their preoccupations: 'Now do not think for a moment that I am trying to persuade you to remain with us for anybody's sake *but your own*,' she would say. 'I am working entirely on your behalf, I am not seeking your personal friendship, I have no reason to do so.'[86] She had a great sense of humour. One member said that at chapel meetings, 'Octavia would be very amusing and they would be rocking with laughter. Then Octavia would bring everyone to order.'[87] She disliked anything sanctimonious or any show of piety.

Rachel Fox recalled her saying, in the middle of reciting a psalm in chapel, 'I do not know in the least what this means, why do you all look as if you do.'[88] She also had an Anglo-Catholic's love of ceremonial, and the women swung incense with all due order in the chapel. She was practical and matter-of-fact: all theological doctrines had to have a practical outcome. She described herself as an ordinary person, 'like any lady you might meet anywhere'.[89] But she also believed that she was the daughter of God. She gave herself and other frustrated women new roles and new opportunities, but she repudiated feminism and female suffrage. She was self-taught but widely read, and naturally intelligent. This she knew about herself, and, while her husband was alive, she found it difficult to manage because she thought she was cleverer than him and admitted that she let him win at games sometimes because he liked to do so. She also believed that her intellect had let her down, and the road to trusting her 'inner ear' and direct inspiration had been a long and torturous one. She was deeply aware of social niceties and concerned to observe them, as the rulebooks of the Society show, and she liked to emphasise her own literary and social connections. But she also believed that a prophet must have 'a discontent with everything then existing, an ability to cease from man, himself included, a disregard of social conventions, a brave and truthful spirit'.[90]

She was utterly single-minded about her mission, her 'Visitation' as she called it, at the expense of everything else. Her followers may have called her Mother, and found in her both a mother figure and a maternal affection for which they had long yearned, but her children were largely neglected in the face of their mother's preoccupations. Her two surviving sons, Ivan and Adrian, moved halfway round the world to avoid what was going on in the front parlour of their family home, to Canada and India respectively. Ivan seems to have cultivated a genuine uninterest or indifference; Adrian was agonised by his mother's religion. Dilys, her only daughter, was just twenty-one in 1919 when the Society began and by the end of that year was already weeping to her mother that she could not bring any of her friends home. This was just the opening sign of years of depression, misery and loneliness for a young woman who never married, who inherited her mother's mental illness and who grew old in a strange religious community about which she had deeply ambivalent emotions but from which she seemed unable to escape.

If the 'Visitation' was centre stage in Octavia's life, then mental illness was not far behind in her preoccupations. She suffered from a range of physical ailments and illnesses but it was her mental agonies, the depths of despair to which she could fall, that affected her life on a daily basis, as the members' personal diaries – full of notes that 'MB was depressed' or 'suffering mental agonies' – indicate. In order to withstand this mental illness, she had to believe that her suffering had a greater purpose: it was for the salvation of her followers. She wrote one day to Ellen Oliver, who was staying in Worthing with the Hodgkinson sisters, 'Well, I once felt so bad I didn't know what to do and I thought of you all at Worthing. Then I prayed, "Lord help me to be glad to suffer for them to have all this new thought." And of course He helped me – but I think He has to let me suffer. I think it is the death of death perhaps.'[91] Her dislike of pretension in religion was related to this; she believed her suffering to be like that of Jesus, and she *felt* how awful it was. Writing of her mental illness to Ellen, she said: 'I want to make this clear that I do not feel any Presence, it just has to be suffered in the ugly, drab way that a FACT has to be borne. This I think is to show up the absurdity of much in the Church. Even Good Friday has a "dressing", a staging that has helped to take away the awful FACT of the Blessed Lord's sufferings . . . I admit to faith sinking down into my very boots sometimes and to anything but a heroic demeanour & all has to be borne in a household which runs in the ordinary commonplace conventional way, an additional trial.'[92] One of the central paradoxes in Octavia's life as a leader, and as a leader who liked to be fully in control, was the fact that she came to believe that if she went 77 steps beyond her house, Satan would attack her. This meant that from 1918 until her death in 1934, she was a virtual prisoner in her own home, only being able to walk as far as the gardens and chapel, unable to do her own shopping. There were many community homes she could not visit because they were too far down the street. A modern, medical diagnosis of this would be obsessive compulsive disorder. For Octavia, Satan was a real threat, and she believed that her imprisonment in her home was part of God's 'great plan of redemption'.[93] This great plan was to live for ever on earth, the goal towards which all community life was directed.

6

How to Live For Ever

'The whole *raison d'être* of the Society is to get together THOSE WHO WILL NOT DIE – those who are predestined to live,' announced *The Panacea*.[1] The aim of Panacea life was to prepare for immortality by a practice called 'Overcoming'. Overcoming was an active process; it was about trying to rid oneself of one's personality, of one's very self. In a paper written for members of the community, Octavia wrote, 'Were it required of me to emblazon a Legend over the gates and doors of these buildings, one which set forth fact and not fiction, it might run thus: "Leave Self behind, all who enter here!"' The aim was to overcome sin entirely, so that with the Second Coming of Christ, one might enjoy immortal life on this earth; and to do this one had to reduce the self to 'vanishing point'; the ideal was to be 'zero'.[2] To do this, to leave the self behind, a person had to change her whole character: 'the things that nobody troubled about, but which make it difficult to live peaceably with some people, are the things that must be altered, for they are worse than sins, because they make other people sin.'[3] The process of leaving self behind was ideally a communal practice, and certainly one that could only be worked on in relation to other people in the stresses and strains of daily life. The 'Manners Paper', one of a series of papers given to residents to guide their daily living, stated: 'to learn to be a comfortable person to live with, should be the aim of all Panacea People'.[4] Ellen Oliver put it like this, in a letter to a prospective member: 'We down here are all pledged to fight the evil within ourselves and so prepare for His Coming; we must overcome our faults and failings and there for [*sic*] we must live together and help to polish each other.' The aim, wrote Ellen, was to become 'colourless or passionless or lost to the devil'.[5]

If Jesus taught ethics through his parables, then Octavia taught them through the sensibilities of Edwardian middle-class etiquette books. Panacea community life was rule-bound, and its parameters very precisely determined. There is a staggering attention to detail in Octavia's papers on how to treat visitors, how to lay the table, how to run the communal households, how to treat servants and how to conduct oneself, all with the express aim of overcoming the self and its whims, its likes and dislikes. Many of these instructions are about food and meals. Toast, for example, could cause trouble. The Manners Paper declares: 'Any person who makes an undue noise when eating toast, and declares they cannot avoid it, must leave off eating toast and must not take any other food which causes them to make a noise.' Similarly, teeth could be tricky: 'Teeth that click must be attended to: there is a remedy that can be asked about.' Eating sweets or candies could make you unpopular: 'People who go about the house with a sweet in their mouth or suddenly scrunch a sweet in one's face, can easily get disliked. Indeed all ugly noises and all ugly ways of eating and drinking tend to make people unpopular, however good they are.' Some of the instructions were simply about making sure everyone adhered to the same middle-class table manners and are indicative of Octavia's snobbishness: 'Never take butter with your own knife. Do not call a dinner napkin a "serviette". Eat asparagus with your fingers, and it is correct to take a baked potato with your fingers and to break it, not cut it.' And 'no person is to put the tip of their fingers in their mouth after taking buttered toast, scone or jam, on any account what-ever'. But Octavia's sense of humour sometimes shone through her endless instructions: 'Do not search carefully for foreign objects on your plate and when found, arrange them on the side as if it were a museum.' The aim was moderation: 'Over-religiousness, sanctimo-niousness, asceticism on one side, carelessness, laxity, luxury on the other are equally wrong. Use all God's gifts, abusing none.'[6] Therefore both over-enjoyment and under-enjoyment of food were wrong, as was appearing too interested in one's food. Meals were to be regarded as a 'domestic sacrament': it was forbidden for 'any person to give an impression of hurry because they wish to get to their work, or of boredom because they do not want the meal'.[7]

As others came to live in the Bedford community, more communal households were set up, and the heads of each household were given clear instructions on how to run them. Most of these guidelines date from March 1921, as houses were being formed, though they were from time to time revised and refined. There were instructions about the food to be served in the community homes; the specific shops in which groceries were to be bought – from a 'list of tradesmen employed by us'; the menus to be prepared on certain days; what could be eaten and what could not; hints on effective shopping; and how to treat visitors. Heads of households were reminded that, in planning break-fast, 'there are 50 ways of serving eggs', not only boiled, scrambled and poached, but also curried and savoury with Marmite or anchovy. Other dishes redolent of the time are found on the breakfast menus: kedgeree, potted chicken, green corn fritters and cold herrings. The main meal of the day was dinner, and there were special menus for special days: on St George's Day, because he was the patron saint of England, they had Yorkshire pudding, good gravy, roast potatoes and horseradish sauce – but no roast beef, because the members did not ✓ eat red meat. On Palm Sunday, they were to eat date pudding because 'dates grow on palms'; on Whit Sunday it was 'usual to have goose-berry tart'. Specific recipes were given for some items, such as Christmas pudding. Certain foods, such as tinned peas, were consid-ered a luxury and reserved for Easter Sunday and Whit Sunday and were to be served with one lump of sugar, mint and a pat of butter. There were very detailed instructions about where to buy the hot cross buns for Good Friday, which were 'very good from Mr Northwood, Castle Road, but he is always told distinctly what is wanted' and the instruction was 'to state clearly that you want them all spiced and currant, not some spiced and some currant'. There was a single-spaced typed page on how to make tea, because 'few people can make tea, and fewer still can pour it out' including what tea to use: 'The Palace Tea' from Dickins on the High Street, which was to be used from the packet kept in a tin, not to be emptied into a caddy or tin. There were two pages of notes on what to serve at tea if a visitor had been invited: hot buttered teacakes and scones in winter, sandwiches with cucumber or anchovy and watercress in the spring. Cakes should be home-made, because 'Bedford cakes and buns are not good.'

The tone of all these notes and papers was didactic and patron-ising. Octavia knew best. Take these notes on cake-making for example, written for women who had been running their own households for years:

Few home-made cakes are sweet enough; they are too dry made with margarine – better use cooking butter. As a rule, not nearly enough fruit is used – peel and grated nuts could be used sometimes with the currants and sultanas; no essences should be used in cakes at all, except Essence of Lemon in ground rice cakes . . . A huge mistake is to suppose that chocolate sweetens; it does not sweeten – chocolate cakes and puddings need a lot of sugar . . . The same applies to gingerbread made with treacle; *treacle does not sweeten*; it is often bitter and sour, but do not use golden syrup for gingerbread; you must have real treacle and plenty of sugar . . . If cherries are put in a home-made cake, it wants *a lot* of cherries, or add cherries to a lot of other fruit with it; hardly ever are there enough cherries in a cherry cake.[8]

Such instructions indicate Octavia's exceptional, even obsessive, attention to detail, but they also illustrate three important principles of the Society: obedience to the centre; uniformity in the houses; and a willingness to accept instruction. The whole purpose of the community's religion was to get rid of sin – which was derived from the Fall. This was essential if a person was to achieve immortality. Members had to leave everything behind that had anything to do with the mortal soul and the mortal mind: 'that creature which has succumbed all the time to the temptations, whims, fancies, peculiarities of the mortal realm'.[9] While the detailed instructions about how to make cakes may seem astonishing when viewed at a distance, they become more understandable as part of a larger enterprise in which obedience and a willingness to become 'zero', to fall into line without asking questions, were directed at the ultimate prize: immortality.

Consideration for others was also paramount, not only at table but in communal living generally. 'Persons sleeping in a room above another bedroom, should immediately on entering their room to go to bed, take off their shoes, put them (not throw them) into their place and put on bedroom slippers, being careful even then, to make no unnecessary noises, or to make all necessary ones, such as much opening of drawers and wardrobes, early in the proceedings. There is much cruelty in thoughtlessness.'[10] This was repeatedly reinforced in all the Society's literature, not only in lists of rules but also in its wider literature. The short stories, written by Octavia and other members and published in *The Panacea*, the Society's monthly magazine, were full of characters who had rid themselves of their annoying dispositions when they converted to the Panacean way of life. In 'The Wayfarers', a serialised story by resident member Brenda Greig, two sisters discuss with another young woman the difference that the Panacea Society has made to their lives. One remarks of the other: 'And Phyllis doesn't scrunch toast now as she used to, and doesn't hum and whistle when she is doing anything.' When they recruit their brother, Roger, he mends his ways, and that leads to more converts: 'The two elderly sisters from the flat below, who used nightly to battle with sleep until Roger had dropped both his boots over their heads, were very pleased to come and hear of this "New Religion", as they called it.'[11] Octavia's didactic tone influenced everyone's writing – but then, she was the editor of the magazine.

Rituals were important in the process of Overcoming from the earliest days of the community's existence. These came to be codified as a series of Acts, and a member's progression through these Acts marked their spiritual progress on the path to total Overcoming. The primary Act was the Life Confession: 'Confession was shown to be the preliminary stage of release from sin, and the more thorough the confession, the worse for Satan.'[12] The confession was based on a distinct theological understanding of judgment. The end of the world as we know it was not to be marked by a great judgment pronounced on each and every soul (as traditional Christianity would have it) but by the trial and conviction of Satan, as 'the cause of that effect called Sin'. The person who confessed was therefore bringing accusations against Satan, the Great Tempter and Accuser of Humankind. Making the Life Confession was a practical Act: Octavia always emphasised the practical nature of her religion. A person said Psalm 139 (dwelling especially on verses 23 and 24: 'Search me, O God, and know my heart; try me, and know my thoughts; And see if there be any wicked way in me, and lead me in the way everlasting) and Psalm 51, and asked that the Holy Spirit bring all the necessary things to their memory. Then the person sat down and wrote as instructed:

(1) Review your life, dividing it into periods of Child, Youth and Maturity.
(2) Set down the outstanding sins that come to your mind and during those periods, also your besetting sins.
(3) Write down in actual words any sins of impurity. The Fall was in the matter of sex relations, and the seat of Satan is the sex question.

(4) Do not spare – make your evidence as condemnatory as possible, for it is required in order to smite the Enemy down to hell.

(5) Any serious sins fallen into after confession must be added to the confession as time goes on, but you must endeavour steadily to overcome habitual sins and defects of character.[13]

Letters sent by members to the Society indicate how people experienced this rigorous work of confession. Ethel Castle, a non-resident member and a governess in Loddon, Norfolk, wrote to Octavia in April 1927 that she had made her Life Confession and read it aloud, following the advice exactly, and 'it was indeed a miserable & painful experience'. She continued, 'What courage it does need to be an Overcomer,' but finished her letter, 'how deeply grateful I am for such hard work & such understanding & sympathy from you & from all at the Centre.'[14] In October she wrote to Hilda Green (by then working as Octavia's secretary): 'Everything is going much more smoothly & easily for me, & it is such an immense relief to have lost that feeling of worry & uncertainty & consequent headaches. I've always longed to be completely healthy & really I think I shall be quite soon.'[15] And later that month, 'My general health really is wonderfully improved & I am a great deal happier. I had no idea that a mental & physical "spring clean" could so completely alter everything as it is doing for me.'[16] Nine months after becoming a member of the Society, Mary Beedell, in Eastbourne, wrote to Octavia of the whole experience of Overcoming, 'I am a very different woman altogether, but one feels there is a lot of self left – but oh the relief I have experienced – it is hard to put exactly what I feel on paper – but may I put it like this & I think you will understand. I do not need any props. I feel quite able to stand alone with the Divine Power at the back of me always – & I try very hard to be a nice sort of person to live with.'[17]

Confession has always been at the heart of the Christian tradition and can be given scriptural basis: in the Book of Numbers, the Israelites are told to confess their sins. The medieval Church had developed an elaborate set of rituals around penance, and in reaction to this the sixteenth-century Protestant Reformation had rejected the notion of confession as a sacrament, though had retained the general confession in worship. The sacrament of penance and individual confession to a priest made a controversial reappearance in the nineteenth-century

Church of England. The rise of Anglo-Catholicism had seen the introduction of more elaborate liturgical practices in some churches: more frequent Eucharist services (renamed Mass); the use of candles, incense and processional crucifixes; the wearing of vestments such as chasubles by the priest; gestures of kneeling and genuflecting at the altar, and facing east (rather than north) while presiding at Mass (not Holy Communion); and sacramental confession. Confessions were made individually to the priest, in the Roman Catholic manner. It was to this, the High branch of the Church of England, that Octavia had been attracted on aesthetic grounds, as a child and young woman, and therefore it is no surprise to see her developing the practice of individual confession as a part of the Society's theology and practice. In a pamphlet on confession, she wrote, with an admiring tone, of Fathers Mackonochie and Stanton, 'men of blessed memory'.[18] They were in fact two of the most well-known ritualist priests of the later nineteenth century, working in the Anglo-Catholic parish of St Alban the Martyr in Holborn, London, in which confessions were openly held, and where Mackonochie specialised in hearing the confessions of women.[19] Mackonochie had been prosecuted for his ritualist practices, and in 1877 had been involved in a controversy about a book compiled by the Revd J. Chambers, *The Priest in Absolution*, which advocated auricular confession and gave instructions to Anglican priests on how to hear confessions.

Sacramental confession was controversial because it gave the priest – the confessor – an authoritative role as the one who could absolve sins. This upset those of a Low Church stripe in the nineteenth-century Church of England, who wanted no intermediary figure between God and the believer. It also gave the priest considerable power. Confession turned out to be particularly appealing to women, perhaps because it provided a safe place in which they could talk about their marriages, family life and husbands, subjects they could not always discuss with any intimacy, safety or truthfulness in other settings. In a society where men were head of the household, they were outraged that a celibate priest might know the details of their family lives and marriage beds, and suspicious that priests might lead their wives, daughters and sisters astray. As the Earl of Redesdale put it in the debate in the House of Lords about *The Priest in Absolution* in June 1877, the questions, especially those about sexuality, put by the confessor to the woman might 'bring about [rather] than avoid the evils to which they relate'. The Archbishop of Canterbury at the time, Archibald Tait, entirely disapproved of confession and thought it was all about 'prying into the secret thoughts or hearts of those' who sought absolution. This meant that the confessor, with so much knowledge, could become a powerful and controlling figure.[20]

The Anglo-Catholics argued back, saying that only sacramental confession and absolution, one-on-one with a confessor, could heal spiritual sickness.[21] This was entirely what Octavia believed. She wrote of 'the beneficial effect of Confession to mind, soul, and body'.[22] By the time she was organising her Society's rituals and practices in the 1920s, confession had become far more generally accepted in the Church of England. Percy Dearmer, the vicar of St Mary of Primrose Hill, and later Canon of Westminster Abbey, wrote one of the best-selling handbooks of the early twentieth century for priests, *The Parson's Handbook*. Dearmer could not be called an extravagantly High Churchman, so it is revealing of changing attitudes that even in the first edition of the *Handbook*, published in 1899, he was advocating sacramental, auricular confession and reminding the parson that church law 'charges the clergy to keep rigidly the seal of confession'.[23] In 1916, Francis George Belton, a priest in the diocese of Birmingham, wrote *A Manual for Confessors* as an Anglican work of practical guidance, which went into six editions. And by 1931 an Anglo-Catholic priest named Embry could write with some bewilderment of the controversy of the 1870s, in the light of practices in his own day: 'in the recognised acceptance of the Sacrament of Penance to-day . . . the opposition which [Anglo] Catholics encountered . . . seems almost incredible'.[24]

Crucially, Octavia understood that people – women especially – *liked* making confessions. Amongst her closest adherents she had High Anglicans who were used to the practice, such as Kate and Elizabeth Hodgkinson, and William Hollingsworth, who ran the Society's printing press and had been a lay member of an Anglican religious community which had a particular association with the High Church. While many people, like Ethel Castle, wrote to the Society saying they found making the confession painful at first, their subsequent letters indicate that they ultimately experienced great relief, and the bundle of surviving confessions in the Society's archives show that members strove to be transparent and honest about all matters. The Victorian Church of England might have been horrified that a handbook such as *The Priest in Absolution* frankly recommended asking questions about sex, albeit often in a circumspect way, but by the 1920s Octavia was entirely open about the need to confess 'matter of sex relations', and members were candid in their confessions. They admitted to ongoing attractions to other members (even though liaisons and marriage between members were forbidden); they confessed past relationships outside marriage (same-sex and heterosexual) and revealed the details of painful, sometimes abusive and dysfunctional marriages, on which Octavia usually (though not always) gave them sensible and practical advice.

Octavia was not alone in developing, along new and distinct lines, this confessional mode. As popular psychology and psychotherapy spread amongst the middle classes in the interwar years, it was adopted by religious groups who focused on inner conversion and self-reformation guided by public confession, often known as 'sharing'. Practical psychology was taken up and given a spiritual dimension by individuals such as the unconventional Anglican, Maude Royden, who began a series of groups or 'companies' in 1919, at her worshipping community in London, The Guildhouse, which she ran with Percy Dearmer. Frank Buchman, an American Lutheran minister who had come to England in 1908 and been influenced by the conversion testimonies at the evangelical conventions he attended at Keswick in the Lake District, began the Oxford Group in 1921. This was a relaxed, religious movement – the groups met in house parties, and in people's sitting rooms – that emphasised spiritual recovery through groups of people working together under the guidance of God. Public confession of sins was central to the work of such groups: 'sharing for witness', as it was called (based on Paul's letter to the Ephesians 4: 25), was combined with popular psychological understandings of the self. The Group Movement became both enormously popular, especially amongst the middle classes, and influential, most notably giving rise to Alcoholics Anonymous and the twelve-step recovery programmes. Women were particularly attracted to such groups, and the communal confessions often concerned sex. Overall, the leaders of these groups saw themselves as providing the means by which the world might be revitalised – through spiritualised group therapy.[25] These groups and their mix of orthodox and unorthodox Christianity, sometimes with elements of Eastern religious philosophy and practical psychology thrown in, exemplify the eclectic nature of much spirituality in the interwar years.

Octavia was fully aware of the Group Movement. She read voraciously, was intellectually curious, kept abreast of all movements, was herself eclectic in her beliefs and was aware of ongoing developments in psychology. She wrote, 'It is part of our policy never to refuse to look into movements which appear to catch hold of the public imagination.' What this meant was that she was always on the lookout for individuals or movements which might rival her own. *The Panacea* was full of refutations of other unorthodox religious groups and ideas, especially those which might seem to share many of the same beliefs and practices as her own community. It is no surprise that she wrote an article for the magazine refuting the claims of the Group Movement, which, she admitted, was 'extraordinarily successful'. She addressed the idea that 'new readers' might be attracted to it, and indeed might think: 'Confession is a strong point with The Panacea Society – perhaps the Group Movement is going to turn out to be what the world is waiting for!' Octavia's answer was of course no, because the Group Movement was a 'human effort', while the work of the Society was, she asserted, of entirely divine origin. She also believed that the Group Movement's practice of sharing one's offences with a friend or roomful of people was 'a most dangerous proceeding'. She was worried about the power of suggestion and alert to the possible misuse of shared information: 'For one human being to tell another of sins which they have committed – sins which the hearer has, perhaps, never dreamt of – is to sow ideas the results of which it is quite impossible to foresee . . . Secondly, confession made to another human being is not certain to be confidential, everyone is not to be trusted; a one-time friend can become an enemy, and may do incalculable mischief by using the confession to defame the character.' Octavia understood that confession could be used as a tool for control; as we shall see in later chapters, as the Society became bigger and its structures more set, confessions were used as a means of acquiring information and therefore maintaining control in the community – for knowledge is power.

The Panacean understanding of confession was distinctive. While Octavia agreed with the mainstream churches that the main object of confession was not to obtain relief from the burden of having

something hidden, but rather to obtain assurance that there is forgiveness, she also believed that 'a far greater object is to be assured that
power will be given to overcome sin'.[26] Panacea members 'instead of
being Penitents . . . shall be Overcomers, systematically reversing all the
dispositions that they know to be sinful or temperamental or even
peculiar'.[27] Octavia gleaned this religious practice of Overcoming from
an earlier prophet, an heir of Southcott named John Wroe, but she also
found it in the Book of Revelation, where the idea of 'overcoming'
occurs numerous times. For example, 'To him that overcometh will I
give to eat of the hidden manna' (2:17). Or: 'He that overcometh the
same shall be clothed in white raiment; and I will not blot out his name
in the Book of Life, but I will confess his name before my father and
before his angels' (3:5). In Octavia's heavily marked-up study bible, the
word 'overcometh' is underlined in red every time it occurs. The Greek
word translated here as 'overcometh' is *nikan*; two-thirds of the twenty-
five New Testament instances of this word occur in the Book of
Revelation. This is the language of the Christian *life*. Interestingly, the
Greek word *pisteuein*, meaning 'to believe', never occurs in Revelation.
'Faith' or 'belief' in terms of Octavia's aims (and indeed in the context
of what the author of Revelation is trying to say) may imply a merely
mental process; believing may be too passive. The question for Octavia
was, rather: are you active? Are you engaged in Overcoming, in
conquering the evil one? Overcoming was, above all, a religious activity,
a practice.[28] Creating a practice for Overcoming was central to the
community's life.

Not surprisingly, Overcoming did not always go as successfully as
Octavia hoped. The answer was usually more confessions. Sometimes,
the inner core of members of the community (mostly the resident
members) would be called to make an additional confession on a
particular occasion. In 1933 Octavia was worried that the bishops had
still not come to open Southcott's Box of Prophecies and decided that
it was because it was 'impossible for the Bishops to come while any
resistance to reproof and correction' remained in the community. 'Let
it be well and truly understood that these are truly the "last days" for
successfully condemning the Mortal Mind,' she wrote, as she exhorted
all members to make another full written confession in 1933. These
additional confessions were sometimes kept – though we do not know
why – and sometimes burned ceremonially in the garden.

Along with the Life Confession, prospective members had to undertake further acts: the Oath of Allegiance, a promise to be led in the
future not by man's teachings about God, but only by his Prophets
(that is, the teachings of Octavia and the earlier Southcottian prophets),
and the marriage vow, asking for their present bodies to be made a
tabernacle for the spirit of God to dwell in. After the Life Confession
had been made and these oaths had been taken, a person was ready
to be sealed as a member. All members of the Society, whether residential or non-residential, were sealed, and the initial – one might
even say *initiation* – rites were a part of this process of sealing. The
idea of sealing was taken from Revelation 7 and 14, and had been
regarded by Southcott as a method of protection from the evils about
to come into the world. Southcott had sealed her followers simply by
giving them a membership certificate that she had signed and sealed
with red sealing wax. Octavia took it much further, and as the community grew, the sealing became ever more elaborate. The script for July
1919 ordered that all members should be sealed. In August, the female
apostles received the White Seal and this was quickly translated to
the Royal Seal in one of those random moments that seemed so
serendipitous and meaningful to Octavia and her followers. Octavia
found some notepaper which had belonged to her son, Ivan, and this
had the royal arms on it; finding that there were just twelve sheets of
it left, she took this as a sign that each apostle should sign each sheet.
When a prominent member of another of the Southcottian groups,
Francis Clark, sent Octavia a crystal seal with the royal arms of France
and England on it, which had supposedly belonged to Mary Queen
of Scots (though this seems highly unlikely), this merely confirmed
the idea that they were right in what they were doing. A vellum book
was bought for the names of the sealed, and used, along with the
recently acquired Royal Seal, for the first time in November 1919, when
Gertrude Hill (who stood for the Church, being a vicar's wife) was
sealed first.

This sealing process was adapted and changed as the community grew.
In June 1924 the first circle of sealing was closed when it reached 153
sealed members, and a new circle was begun. Before 1925, everyone who
wished to be sealed had to come to Bedford to gain the full sealing. From
1925, arrangements were made for this to happen by post, with new
members having the option of doing the sealing ritual for themselves at

Mabel Barltrop, happy, with her
first-born son Eric, 1890.

Mabel and Arthur Barltrop with their
sons Eric and Ivan in the early 1890s.

Arthur Barltrop, curate, in the 1890s.

Aunt Fanny Waldron who helped raise
the young Mabel and always lived with
the Barltrop family until her death in 1923.

Mabel with bicycle.

Mabel in her widow's mourning clothes on a picnic with Ivan (*left*), Dilys and Adrian *c.*1907.

The Barltrop family *c.*1909.
Back row from left: Ivan and Eric; front row: Mabel, Dilys, Adrian.

Mabel and Dilys with the family dog *c.*1910 (pets would be banned from the Panacea Society).

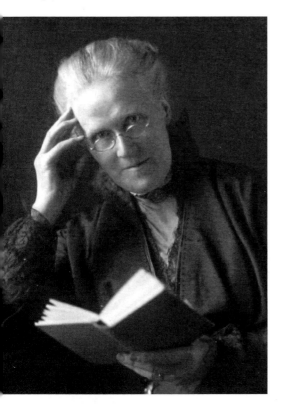

Rachel Fox: Quaker,
Spiritualist and author.

Helen Shepstone, who wrote from
South Africa to Rachel Fox about
Southcott's prophecies.

Ellen Oliver, the former suffragette
who named Mabel as 'Shiloh'.

Mabel Barltrop c.1919
when she became Octavia.

Number 12 Albany Road, Bedford: the Barltrop family home where the Panacea Society began.

The front parlour of 12 Albany Road, the room out of which the Society was organised for several years.

Gertrude Esther Hill, apostle and vicar's wife, milking a cow at home.

Winna Green, apostle, dressed as the Knave of Hearts in the Society's production of *Alice in Wonderland* in 1929.

Kate Hodgkinson, apostle. Octavia criticised her for wearing ugly hats and being dishevelled in her dress.

Alice Jones, apostle, dressed as the King of Hearts in *Alice in Wonderland*.

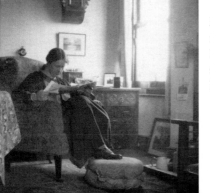

Evelyn Gillett reading at the home in Bedford she shared with her sister.

Peter Rasmussen in Pierrot costume for one of the Society's entertainments.

Peter Rasmussen burning members' confessions in the Society gardens. Note the toy lamb representing Christ, the lamb of God.

Members at a Society garden party in the late 1920s. The Edwardian dress of some of them highlights the relatively elderly membership of the Society.

Garden party in the late 1920s. Dilys Barltrop, hatless, looks directly at the camera from a central table.

Octavia (left in shawl) walks across the tennis courts to greet members at a garden party, late 1920s.

Members dressed for country dancing at the garden party in 1928.

The chapel before the stained glass window was installed behind the altar at the east end.

(*Below left*) John Coghill's painting of croquet in the Panacea gardens, showing the clock tower and the exterior of the chapel.

The stained glass depicting the female aspect of the divinity, Mother Jerusalem, or the Divine Mother.

Muriel Gillett working in the Society's printing press alongside William Hollingworth.

William Hollingworth in the storage area of the Society's printing press. The brown-paper parcels of books and posters, ready for those who request them, are still in place today.

home, to avoid the need to make a visit to the Bedford headquarters. This was clearly a practical necessity once members were recruited in the USA, South Africa, Australia and New Zealand. The Royal Seal was used until 1925, then replaced by the Royal Red Sealing, and then by the Blue and Green Sealings (May 1926 to October 1928) and finally by the Crimson Sealing in 1930. The reason for these changes in colour is not clear, but certainly the whole process of sealing became more complex as time passed, Christ did not come, and people still did not fully overcome their selves; and as numbers grew, the process was also increasingly bureaucratised. Later, to keep count of the membership, the Society divided members up into companies of fifty. One reason for the meticulous records was that the Society wanted to keep track of its progress towards gathering the 144,000: the number in the Book of Revelation of those who would be saved at the Second Coming of Christ. The seal was a sign that you were one of that number, destined to inherit life immortal, sealed to live and not to die.

Once a person had been sealed, the process of Overcoming had only just begun. A sealed member continued to monitor her faults and failings, going through them each night, making a list – to be given into headquarters – of their 'inhibitions, peculiarities, weak points and drawbacks' that might include the following:

Nervousness,	Any kind of Temper,
Sensitiveness,	Sulkiness,
Shyness,	Moroseness,
Fear,	Procrastination,
Selfishness,	Discontent,
Self-opinion,	Love of money,
Doubt,	Fear about money,
Jealousy,	Meanness,
Pride,	Extravagance,
Untruthfulness,	Untidiness,
Exaggeration,	Carelessness,
Criticism,	&c, &c.[29]

The reaction of one member is quite amusing: having experienced the making of her Life Confession as a spring cleaning which gave her great relief, Ethel Castle wrote a few months later, worried that

'I don't seem able to bring enough faults and failings to my mind each night.'[30]

Those who made their confession were also recommended:

(1) To search your property and to be careful not to retain things that do not properly belong to you.
(2) To endeavour to pay all debts, to be careful to keep out of debt, and to try to be in front of your expenditure.
(3) To exercise moderation in all things, spending moderately and saving moderately.
(4) To live as one who hopes to be among those who will hear the words: 'Come, ye blessed children of my Father, inherit the Kingdom prepared for you.'

Point (2) on the matter of debt was important. No one who was in debt could come to live in the community, and members had to declare their financial situation honestly when making their application for residence. Members came to live in the community in three ways. First, if they had the means, they might buy a property close to the community headquarters. Secondly, if they could not afford to buy a house – or did not want to do so – they might rent a room in another member's property and pay for their meals there. But even then they had to have some source of income, for once they became resident members, they were not working outside the community; all their labour was devoted free to the Panacean cause. The organisation of community houses was done centrally, with Octavia assigning the houses that people should live in. Thirdly, if a member had no income at all, then she could become a servant in one of the community houses, receiving a small income in return for domestic work.

Debt could make for a delicate situation, and Octavia was keen to avoid the complexities it might cause for a resident member. Agnes Hilson had been in contact with the Society from its earliest days, corresponding with both Ellen Oliver and Octavia. She desperately wanted to come and live in the community but she was heavily in debt: she had borrowed money from the Yorkshire Loan Training Fund for a course in Physical Culture. The scheme was designed to help women, who could not otherwise afford any higher education, to pay their fees by giving them no-interest loans. Although Agnes still had this outstanding debt, Octavia relented and let her come to stay in the community; this was early in its history, when the rules were not as hard and fast as they became later. The problem was that in 1925 another non-resident member, Ethel Cooke-Yarborough, who also had a loan from the Yorkshire Loan Training Fund, and was obediently paying it off before she came to live in Bedford, learned about resident member Agnes Hilson's unpaid debt to the same fund, and was most unhappy. She wrote to Octavia to complain. Octavia's reply is interesting because she does not address Ethel Cooke-Yarborough's sense of grievance but focuses rather on the community's response to Agnes Hilson, revealing a kindness and flexibility that is not always apparent in the official documents. She wrote that Agnes Hilson is

> a very difficult and sad case to deal with and has been an almost daily anxiety since October 1920. Our treatment of the case has been charitable and patient in the extreme, for she dealt most unjustly with certain matters of money here. She is not a girl; she is over 50; she was 30 in 1902 when she began the Training . . . We have offered her travelling expenses back to Edinburgh and enough money to make a fresh start, but she wishes to remain . . . We consider that neither the Committee [of the Loan Fund] nor we are blameable but that it is a case of an unjust nature with which only the Almighty can deal, and, naturally, to lend such a large sum of money to such a person is to court disaster.[31]

There was of course a paradox to Overcoming. The very practice of trying to rid yourself of your personality means that your distinctive characteristics emerge ever more clearly. It was this practice above all else that drove the dynamics of the community, and thus the rhythms that arose from that practice formed the ups and downs of the community's interactions, creating their *gathered* life. Furthermore, the normal tensions of community life were exacerbated by the injunction to members to report not only their own faults and failings, but also those of others. 'This is the House of Correction, this is the Era of Reproof,' wrote Octavia.[32] Members had to be willing to be reported by others and to have no malice against them for doing so; nor must they misjudge them in the performance of this duty. They also had to report anyone who fell short of the standard which they knew was required of them. The consequent atmosphere of spying on one another could be really unpleasant at times, especially when potential dissidents emerged in the community.

At the centre of this way of life was Octavia, the dominating figure to whom obedience was due, for whom (as she was regarded as the daughter of God) the practice of Overcoming was deemed unnecessary: 'she had never sinned *spiritually*, even though she had had to enter a body which knew sin'.[33] She was the one who initially set the exacting guidelines for community life, and corrected and reproved members. Brenda Greig and Irene Mellor, two members close to the centre of resident community life in the late 1920s, wrote in *The Panacea* (which was, we must remember, edited by Octavia): 'our Leader . . . [is] sensitive to a degree, she can sense in a moment if anyone is in disagreement or opposition. The pleasant way would be to steer clear of the tender spots in character, but that is never done: if faults and failings are exposed unsparingly, our Leader is unsparing of herself and her feelings.' If 'some fault has shown itself plainly during the day', the subject could be raised at the evening chapel meeting: it was done 'exquisitely' and 'severely probably, but always usefully, so that not only the culprit (who, of course, is never named), but all of us can see what must be avoided, and how to build the opposite virtue. Until it is brought to their notice, few might stop to think what it must cost our Leader to buffet daily with the failings of 30 or 40 persons.'[34]

The surviving correspondence between Octavia and Panacea members shows how many different people she was counselling at any one time; how many tricky family dynamics she was helping people to negotiate; and how much advice she was dispensing on a daily basis, much of it sensible and down-to-earth. This correspondence was with both non-resident and resident members, for these middle-class women, long in the letter-writing habit, continued to write to each other even if they lived only down the street from each other. To read through these letters is to understand how much of Octavia's time was devoted to helping needy people, and how many people's problems she was juggling at a given time. For when a person joined the Society and began the process of Overcoming, he or she entered a psychological process of rooting out old wounds and deeply ingrained habits of being, and often also brought with them complex family dynamics. The latter was particularly the case if more than one member of a family joined. Take, for example, the Gillett family.

When Mary Gillett and her two daughters, Muriel and Evelyn, joined the Society in 1921, and the sisters became resident members, they brought with them their own family drama, upon which Octavia was constantly advising them. Mary Gillett was a needy, ill and overbearing mother, who had relied heavily on Muriel from an early age. In turn, Muriel was an over-sensitive young woman, who resented the duties imposed on her; joining the community gave her the opportunity to be free of her mother's control. In January 1924, she wrote to Octavia that 'the chance came this morning for me to try to explain to Mother how I still feel bound up by her & that I want to be freed'. In May, she was still writing of her problems: 'it seems to me that she loves me for her sake, and not for mine'. Octavia sensibly advised Muriel not to expect more of her mother than might be possible. She also recognised that Muriel had not been properly mothered, and suggested she turn to Octavia herself for that maternal nurturing, something which Muriel strived to do.[35] Muriel appreciated Octavia's guidance, writing to her: 'When you asked me yesterday if I am happier than I used to be, I know that by my reply I couldn't have given you any idea of how enormous is the difference . . . but I would like you to know, and it is due to you too to know it for it is you who have done it for me.' She went on, showing that she understood Octavia's role in the community: 'You see so much of the side of having to deal sharply with people & feeling that you are paining them, that I would like to tell you that the little bit of hurting you have had to do for me, and may have to do, don't count anywhere by the side of the help you have been to me and the comfort.' Finally she had someone to turn to with her problems: 'I have longed for years for someone to be able to tell me where I am wrong & to put me right, & when at last I find that person in you I am truly thankful.' And she believed the advice to be not simply that of a friend or spiritual mentor, but of divine origin: 'This power of yours to alter the whole outlook & events of my life, seems to me to manifest Christ with you so much more than what the world calls miracles do.'[36]

However, not everyone appreciated Octavia's advice and straight talking. Muriel's mother, Mary, felt misunderstood by her. When she went to Octavia for help, she felt that Octavia talked about irrelevant matters, and was particularly perplexed when Octavia interpreted a case of sunburn as a sign that she 'had Lucifer'! The consequence was that Mary Gillett left the Society in May 1924, and went back to live permanently in their old family home in Banbury.[37] This was a liberating moment for Muriel, who was intent upon staying in Bedford. But then she had to face up to another difficult family dynamic: her resentment of her younger sister, Evelyn, who, she felt, had evaded the duties of tending to their mother for many years. She called upon Octavia to help with another layer of unravelling, so that the sisters might live peaceably together now that the 'glue' – albeit dysfunctional glue – of their mother had gone from the home. Octavia got them both to tell their story: Muriel's was full of sensitivities, long and tortured; Evelyn's was breezy and short – she had always escaped from the problem by getting out of the house. But Evelyn did reveal her difficulties in dealing with the passive-aggressive Muriel who felt herself to be so burdened: 'my great idea in those days was that what Muriel wanted done should be done, but the difficulty often was to find out, as she was rather silent, inclined to sulk and considered I made too much noise.' While Muriel felt that Evelyn had evaded the care-taking duties, Evelyn found it difficult to deal with Muriel's desire for control: 'Later in life, Mother being so ill, Muriel practically took her place and nothing was done without consulting her which rather got on my nerves.' Octavia's conclusion was that 'Both like to be a *centre*. Evelyn likes to be important. True importance does not have to assert itself.' Her conclusion was that both had to rid themselves of 'self'.[38] They took Octavia's advice to heart. Both remained in the community until their death, eventually running a well-oiled community house, exercising the gift of hospitality on behalf of the community.

Evelyn, however, always remained exuberant, independent-minded and high-spirited, which meant she was told she had a lot of Overcoming to do. In 1932 she wrote a shrewdly perceptive document entitled 'Reminiscences', detailing many of the criticisms of her character supplied by her fellow members in the nine years since her arrival in Bedford.[39] She was very close to Dilys Barltrop, simply because they were two of the very few young resident members. But Dilys was a hypersensitive individual for whom Evelyn was probably the most unsuitable best friend, wearing the 'wrong clothes' in public (her gardening clothes), the 'wrong shoes', eating messily, being at times over-enthusiastic, at other times sullen. Evelyn managed to rub people up the wrong way just by opening her mouth. She once declared innocently to Winna Green that she found everyone at Panacea 'boring', then wondered why Winna avoided her after that; she passed on a message she thought she had had from the deceased Eric Barltrop, upsetting Octavia. She was a tomboy, who liked nothing more than working at her car or gardening, and in the fifty years she spent in the Society, it seems that her personality was never smoothed down. She retained her unpredictable spiritedness and what the Panaceans would have regarded as her rough edges.

The process of Overcoming could make community life tough and complex, especially with members reporting each other's faults and failings to Octavia, but most of the members were grateful that someone showed such an interest in the smallest details of their lives. And the Panaceans also had fun. Sometimes there was a foretaste of the paradise towards which they were all working. Their diaries abound with details of musical evenings, garden parties, cycling trips and painting expeditions into the surrounding countryside. They were not cut off from the most popular form of entertainment of the time: 'the pictures'. Members were allowed two visits a week to the cinema in town, joining the other half-million or more Britons who went to the cinema twice a week.[40] 'After supper took Amy [the servant] to the pictures again to see Mary Pickford in "Little Annie Rowney"', wrote Kate Firth in her diary, and the next day she recorded that she had been given special permission to go to the pictures a third time that week, to see Harold Lloyd in *College Days*, which 'was too funny for words'. These were, of course, American films, for America dominated the 'talkies', and Panaceans were no more immune to the American domination of the interwar cinema market than any other cinema-goers, though they had a certain disdain for the Americanisation of British culture, which represented modernisation. Other leisure activities were more home-grown: the 'wireless room' in the Society's gardens was dedicated to games – darts, cards, games with dice – and listening to the wireless. Home movies show members playing tennis in the gardens and leaping about with real exhilaration. A watercolour by member John Coghill conjures up the atmosphere of a game of croquet in the gardens. The women are dressed in their elegant red and blue frocks with matching hats, while their male companion – Peter Rasmussen in bow tie and linen blazer – stands back with his croquet mallet over his shoulder. The sun is shining brightly; the chapel clock has just struck twelve; and the garden is gloriously in bloom with lavender bushes, climbing roses and hydrangeas.

In the early days of the community, informal musical soirées, where Octavia played the piano and others sang, took place in Octavia's home. 'Musical evening 7.30 M.B.'s,' Gertrude Searson wrote in her diary in 1919. As the community grew, social events were more formally organised. There were evening buffet suppers and garden parties for the whole residential community and selected non-resident members. Rachel Fox described the first of the garden parties: 'Octavia gave a Garden Party to all at the Centre, in the Garden of *The Haven,* on the 18th – a most perfect day. Tea was served under the big weeping ash-tree named Yggdrasil. After the Meeting, twelve of the party danced country dances, dressed as country people in smocks and panier dresses.' For the official account, Octavia reflected: 'we have advanced from such a small affair, to the beautiful gardens in which we have just been having tea under the shade of the wonderful tree Yggdrasil. Most of us have been taught that we must not enjoy ourselves too much; but now we are beginning to find that God wills us to enjoy His gifts as much as we can'.[41] She wrote more informally in her diary, 'great success, lovely weather', having noted the previous day, 'jelly ready for the party'.

Annual garden parties were thereafter held on the second Friday or Saturday in July between 1929 and 1932, close to the General Council Meeting of the Society (so that those travelling to Bedford could stay for both). The programme for the 1930 party features such high jinks as a potato race, clock golf, and country dancing organised and led by Gertrude Hallwood. In 1931, there was tennis, darts, rings and putting, and in 1932 tennis, darts, a ring game, croquet, badmington (*sic*) and clock golf. Buffet suppers were held annually in January. Hilda Green described the party held on 27 January 1927, in her diary:

> After the service all went over to The Haven . . . all assembled to the number of 43 in the Blue Room; various ladies contributed songs and music. Peter appeared in costume as a Chinese lady, then as 'her husband', later as 'Miss Montmorency'. Guests went into supper in 2 parties after which a hunt for treasure took place, then crackers were pulled. Before leaving, each had a glass of port and a piece of Christmas cake.[42]

After the January buffet supper in 1929, members performed a two-act play based on *Alice in Wonderland*.

Octavia choreographed all these events down to the last detail. In preparation for the 1930 garden party she typed up six pages of notes detailing which tables, chairs, cutlery and china would be used from which community houses, and made a sketch of how the place settings should look. After every party she typed up notes outlining what was good and bad about it and what should be different next time. After one January buffet supper she wrote a long list of complaints to Jessie Tweedie, a resident member who had been responsible for much of the organisation: 'Crackers dreadfully disappointing, ugly colours & nothing much in them. The Red Jellies and Large Glasses very ugly . . . Table looked flat and ugly – CAKE vulgar – merangues [*sic*] too difficult to eat . . . Lemon-ade too much and too weak. Claret cup not strong enough – there was fruit in the bottom.' In preparation for the January 1928 buffet supper party, she noted:

> No cider cup. More sugar in claret cup. No plum cake. Another kind of sandwich. Learn waltzes. Must have sufficient chairs for all in blue room. Servants should dress better. More light in supper rooms. Get all the plates very hot & each set out before they come to table.[43]

We can only imagine the fear and trembling with which members prepared the party food and set up the rooms, hoping against hope to get it right this time, accepting the instructions as part of their regime of obedience and Overcoming.

All of these social events were happening, the Panaceans believed, in the original Garden of Eden, which extended for a three-mile radius from the chapel. It was land that had 'never belonged to Satan', a place where 'the Lord retained a pied-a-terre or foothold' (while Satan was busily ruling the rest of the earth).[44] To the outside observer, this is an incredible claim, but it is just one of many instances in which a metaphysical idea was conceived as a concrete reality in the life of the Panacea Society. Octavia had a vision that when Jesus came again, they would be strolling around the Garden of Eden with him and chatting on a first-name basis with God, eating delicious foods. The garden parties were just a precursor to that moment: the first garden party was 'only the beginning of the pleasures that would be ours'.[45]

Getting the details of the garden party just right was vital: it would hasten the Second Coming of Christ, but it was also a foretaste of their immortal life. The meringues in paradise would not be too difficult to eat, and the table settings would certainly not be flat and ugly. These were people with radical theological ideas, but a largely conservative attitude to almost everything else. Their idea of paradise was a tea party, with all the proper etiquette observed.

Garden parties and buffet suppers were very special treats. The main work of Overcoming and ushering in the millennium was woven into the community's daily routine. The day began in the community houses with the delivery – by the household's servant – of hot water to a member's room, for washing, at 7.30, followed by breakfast, after which the head of the household read a script and the day's reading from a compilation of biblical texts, *Daily Light*. Then everyone went to their jobs; as one member put it: 'the Housekeepers to their larders and kitchens, the Printers to the Press, the Gardeners to their gardens, the heads of the Healing Department and Publication department and the Typists to their cheery, well-equipped offices, where some of their helpers arrive a little later, having done some housework first.' Lunch was held in the community houses, and then members worked again until 4.30, when they went home for tea, 'a jolly meal with home-made jams and cakes, fun, and chat, and the day's work done'. On Saturdays, when members only worked in the morning, there might be tea in the town or a picnic on the river (which was a short walk from the community). Sunday was a day of rest.[46]

The highlight of the day was the evening meeting. In the early years, worship was held in 'the upper room' in Octavia's house. In 1920, a shed behind her house was converted into the Garden Room, and this eventually served as the chapel, with the capacity to hold about fifty people. Chapel services or 'the meeting' took place at 6.30 every evening. Much of the evening service was culled from the Church of England's Book of Common Prayer. The script, which Octavia had taken down that evening, was read and discussed. Octavia did not preach a formal sermon; she led the service, and anyone could make a comment. Sometimes cuttings from newspapers on topical church or world events were read, or recent influential books talked about. Members constantly stressed the relaxed atmosphere: 'sometimes the little community enjoys a good joke much to the surprise, I know, of

some visitors who have expected a much more "religious" atmosphere,' wrote Mary Warry, a non-resident, when describing a visit.[47]
Brenda Greig and Irene Mellor, resident members, wrote that sometimes the meetings 'run in such a funny vein that one gets weak with
laughter. No one can tell a whimsical story more dramatically than
our Leader. Her memory for them is boundless, and her witty way
of putting a thing is most entrancing, while her laugh is infectious to
a degree.'[48]

Non-resident members had their own local meetings, usually once
a week, and always at 6.30 p.m., and they followed a similar worship
service to that at headquarters. The leader of the group read out notes
from friends who were resident members in Bedford, and members
of the local group who had recently been to Bedford were pressed
for news and a report of their visit. One non-resident member,
Josephine Low, ended her account of such a local meeting, in
Eastbourne on the south coast, where there was a sizeable group of
non-resident members, saying: 'there is no time limit to our meetings.
They last for about an hour and a half, and are ended quietly and
informally with parting remarks and messages. As we go on our
different ways homewards, over the hills, or down into the town
stretching itself to the sea, I think we realise anew each week how
we who belong to The Panacea Society are indeed a Blessed people.'[49]

There were many reasons why people – women especially – found
the Society appealing, and why Panaceans believed themselves to be
a 'Blessed people' but the primary attraction must lie in the Society's
theology. It is important to take at face value the members' belief that
they were witnessing the coming of the divine daughter in Octavia,
and were thus engaging in a set of religious practices which would
enable them to achieve immortal life on earth (not merely in heaven)
with the next coming of Christ, however hard those practices and
community life were at times. The individual members of this community were bound together by the promise of eternal life and by
the communal and all-consuming project of establishing the kingdom
of heaven on earth, which, they believed, would occur in Bedford
itself. Each was called to be one of the 144,000 chosen and foretold
in the Book of Revelation. They felt special, chosen, and they believed
that they would not die.

There was a day-to-day appeal too. Octavia was an emotionally shrewd woman, a good reader of character who realised that, at heart, the vast majority of people simply wanted to make themselves better. In this sense, she pre-empted the self-help trend of the later twentieth century. Members picked up on this practical element. Mary Warry wrote enthusiastically, just six days after her initial contact with the Society, 'I positively enjoy being an "overcomer", it's something practical one can get on with without any wondering, & every time I succeed I cock a snook at the devil.'[50] She was exactly the kind of person to whom this possibility of self-improvement, this training to become a nicer person to live with, might appeal. Married to a retired colonel thirty years older than herself – she was twenty-eight in 1924 when she was sealed and was therefore one of the younger members – she lived with her husband on the edge of his family estate and her days were spent in good works with the tenants: reading the Bible with them, praying with the sick, teaching the girls and young women to read their Bible and pray regularly.[51] Her way of life reflected a pattern that many thought was being eroded but which Panacea people believed to be the proper ordering of society: she was part of village life in which she and her husband were, as she put it, 'the only gentle-folk in the village' but in turn they were expected to be charitable and benevolent.[52] Mary Warry was also emotionally intelligent enough to come to an understanding that the spiritual and psychological process in which she was engaged was more complex than she had, in her initial enthusiasm, realised. Ten months after being sealed, she wrote in a more thoughtful vein: 'I will settle down once more to deal with that extraordinarily subtle thing "self".'[53]

As ever, Octavia's vision was both conservative and radical, combining a nostalgic desire for the past and its values with a startling awareness of the issues of the day. In appealing to others, she tapped into this paradoxical current – into people's desire for the security of the past combined with a wish to rise to the challenges of the future. It is no surprise that there were resonances between what Octavia was doing and what others were advocating, whether in the Group Movement, the various strands of psychology that were popular in the interwar years or other religious movements: all were attempting to think through that complex phenomenon of the 'self' with which the modern world had become so obsessed. All were attempting to work out how that 'self' should operate in the world. If there ever was a walking advertisement for Octavia's way, it was John Coghill, who joined the Panacea Society in 1934 and was engaged in the practice of Overcoming from then until his death in February 2008. I spent a lot of time with him at the Society while I was researching this book. His kindness and gentleness made him remarkably easy to rub along with, and his humility, in all its easiness of spirit, made this observer wonder if there was and is just something to this spiritual practice after all.

7

Trouble in Paradise

In the spring of 1922, a flamboyant American named Edgar Peissart arrived on the Panacea doorstep in Bedford. He immediately charmed the ladies. He was sixty-three, about the same age as many of the apostles, and he cut a striking figure, despite being quite short and rather deaf. He wore rings on his fingers, a dapper bow tie and top hat, had a stirring and authoritative voice and a charismatic air about him. Octavia commented: 'his voice is one of his assets – he recited parts of the "Merchant of Venice" at one of our social evenings, and truly, I never heard anything so tremendous.' But just one year after his arrival, he was dramatically expelled from the Society. He had made a bid for power, seeking to co-rule with, or possibly unseat, Octavia, and he had set up a male homosexual subculture in the community, which, when it was discovered, was regarded as a threat to the theological claim at the heart of their beliefs – that it was Woman who would ultimately redeem the world.

The episode was a turning point in the community's history. For his expulsion brought about an extraordinary event. Panacea members came to believe that one of their own, the rather ordinary woman named Emily Goodwin who worked as nurse to Mabel's aunt, could speak as the Divine Mother, the second person of the foursquare Godhead. Through that 'Instrument', as she was called, the Society's structures were reinforced and discipline was tightened in an effort to manage this now fast-growing community. By the beginning of 1923, the Society had three community houses, and its non-resident membership was rising. Six months later, there were 122 sealed members, and another 85 provisionally sealed, bringing the total to 207.[1] And with growth came the greater possibility of dissent and tension.

Edgar Peissart first wrote to Rachel Fox early in the Society's history, in March 1919, three years before he finally arrived. He presumed that she was the author of the little book, *The Truth about Joanna Southcott* (which was in fact written by Alice Seymour's acolyte, Mary Robertson). Soon after that, he was reading all of the available Panacea literature and writing to Ellen Oliver and Octavia as well as Rachel Fox. He was full of words and full of himself. The letters were written in his large swooping handwriting, and in his distinctively wordy style, with constant allusions to biblical and esoteric teaching, astrological discussions, pseudo-scientific theories, mystifying calculations and numerology. It is hard to make much sense of them, but his chief message was that he was 'the Man' for the Visitation, who would need to be present for the Box to be opened. Rachel Fox replied firmly, 'we women have been instructed not to listen to the opinions of any man at this crisis, lest we should be led astray' and she recorded that the letters received 'scant attention from Octavia'. Kate Firth, in looking at the letters and at the photograph that Edgar Peissart sent of himself, 'declared that he was the devil himself'.[2] Certainly there is something rather creepy about the photograph of Edgar in theatrical outfit of cloak and top hat.

By November 1920, Octavia and those at headquarters were sick of being bombarded with his long, rambling letters and Octavia wrote to him: 'I must close my efforts to make you see the simplicity of our teachings compared to your complexity,' but she let him know that she had put him in their prayer request book that the Lord might 'deliver E.P. from the psychic control which is leading him astray from the path of Life. O Lord, help him to become as a little child.' There is a similar prayer in the request book in the same year, for another American man, Jesse Green, who had been writing to the Society from Chicago. At that time, Octavia had written back to him, telling him just to read the Prophets and pray, and leave dreams and other writings alone. 'You have wasted God's time terribly – do – I pray you cease all this writing,' she wrote. In the book of prayer requests, she wrote: 'O Lord we beseech thee to act powerfully to deliver Jesse Lawrence Green from psychic spiritual control – Grant that his flesh may come with him as that of a little child, that he may take the lowest place cheerfully and wisely until thou doth bid him to come higher. Aid him to bow before Thy requirements that he shall obey the Woman – both in word and in deed.' The prayer ended, rather wryly, with Octavia's trademark sense of humour, 'Deliver him, O Lord, or deliver us from him. Amen.' A little while later, someone wrote in the request book that the prayer had been answered: 'he is much more child like and endeavours to obey the woman. The Lord delivered him'.[3] But they were overly optimistic: this man was to figure in the 1923 drama surrounding Edgar Peissart.

Despite Octavia's letter, attempting to bring a close to the correspondence, Edgar Peissart continued to write to several of the central women of the Society. In January 1921, he wrote to Ellen Oliver asking where his Royal Seal was, and why he had had no reply from Octavia about his request to come and live in the community, repeating that he had indeed accepted her call. Never one to take a hint, or indeed accept a bald truth, he asked plaintively, 'What is the matter?' The answer, drafted by Octavia the following month (they did not rush to reply), stated, 'the reason we have never sent you a seal is that it would be impossible to anyone who makes the claims that you make'. He believed Octavia's status as the daughter of God, but his own claim to be a messiah figure went alongside it, and the women could not accept this. They made it clear that they followed Jesus Christ, 'the immortal man' who 'has a body' that 'can walk on water & pass through doors' and is 'Father, Husband, Brother, Friend'. They had no need of another divine man. 'Therefore it would be no kindness to you to allow you to ally yourself with women who are pledged by an act of homage & a most solemn oath' to Jesus Christ. Edgar was told firmly to endeavour to overcome his deluded claims and 'come face to face with yourself as a man'.[4]

Edgar Peissart was a religious seeker, mixing ideas from many different belief systems. His life was a perpetual quest for the truth, and thus a perpetual disappointment as his attempts to find it – or explain what he thought it was to others – were frustrated. His itinerant religiosity was remarkable. If any one person could find and attempt to join most of the marginalised Christian communities and heterodox religious groups of his time, then Edgar Peissart was that man. Over three decades, he lived all over America as he went about the religious quest that in 1922 brought him to the Panaceans in Bedford. External evidence of his movements shows him popping up in at least four different religious communities in the last decade of the nineteenth century and first decade of the twentieth, while notes that Octavia made indicate his membership of yet others. He was born in Pennsylvania, and his first recorded membership of a church is in that state, as a member of a Mennonite church in Milford Township, Lehigh County, in Pennsylvania, for a year: he joined in July 1893 and withdrew in 1894.[5] Octavia's notes suggest that he then became a Russellite – a follower of Charles Taze Russell, whose group was a precursor to the Jehovah's Witnesses; in 1896, a member of the River Brethren in Pennsylvania, a Mennonite offshoot; and in 1898, one of 'John Wroe's people', as Octavia put it: the Christian Israelites.[6] He next appears in any external records as a part of the House of David, a Southcottian community in Benton Harbor, Michigan, that had developed out of the Christian Israelites in 1903–4, which also believed they had Shiloh incarnated in their leaders, Mary and Benjamin Purnell. He joined in March 1903, early in the community's history, and stayed there for five years. While there, he was 'man milliner' to 'hundreds of their females!!!!' as he put it. The Benjamin and Mary community set up an extraordinary tourist resort in their grounds, to which thousands of visitors and holidaymakers thronged, arriving by boat across Lake Michigan or on the train from Chicago to the funfairs, cafés, concerts, baseball games (they had a famous team), jazz concerts and miniature railways. Early in the days of that resort's development, Edgar worked as a cashier at the ice-cream parlours, restaurants and miniature railroads, and was head of their greenhouses where, he boasted, he grew thousands of different geraniums. He was one of the people sent to New York in 1905 to greet a group of Christian Israelites arriving from Australia, led by William Bulley, on behalf of the Benton Harbor House of David. In his typically self-aggrandising style, Peissart claimed he was 'the means used by Jesus, to cause Wm Bulley, an old man, and 83 souls, to leave Australia on a seven weeks sea voyage, via Palestine, for N.Y. City, America, where Mr Peissart and the Manager of the Colony awaited them, with a special train, to go about three more days journey to Michigan.' The Australians brought $100,000 with them, for the House of David, and Peissart implicitly claimed responsibility for that wind-fall, as well as attracting many others to the colony.[7] His personal style was remarked on by others: Joseph Hannaford, an Englishman who went to be a member of the Benton Harbor House of David community in 1905, alluded to Edgar Peissart's flamboyancy when he described someone's dramatic gesture as 'à la Peissart'. But when Hannaford wrote that in 1911, Edgar had long ago left the House of

David, and in 1909, the year after he left, he was writing a letter complaining about the House of David colony.

Edgar's next move was to the Koreshan Unity community on the banks of the River Estero near Fort Myers in Florida. When he arrived there he had the trademark long hair and beard of the Christian Israelites, and was remembered by members of the Koreshan community as a bit of an 'oddball'.[8] This community had moved to Estero in Florida in the last decade of the nineteenth century, having formerly been in Chicago. Its leader, Dr Cyrus Teed, known as Koresh (the Hebrew title of the biblical King Cyrus), in a syncretistic style that was typical of the late nineteenth century, mixed Christian, quasi-Hindu and scientific beliefs, teaching that the world was hollow and the human race was living *in* it. At its height, between 1904 and 1908, the community had about 250 members, as well as homes for the members, a community dining hall, a sawmill, a printing house, concrete works, post office, general store and bakery. Edgar next appears attempting to join the Florida Shaker group, near Ashton in Osceola County, which had been established in the area in 1894.[9] He declared that he was in sympathy with the Shakers, but they found him quite unsuitable. Shaker Ezra J. Stewart wrote in May 1911, 'As a result of an interview with the elders here . . . [it was thought best] that Edgar should depart [for Estero] next morning by train . . . as his views were found to be quite different from ours . . . He evidently hoped to set up a little kingdom here with himself as leader. [He] wears finger rings, and has much distaste for work, altho fairly strong and in good health'.[10] Octavia made a note in her records that he had stayed with the Shakers in 1910 for a year. Edgar did not have the taste for simplicity, which was a hallmark of the Shaker way of life. The point about work was also significant. For the Shakers, work had spiritual meaning and they supported themselves financially by farming and business ventures; they grew fruit and were widely known in the area for their excellent pineapples; farmed cattle; fished and sold timber from their estate. Edgar, however, was interested more in power and his own special calling. When he left the Shakers he returned to the Estero community in Florida.

While Edgar was clearly a religious seeker, and a seeker of power, and in that sense any religious community was game for him, there were similarities between the doctrines of the Koreshan Unity community, the Shakers, the House of David and the Panacea Society, all of which he found attractive. Cyrus Teed, the Koreshan leader, like the Shakers, taught the inner circle of followers that their celibacy would lead them to immortality, and certainly claimed immortal life for himself, and Octavia likewise advocated singleness and celibacy as the best way forward on the road to immortality. All three groups taught that God was both male and female, and that both male and female elements of the divine needed to be manifested on earth. Teed differed from Ann Lee of the Shakers and Octavia in that he also taught regeneration (or reincarnation) and he believed that God had sent six messengers to earth (Adam, Enoch, Noah, Moses, Elijah and Jesus); he – Koresh – was the seventh. Cyrus Teed died on 22 December 1908, and was not raised on the third day (Christmas Day) as he had told his followers would happen. The community kept Cyrus propped up in a bathtub, with high hopes that he would be resurrected or regenerated, but finally on 27 December the county health officer ordered the body to be taken away and buried.

Edgar, who had arrived at Estero just in time to know Teed for a month before he died, believed that Teed's spirit had passed into him on Teed's deathbed. He wrote that Teed 'consciously passed over to me, all the Spirits of the new Jerusalem' whom he had gathered into his bosom. Edgar believed that these spirits were now the inspiration of his teaching, 'full of wisdom because they possessed the kingdom of God within'.[11] He took to calling himself Cyrus or Koresh and had a flyer made up in which his own picture was superimposed on Cyrus Teed's, as Teed's receded into the background. He also made similar claims about the Shakers' leader Ann Lee, suggesting that he was the true heir to *her* leadership, and made up posters to the effect, titled 'Projection of the Mother Lord Ann Lee'. Mother Ann Lee had been long dead; the Shakers were having none of it; and they saw through him. But the period just after the charismatic leader of a group dies is a vulnerable one: it often fractures, with individuals claiming to take on the dead leader's authority. This is exactly what happened with the Koreshans.[12] Edgar Peissart was leader of one of the splinter groups, and spent his time corresponding with various members – he had long, annotated typed lists of people he thought sympathetic to his cause – who might support his claims to have inherited the spirit and leadership of Dr Teed. He wrote theological tracts in which he presented his claim to be the 'Son of Man' or the 'second cherub', and published a newsletter called the *Messenger* in which he detailed the treacherous antics of other Koreshans. It is no surprise that once he had established himself in the Panacea Society, he made a bid for power there too. A picture emerges of a man who went from community to community, seeking not only truth but also power, disgruntled and dissatisfied when people did not recognise *him* and his gifts, but not above returning to a community he had rejected if he saw a further opportunity to get into the leadership.

When he arrived in Bedford, he had been perpetually travelling, never settled, but constantly in contact by letter with other disgruntled Koreshans and Shakers. In the ten years before arriving in Bedford, he had lived in Atlantic City (1911); Cuba (1914); Arkansas and St Joseph's City (in Michigan) (1916); Rock Island Pacific (the Chicago railroad) (1917); and finally California (1917–19), particularly San Diego and Los Angeles where he was in touch with a spiritualist minister, the Revd Edward Earle, and Florida (1919–21). Octavia's notes also indicate that he was in prison for three months in 1909, but no further details are given: this was just after his attempt to replace Teed as leader in the Estero community, and before he spent some time with the Shakers.[13]

By 1922 Edgar was looking for another place to settle; and his final destination was Bedford. His arrival there marked the end of a long quest, and the culmination of his two decades of religious and geographical wanderings. But before making his bid for leadership in Bedford, he bided his time, remaining discreet about his own special understanding of himself as the chosen Man, and his need for a female counterpart. The Koreshans – with their idea of the male and female in the Divine – had been taught that 'the Woman' must be found, and that this would happen before 1925. He had written a little flyer called *Verbum et Sapienti!* in which he articulated the importance of this quest to those communities with which he had been most closely associated: 'Whilst ye followers of Koresh, Ann Lee and Mary and Benjamin, have believed in the triunity of Father, Son and Holy Ghost, also in the Bride and Motherhood of God, ye have sadly neglected "The Daughter of Zion" of "the fourth dimension" – the fourth heaven of the Tetragrammaton – the Godhead of the Universe! It is "unto Shiloh (or the Daughter and twin sister of Michael) that the Gathering of the People is to be."'[14] On reading the Panacean literature, with its talk of a female Shiloh, and its own adoption of Theosophical language of the fourth dimension, Edgar came to believe that Octavia was that woman, and so, in 1922, he set sail for England on the Cunard liner, the RMS *Aquitania*, recently refitted after its wartime service in the Navy. A surviving menu from his voyage has his notes scribbled all over it, and like all of his other papers, it is full of numerological calculations and the interpretation of esoteric teachings, showing that his restless mind and ceaseless religiosity were busy even while he was enjoying a comfortable, second-class voyage across the Atlantic in one of the most popular liners on the North Atlantic route in the 1920s. Having docked in Southampton, he went straight to Bedford, and signed his application for the Royal Seal that very evening, 11 March, while staying at the Swan Hotel – which was just around the corner from the community. Two months later, he sent a letter to two of his Koreshan associates, Henry Rahn and Helen Lemke, saying: 'Be well adviced [sic]. I have found "the chosen woman, to be revealed" as Cyrus said she would be! "She" has "the secret of the Lord".'[15] He had found the Woman who could help him fulfil his own call as 'the Man', but for the moment she remained blissfully unaware of his agenda. He kept it a secret from all but a trusted few.

When Edgar Peissart arrived in Bedford, Octavia had a choice. She could send him away – and she was not above doing this if she thought people did not belong in her community – or she could incorporate him, test his ideas, appropriate them for herself if they were useful, and hope that he would become obedient as others had before him. Peter Rasmussen's arrival from Australia had been invested with great meaning, and his presence a success, and in the light of that Octavia regarded Edgar's arrival from America as symbolically important. On that basis he became part of a new, inner group known as The Four, who met for private worship after the evening chapel services in the newly expanded Garden Room, from April 1922 to the end of January 1923. The choice of the four who surrounded Octavia and formed this group reveals who had risen to prominence in the community in its first three years and whose personality was deemed suitable for esoteric rituals: Kate Firth, as might be expected – but she was the only one of the original female apostles in the group; Peter Rasmussen, who had by 1923 become Octavia's right-hand man; Emily Goodwin, who was subtly making herself more central to community life; and Edgar Peissart, the interesting new arrival.

The inclusion of Edgar Peissart was perhaps surprising. Rachel Fox, in her diary, recorded her visit to Bedford on Whit Sunday, in June 1922, when The Four had been worshipping together for two months. She described The Four as 'the foundation pillars of the Church' and of Edgar Peissart she remarked 'I . . . heard all the wonderful story by which Mr Peissart was led to Octavia to lay all his wisdom at her feet.' Rachel explained the theological significance with which his presence had been invested: 'he came at the right moment to support Octavia the daughter as the representative of the Father'. Four was, of course, a significant number for the Panaceans because God was for them no longer just a trinity but four: Father, Mother (Holy Spirit), Son and Daughter (Octavia). Therefore, wrote Rachel Fox, 'the perfect earthly Family is comprised of 4 – & revelation has shown us these are 4 who had been witness from heaven to this being the Divine ideal'. The Four were also regarded as the four living creatures of Ezekiel's vision; the four creatures around the throne of God in the Book of Revelation.[16]

In Ezekiel's vision, in the Hebrew scriptures, the wheels move as if one living being, and the meetings of The Four in the Garden Room began to incorporate movement into their worship.[17] Rachel Fox gave a very respectable account of their activities: 'the Four moved by one Spirit, without any plan. It was wonderful to see them as they formed and reformed with marvellous swiftness into figures and groups portraying scenes that could be specified. There was no music heard yet Octavia was able to play on the piano some of the music of the movements and very often today those who participated, say they would give much to see it all again.'[18] The Four kept a diary of these liturgical movements, and that gives a much more chaotic impression of the whole thing, as they crawled on the floor, chased evil spirits in the air and dragged themselves around the room in a peculiar manner. Not surprisingly, they kept their activities secret from the rest of the community. Octavia wrote to Henrietta Leach, by now a rather semi-detached apostle, that she should not expect Kate to talk of her activities. 'So dear I ask you to bear with me & Kate if there is much silence on our chief work & to give her complete freedom. In fact you must reckon that she hardly exists & that she is under a necessity to do as she does – as one of the 4 she must do exactly as they do.'[19]

Edgar Peissart was keen to make a good impression and thrilled that he was part of the inner circle. In June 1922 he wrote to a friend, enclosing a letter he had received from Kate Firth, 'to show you how very much they appreciate me!' He continued: 'It is very wonderful and very encouraging, to make me feel "free indeed".' But it was in his nature to scheme and plan, and it was hard for him to abandon the habits of a lifetime. Two months later, he was writing to a non-resident member of the Society, Helen Morris, whom he had befriended and taken into his confidence, 'my work and capacity are beyond mortal comprehension!'[20] A letter to the same correspondent a month later written hastily in the dark (there was always a furtive element to everything he did) showed that he was struggling to fit into the community that had embraced him so warmly. 'I did lay aside all past teachings in coming here; but, when I was made representative of the Father, I began to speak of my past teachings; even to you as well, and in this letter at that; for which Mrs Webster [another Koreshan who had become a Panacean, and knew Edgar from before] chided me tonight!' He suggested they discontinue their writing on these matters, for he wished to be obedient to the Woman and stay true to the household of faith. But this was temporary: his wisdom told him that he was merely laying aside his truth 'for the present'.[21]

Edgar's obedience lasted only so long. By the end of 1922, the Panacea members were losing confidence in him, and by December Rachel Fox wrote, 'we had had several strong indications that all was not well'. Already Octavia had decided that she had made a mistake in allowing him to represent America (and, indeed, God the Father) in the Four. She replaced him with Monsieur Monard, a Frenchman who had known Rachel Fox for many years, who had been brought up a Roman Catholic and was later a spiritualist and Theosophist before reading Rachel Fox's writings and coming to Panacea beliefs through her. Octavia made EP – as the Panaceans referred to him – the record keeper of the group's movements. His displacement only helped to foster his sense of resentment and jealousy. Gradually, the women began to suspect he had designs on the leadership of the Society. They gave the whole thing a theological spin: their community was at the heart of a cosmic battle between good and evil and so EP 'began to show himself conclusively as the emissary of Lucifer the Angel'. Octavia believed 'that it must have been in the plan of

God to put Satan in her precincts and power, in order that she, to whom the Mystery of Godliness has been revealed, should meet and defeat in deadly combat, the author and instigator of the Mystery of Iniquity.' The Panaceans were preparing for battle with the evil one.

As events unfolded, they were interpreted as the actualisation of biblical prophecy. What was predicted in the Book of Revelation was coming true in Bedford, and would lead to the millennium and the Second Coming of Christ. Octavia thought that Edgar was the red horseman of the Apocalypse in Revelation. The four horsemen of the Apocalypse appear in chapter 6 of Revelation, where it is prophesied that these horsemen will wreak havoc on the world. The second, riding a red horse, represented war: 'and *power* was given to him that sat thereon to take peace from the earth, and that they should kill one another: and there was given unto him a great sword.' (Revelation 6: 4). This was in fact what Edgar also believed about himself. He wrote that 'I as the red horseman "took peace from the earth" in 1913–14.'[22] In other words, he believed that he had brought about the Great War. In Edgar, Octavia had met her match. He had an ego as great as hers. Here was someone who believed that he had a divine purpose and his actions had cosmic significance, just as she believed that she embodied the divine and members of her community were biblical characters. They believed that they were living the biblical prophecies in order to bring about the last days. Edgar would bring war to the community, but that was as prophesied. A cosmic battle between good and evil was about to take place in Bedford on behalf of the rest of the world.

On Octavia's fifty-seventh birthday on 11 January 1923, Edgar was still part of the inner circle, joining in a special ceremony with Octavia, Peter, Kate, Emily and Monsieur Monard to consecrate four rooms with incense and holy water, and say psalms together. But it was on that same day that Octavia 'began to see him as the Image of Jealousy sitting in the Holy place with his face to the North – where he always sat'. Four days later, there was a confrontation between EP and Octavia when she made it perfectly plain that she did not accept his 'call'. 'You are nothing more than the others to me,' she told him, and she begged him to become childlike, and give up what he thought was his call; but when she saw how angry he was, she chased him out of the room with a paperknife – with 'Jerusalem' engraved on it. Hilda Green, in her diary, wrote of the 'terrible scene' and described EP's encounter with Peter at the door, as Octavia chased him away: EP said 'Thank you for your kindness, you can send for me when you want me – . . . [he] offered his hand to Peter who refused saying "not until you shake hands with O".'[23]

The Panaceans were right to believe that Edgar was a threat. He had started to cultivate other members, hoping they would accept his call as the Man, in particular the prominent non-resident member, Helen Morris, whom he had met in Bedford, and who shared his interest in esoteric spirituality and was, like him, a religious seeker. She shared her religious experiences with him, and her problems with her bullying husband. He sensed in her a ready disciple for the gospel according to Edgar.

Edgar was also involved in more complex intrigues, quite beyond the imaginings of the ladies. He had fallen in love with the 'dear boy' Thomas – known as Donald – Ricketts, a twenty-five-year-old Cambridge undergraduate studying forestry at Trinity College, who had joined the Society in January 1922.[24] Rachel Fox had first met him in the summer of 1922, and described him as 'a keen worker for us'.[25] Donald came to stay in Bedford just after Christmas and before the Lent term at Cambridge began, arriving on 29 December. By New Year's Eve, Edgar had made his feelings known to Donald, pulling him on to his knee and kissing him, and as the new year began, so did their affair. They spent the nights together, and as much time as they could in the days, so far as the routine of the community allowed, until Donald had to go back to Cambridge six days later. But he was back on 11 January – Octavia's birthday, the moment when she began to get really suspicious – and stayed for another week. By this time, Edgar was more on his guard, and just before Donald left for Cambridge, 'told him that he was not to tell "those women" what had passed between them and that if D were asked he was to say that certain friendly relations had passed between them only'.[26]

Edgar imbued his sexual acts with sacred meaning. Donald's confession and the surviving correspondence between Donald and Edgar reveal how EP interpreted his homosexual activity – both theologically and in terms of his own 'call'. Kissing was understood as the exchange of 'breath'. Breath was given divine significance in many of the new religious movements that had emerged in America in the late nineteenth century, and Octavia herself was said to have divine breath. Edgar gave it his own particular religious twist, speaking of the exchange of 'ecstatic breath'. And in order to make religious meaning of male same-sex acts, he took the prevailing discourses on celibacy in the groups he had joined, especially the Koreshan under-standing of celibacy, and gave them new meaning. Cyrus Teed had taught that 'the ultimate, potential energy of man's being is in the seed of man. . . . It is the supreme potency in man that gives him that essential and vitalising substance.'[27] Edgar marked up his copy of Teed's writings on celibacy, heavily emphasising the sections on the 'seed', but reinterpreted it for his own ends, telling Donald 'his seed had to be opened and given to D' so that 'D could obtain life'. Indeed, 'the covenant David & Jonathan made together was this exchange of "seed"'. It was the *exchange* that was necessary and, Edgar believed, in his unusual understanding of things, that kept him and Donald from transgressing.[28]

That Edgar believed that the rules and writings on celibacy applied only to heterosexual relations is evident from his correspondence with Helen Morris, who wrote to him about her marital problems. In particular, she wanted to live a celibate life, with separate beds and separate rooms for her husband and herself. EP proved a sympathetic ear ('you made no mistake as to arranging for separate rooms, if he was prepared to meet the conditions!'[29]) as she described the occa-sions on which Mr Morris tried to force her to have sex. She was always victorious in her resistance, but she lamented to Edgar: 'Why should I have to go through all this? I feel you know, I only guess, tell if possible please, but it makes the burden easier: and tell if the stand I take [celibacy] is correct?' She added as a postscript: 'I would suffer death if need be sooner rather than falter, but it strengthens me to hear from you that my attitude is the correct one.'[30] In turn, EP gave her the theological ammunition for her cause, sending her the Koreshan pamphlet that advocated celibacy as the route to immortality. And he gave the impression that he was celibate: 'If Jesus our example was celibate in eat [i.e. he fasted], in word, in deed, in life, why should we do otherwise. That settled the question with me!'[31] And in his own terms he was, for he interpreted celibacy as the separation of the sexes. A passage from the Koreshan pamphlet, selected for quotation by Helen Morris in a letter to Edgar, illustrates this mentality: 'there can be no immortal life without the conservation of the sex energies ✓ of both male and female. This must come through the separation of the sexes on the place of sensuality'.[32]

The exchange of seed between men was not, in EP's mental universe, a waste of the 'sex energies'. On the contrary, it was necessary for the fulfilment of his call as 'the Man'. It was all 'the part of the work which woman could not do & which O would have to accept'. He had a complex numerological interpretation to emphasise why he and Donald were *the* two men who should engage in this exchange of seed and further Edgar's call, explaining that Donald was 7 (regarded as a mystical number in many religious traditions) and Edgar was 8 (a number of fulfilment – just as Octavia represented the octave, or 8). The exchange of seed, the sexual act, created a spiritual bond between the men and confirmed EP's call. He wrote: 'The very same feeling that you experienced ran all over my interior as though you were all alive within me! I saw definitely in it, how greatly our souls or seed are knitted as one man!' He continued, 'There exists a life in us that can never be broken again! And I thank you greatly for the manner and way you expressed your faithfulness towards myself and the work ahead!'[33] Edgar's seduction of Donald was entirely intertwined with his presentation of his claims to be 'the Man'. Donald was not merely a love object but another potential convert – and, extraordinarily, the sexual vehicle to the fulfilment of EP's call.

This was not merely an affair between Donald and Edgar. There were the beginnings of a male homosexual subculture developing in the community, largely revolving around Edgar. As soon as Donald slipped away, Edgar would find Jesse Green outside his door, holding a 32-page letter in which he demanded that Edgar follow his desires. Jesse Green threatened that if Edgar did not do as Jesse desired, then God would take from Edgar some of his gifts and give them to Jesse. Edgar reported all of this to Donald, who was the one that had captured his heart. Jesse and Donald were not unknown to each other – though whether they engaged in any kind of intimate or sexual relationship is not clear – because they worked together in handing out Panacea leaflets in Cambridge. EP also argued that Jesse had sinned because he had spilled his seed on the ground. While EP gave sacred meaning to his sexual acts with Donald, he was evidently happy to have sex with Jesse Green when that option was open to him, and in his gossipy letters to Helen Morris he conveys a sense of the ways in which he was monitoring the sexual histories and activities of other Panacea members, not least to have power over them. He went to tea with apostle Mildred Hollingworth, and her husband William, the Society's printer, and he detected in Mr Hollingworth a particular sexual past; whether homosexual or not is not known though the insinuation is there. 'By intuition or otherwise, I felt I knew a secret of his former days; so I talked to him and he acknowledged same; thus, I am made a sort of Saviour, to cause him to become a full celibate!'[34]

This same-sex subculture amongst some of the few men in the Society remained covert for only a few months. Once Octavia's suspicions were aroused, she exerted pressure on all members to report anything they knew. Octavia and the inner circle gathered their evidence as 'accounts of his evil deeds began to be revealed'. Octavia learned that Helen Morris had been taken into Edgar's confidence about his call, and had corresponded at length with him. This was a serious betrayal because when Octavia had first met Mrs Morris in late August 1922 she had marked her out as someone who could help her. Octavia had written to Rachel Fox with enthusiasm:

> I think the Lord is going to give H.M. a view of the awful deeps in which I practically reside: it needs a person coming straight out of the world and of a particular calibre to realise this. Her 'you poor creature,' after she really grasped my position, was helpful . . . Useless sympathy I cannot endure but as HM said, 'You must have an understanding people and they must use the understanding as a weapon of your deliverance.'[35]

Yet more galling, it was Octavia who had introduced Edgar to Mrs Morris, unusually allowing him in on an interview with a non-resident member. The correspondence between EP and Helen Morris continued into early February 1923, when Mrs Morris wrote to him of the 'misunderstanding' in which he was involved and reassured him that 'I am absolutely on my guard, have no fear or worry about that!'[36] Edgar had kept all of Helen Morris's letters. He now ripped them up and threw them away but Octavia requested that they be stuck back together again: Peter Rasmussen did this with sticky tape or the edges of stamp paper. Octavia commented that the task made a jigsaw puzzle seem easy, but it was worth it for they were such 'incriminating evidence'.[37] As the tide turned against Edgar, Helen Morris tried to please Octavia, writing to her that she had never really believed Edgar Peissart's claims anyway, a direct contradiction of what she had written to him.

Octavia and the inner circle of members found every bit of incriminating paper that they could, collecting it in a big black metal box that had belonged to Ellen Oliver (the papers were all still in the box when I arrived), and exerted pressure on others to confess their own part in the EP scandal. One member observed that Donald Ricketts had been seen a lot recently with Mr Peissart, and so he was summoned by telegram to travel from Cambridge across to Bedford immediately. On 17 January, Kate Firth took down a statement of 'the Iniquity'. Donald quickly buckled and gave all the details of his and EP's sexual relations, and EP's claims to theological authority. Jesse Green was also summoned. He had already sent a letter to Octavia confessing all: when she received it, she had thrown it on the table because it was 'so foolish'. He admitted to having sex with many men, including the younger brother of Muriel and Evelyn Gillett, who was a teenage schoolboy, though he asserted that he had never engaged in anal sex. Now he had a tense and awkward interview with Octavia and Emily Goodwin – who was quickly becoming her right-hand woman. Eventually, they got him to kneel down and pray for forgiveness. The scene was a dramatic one. Octavia went to get Emily's knife and when he saw it, Mr Green started praying very hard because he thought he was about to be sacrificed. But Mrs Goodwin was simply attempting an exorcism, shaking him furiously to get the devil out of him. 'He won't go out, he won't go,' she screamed, and then she shouted, 'I command this devil to leave him, get out.' And in a phrase that hinted at things to come, she said, 'I the DIVINE Mother JERUSALEM command this devil to get out.' By this time, Jesse Green was on his knees, weeping like a child; Octavia began to nurse him, and gave him some milk to drink and cake to eat.[38]

This episode reveals the developing roles of Emily Goodwin, administering judgment, and Octavia, administering pastoral care, and foreshadowed what was soon to come. The events of the last few days of January 1923 changed the shape of the leadership in the Society for

the rest of Octavia's life. But Octavia still did not know what to do
with EP. As Rachel Fox put it, 'It was a terrible moment when Octavia
grasped the fact that the Man of Sin had appeared here within her
doors.' This did not mean that her sense of humour left her – she
gave him the nickname of Mr Pie-Crust – but she was, as Rachel Fox
put it, 'Distressed beyond measure and totally unable to think what
to do with a person too wicked to keep or to send away' so 'on January
28th . . . she prayed at the luncheon-table for some Divine interven-
tion'. Emily Goodwin – or God, depending on how you see things –
came to the rescue. She went into a trance and claimed to speak in
the voice of the Divine Mother, 'My Daughter . . . I have come to
your help . . . I have come to establish the kingdom of My Son. Send
the man to New York, he will die.'[39] This prediction was not only a
turning point in the Edgar Peissart saga; it was a turning point for the
Society. From that moment, Emily Goodwin would regularly go into
a trance and, as members came to believe, speak as the Instrument
of the Divine Mother. She thus came to exert enormous power and
control over the community.

Octavia now knew what she must do. The community would put
EP on trial. The outcome was already decided: he was to leave the
community but he was not to know this ahead of the time. Octavia
was not above dissimulation to achieve her ends, and she appealed to
his sense of importance by inviting him to a private meeting in the
Garden Room on 26 February with some of the inner circle.
Meanwhile, his room was emptied of his clothes and personal effects,
and these were moved to another room in town, which was prepared
for his return after the trial: the fire was lit, a meal laid, his clothes
put tidily away and the bed aired. The Society kept all his papers and
books.

In the context of worship – two hours of silent prayer and the
reading of psalms – Satan was put on trial. It was not EP on trial here
for he, like Jesse Green, was thought to have been under Satanic control.
Satan was being prosecuted in the Panacea court that afternoon for
male homosexuality, which, Octavia argued – making the case for the
prosecution – had been administered to and by Cain. Biblical stories
were recast in the light of male homosexual activity. 'We come to the
Secret Male Combination which Cain tried to force upon Abel[40] &
which Irad the son of Methuselah betrayed to the sons of men & for

which Lamech slew him. We come to the Secret Male Combination which existed between Jonathan and David producing Love called Erotic Love, which is worse than Lust; the love which is unproductive Soul Passion – whereas the love between man & woman (normal) is body passion, safe because productive.'[41] While celibacy was regarded as the higher good in the Panacea community, Octavia took the standard Christian line on the goods of marriage: that marriage was not only for companionship but also for reproduction. Sex between man and woman was 'natural' because it was productive and she was, like all the mainstream churches at this time, opposed to the use of birth control (the Anglican Church reversed its policy on this at the 1930 Lambeth Conference).[42] She held to the strong nineteenth-century belief in a clear-cut sexual difference: marriage was between 'a Male Masculine Man and a Female Feminine Woman – of a union which brings forth normally, male sons and female daughters'.

We can only understand the construction of the trial as the prosecution of Satan if we remember that the Panaceans believed they were engaged in a cosmic battle between good and evil and that EP was 'the emissary of Lucifer the Angel'. The Panaceans knew their task was to defeat Satan. By casting Satan out of EP, they were effectively casting Satan out of their community – the true Church. In preparation for the trial, all the Panaceans had been urged to confess their sins, to purge themselves and purify the community. At the trial, first Lucifer, then Satan and then five other 'controls' (evil spirits) were cast out of EP and 'the victim was completely broken down, and was truly penitent'.[43]

The issue here was not so much male homosexuality – though Octavia regarded that as entirely unnatural and 'an iniquity' that was 'a million, million times greater than the sin of the Fall'[44] – but what it represented: the rejection of Woman when Woman was the ultimate redeemer of the world, the only one who could bring true immortality to the gathered 144,000 and, so she believed, fulfil the scriptures. EP's sexual liaisons with men and his bid for power amounted to the same thing: a rejection of the special authority of women that was the hallmark of the Panacea Society. In that sense it was a rejection of the late-Victorian feminine domesticity that the Society epitomised, which was accompanied by the emergence of a more public homosexual–homosocial culture at the turn of the century as a flight from that domesticity.[45] In Panacean terms, Edgar Peissart's greatest offence was that, although he came to Bedford searching for the Woman, in the end he did not need Woman, either as an authority figure or as a romantic partner. As Octavia put it in a letter to Henrietta Leach: 'All women . . . were in danger till the man of sin was revealed and the peculiar nature of his sin revealed also, for it did away with the need of womanhood.'[46] This was a cosmic drama that the community believed it was playing out on behalf of the rest of the human race. Rachel Fox wrote a fantastic bit of hyperbole when she said, after the 'trial' of EP: 'Thus ended what we felt was the greatest event next to the trial before Pilate that has ever taken place.'[47]

The community did not ask that criminal charges be brought against Edgar Peissart, Jesse Green and Donald Ricketts, nor did they report their activities to the police, even though male homosexuality was then still a crime. This was a matter to be dealt with by the community, and it was understood not primarily as a crime, but theologically as a sin. There was also the reality, of course, that such a criminal case would have brought the whole community into disrepute. Nevertheless, when Octavia sent Edgar to his new quarters – 'where you may be sure I had arranged a nice room with a good fire and a meal laid', as she wrote to one member – a letter was given to him in which she made it clear that she had communicated certain matters to the Chief Constable, and said that for his own sake he should remain indoors until he went to America. Edgar did not stray out of his new home, and was visited daily by Emily Goodwin to whom, in her guise as the Divine Mother, he made a very full confession. On 24 March, Edgar Peissart set out on the ten-day voyage back to New York City.[48]

Jesse Green left England for America four days before Edgar. After he had left, Octavia met with a disgruntled Society member named Frederick Ibbotson who complained to her: 'He [Jesse Green] led me into evil knowledge', while his mother protested that her son 'wouldn't have been led into all this mischief with Mr Green'. Octavia protested back, claiming that she had not known what Jesse Green had done with Frederick Ibbotson at the time: 'do you dare suggest that I, the mother of 3 sons, have used him in the work [for the Panacea Society] knowing that he led an impure life'?[49] In fact, she did know, at least by late January, as Jesse Green had confessed it, and she was following his suggestion that if Mr Ibbotson should mention anything as having occurred between them, then 'you can act as tho' you know nothing of it, if you wish', for 'Mr I has no proof and I am used to dealing with cross examiners.' The fear must have been that Mr Ibbotson would bring charges.

Jesse Green continued to write in to the Society from the USA and to do some evangelistic publicity work there for the Society. Two months after leaving Bedford, he wrote to Octavia declaring his intention of keeping rather than repaying the $100 passage money the Society had given him because he had put it towards buying a Ford furniture truck with which to get about and evangelise on the Panaceans' behalf. He married a woman called Marie in 1924, a widow who already had two children. She did not share his faith: she was a member of the city's Faith Tabernacle and thought the Southcottian writings were from the devil. She was annoyed by his evangelising activities – carrying a Southcott banner and using a megaphone, which he had bought deliberately to annoy her – on the streets of Philadelphia. He seems to have enjoyed flouting her. 'Well, when my wife had nigh wearied me to death as I was saying I then purchased a megaphone and held a most delightful meeting.'[50] They had a child in 1925, but Jesse Green was still planning on travelling around in his Ford furniture truck, with a male friend, a Mr Schultz from Newark, spreading the Southcottian word. He called this 'trucking with my truck'.

Jesse continued to evangelise to the detriment of his family life. He and Marie had two more children and very little income. With a household of seven to feed, in June 1928 Marie finally wrote to the Society distressed that Jesse seemed unable to hold a job and spent any money they did have on Panacea books which he was singularly unsuccessful at reselling. He had even resorted to using another address to receive the books, which Marie had eventually discovered. Furious, she burned some of his Southcott literature. She begged the Panacea Society not to send him any more books. He was in fact a terrible evangelist for the cause. Even his own mother wrote, 'He is not adapted to that kind of work – he repels those whom he would convince – and many think, too, that he has lost his mind.' She had been paying their rent and helping them for the past year, and she now wrote to Hilda Green in Bedford: 'he robs his family of food whenever he sends you money' and proposed that she and Marie send all the books back to the Society and asked that they 'do not take a cent from him and return cash for what we return if possible'.[51] The issue was resolved and the Panacea Society sent him no more books, and promised to support him in working for his family but not in distributing their literature. A month later, he and Marie wrote separate letters to the Society, asking both Octavia and Mrs Goodwin whether they should buy a house, for houses were cheap and they could pay off a mortgage in ten years. Octavia, with her distinctive sense of the imminence of the end times, wrote that it was not wise to buy a house under present conditions in the world. Things were getting worse and it would be far better to save the money, to have something to fall back upon, as bricks and mortar would not be of any use. It was not advice she followed in her own life, for in Bedford she was building and growing the community house by house.

In the correspondence between Jesse Green and the Society, few of his letters allude to what had transpired in the Society in 1923 or his part in it; none gives any hint of embarrassment, anxiety or guilt about it.[52] His attitude towards his same-sex activity was equally casual: it was just sex, a physical act. He chanced sex with other men as and when opportunity arose, like many men in the interwar years.[53] Such encounters constituted a precursor to marriage, and possibly a side activity within marriage (Jesse Green was, after all, always planning to go trucking with his male friend) but not an identity.[54]

Donald Ricketts remained a member of the Society and adhered strictly to its beliefs and practices. He completed his undergraduate degree at Cambridge in the summer of 1923, then went out to Rangoon in Burma as part of the Indian army, and was made a captain in June 1924. A couple of months later, he sent his confession into the Panacea Society from Burma. Most of the confession was routine, but under the heading of 'Doubt' he wrote that he had fear 'after the matter of EP; fear of what might happen to me; fear of whether or not I might have to die etc; fear in regard to the future'.[55] He continued to have a sustained belief in the Society, despite everything that had happened, and wrote several articles on life in Burma for The Panacea magazine. His faith was enough for him to encourage his mother Annie to join in February 1925. After living first with her daughter in Australia and then with Donald in Burma, Mrs Ricketts returned to England with Donald in 1929 and became a resident member of the community in

Bedford. Donald often visited her there. In 1943, he was awarded the OBE for 'bravery and distinguished services in the evacuation of Burma', where he was, by then, Deputy Director of Evacuation and Deputy Conservator of Forests.[56]

These men were having sex with each other in the 1920s at just the moment when medical and psychological explanations for homosexuality were being developed. At no point did any of the players in the drama explain what was going on in those terms. Octavia may well have been familiar with this literature, being a voracious reader and having worked as an editor for a number of writers in the early part of the century who were translating psychological and psychoanalytical works from the German, but if so she never alluded to it. There were echoes of other prevailing understandings of homosexuality: EP's love for the younger Donald, expressed in terms of purity and soul-bonding, resembled the Hellenist ideal so popular amongst male literary figures of the late nineteenth century. But in the end, theological interpretations – sometimes wildly clashing interpretations – won out. The episode also demonstrated how intense, indeed sexually intense, life could be in that small community (think of Jesse Green hovering outside EP's door until Donald left). The Panaceans believed in ongoing prophecy and revelation, and it was this that enabled sexual behaviour of all sorts to be explained in terms of religious belief, even if the explanations went against Octavia's authority and the prevailing teaching of the group. Edgar Peissart believed he had the authority to reinterpret celibacy in his own terms. Furthermore, this enclosed society, separate and separated from the outside world, gave a certain kind of shelter to these men who engaged in (criminalised) same-sex activity, and enabled them to dignify their sexual activities and desires with theological meaning.

The episode has some affinities with a case that occurred in Theosophical circles some years earlier. In 1906–7 a scandal arose around Charles Leadbeater, one of the leaders of the Theosophical Movement, when it emerged that he had taught boys to masturbate, and had shown a preference for the company of young men. Leadbeater resigned from the Theosophical Society but was readmitted in 1908. Former Theosophists in the Panacea Society, such as Monsieur Monard, may have remembered the case.[57]

Immediately after the events of February 1923 that had culminated in EP's expulsion, as the men went their separate ways, the community set about rebalancing the structures and purifying itself. On 1 March a procedure called 'Casting the Controls' was begun. This was essentially the exorcising of demons, the casting out of evil from the community. Ahead of time, everyone was commanded to confess their sins, clear up all debts and return all borrowed things. Emily Goodwin – EG – and Octavia then met with each person, and EG as the Instrument of the Divine Mother, exorcised the controls from them. A ritual was quickly developed in which the community member sat in the middle of the Garden Room, holding a list of their defects. Octavia read words from Isaiah 35 as the members prepared for the list of their inhibitions, peculiarities, weak points and drawbacks to be read out before the Divine Mother: 'Strengthen ye the weak hands, and confirm the feeble knees. Say to them that are of a fearful heart, Be strong, fear not: behold, your God will come with vengeance, even God with a recompence; he will come and save you' (Isaiah 35: 3–4). Once the list had been read out, the Divine Mother then asked the person whether they wished to be delivered. When they replied in the affirmative, she said, 'You are to condemn these failings as being no good, NOT OF GOD.' The casting of the controls would follow. EG had a heightened sense of drama and she would physically enact struggles with the 'controls', which were named by Octavia and commanded by her to depart. EG chased the invisible spirits, as they came out of the person, around and out of the room, sometimes cutting at them with a knife in the air. Not surprisingly, the onlooker could never see the 'control'. Instead, they saw EG's battle with it, 'parrying and thrusting, and warding off the attacks of creatures of which one could quite easily judge the size, height and form'; this was 'sufficiently distressing, especially when they would try to strangle her – to sting her – to fling darts at her and Octavia soon found out that one and all had a purpose, which was to get her down on her knees, and this became the thing to avoid as if for life or death.' This might go on for fifteen or even thirty minutes, and then the penitent member could be declared free of the 'controls'.[58]

The increased number of confessions and the new rituals were aimed at cleansing the community. Their practical effect was to tighten the structures of authority and bring the growing number of members under greater control. Emily Goodwin's claim to speak as the Divine

Mother had already given her enormous power. On 3 May, her authority was sealed when her first words as the Instrument of the Divine Mother – 'send the man to New York, he will die' – were revealed to have come true. The community received word that Edgar Peissart had indeed died in New York City on 12 April, soon after he had arrived there. Pitiful letters to members he thought might be sympathetic to his cause – he had no money and had caught pneumonia in the third-class cabin he had had to share with rough Irish immigrants on the boat over – reveal that he was very sick on arrival. This did not make his death any less startling a fulfilment of the Divine Mother's oracle for the Panaceans.

Obedience to the centre now entailed obedience to the Divine Mother as well as to Octavia. The members' explanation was, of course, that the Divine Mother had come to dwell amongst them, and, if this were not enough, on 1 February 1923 it was declared that Emily Goodwin was Eve, the first woman in the Book of Genesis. In her trance, she was the Instrument of the Divine Mother; as Emily she was Eve embodied. If we look for the motives of Emily Goodwin herself, it is hard to know precisely what was going on. She did not keep a diary; nor is there any significant correspondence between her and Octavia, because they lived in the same house: their conversations remain lost to us. But how did a woman who came as nurse and housekeeper to Octavia and her aged aunt come to exercise so much control and power? That she did so suggests that she was an acute observer; that in living with Octavia she saw she was lonely in her leadership, and often privately uncertain as to the best course of action to take. Whether Mrs Goodwin's motive was simply to acquire power for herself or genuinely to help share the load with Octavia, whose suffering she wished to relieve, the episode reveals that she was a shrewd operator. She retained her simple and friendly personality as Mrs Goodwin; she exercised enormous control over the lives of hundreds of people when she put her hands in her lap, went into a trance, and professed to speak with all the authority of God, the Divine Mother.

The year 1923 began with Edgar Peissart's bid for power. He was a man whose appeal to Octavia, when he arrived the year before, is understandable: he had a ready theological language, he was cultured, and he shared the apocalyptic hopes of the community. She even

allowed him into one of her interviews with another member, a rare
event. But her attempt to get him to conform – to put him and his
form of theological discourse into her own religious understanding
of the world and her community framework – failed, and everything
exploded. So by the middle of the year, it was not the cultured and
theologically literate (if eccentric) Edgar Peissart who had come to
share power with Octavia, but a lower-class woman, who had been
nurse to her aunt. Emily Goodwin was not one of the inner circle of
propertied Victorian gentlewomen who made up the core of the early
membership. She was the daughter of a gardener, widow of a baker,
whose sons worked as a joiner and a labourer, and whose daughter
was a housemaid. Given Octavia's strong sense of social status (some
would call it her snobbery) it is remarkable that Emily Goodwin, of
all the people in the community, rose to this position of unquestioned
authority.

What did Octavia gain by the transfer of power? She was certainly
not a mere cipher in this sequence of events. She participated fully in
it. But she also worried incessantly about what to do. Her community was growing and problems that caused her anxiety were inevitably
multiplying. She was now able to hand over the responsibility for
correction to someone else. She could be 'good cop' while the Divine
Mother was 'bad cop'. Emily Goodwin – as the Divine Mother – was
in that sense her alter ego: the part of the divine family (or Godhead)
that could put the boot in and discipline people as and when required.
The class difference between the two women was important here.
While we have seen that she was not afraid to be direct and voice her
opinion, Octavia nevertheless set much store by the proper appearance of things. She was thus able to retain her gentility while the
working-class Emily Goodwin would go into a trance and admonish
the troublemakers brought before her.

What Octavia did now was consolidate her charismatic power. As
if the year had not produced enough extraordinary revelations, at the
end of May she came to an understanding that her husband, Arthur,
had been Jesus in Christ's second incarnation on earth. This was
revealed to a chosen few: on that evening in May, just Rachel, Peter
Rasmussen and her daughter Dilys.[59] Octavia now wore her wedding
ring (removed on that evening in June 1919) again. The idea that Arthur
was Jesus remained an unwritten 'secret' carefully passed from member

to member, orally. I was allowed into the secret knowledge one day by one of the members, who sought me out in the archive room of the headquarters to tell me. It was hard to know just how to react to the news. In 1924, when Octavia published her memoir, she gave a hint to readers in the know with a phrase from the hymn, that Jesus was 'Prophet, Priest and King'. Christ had already come as Prophet, as Jesus, in the first century; he had now come as Priest, as Arthur Barltrop. His coming as King had yet to happen, and the Panacea Society was therefore awaiting the third coming, not the second, of Christ. All of this gave a (startling!) new understanding of the theological phrase, 'very God and very man'. In her memoir Octavia emphasised Arthur's *ordinariness*: 'He had no high flights nor was he at all mystical nor occult, nor even what is called very spiritual.' He was 'what might be called a *good* man – nothing more'. But all of this was simply to stress the naturalness of his life in contrast with the reality of who he was: 'I always felt there was something very mysterious about him, but nothing uncomfortably mysterious.' Furthermore, she wrote, 'I had always the strong conviction that there was something very much "ordained" about our marriage.'[60] With this revelation she sealed the importance of her family unit, or so she hoped, in the life of the community. Her children were now God's grandchildren. What this revelation also ensured was that no man could claim to be 'the Man' – a male messiah figure – ever again. 'The Man' had been Arthur Barltrop, who was – staggeringly – also Jesus.

In the wake of the Edgar Peissart incident, Octavia could however be assured of the total devotion of the other man at the centre of the community, Peter Rasmussen, who had stood by her throughout. His role as the good man was reinforced by all of this drama. In return he was elevated to the position of the biblical figure of Jesus' disciple Peter (just as Emily was Eve). It was, significantly, on the night before Donald Ricketts arrived to make his confession about Edgar that Octavia washed Peter's feet, as she had washed her female apostles' feet, indicating that he was one of her closest disciples and confirming his apostolic authority.[61] But there was also a sense in which he was the son that never escaped (unlike Mabel's actual sons who went as far away as possible). He was young – in his early forties – when he arrived, and he remained in the community until his death in 1988. She was a maternal figure to him: a small, sensitive man, prone to depression, and overly sensitive to criticism, which made life difficult for him in a community in which responding positively to criticism and correction was part of the religious discipline. In 1921, after a time of unhappiness when he had threatened to leave the community, he had written to Octavia: 'But I will be quite happy where you are, and will never go away and leave you!! I want to stop where you are and will try to do whatsoever you want me to do.'[62] That is precisely what he did, and Octavia could always be assured of his childlike loyalty and devotion.

But with Emily Goodwin taking a share of the leadership, for Octavia the claim that her husband was Jesus was still not enough to distinguish her. She needed something else to mark out the fact that while Emily Goodwin was merely the *Instrument* of the Divine Mother, she was *herself* divine – the daughter of God – and it soon emerged. Octavia now consolidated her power and displayed her charisma by the establishment of a new healing ministry, in which ordinary tap water was given healing properties by her divine breath. Through this ministry, thousands of people were brought into contact with the Society. The Panaceans were about to go global.

8

Going Global

On 6 May 1923, the Divine Mother proclaimed that Octavia had the power to heal. The proclamation heralded two important features of the Society's future. First, Octavia's capacity to heal was developed into an international healing ministry, which increased its numbers exponentially. This in turn led to an increased codification of its structures and greater bureaucracy in the administration of its various burgeoning 'departments'. Secondly, the very fact that the Divine Mother had made the proclamation pointed to the way in which changes would be marked and new things done from now onwards. The Divine Mother would speak, creating and giving authority to all new activity.

The inspiration for the healing had come two years earlier, before the advent of the Divine Mother. On 17 February 1921, Octavia had been about to take a tabloid (a codeine-based effervescent tablet much promoted after the war as suitable for nerves and tension) for her neuralgia, when it had shot out of her hand and rolled across the room. Surprised, she nevertheless characteristically made meaning out of a seemingly random act. She said to herself, 'Perhaps I am not meant to take it!' Maybe, she thought, it was a call to 'cease from every means' and rely on God only? So she simply drank the glass of water, with which she had been going to take the pill, after saying a prayer over it: 'O Thou who didst make the water wine at Cana of Galilee, I beseech thee to cause that this water be made effectual in place of the tabloid. Amen.'[1]

From that day, Octavia used no medicine, ointment or lotion, and some of the apostles began to imitate her in this. By the end of 1921, Rachel Fox, witnessing Octavia's improved physical health under this regime, felt they should get a medical opinion: 'in order that the progress of the changes which were going on in Octavia should be witnessed to by an entirely outside person whose evidence the world would respect.' She tried two eminent doctors, one of whom said it was merely the phenomenon of 'healing spiritualism'; the other, Dr Wallace of Harley Street, wrote to say that he did not have time to undertake the necessary examinations. Octavia's own doctor demonstrated a brief flurry of interest. 'He sees the affair as obviously medical rather than clerical,' Octavia wrote to Rachel. She went on: 'It is quite a new thought that the clerical job has been to teach people to die (salvation of the soul) & that the medical fraternity which certainly has tried to prolong life, would obviously be the most likely persons to whom the great Hermetic secrets would be confided.'[2] But no doctor took up the matter seriously, and Octavia and Rachel decided to let it rest. The medical authentication they longed for never came, but very soon the testimonies of those taking the water were witness enough.

After the Divine Mother's proclamation in May 1923, Octavia's capacity to heal – by breathing on and praying over ordinary tap water – was put to the test amongst the resident members and closely connected non-resident members. They began to drink water that had been blessed by Octavia and also applied it to their bodies. But the process was cumbersome. Rachel Fox recalls hauling great bottles of blessed water back to Cornwall.[3] How could those who lived away from Bedford receive the blessed water? A solution quickly emerged. Small sections of card, breathed on by Octavia, were sent to people in the post, with exact instructions on how to put the card into a jug of ordinary tap water, and with the words to say over the jug to bless the water. Cardboard was later exchanged for linen that could be more easily dried out and reused many times over. The Society bought great rolls of linen over which Octavia breathed her divine breath before it was cut into small squares with pinking shears. These linen squares are still used to this day (and Octavia prepared many rolls in her lifetime, so it is unlikely that they will run out any time soon). The Society had developed a healing scheme which anyone could use anywhere, as long as they had access to water.

In February 1924 they went public, placing an advertisement in various newspapers: this ad ran regularly and the response was steady. Those who wrote in received the cardboard – later the linen – section, along with precise and detailed instructions on what to pray and do.[4] The water was to be drunk, bathed in, and applied to the parts of the body afflicted with ailments. In return the water-takers had to report regularly, tracking their progress, stating whether their ailments had improved or not. The Society promised not miracles but rather 'slow but sure deliverance' of both a physical and spiritual nature, for the water aided the vital work of overcoming one's disposition or self. Not only sin but now also sickness was to be overcome. Only obedience to the careful instructions on how to carry out the healing with water was required – not even faith, and certainly no money.

The popularity of a healing ministry in the interwar years is not surprising. There was no national health service and many illnesses were still untreatable. Furthermore, given the 1918–19 influenza epidemic, which had killed between twenty million and forty million, attacking the young especially, the possibility of healing was attractive. There had been a widespread revival of spiritual healing in the early twentieth century in many churches and religious groups, including the Church of England. The well-known hymn writer and Anglican vicar, Percy Dearmer, was Chairman of the Guild of Health, founded in 1904, and was one of many Anglican clergymen keen to promote the ministry of healing, primarily through prayer. In 1909, he published *Body and Soul*, exploring the effects of religion on health and citing examples of spiritual healing from the New Testament to his own day. In 1916, a prominent member of the Guild, Lily Dougall, published *The Christian Doctrine of Health*, a practical manual on how to pray for healing, which went into three editions.

A year after the foundation of the Guild of Health, James Moore Hickson, an Australian Anglican layman living in England, founded The Society of Emmanuel, which aimed to bring together Christians who were 'in sympathy with the Scriptural practice of the laying on of hands with prayer for the sick in the name of Jesus Christ'. He led prayer groups up and down the country, and in 1911 had come to Bedford. Kate Firth and Mabel were involved in a prayer group at their parish church, St Paul's, and had held prayer meetings for his work. From 1919 to 1924 Hickson went on a world mission, holding packed spiritual healing rallies in churches and cathedrals wherever he went. Hickson was Low Church; Dearmer was Broad Church (Modernist); not to be left behind, in 1915 the High Church founded its own healing society, with the use of healing oil and prayer, the Guild of St Raphael. This quickly spread to other parts of the Anglican

Communion, and by 1920 the Guild had branches and members in Africa, Canada, New Zealand, India and China. By 1920 spiritual healing was causing enough of a stir for the Lambeth Conference (the once-a-decade meeting of Anglican bishops from around the world) to call for a committee to report on the subject. There were, too, the heterodox groups that advocated spiritual healing, most notably Christian Science and followers of the New Thought movement who set up healing groups, as well as those, such as the Theosophists and Spiritualists, who were simply sceptical that science could answer all questions, in medicine as in other spheres of life.

The Panaceans observed the activities of these other groups, and clearly separated themselves from them. James Hickson's mission to Bradford in October 1924, much reported in the newspapers, was the subject of discussion in the Society, and was declared by the Divine Mother to be a 'false healing'. When he came to speak at the church close to the Panacea Society's headquarters, the Society 'felt it a kind of challenge on the part of Lucifer to send him into such close proximity to the True Healer'.[5] Octavia directed followers to put the Divine Water inside the church, and to sprinkle it all around the building. Some of the apostles attended Hickson's service, clutching their seals for protection.

There was, however, a feature of these movements that deeply appealed to Octavia: their global reach. The Church of England had a ready-made constituency around the world – the Anglican churches that made up the Anglican Communion. Heterodox movements such as Theosophy, New Thought and Christian Science had worldwide networks. It was now time for the Panacea Society to extend its tentacles more rapidly and efficiently, not only through Britain but also beyond its shores.

Family and friendship networks throughout the British Empire had already created some Panacea members in the countries that made up 'Greater Britain' such as Australia, New Zealand and India. A keen member in India, Captain Richard Maguire at the Army Signal School in Kakul, Abbottabad, learned about the Society from Octavia's son, Adrian, who was in the army in India. He wrote: 'it has satisfied a very deep felt longing and given me an object for reform, as I could never feel for the church teaching, as it said one ought to feel.'[6] Hearing of it from Adrian Barltrop, someone who was so respected and appreciated, made him take the idea seriously, especially in a place where the clergy were so aloof. The irony was that Adrian Barltrop later totally rejected the Society and had fierce battles with his mother about it. But in Maguire he made a very keen convert, who was always trying to spread the word amongst the officers and other men, usually with little success, especially amongst the NCOs. But he succeeded in winning at least two others over to the cause: Lt Killingley and Lt Douglas Harris, both of whom wrote into the Society in 1922, wishing to be sealed as members.

The Panacea Society had from its beginnings attracted members from existing Southcottian groups in the colonies and former colonies. Peter Rasmussen, who came to live in Bedford, was perhaps the most prominent of such recruits. Others were actively discouraged from coming to Bedford, however: Octavia told Mrs Louise Coventry from Newtown, a suburb of Sydney, who had written at length about her 'angelic' experiences, 'Not to come here' but to prepare the way in Australia by selling books.[7] The Society needed workers around the world. Many therefore joined and remained non-resident members in their home towns in Canada, the USA, Australia and New Zealand, where the range of Southcottian groups had roots. In Canada, there were Southcottian groups in Ontario and British Columbia who became interested in the Panacea Society. Joseph Gardner in Temperanceville, Ontario, who had been reading Southcott since 1914, held meetings at his house to study the writings, and a small group of men attended from towns up to a hundred miles away. He was in touch with other Southcottians in Ontario, such as George Marlatt and his wife in Toronto, who held meetings on the Toronto streets in summer, and Sunday-evening meetings to read Southcott's writings in Brown's Hall in the winter when it was too cold to meet outdoors. Gardner and the Toronto group were also in touch with Florence Cullum, a prominent Southcottian in Cleveland, Ohio, and had crossed the border to see her. One of the members in Toronto, Jane Davidson, wrote that her grandmother had known Joanna Southcott 'but like most people at the time did not believe in her'. She concluded that 'it is the Lord's work that I should come to Canada to find out this truth and accept it with all my heart'.[8] Ethel Scales in Kamloops, British Columbia, had read the works of Southcott, Wroe and Jezreel, and was now interested in the writings coming out of Bedford. She wrote to Miss Oliver in January 1919 to receive them, and in turn introduced them to others, such as Alfred Bradley from the same town, who became a sealed Panacean.

This kind of networking, which had so successfully enabled the Society to grow in its first few years, had its limitations. There were only so many friends and family members whom the Panaceans could interest in their ideas and practices, and by 1923 members of the existing Southcottian groups had largely worked out whether they were interested in this particular newcomer or not. Furthermore, the advent of the Divine Mother had not been pleasing and plausible to everyone. In February 1923, soon after her manifestation as the Divine Mother, Emily Goodwin went to visit the New and Latter House in London, where she had sometimes worshipped in the past. This time she went into her trance-like state and spoke as the Divine Mother, berating the congregation for not accepting Octavia as Shiloh. She portrayed them as the five foolish virgins, from Jesus' parable in the Gospel of Matthew (25: 1–13); they had lamps but no oil and were unprepared for the arrival of the bridegroom. They had waited for something to happen and, now it had, they were ignoring it – namely, the coming of the Divine Daughter, Shiloh incarnate, Octavia. When she went on to say, 'You are teaching the commandments of man, your church is built on a rotten foundation', one of the leaders decided they had had enough, and tried to stop her speaking. Having no success, the leaders switched the lights off. 'Thus,' wrote Rachel Fox, 'these foolish people showed that they choose darkness rather than light.'9 What it meant, practically, was that the British members, at least, of these related Southcottian groups had largely closed the door on the Panacea Society and were no longer a possible source of converts.

The healing ministry came to the rescue. Crucially it could reach people who had no contact with Panacea members, and no prior knowledge of the Society. The Panaceans referred to the healing as the hook and the bait, 'which the Lord gave us to use in our call to be fishers of men'. Octavia believed that the world was her parish and she had grand ambitions. Her little society would not only manifest locally and nationally but, she believed, would eventually appeal to the whole world.10

Advertisements were vital in spreading the word initially, and they remained important, though the healing also quickly began to spread by word of mouth. Soon after the very first advertisements were placed in British newspapers at the beginning of February 1924, the responses started to roll in. The advertisement told applicants to 'state all your complaints at once in as few words as possible'. They would receive a reply from the 'CSS' department – not signed with any Panacea member's name – with the cardboard (later linen) section and directions on how to prepare the blessed water. (CSS stood for the initials in Latin for Community of the Holy Ghost, the Panacea Society's name then.) Two sorts of blessed water were to be made up, one for internal (A) use, the other for external (B) use. Water A for internal complaints was prepared by placing the linen section 'which will never lose its virtue' into a large clean bottle, which was then filled with water from the tap. While doing this, the person was always to say: 'I ask for Healing by Water and Spirit, and for other benefits.' The linen section could be placed in boiling water from time to time to keep it sterile. When travelling, the person should take the linen section along, and drop it into a glass and count to four. To prepare water B for external use, some of the blessed water A was 'diluted': two wine glasses of it were to be put into a similar large bottle and this was filled up with tap water. For all complaints, four wine glasses of water A were to be drunk daily, the first before breakfast, and the others at 11 a.m., 3 p.m. and 7 p.m. This could be increased to seven glasses per day in cases of very severe illness. The blessed water B was also to be used in the water-taker's baths, for sponging rheumatic limbs, for inhaling if one had asthma, catarrh, bronchitis and similar complaints, for bathing sore eyes and treating wounds, and so on. If in any kind of trouble, the person should drink an extra glass of water A. Other general, sensible advice was given: to take exercise and be moderate in all things, eating wisely, though red meat, shellfish and fish without fins or scales were not recommended (they were forbidden to sealed members). These instructions were translated into multiple languages as the healing ministry expanded internationally.[11]

In return for this, the water-taker was required to be obedient, reporting back one month after first receiving the treatment, and thereafter every eight weeks. This changed to every quarter in 1925, because of the numbers of people writing in. Replying to the sheer volume of mail that arrived at headquarters kept an army of Panacea ladies busy. They had received 203 applications for the water by the end of

March, just two months after the first advertisement, and 3,389 by the end of the year.

To spread news of the healing further, the Panaceans held public meetings, usually in London, with members such as Alice Jones and Rachel Fox testifying to the efficacy of the water. A meeting in Mortimer Hall in August attracted an audience of 250 and as a result 217 letters of application came in,[12] and a meeting the next month in Kensington Town Hall, organised in part by Frances Wright, a newly sealed member, produced similar results; Kate Firth, Winna Green, Alice Jones and one of the Gillett sisters were speakers. Mrs Wright wrote to Octavia, describing the meeting as a 'real success' but noting 'it was pathetic to see the eagerness of the people who surrounded us when we left the platform'. The members who spoke looked 'so attractive' and 'were so well dressed' (which would have gladdened Octavia's heart) and 'Mrs Firth made a very nice speech. Very much to the point & earnest.'[13] They continued such meetings into the next year, with another one in Kensington in April 1925 and one in Eastbourne (where there were many Panacea members) later that year. Rachel Fox described the April meeting in Kensington Town Hall in her diary, noting that after she and Kate Firth, Alice Jones, Frances Wright and others from Bedford had made their speeches, many people came to talk to them: 'the result of such was that we got hundreds of applications from simple folk, many hardly able to find a scrap of paper – and the week after the meeting they [Bedford HQ] actually treated 641 cases!' Ever the optimist, she wrote: 'the newspaper articles, intended to make fun of us, on the contrary caused a great interest in our work'.[14]

Rachel was referring to the reports, in both the national tabloid and regional newspapers, of the meetings. Despite her propensity to look on the bright side, these reports usually focused on the sensational or quirky audience questions and members' claims. The *Daily News*, under the heading 'The Little Daily Dose in Someone Else's Tea', reported one concern. A well-dressed woman at the meeting asked, 'Can I really cure my husband [of his bad temper] without his knowledge?' The reply came: 'Absolutely; you can put it [the water] in his tea.' Women from the middle and upper-middle classes wanted to tame not only their husbands but also their servants. One audience member asked if the cure would work on her servants, and another replied that she had tried it on her ten servants and 'they are now so loving and delightful that she doesn't know what to do with them'.[15] The *Daily Mirror* noted that even overdrafts and baldness might be cured.[16] The *Daily Mail* had the headline 'Divine Healing by Post' and reported that one of the 'Panacea folk' testified that both she and a 'dear dog' had been healed.[17]

Buoyed by the success of the healing in its first eight months, Octavia, who was usually keen to protect her anonymity, even allowed a small number of journalists to come to the Bedford headquarters. But she was not happy with the results – she wrote to Rachel Fox that it was 'a veritable crucifixion of her sensibilities'[18] – and it was an experiment not to be repeated. The *Daily Sketch*, a British tabloid newspaper at that time owned by Lord Rothermere's Daily Mirror Newspapers, ran an article with the headline 'Crank Society's Secret'. The journalist described his arrival: 'No distinguished person was ever conveyed more secretly to the Allied Fronts in the War than I was taken to-day to the secret headquarters of the Panacea Society.' He went on, 'Not for worlds would I divulge the whereabouts of the Panaceans. I only succeeded in persuading the Eighth Prophetess to lift a corner of the veil of mystery that surrounds her society by giving my solemn word that I would not disclose its locality.' But the journalist did everything else that Octavia asked him not to do. 'Don't call me a "high priestess" or make fun of our beliefs,' he reported her as saying, and then proceeded to do both, describing her as 'high priestess of her cult'. But Octavia, always sensitive to class, was surely pleased when he quoted her as saying, while he looked around the 'big roomy residences with pretty gardens', that 'You won't be far wrong if you put us down among the upper middle class.'[19]

Once the healing went public, the press was the medium by which scoffing sceptics and rival Southcottians could attack the Society. Mary Robertson, Alice Seymour's right-hand woman, wrote numerous hostile letters to a range of regional newspapers about the Panaceans' 'startling propaganda' saying, 'The Southcott writings plainly foretell the coming of strange healers at the end: we are warned that these will perform "lying wonders", that the cures will not be permanent'.[20] Mary Robertson spent a lot of her time obsessively tracking any mention of the Panacea Society in any newspaper, local or national – or she or Alice Seymour went to the expense of employing a press cuttings service – and was relentless in refuting the Panaceans' healing claims wherever they were reported, whether in the *Birmingham Gazette* or the *Eastbourne Chronicle*.[21] The Panacea Society certainly employed a press cuttings service, and members working in the office at head-quarters also spent time combing the newspapers for references to themselves or a related interest. Sometimes Rachel Fox, as the public face of the Society, wrote a letter to correct misinformation, and she quite often wrote to refute Mary Robertson's claims. The busy office workers in the Panacea headquarters kept all the articles about their healing in a large scrapbook, and pasted them alongside items on the Church of England's disagreements about spiritual healing and the controversial healing rallies and meetings of James Hickson.

The flurry of newspaper discussion about the Panacean healing was largely British-based. Meanwhile, the Society was busy advertising the healing around the world, and the first application from beyond Britain came from Mr Ernest Gideon on 12 February 1924, from Hyderabad, India. An Indian and a member of the Society, he had first written for information when he had been a student at Jesus College, Oxford, and had been sealed in 1923. After he had applied for the healing, the Society did not hear back from him and assumed he had lapsed in his reporting until another Panacea member wrote in a year later from Eastbourne, where some of Ernest Gideon's family lived, to say that he had caught dengue fever and had been taken under medical care and had therefore been unable to keep up with the water-taking regime. Mr Gideon wrote to Octavia several months later in July, to apologise that his 'long silence has strained your faith in me' and tried to explain his family circumstances. While his Indian family was generally liberal-minded, and did not mind his unorthodox religion, his refusal to take medicine had caused all sorts of fraction, especially as one of his uncles was a doctor. This tension had been exacerbated when, after recovering from dengue fever, he had contracted a severe case of conjunctivitis, and was whisked off to see a specialist in Bangalore. He had been in total darkness for three months and had only just had his bandages removed. The power of his family and the respect required even of adult children for their parents and their views, coupled with the fact that he and his family disagreed both on medicine and healing and on the thorny issue of denation-alisation, made for a difficult context in which to be an obedient water-taker. The Society advertised in local newspapers such as the *Rangoon Gazette*, which not only prompted Ernest Gideon to apply for the healing, but also one D. Cooper to write in from Insein in Lower Burma on 15 March, with nerves and deafness.[22]

Specific groups were targeted through the choice of advertising venue. Knowing that they might attract followers from other heterodox groups, the Society published in Theosophist magazines, especially the *Herald of the Star* which had carried an article on Joanna Southcott in its November 1923 issue. The *Herald of the Star* was an international publication so it was via the Panacea Society's advertisement placed there that the 'news of the Healing went into all nations'.[23] The first applications for the healing from Australia and New Zealand – where Theosophy was enormously popular, especially since the arrival of Charles Leadbeater in Sydney in 1915 – came in because of that advertisement. Some of the initial enquirers wrote from the Melbourne Theosophical Headquarters but letters came in from all over the country from May 1924 onwards. F.H. Layton from Preston Apiary, Donnybrook, Western Australia, wrote to say that his wife had 'pyorrhoea of the gums and a friend had a fibrous growth internally'. He reported three months later that 'the directions are being carefully followed, but it is too early yet to note any perciptable [sic] result. I'm also suffering with bleeding piles. Could you treat me for same?'[24] J. C. Woodward from Ladbrooks in New Zealand wrote in with a strained heart, which he had had for thirteen years, and torn ligaments. He reported faithfully, at first saying that he was better and able to do some work for the first time in years, had more energy and was happy. He had had a relapse by the second report, but was 'keeping exceptionally well' by the third. His letters continued with positive reports so that a year later he had recommended the water to his mother and several friends, even though he lived in the countryside where neighbours were two miles apart, so he was not naturally part of any network. He sometimes had relapses; 'but your letters always seem to give me fresh heart', he wrote,[25] and he missed the healing water if he was not in a place where he could take it at the designated times.

Theosophy was of course popular in India, and the advertisement in the *Herald of the Star* brought in further applications from there. Mr Alpaiwalla wrote in from Bombay in May 1924 with a disease of

the retina, and after taking the water, reported a slight improvement
in his vision. Mrs R. Darhvierwala wrote in from Ahmedabad, India,
on behalf of her seven-year-old son who had lost the power of speech
and hearing during a bout of fever three years earlier.[26]

Water-takers often treated others with their water, thereby bring
them into the healing. The Panaceans had always relied on networking,
and they continued to do so, with new water-taker applicants and new
members opening up new networks. Peggy Geyser, writing from
Hawkes Bay in New Zealand, noted that she had received the treatment from Mrs Cecil Smith in Napier, close to Hawkes Bay. Amongst
some of the early applicants from Australia were several women from
Coogee, a tight-knit coastal community in the eastern suburbs of
Sydney. One can imagine word spreading of the new cure that one
of them had discovered and acquired through the post from England.
Sixty-one-year-old Mrs Annie Leather wrote in from Adelaide, Australia
in 1926, suffering from 'rhumatism' [sic], stiffness of the joints and
tonsillitis, because her sister had told her about the divine healing.
Bertha Roberts from Heathcote Valley in Canterbury, New Zealand,
who sold flowers for a living and had also seen the advertisement in
the Herald of the Star, wrote in not only about her catarrh and
bronchitis but also about her son, Lincoln Russell Roberts, who had
fought in the war and was run down and nervous, and had carbun-
cles on his arms. 'He is real down, but works too hard. Please help
him if you will or can.' She reported regularly: her catarrh had cleared
up, her sight became better so that she could read without glasses,
and she introduced her eighty-five-year-old father and seventy-year-
old mother, as well as her daughter and her brother to the water, but
she could not get her son interested in it. She started to read the
Panacea literature, described her psychic experiences and visions and
her complex family dynamics at length in her letters to CSS, and asked
to be sealed. She put the water in her son's tea '& he is better tho I
do not say a word'.[27]

The millions of letters received to date, and now in the Panacea
healing archive, open up worlds of discomfort, suffering and embarrassment, often caused by poor medical treatment or botched surgery.
Mrs Mariane Winterton in Swanbourne, Western Australia wrote: 'My
complaint is an injury through childbirth, neglect of which has caused
a weakness of the organs of elimination, the bowels especially having

lost their retentive power.'[28] She wrote in later to say that she thought she felt a benefit but it was hard to say, given that the trouble was of such long standing. Mr James Albert Robins wrote from Perth in Western Australia to say he suffered from bladder troubles and deafness. It was painful and scalding to pass urine, and sometimes he passed blood and mucus. He had received numerous diagnoses from different doctors – acute cystitis, chronic cystitis, a growth at the bottom of the bladder – but, as Mr Robins sadly reported, the only thing all the doctors agreed upon was 'there is inflammation from some cause & that it can't be cured'. His own opinion was that 'it was a faulty operation or want of care afterwards, the Drainage tube fell out of the wound after two days (I was operated on for stone in bladder), it fell out of 3 others & they all died within a year, one after a month of terrible pain in hospital. It was at the close of war, Drs & nurses very scarce.' He was a dutiful, regular reporter, saying that his deafness remained the same but his bladder seemed to be steadily improving, if still painful. However, his wife wrote on 21 January 1925, when he had been taking the water for some months, to say that he was much better. In particular his temper had been 'very severe & continual before taking your cure, [and now] he has improved in every way'. She was recommending the cure 'to several people that doctors cannot do more for them'.[29] Some sought relief from less severe but embarrassing symptoms, for example J. T. Elhart in Colombo, Ceylon, who wrote in September 1925 with dyspepsia and constant flatulence – 'I keep on belching and passing wind almost the whole day.' He wrote two months later to report: 'the flatulence and wind is much better.' Across the top of his original letter, a CSS office worker in Bedford has written in red letters 'LIVER'.

By March 1926, just over two years after the healing had gone public, 4,339 people had applied to take the water. Not everyone had continued to report faithfully every eight weeks, but still the volume of enquiries and regular letters that the CSS department at the Panacea headquarters had to handle was getting beyond the capacity of the ladies, industrious as they were, and highly organised as the CSS leader, apostle Mildred Hollingworth, a former nurse, was. That month the Panaceans at headquarters decided that they simply could not reply to everyone each time they wrote in to report, and they enclosed slips with their replies to the water-takers saying that 'Owing to great increase of work

in the various Departments we are obliged to reply very briefly' and
'The work is growing so rapidly that now we are going to ask you NOT
TO ENCLOSE AN ADDRESSED ENVELOPE unless you want a reply.
You can help this great work by patiently going on with the Treatment
and reporting every two months. We shall rejoice in your reports but in
future we will not reply unless you ask for advice.' In August they required
non-residents now to report quarterly, instead of every eight weeks.

Nevertheless, the Panaceans knew that they were performing a vital
pastoral ministry across the globe. People wrote about their most intimate medical problems as well as difficulties with their marriages,
families, sexuality, jobs and money, and might have had no other outlet
to discuss them. So the Society allowed for occasional letters about
such problems that required replies from CSS. There was also the
Confidential Department nominally headed up by Mrs Goodwin
herself, though in practice Hilda Green maintained much of the correspondence. The Confidential Department dealt with all the intimate
matters related to membership: making the Life Confession; baptism;
the various rituals in the progress towards immortality; and tithing
and other financial issues. People wrote to Mrs Goodwin about a
variety of concerns: in the economic recession of the late 1920s, men
and women wrote from Britain and the States about the difficulty of
getting employment, often desperate about how they might feed and
house their families; women wrote about abusive husbands; men wrote
about trying to control their urge to masturbate (at a time when this
was regarded as self-abuse); some wrote about complex family
dynamics that they simply did not know how to sort out; others about
their spiritual puzzles and doubts. As one man wrote, disappointed
that he had had no reply to his most recent letter and still longing for
help: 'You understand people.'[30] The Panacea Society had an important role as 'agony aunt' to the spiritually, physically and materially
despairing in the interwar years.

The great success of the healing abroad brought not only a huge
volume of post, but the additional problem of the slowness of the
mail coming by boat from places such as New Zealand, South Africa,
Australia and North America. As one water-taker wrote from West
Australia, 'as it takes a time to receive a reply, Australia being so far
away, I am writing to ask you if you would please send me a further
supply of perforated card'. The solution was to set up 'Towers' abroad.

These were trusted and responsible sealed Panacea members who would head up satellite healing headquarters of the Society. Water-takers would write into the Towers, who would then compose a summary report of the water-takers and send it into the Bedford head-quarters every month. Supplies of the case papers, linen squares and Panacea literature were sent out regularly to the Towers for distribu-tion. Mrs Christina Bridges, in Fort Victoria, Southern Rhodesia, was the Tower for Africa in the 1920s and '30s, and she wrote meticulous, brief summaries of 'her' water-takers' reports. She wrote that she wished to bear the expenses of the healing ministry in her area, as did some other Towers, by way of a gift to the Panacea Society. But in August 1927 Octavia wrote to all the Towers abroad, saying that they should submit all expenses (postage, stationery, etc.) to the Bedford headquarters, and they would be reimbursed. This was largely because the Society had recently become a charity and had to present a balance sheet to the Charity Commissioners, and therefore wished to be entirely businesslike about everything.

Other Towers wrote more chatty reports, with various asides, and even sent sample letters to Bedford. Elinor Partridge from Burwood in New South Wales, the Tower for Australia and New Zealand in the 1930s, noting that a lapsed reporter had begun to report again, commented, 'Another case of husband's opposition. What a number there are! One woman said her husband was "very stagnatic"! It is such a helpful harmless religion to oppose.'[31] She put up with unex-pected water-taker visitors who talked a lot, and in turn told the Bedford ladies a good deal about her own family and household: comments such as 'Rod continues to ride in Cycle Races and gets bad colds fairly frequently' surely foreshadowing the content of the much-despised Christmas round-robin letter of our own day.[32]

Towers were set up in all the major countries (or in some cases continents, notably Africa) where there were water-takers – except the British West Indies (BWI) and parts of the USA. This seems to have been because there were no suitable sealed members in some parts of the USA and the BWI; though the Society's belief in the superi-ority of white people – discussed later in this book – may have informed their decision about who was 'suitable' in the BWI. Nevertheless, there were far more water-takers from the USA and BWI than most other countries. Despite the conscientious work of the Towers, this suggests that direct communication with the CSS department in Bedford was more satisfying and effective.

Water-taking sometimes turned into membership, and that was certainly the Panaceans' hope. On 4 September 1924, Octavia sealed the first three persons brought in by the healing water. Octavia's illness in the days following that sealing was attributed to an attack by Lucifer, for surely by the healing they 'were penetrating into Satan's Kingdom in a very definite way'?[33] Ethel Cooke-Yarborough, from Wyberton in Lincolnshire, was sealed a month later. She had written in March 1924, and then started to read the Panacea literature. She was in correspondence with Miss Green from June of that year, seeking answers to her theological questions. Once she had discovered the Society and the teachings of Southcott and the previous prophets, the new knowledge was truly a revelation to her. She was converted and found it 'awful to think that the Bishops & Priests in the Church have never taught these things'. But she was worried about rushing into membership. 'I meet many church people (Church of E) who have never even now heard of J.S. how can they understand the teachings enough to be sealed in a very short time? These things have to be prayed and pondered over. The redemption of the body is an entirely new teaching to church people.'[34] She continued to ponder the writings she had been sent, visited Bedford in September to 'make the acquaintance of those who understand J.S.'s teaching so much better than I do',[35] and was convinced enough to be sealed on 1 October 1924. She continued to write in with her theological questions long after that and remained a member for the rest of her life, briefly becoming a resident member before her death in 1935. She was always a questioner: this was the member we met in Chapter 6, passionately quizzing Octavia about why someone else who had a debt with the company to which she also was indebted had been allowed to become a resident member when she had not.

Those who went on from the healing to be sealed did so for a variety of reasons: some because they believed that the water had successfully healed them, some because it seemed the natural next stage and others because they had read the Panacea literature. Miss Maude Helms of London wrote in 1926 to report that her various aches and pains were gone, and her vitality and energy renewed. 'Truly, the water is wonderful . . . I am thankful to Divine guidance for having directed me to the Panacea Society.' She continued: 'I would like to feel that I am ready to be sealed if it is the Divine Will.' Many people wrote in with this sense of *progressing to* the sealing. Mrs Betty Rossiter from Bromley in Kent wrote in 1926, after taking the water for two years, to say that her indigestion, legs and heart were all much better, but she was still having pain on her left side and attacks of giddiness. Nevertheless, 'I am pleased to say that there is no comparison between my case now & 2 years ago – I have learnt to overcome more than I thought possible. My life is much more harmonious & I have almost lost the sense of fear.' She therefore asked for the sealing, if the Society thought she might have it now. Others discussed it with friends who were already members, such as Mrs Edith Jenner from Eastbourne, who talked it over with Mrs Beedell, an enthusiastic non-resident member there who brought many people into the Society. Mrs Jenner wrote: 'I am sorry to have delayed so long, but Mrs Beedell has greatly helped me, and I desire my name to be written in the "Book of Life".' Some had signed one of the petitions to open Joanna Southcott's Box of Prophecies, begun reading the Panacea literature and felt the next stage was being sealed, for example as Mrs Kathleen Hanson-Abbott from a farm in Tring, Hertfordshire, who wrote that she was reading Rachel Fox's book, *The Suffering and Acts of Shiloh-Jerusalem*, and 'it makes me long to be a true member of the Panacea Society'. Bertram Durant, a student at Exeter College, Oxford, who came from Plymouth in Devon, wrote to say that he had studied some of the Panacea Society publications and was applying for 'the privilege of being sealed'.

But the Society was the victim of its own success. So many people wanted to be sealed, after taking the water for a while, but were clearly distant from the Society's day-to-day activities, and – not having entered via any existing networks – were adrift even from other non-resident members, that it was decided there should be a less demanding form of sealed membership. These people were vital for getting member-ship up to the required number of 144,000, but they were not part of the inner circle of sealed members. From 1927 the sealing was there-fore made less onerous for this kind of member. A little pamphlet called *Healing and Sealing* was issued, which stated that the require-ments for being sealed 'are no longer as severe as they have been for those who compose the Foundations, for we are told that time is short and that now all are to be sealed first and taught afterwards, according to the words, 'They shall be taught of God".' The requirements were described 'as not more than those of ordinary Christians'. 'All you have to do is believe in God the Father, the Sacrifice of His Son upon the Cross for the Soul, and in His Coming again to peace. In view of His Coming you would naturally endeavour to live a Christian life.' The booklet continued: 'Please note that if you do not wish to be sealed, it makes no difference whatever to your position as our patient – you can go on taking the Water just the same. Taking the Water is part of the great work of preparing you for the Lord's Coming, for all who have "the hope of His appearing" must purify themselves even as He is pure, and the Blessed Water will help you to overcome your sins and your failings as well as helping you to overcome disease.'

The wording of the pamphlet suggests that the Panaceans were being as elastic as possible in allowing people to become sealed, but even these demands were too much for some. In December 1927, Gertrude Pike from Southend-on-Sea in Essex annotated her copy of this pamphlet and sent it back in to the Society. She wrote: 'What is a Christian life? I live quietly and peacefully. I ask every day for faith to believe. I want to be sealed, but cannot conscientiously say I am a Christian.' For others, the simple declaration they had to make was just what was required to draw them in.[36]

Now that there existed such a basic form of sealed membership, a more complex form was needed to separate out more committed members. New rituals and formal stages of membership were added to a person's spiritual journey in the Panacea Society, all of them opportunities for Emily Goodwin, both as herself and as the Divine Mother, to exercise further control. It was now the Instrument of the Divine Mother who read and replied to the Life Confession – 'burning the confession as soon as it has been read, and [as Mrs Goodwin] knowing nothing whatever of its contents', as the Panacea literature claimed. Before the member was sent their seal, a new act was introduced called the destruction of the mortal soul, accomplished by the Divine Mother on the incoming member's behalf. This indicated that a person could live and not die, that they could be changed and dwell immortally on Earth in a new and happy world.[37]

After being sealed, members were now expected to tithe: to give a portion, usually a tenth, of their income to the Society. The Divine Mother first commanded Octavia to set up a system of tithing in April

1923, and it was introduced to all sealed members in September 1924. It was explicitly stated that this was to 'secure an income upon which the Kingdom of Her Son and Her Daughter' could be established. Octavia had always been scrupulous about money, operating within the means she had to hand and according to the gifts she was spontaneously given. Tithing marked a new departure: it was a direct request, indeed a demand, for regular gifts of money from members, though it was represented as advantageous to the giver. The payment of the tithe was said to bless a person's income – it was quaintly called 'the Protection of Pecuniary Affairs'. Further, the Divine Mother reminded members, *she* had given them all they possessed anyway, and would now guard it *if* a tithe were paid. Octavia backed up the practice with a short theological and biblical history of tithing, but the impulse for this new 'Divine Obligation' came from Emily Goodwin as the Divine Mother.[38]

Once committed members were sealed and had settled in tithing, the next stage was baptism in the Church of England, followed by the destruction or withering of the mortal mind, 'that terribly active possession of ours which is the root-cause of every sin, disease, affliction, and disability; that enemy to peace which must at least give way to a new mind, in which the peace of God will dwell for ever'. This was to be done in five ways: (1) by using the formula 'I will not'; (2) by drinking an extra glass of the healing water in times of difficulty; (3) by making a Daily Record of ones faults and failings; (4) by sending this Daily Record in to Mrs Goodwin every month; and (5) by studying the scripts on this subject. This constant feeding in of personal information gave the illusion of divine omniscience to Mrs Goodwin, as did other features designed to 'help' with this withering of the mortal mind. The Court of the Immortal Mother Jerusalem was set up, so that members could present themselves as faulty persons to the Divine Mother and be judged by her. And finally, an act known as the cursing of the fig tree was initiated, in which the Divine Mother cursed at the root all unwanted and hateful thoughts. This was based on Jesus' cursing of a fig tree (Matthew 21: 17–22 and Mark 11: 12–14 and 20–26). To prepare for this, a member had to use the formula 'I blame myself' at every return of the thoughts they wanted to get rid of. They would receive notice from Mrs Goodwin when the cursing of the fig tree would happen on their behalf. She controlled when they progressed to the next stage in their spiritual journey of Overcoming and the quest for immortality, and thus when they moved to the highest level of membership by virtue of the rites of passage they had been through.

Mrs Goodwin accrued enormous power in the community through such intimate knowledge of every member who chose to go through these stages. Her control over the inner circle of members tightened. The Society also became increasingly hierarchical with more exclusive groups towards the centre though, paradoxically, the closer you were to the centre, the harder you had to work spiritually on yourself. One bureaucratised outward sign of these different gradations of membership was that people said different prayers over the water and when taking the water, according to their membership 'stage'.

The cardboard/linen sections and the blessed water were used not only for healing but also for other forms of protection. The blessed water was sprinkled around buildings to protect them. At the end of February 1924, non-resident members were commanded to sprinkle the entrances and gates to their houses with water B. This was given theological significance: it was a re-enactment of the command in Exodus to the Israelites to smear blood on their doorposts and lintels so that the Lord would pass over their houses when smiting Egypt with plague (Exodus 12: 1–13). 'You are to regard this as a sprinkling of the Blood of the Lamb, as in the days of the Passover and you are to say Psalm 91 when you return into the house after performing the act.' (Psalm 91 is about the assurance of God's protection.) The Divine Mother commanded this to be done before 'the destroying angels passed over the land'; the blessed water would be 'as a protecting angel for each house'.[39] People adapted this for their own purposes and circumstances. John Coghill recalled running a dance at Aberdeen University in the mid-1930s when he was still a student, and being worried about a rowdy element: he sprinkled the entrance to the building and the edges of the dance floor with the blessed water and everything went smoothly.[40] Bertha Roberts in New Zealand was anxious about a train she was travelling in, so sprinkled her carriage with the blessed water and was safe. While most of the reports were glowing in praise of the water and its protective capacity, sometimes the Society received reports of the water failing, which puzzled faithful members. Non-resident member Gertrude Austin wrote in, very shaken, to say that the two houses she and her husband owned in Surbiton and Shoreham-by-Sea in southern England had both been burgled even though they had been sprinkled with the water. 'I on my part should be very grateful to have explained to me how evil went past the threshold, even into the bedroom on both occasions where a Section and the Healing water were?'[41]

There were sprinkling projects, co-ordinated from the Bedford head-quarters, to protect public buildings. On Hallowe'en in 1925, which was damp and murky with a dense, wet fog, five members set out to sprinkle the churches of Bedford. Rachel Fox, who was one of the five, wrote: 'we felt like conspirators, glad that we could hardly be seen by each other or by the public'.[42] The following month, other buildings in the town were sprinkled: the post office, bridges, the electrical, water and gas works, the town hall and corn exchange, the Chief Constable's house, railways and even the Cardington aerodrome, five miles outside Bedford where airships were built and flown. Members from headquarters were also charged with sprinkling major buildings in London: the Houses of Parliament, St Paul's Cathedral and Westminster Abbey, Buckingham Palace and other royal palaces, concert halls, major museums and galleries, the Bank of England, Scotland Yard, the War Office and other useful public buildings, as well as railways, bridges and post offices. The background to all of this was that the Panaceans were constantly expecting the Second Coming of Christ and accompanying apocalypse. Their selection of buildings and places for protection indicates what they thought important to save.

The water was used for other purposes too. Non-resident members who had animals – 'cattle, horses, dogs, cats, fowl or birds etc.' – were instructed to give them a teaspoon of the Blessed Water in their drinking water once a day, and were provided with a special section of linen for this very purpose. Many people wrote to report the success of this. Geraldine Bartup from Upland Farm, North Shepstone in Natal wrote in to say that they had had an infestation of locusts on their farm. They 'beat them off with Police Whistles, Tins, Bills, etc.' for a fortnight and had then sprinkled the crops with Blessed Water, saying the 91st psalm all the time, and the locusts 'have not done any damage as far as we know'.[43] Elinor Partridge, the Tower in Australia, reported that Mr Archie Clark's sheep were dying of some sudden disease, so he sprinkled the paddocks with water B and only one more sheep died. She also noted that Miss Y.S. Irving used the water when bitten by a poisonous red-backed spider and was saved from serious results.[44]

The cardboard or linen sections could also be used for protection. In February 1924 the Divine Mother – ever concerned about financial matters – commanded that anyone who had money in a bank should take one of their card sections and drop it anywhere in their branch of that bank so that 'their money, passing through that bank, may be protected'. This conjures up a wonderful image of Panacea members and water-takers dropping the sections, as if by accident, while passing through their bank. Those who had money in a Post Office savings account were commanded to do the same thing there. The instructions continued, 'It does not matter if the section is swept up, but many have put a little gum on their section before starting and have stuck it under the counter or in some odd corner.' They were also to put gum on another section and stick it into their bank books.

Members adapted this use of the sections for their own purposes. Mary Warry wore the linen sections in her shoes when she was presented to the King and Queen at court. She also cut two small squares off a protection card and dropped one in the throne room, where the King and Queen were receiving people, and the other in the supper room after the presentation. As a result she felt the whole event – which she described at great length to the royalist Octavia – was 'almost holy somehow' and her brief presentation to Queen Mary seemed to last longer than that of others and earned her a glowing smile from the Queen. She believed that the Queen might possibly have had some memory of her, as her cousin's husband was a court official, and she felt that could be 'useful later' to the Queen, presumably when Christ came and all the action, even for the King and Queen, was taking place in Bedford.[45] Delighted by the royal connection, Octavia thought Mrs Warry was still to be corrected and replied, 'Do you not think it would be wiser to attribute the Queen's bow and smile to the important fact of your being one of the Lord's adopted children – as thus it is useful to you, to us, and to the Royal Family and has a permanent value – whereas the other supposition is of no moment, and goes no further, ending with mere personal interest to you and your family – indeed the Divine Mother says what I say is so.'[46]

This protection work was formalised in 1925 by command of the Divine Mother, who ordered Octavia to prepare special small cards bearing the words 'Divine Protection' just as she prepared the sections for healing, breathing her divine breath over them. These were to be given to applicants, but the Divine Protection work never attracted as many applicants as the healing, and its administration at head-quarters was rather less efficient, at least at first, than that for other areas of the Society's work. It was not particularly successful in drawing in new water-takers or members, but the use of sections for protection was always popular amongst existing water-takers and members.

As part of the formal protection work, wardens were appointed in each county in England, such as Ethel Cooke-Yarborough for Lincolnshire. They were to be sealed persons, fully conversant with the teachings of the Visitation, and were conceived of as 'Bricks for the Towers of Refuge'. Their duties were to tell people about the possibility of divine protection, though not to press anyone into asking for it; distribute the protection cards to those who asked for them; post handbills and flyers in village shops and on billboards, when directed by the Bedford headquarters; support the Protection Department through monetary gifts; and also make preparations in times of national difficulty or emergency.

In October 1925, a very special bit of protection work was done to protect the Garden of Eden and its environs. Those at the Bedford headquarters drew a circle with a radius of twelve miles from the Panacea Society chapel. At eight points on the circle they buried linen sections. Thus, they believed, the Daughter Shiloh took possession of the land and created an ark of protection for all those in the Bedford area, which was referred to as the Royal Domain. There were four expeditions and Ernest Ashleigh Boddington, the Director of the protection work, led each of them. He was responsible for digging the seven-inch-deep hole for each linen section. Evelyn Gillett, gardener for the Society and – crucially – owner of a motor car, drove them and was the person who covered the section with soil. Dilys Barltrop accompanied each trip as a representative of the Divine Mother and poured divine water over the section. A different apostle went on each expedition and put the section in the hole. Photographs of the occasions, taken by Evelyn Gillett, show Kate Hodgkinson, untidy in dress as always, with her coat flying open and wisps of hair emerging from her hat, at the north-eastern points on 17 October; Jessie Paterson, neat and matter-of-fact, at the south-eastern points on 21 October; Gertrude Searson, suave in a fur-trimmed coat and gloves and fur toque, at the south-western points on 24 October; and Winna Green, earnest in her spectacles, on the north-western trip on 28 October. Ethel Castle, a non-resident member, accompanied the group to six villages, giving out a Panacea leaflet when she bumped into a 'jolly old workman' and a man whom she mistook for a gardener but turned out to be a clergyman who 'had a cultured voice but was most domineering' so she fled.[47]

Print culture remained vital to the Society's missionary activities. The year 1924 saw both the launch of the healing ministry and two important publications that supported and promoted it. One was Octavia's book *Healing for All*, published two months after the healing went public, at the end of March 1924, which advertised the healing, and summarised the Society's beliefs. The other was the foundation of *The Panacea* magazine. This went hand in hand with the healing ministry. It was a monthly publication designed as a gentle way in for enquirers and those who had entered the Panacea world via taking the water. The first few copies did not even mention Panacea beliefs. As Rachel Fox put it, 'the first three numbers contained attractive matter of a non-alarming but sparklingly suggestive nature'.[48] Only in the fourth copy was the healing boldly declared as a new discovery. Water-takers as well as members subscribed to the magazine, which contained an editorial by Octavia; articles on Panacea life; short stories by members; poems, often by Dilys Barltrop; special pages for the sealed; reports from the Towers around the world; articles on current theological controversies; Pen Pictures from Panacea people (descriptions of their home towns by non-resident members, usually) and – importantly – excerpts from the healing reports (made anonymous of course). The magazine was an important vehicle for publicising the success of the healing.

The whole tenor of the magazine was one of cosy middle-class English life, which sat rather uneasily with the Society's extraordinary theological claims. But to read *The Panacea* is to step inside the mindset of Panacea members, to understand their assumptions about class and race almost instantly, to understand their paradoxical and yet intoxicating combination of nostalgia with a longing for change.

The colour plates and illustrations of English gardens, abbeys and cottages appealed to a mythical, rural, decidedly southern form of Englishness. The poetry and short stories conformed to the genre of domestic popular literature of the period, targeted at women. Octavia's two novels, serialised in the magazine before they were published as books, were a cross between that form of domestic literature and Anthony Trollope's novels, containing as they did rectors, archdeacons, deans and bishops, divided into baddies (who lived a complacent, self-satisfied life, never asking questions) and goodies (who stumbled across Panacea ideas and beliefs and accepted them with alacrity).[49] Members contributed articles and letters, poetry and short stories, but Octavia did much of the writing, some of it appearing in the form of editorials, some under her own name, and yet more – especially the articles on the Church – under the male pen name of Mark Proctor. The Church often came under attack as wanting, but another favourite theme of hers was the error of the heterodox religions that were potential rivals to the Panacea Society. Octavia knew that members of those religious groups were ripe for the picking, and that the Society had already enjoyed much success in gleaning from such groups, but she also knew that she needed to separate the Panacea Society out from them and explain why it alone had the Truth.

The Panacea Society undoubtedly targeted such heterodox groups, not least by advertising the healing in their magazines as we have seen, but there were limits beyond which even it would not go in the quest for members. A request from a Miss Absell in Eastbourne to speak at her Animal's Friend Society met with frostiness at headquarters. Meanwhile, non-resident member Gertrude Hallwood had written to Miss Green to say that the members of the Animal's Friend Society were 'children over the age of six' and 'the adults are a few cranks of the RSPCA all tutored by Miss Absell . . . who usually speaks to them.' So, she advised, 'it would not be of any use for any of us to go & speak to them.' CSS wrote back to Miss Absell to say, 'we are very sorry, but realising more particularly now what you want . . . we think the days are too early for us to speak at the meetings of the Societies that you mention. We do not think that average people would believe in such a work, indeed if it comes to that there is very little to say on the subject – except to say that if the animals are ill, they should have the water given to them.' This last part was corrected by Octavia to give the ending a friendlier tone, as the CSS correspondent had originally written: 'except to say that if the animals are ill, and take the water, they will die or get better'.[50]

After the Church of England, one of the most frequently occurring former affiliations amongst the Panacea inner circle was Theosophy. For a while in 1924 the Society deliberately cultivated Theosophists. Theosophy had grown in Britain during the war (rising to a membership of 4,155 in 1918) and continued to increase through the 1920s, appealing especially to women. But there were simmering resentments and factions, and this meant that many were dissatisfied and might be tempted away to join the Panaceans. Not everyone was happy about the election of Annie Besant as president of the Theosophical Society in 1907, nor about the readmission of Charles Leadbeater to the Society at the end of 1908, after his involvement in the sex scandal about young men (over which American Theosophists had split). There was a disgruntled group in the British Theosophical Society who disliked Annie Besant's 'neo-Theosophy', what they saw as her abandonment of traditional, Blavatsky-style Theosophy, and, in particular, her and Leadbeater's belief that the World Teacher, whom many Theosophists were expecting, would manifest as a young Indian man named Jiddu Krishnamurti, whom Leadbeater had 'found' on the private beach attached to the Theosophical Society's headquarters in Adyar, India. Leading the opposition to Besant in England was a man named William Loftus Hare who by 1924 had brought this simmering resentment to the boil and led a special convention, where the Theosophical Society's leadership was accused of leading the Society astray, and monopolising power through the secretive Esoteric Section.[51]

In the spring of 1924, Frances Wright, a member of that group of disgruntled Theosophists and friend of William Loftus Hare, became a Panacean. Mrs Wright, who lived in Kilroy Castle in County Cork in Ireland, joined the Society after reading an article about Southcott in the *Herald of the Star* and responding to the Society's healing advertisement in the same publication. Mrs Wright was a seeker, like so many who joined the Panacea Society – and, indeed, like Octavia herself. Brought up in India, she had been impressed by the devotion of the religions there; had thought about joining the Roman Catholic

Church; liked the beauty of High Anglicanism but found there no answer to her question about the Lord's Coming; and eventually had settled on Theosophy. But when, in 1924, she applied for the healing and received the case paper and 'the section so carefully pinned to the left-hand corner' she called to her daughter, 'Come here, come here! I have found the right thing at last – I am perfectly sure of it.'[52] She had written to Rachel Fox in April 1924, after she had read her book *The Finding of Shiloh*; first came to see Octavia in May 1924, and was sealed on 5 June. Ever busy and making new plans, bubbling with enthusiasm about her new religious affiliation, Frances Wright began her campaign to bring dissatisfied Theosophists into the Panacea Society, and enlisted Octavia in it. Three days after she was sealed, she was writing to Octavia to say that she was over in London and would bring four Theosophists to see her the following week. All were high-ranking and, like Frances Wright, discontented with Annie Besant. Two were the Misses Debenham, aged twenty-two and twenty-three; they were, as Frances Wright noted, 'rich Debenham & Truebody' – a national department store that had grown in the early twentieth century.

Meanwhile, Frances Wright remained embroiled in the machinations of the Theosophical Society. William Loftus Hare wrote to her to say that he had wanted to cleanse the Theosophical Society for eight years, and although he had heard of dissatisfaction from all directions, 'yet we continue to send greetings to Leadbeater and Raja and rise 5 or 6 times when AB comes into the room. We flatter her when we know she is deceiving us – we tolerate her when we know she is misleading us.'[53]

Octavia realised that she was being drawn into an intra-Theosophical disagreement. She wrote to Frances: 'I can perfectly understand your natural desire to get something going, but the chief thing is for all who embark in the matter to have a very clean sheet, as you are not fighting Mrs Besant really, you are about to enter the lists against the greatest creature there is in the unseen, apart from the Divine Family – that is, the Angel Lucifer.'[54] Nevertheless, she agreed that she would meet Mrs Besant if Mrs Besant would see her. Frances Wright set about planning this, and she herself had a meeting with Mrs Besant. It was disastrously unpleasant, but nevertheless Mrs Wright went on to write and ask her if she would meet Octavia, whom she described as 'a great teacher . . . a woman of intellectual power, a writer, lecturer & literary critic, of gentle birth & deep reading & thought'. She continued: 'I feel very strongly that if you & she would meet, it would be of enormous benefit to the whole world.'[55] Annie Besant did not reply to the letter, and the meeting never happened.

By late 1924, Octavia felt it necessary to be quite firm with the Theosophists who joined the Society, making it clear that they could retain no links to their old religion. They could of course continue with the healing as practising Theosophists, but they could not enter the 'inner circle' of sealed Panaceans. Frances Wright herself retained her Theosophical affiliation after being sealed. As a prominent Co-Mason, in June she was still going to Theosophical Co-Masonic meetings in London, and performing as an officer at them – and being scowled at by Mrs Besant. Co-Masonry was a form of Freemasonry that admitted women and was (unofficially) a subsidiary but important activity of the Theosophical Society. Mrs Wright's letters to Octavia highlight the crackling tension at these Masonic meetings, with different factions shooting mean glances at each other during the ceremonies. At the end of June, she wrote to tell Octavia that she had meant to leave the Theosophical movement but now she would wait for them to throw her out. Others she tried to bring in were too committed to Co-Masonry to join the Panacea Society, or kept going to their Lodge meetings even after they were sealed. By September 1924, at the meeting on the Panacea healing in Kensington Town Hall, which Frances Wright had organised with her usual breathless enthusiasm, only four Theosophists were present. In a letter to Theosophists who were prevaricating, written later in 1924, Octavia described Theosophy as 'Luciferian intellectuality – useless as a religion, and mixing itself up with false religions and bogus Churches because it knows man must have religion.' She sided with Frances Wright's opposition to Annie Besant, the woman who had not even deigned to accept the invitation to meet her. She wrote: 'In addressing five important Theosophists the other day, it was shown to them, that they knew less of Mme Blavatsky than I did. Mrs Besant has nothing to do with religion. She is a political and social reformer, an occultist and philosopher. I do not disagree with her speeches – I repudiate them as old-fashioned and effete. Her ideas have been tried and tried for centuries, while, as a politician, she would wreck the Empire.'[56]

Frances Wright did not resign her membership of the Blavatsky Lodge in London until November 1924, and even then she remained a member of the Cork Lodge for the moment 'in the hope of turning it into a Panacea meeting place'. This was perhaps not unrealistic, given that the principal members of the Lodge were all water-takers. But even that was part of her scheme to 'break' Leadbeater's influence in Ireland. Her motivations in making such plans were always pro-Panacea – she wrote, for example, that she hoped 'soon to have quite a little colony taking the waters here'[57] – but they were often inextricably linked to her remaining emotionally invested in Theosophical disputes. By the end of the year she was seriously working to close her association with Theosophy; she had cleared out all her Theosophical books, giving her best to Octavia and the rest to her local Lodge.[58]

For all of Frances Wright's activity, she brought in few additional members. Theosophists were still attracted to the Society, however, by a variety of routes. Non-resident member Josephine Low joined in 1924 through friends in Eastbourne. Brenda Greig, who became an active resident member in the mid-1920s, had a Theosophical background. The Society continued to define itself over and against Theosophy, as it defined itself over and against the Church of England and other rival religious groups. As long as it attracted members from all those constituencies, it needed to assert that it alone was right.

The Panaceans even went so far as to imagine that their activities were affecting what the Theosophists were able to do. The script of 30 October 1925 commanded that the protective sprinkling of the churches in Bedford was to be done before the meeting of the Theosophists, set for 1 November, at which Krishnamurti was to be announced as World Teacher. This sprinkling was duly done on 31 October. The next day, Panacea members Brenda Greig and Irene Mellor were sent along to the Theosophical meeting in Queen's Hall, London. Irene Mellor went ahead of time and, during an afternoon concert, scattered the linen sections about the various entrances and lobbies, changing her position in the concert hall several times as if to hear the music better but in reality to disperse the sections more widely. As people left the concert she dropped sections under the chairs on the platform where the Theosophists would be speaking that night. During that evening meeting, she and Brenda Greig pressed handkerchiefs to their faces that had been sprinkled with the blessed water, 'to relieve us breathing in such a foreign atmosphere'. Despite her fluent address, Mrs Besant did not declare the identity of the World Teacher at the meeting, and future attempts to put Krishnamurti forward as a Christ met with little success in subsequent meetings in Scotland and America. The implication was that the sections had done their work: Panacean truth was advancing while Theosophical false-hoods receded.[59]

By the end of 1925, the healing ministry, which by then had been public for nearly two years, had had 9,240 applicants. Combined with the protection work and the monthly magazine, it had taken the Society worldwide. The Panaceans' reach had become global. As growing numbers of people wrote in for the healing and joined the Society, Octavia realised that a constant theme in letters to the healing and confidential departments was sex; that a persistent issue in people's confessions was sex. Furthermore, as the outer circle of non-resident members increased, questions about who could and could not marry began to be raised. In 1925, Octavia decided she had to tackle the 'sex difficulties' amongst her members and make her theology on the subject clear.

9

Sex Difficulties

In November 1925, Mrs Emily Carew-Hunt wrote to the Society from Cannes in France, where she had been living for about four years with her husband, Major Cyril Carew-Hunt. They were both Panacea members thinking of moving to Bedford. She told Hilda Green, the recipient of so much post of this sort, that she and her husband had never had sex. She gave four reasons: that he was a virgin; that he did not want a child; that they therefore thought they should not have sex; and they were not quite sure whether the sexual act was of God or of Satan. In a postcard sent to Miss Green some months later Mrs Carew-Hunt obliquely suggests another reason. Noting, as she made practical arrangements for their move to Bedford that they slept in separate rooms, Mrs Carew-Hunt explained that 'my husband has slept badly since the war and the least noise wakes him so we have done this [had separate bedrooms] since being abroad'. Taken together, these two pieces of correspondence give a glimpse into what married life might have been like for many couples in which the man had served in the war and now suffered from what we can, retrospectively, identify as post-traumatic stress disorder – and, as a consequence, found both sleeping and sex difficult. They had been married ten years earlier, in the summer of 1915, in Portsmouth, when Emily Vickers (as she was before her marriage) was forty-three years old and Cyril – then in the Royal Artillery – was thirty-nine.

The matter was considered important enough for Octavia herself to reply to Mrs Carew-Hunt. In her letter, she stated clearly that sex was allowed by God within marriage as long as the laws of chapter 15 of the Book of Leviticus were observed – namely, that sex between a man and a woman could take place only when the woman was not menstruating; and that the 'unclean' period should last during the time of menstruation and for seven days afterwards. Octavia had taken from the nineteenth-century founder of the Christian Israelites, John

Wroe, the belief that the original sin was not the mere eating of an apple but Adam and Eve having sexual intercourse while Eve was menstruating. While Octavia largely abolished the keeping of the Old Testament law that the Christian Israelites adhered to, this aspect she retained. Sex for the Panaceans was thus an 'act permitted by God between man and woman, but under the restrictions of Lev. XV and with the safeguards of a home, in which the children if any, can be reared'. Ultimately, however, bodies 'will be redeemed from the sex difficulties by the water'. Thus Mrs Carew-Hunt was urged to go on taking the water and continue the practice of Overcoming, for 'that is all there is'. The implication here was that sexual attraction would be overcome in due course as a person became more perfect.[1] As Octavia had written to Rachel Fox, 'I have always told you generation will *cease* in Israel, thank God.'[2]

In March that year, Octavia had stated her views explicitly in a confidential paper on 'sex-relations' sent to the non-resident members who made up the second-tier inner circle of the marked-out, important group of 144. The Society's purpose was to re-enter Eden, and so the circumstances of the Fall – in which sex featured centrally – had to be tackled head on. She wrote:

> The obvious reason for this Visitation is the adjustment of the sex-relations which were brought about by the Fall, in order that God may dwell with men on earth.
>
> To belong to the Visitation and not to understand this point, is to show a lack of common sense and of common intelligence, for sex-attraction *is* the serpent that has to be bruised, in order that its power may be taken away, and it is the 'dragon in the Blood' which has to be purified.[3]

The Society therefore permitted those who were married to have sex, as long as they observed the laws of Leviticus. But there was, too, the implicit notion that those who were perfect would not have sex; indeed, through the practice of Overcoming, they would eventually lose the desire for sex.

These somewhat mixed messages about marriage and sex meant that celibacy within marriage was often sought – usually by the female Panacea members – and for a variety of reasons. Some women regarded sex as a duty rather than something to be enjoyed, and their religion gave them a good reason to negotiate celibacy within their marriage. Mary Beedell, a member of the Eastbourne group, wrote to Octavia in 1923: 'I have felt for a very long time that my body is a very sacred vessel for the Master's use – and have felt sexual relationships to be very repulsive – and as I talk to my husband a lot about the Visitation I asked him if he could not give that part up (which he has done) and it has not caused a word of dissension in any way.'4 For her friend Helen Morris, married to a bullying and oppressive husband, sex became a battleground, as she attempted to give it up altogether. Helen had a far from positive view of marriage: 'marriage is nothing but legalised prostitution and it is most obnoxious to a pure-minded woman.' She wrote to Edgar Peissart – then her confidant – that she had been trying to live without sex for several years, 'and have *killed* all desire for sexual intercourse, in fact it has become objectionable'. Despite her husband's promises of 'freedom from the evil thing' he persisted in pressing his conjugal rights, especially as he became more antagonistic to Panacea views, subjecting his wife to endless criticism of her religious beliefs so that 'at times the insults are unbearable' and, she reported, 'he is most abusive'. At the end of November 1922 she had written to Edgar Peissart about 'the toughest bit of trial it has ever been my luck to have & all because I would not give way to him in sexual intercourse at 9 a.m. in the morning – a dreadful struggle but was not overcome, only by his temper which was Vile!' He said he had finished with her, that he hated her, and she was to go, and would soon be begging in the gutter. Not surprisingly, she made herself scarce for the day, at which point 'he really went mad' until, ten hours later, he found her hidden from his sight in another part of the house. Similar struggles over sex occurred, and even though she was always 'the victor' she found it deeply upsetting and trying, so went to a lawyer (a man) who advised her 'to give way to him [her husband] within reason' but, as she declared to Edgar, 'I have no intention of doing so whatever happens, am I right?'5 Religion might help where the law would not. But it was not to be. Octavia's inherent conservatism won out. Several months later, in April 1923, when Edgar Peissart's intentions and actions had been revealed and he had been banished to New York, Octavia wrote to Helen Morris, ending the letter with a response to her persistent questions about celibacy. 'You will have to give up all your ideas re the Marriage question, it has been very bad for Mr Morris, it makes suppression which comes out in other ways, God ordained marriage for the human race as a safeguard, human intrigues have made matters worse.'[6] This was just a part of the obedience required of Helen Morris, now that her covert friendship with Edgar Peissart had been revealed, if she wanted to remain in the Society.

For Rachel Fox, who had a very loving marriage and supportive husband, the decision to give up sexual relations with her husband was 'a living sacrifice', made at great cost and in the pursuit of perfection. She wrote in her diary:

> While at Bedford I felt increasingly that if I was to go on to perfection in understanding the law of Christ for the body so that if immortality were to be my portion as well as the portion of others – 'Israelites' or the overcomers of their own evil in body, mind and spirit – that I must not continue 'in the flesh' the usual marriage connections with my beloved husband. I had long been feeling it time that we should give it up, but at last without any pressure from Octavia or consulting flesh & blood I decided I would write to George and ask if he would agree. And I felt the Spirit helped me to write, and then I prayed that it would help him to decide rightly. I felt it was far more of a giving up for him than for me. His response was a beautiful willing sacrifice, which touched me more than if he had claimed his right as a husband. No one will ever know what this strange decision of our advancing years has cost us, but I believe that it has been the right thing and that both of us will receive reward from our Father which sees the secrets of all hearts and knowest what we do so that nothing may hinder the work of grace in us.

And she echoed Octavia's theological explanations: 'I can understand that as this act of marriage in the flesh is the result of the sin in Paradise which led to the Fall of man into earthly and sin-stained conditions, this will have to be "cut off" for all those who desire the Immortality of the body, as Israel desires it.'[7]

Others found themselves confused as they attempted to work out what was actually required of them by the Society, especially after the 1925 paper had been sent out to non-resident members. In that document, Octavia had commanded all married members of the Visitation to 'place their difficulties before the Divine Mother Jerusalem', who would tell them what was expected of them. Wella and Frank Bauer, non-resident American members who lived in Independence, Missouri, wrote in April 1925, reporting on their sex life. They had been married for fourteen years, had two children and were always an affectionate couple. They had sex observing the laws of Leviticus, wrote Wella Bauer, in a remarkably frank letter. 'Now we cohabit [have sex] in the clean time not for children (for we use precaution) but to satisfy the flesh. Once or twice a month would satisfy me but with my husband it takes oftener, but outside of home and me that desire never bothers him. Often times he has laid down beside or against me in the unclean time until the desire was satisfied or laid a hand on me until I was satisfied.' But their frankness brought about a new dilemma, for the Divine Mother's reply made it clear that 'precaution was a sin'. Mrs Bauer wrote back seeking further advice: 'Then is there a time during the clean time in the month that one can cohabit and not conceive or is the right way a complete separation or bring forth more children?' In a postscript to the letter, she added: 'I would rather not have intercourse than to have children under present conditions, but if more children is the command then I am willing.'[8]

In 1925, the Society's attitude to birth control was consonant with that of both the British Medical Association (which officially condemned it, even though some individual doctors disagreed with that position) and the Church of England: contraception was not to be used by churchgoers. Gradually, medical ideas about contraception changed, so that in 1930 the British Medical Association declared that birth control, and advice about it, should be dispensed where the health of the woman might be affected by any further pregnancies. The shift in medical thinking influenced the Anglican Church: the Lambeth Conference, in a surprise move, cautiously approved the use of contraception in 1930.

Octavia was aware of and interested in the heated debates about birth control throughout the 1920s that resulted, not least, from the publication of Marie Stopes's *Married Love* in 1918. In the late 1920s, Octavia seems to have been in communication about the subject with a non-resident member in Liverpool, Hilda Abernathy, who sent her a booklet on birth control, *Family Feelings*, with the note: 'This little booklet which I am enclosing is one which I promised you, it does not seem to be from the "Marie Stopes" people but it is on the same subject. I have been waiting and hoping I should get something more interesting for you but so far nothing has been sent to us.'[9] When the Anglican

bishops at Lambeth in 1930 changed their mind about contraception
and declared that 'we cannot condemn the use of scientific methods to
prevent conception' where married couples had considered the question seriously and where there were good moral reasons why the way
of abstinence could not be followed, Octavia did not approve. An editorial in The Panacea declared the bishops' 'little excursion into the
dangerous ground of the sex question' to be 'dangerous and devoid of
good results to every person' precisely because they had ignored the
Panacea Society's information – which had been sent to all forty-two
Church of England bishops and the two archbishops, as well as the
Mothers' Union, the White Cross League and the Church of England
Working Men's Society – that it was necessary to keep the laws of
Leviticus 15.[10] Octavia's choice of institutions to which she sent the
Panacean advice is revealing. The Mothers' Union repeatedly took a
conservative stance on marriage and its reproductive purposes, opposing
the relaxation of divorce laws and birth control in the 1910s and 20s.
When the Lambeth Conference revised the Anglican Church's position
on birth control in 1930, the Mothers' Union found itself awkwardly
having to change its own position, especially when the Archbishop of
York, William Temple, pressed them to do so. Its central council now
declared that the use of birth control was a couple's private decision.[11]
The White Cross League had, since the late nineteenth century, advocated 'social purity', campaigning against men's promiscuity and encouraging people into more spiritually uplifting marriages. We can see Octavia
coming out of both of these traditions: she had been a keen member
of the Mothers' Union when she was a curate's wife. As late as 1914
(just before her world was turned upside down by reading Southcott's
prophecies) she had written an article for the Mothers' Union magazine giving advice to mothers on how to explain matters of sex clearly
and practically, but without unnecessary additional detail, to children.
The moral purpose of such common-sense teaching was to ensure
purity as the child developed into an adult, without which an impure
soul would create a life of misery that would take years to cure.[12]

   Back in 1925, Mrs Bauer received the reply that cessation of sexual
activity was preferable to the use of birth control. Four months later,
she wrote that she and her husband were striving to remain 'separate'.
Ironically, however, just as they were struggling for celibacy in their
marriage, she had succumbed to her earlier-confessed desire for her

Mormon dentist.[13] She had written earlier: 'If there are mates in the human family he would be my mate yet God knows I never encouraged him, yet it seems neither of us could overcome the condition and my sin has been with him. I would or must say twice this week I have committed the deed with him (adultery) . . . Both seemed not to be able to endure longer.' She sought advice from the Divine Mother as to whether she could still be an Overcomer, and what she should do. In the meantime, she was drinking more of the blessed water to try and overcome her desire.[14] At the end of August she had received a letter of forgiveness and the promise of help from the Society, with the command not to have any contact with the dentist. By then she had already told her husband, who had found no fault with her and kissed her, saying, 'I forgive you but I fear for you in this visitation.'[15] Wella Bauer kept the command and did not see the dentist again, though was in some consternation a couple of months later, when she realised she had a decaying tooth – 'it had never entered my mind that I would have that to deal with' – but went to her husband's dentist and 'afterwards I felt better for I felt I had obeyed,' even though she found it trying to go elsewhere when her own dentist 'had cared for my teeth for so long'.[16]

Mrs Bauer's letters, giving considerable detail about her marriage and sexual temptations, are just some of the many letters that poured in after Octavia had sent out to non-resident members her March 1925 paper with the request that they write in to the Society about their sex difficulties. Some found this a relief. Mrs Duncan, also from Independence, Missouri, wrote pages about the marital problems arising from her husband's propensity to get into debt and her overbearing mother-in-law and concluded: 'I am thankful . . . that I can tell some human being everything and know that I am telling the right one and the One who will comfort.'[17] Many were still confused about what they should or should not be doing. Anna Summers, who lived in Akron, Ohio, wrote: 'Am writing to ask what the will of the Divine Mother is regarding married believers on the sex question. My husband and I lived "separated" for months not because we had discussed it and agreed to it but – shall I say naturally? – and now I see a tendency the other way again and I am uneasy about it. Will you kindly tell me what is the will of the Divine Mother and what one is required to do?'[18] Others obediently reported that they had trouble with 'sex-relations'; sixty-four-year-old James Hancock of London wrote of it as a struggle with the world: 'one may avoid it for a time – long or short, but travelling, mixing with the world, one is ever open to it and needs be on the move'.[19] People continued to write in with their dilemmas about sex. Norman Winckler, from Kidderpore in Calcutta, India (and brother of a resident member), wrote to the Divine Mother in 1929 that he was having difficulties with his wife. He felt called to give up sex, but she did not, stating baldly to him: 'this is going to mean trouble between us'. He continued: 'Then one night I gave way to her but owing to the rapidity with which I completed the sexual act she remained unsatisfied and was bitterly disappointed and would have nothing to do with me.'[20] He wanted advice on how to proceed in these confusing circumstances.

The world's attitudes to marriage and sex were changing fast. These letters give us a window into the experience of sex and married life in the interwar years, at a time when Victorian and Edwardian ideas about the institution of marriage, and the related question of sex, were being questioned. The circumstances of World War I had led to greater freedom for courting men and women, when chaperones ceased to be practically possible for women and men of the middle and upper classes, and to a new urgency in the matter of love for all classes. Often this resulted in speedy marriages and a generation of children born out of wedlock, as young men were sent to the Front and to the possibility or even probability of an early death in battle. This new freedom was not to be relinquished at the end of the war.

When women received the vote in 1918 and reflected on their experience of work (and the fact that their work was needed) in the war, so they began to think about the possibility of more equal marriage relations. The ideal of companionate marriage, in which a woman and man chose to marry each other for love and companionship, increased in popularity. The artistic and literary elite, represented most obviously by the Bloomsbury group, were experimenting with new forms of marriage and relationship, in which infidelity was recast as being true to one's feelings; openly triangular relations were experiments in the new honesty; and same-sex relations were no longer regarded as morally wrong. Open, frank discussion of birth control was increasing, as exemplified by Marie Stopes's writings and the public response to them. Forty thousand copies of Stopes's *Married Love* had been sold by 1923, and in 1921 Stopes opened London's first birth-control clinic where women could go for advice on contraception and be fitted with the cervical cap. Twenty thousand women visited the clinic in the first three months. The promise of relatively reliable birth control, greater knowledge of it and easier access to it opened up the possibilities of sex for the sake of pleasure alone – for women as well as men. The Victorian idea of sex as a woman's duty to be endured rather than enjoyed (however true or not that may have been in practice) was slowly being eroded. All of this had a utopian ring to it, as people imagined more new possibilities for, and forms of, marriage, and advocated a greater frankness about the realities of married life and sex.

The spectrum of attitudes to marriage and sex in society at large, in this time of uncertainty and change, is present in microcosm in the letters written by Panacea members. Mary Beedell represented a more traditional view of sex as duty when she asked her husband to release her from sexual intercourse. Helen Morris used religion as a means to escape the perennial problem of marital abuse, and appealed to the rhetoric of 'purity', which had been used since the nineteenth century by the White Cross League and feminist groups with which she had contact. Rachel Fox wrote of the warm companionship of her marriage to the gentle Quaker George Fox, in which sex was an important facet. Some women expressed their sexual desire, which may have had something to do with the more open climate in the world and the acknowledgement that women *had* desire, or may simply have been in obedience to the command from Octavia and the Divine Mother to be entirely honest, 'for no one will be able to hide anything that eventually ought to be spoken of'.[21] Even Emily Carew-Hunt admitted that she had 'always struggled against the lust of the flesh'. Married to a man who did not wish to have sex, or was not capable of it after his traumatic wartime experiences, she began to dream of having sex, 'waking up to feel as though this act had been accomplished or was in the process of being accomplished'. Eventually, this began to happen while she was awake and she recorded that 'the same act seems to be trying to make itself felt on the physical body in full consciousness'. She attributed this in part to the fact that she and her husband had previously been persuaded to join an occult order and on seceding from it had been assailed in a similar way: hence her question as to whether sexual intercourse was of God or Satan.[22] Wella Bauer struggled both with the command not to have sex with her husband in obedience to the command not to use birth control, and also with her desire for her dentist, the man she considered her God-given mate in the human family – 'the desire to be with that person never leaves me long at a time' – and when she gave up seeing him, he was often in her dreams. In the end she transformed her sexual desire for him into a desire for him to become a Panacea water-taker. Several months after she had ceased all communication with him, she wrote to the Divine Mother: 'a day does not pass but I find myself thinking, wondering, if finely [sic] he won't apply for the water and take it till it makes a man of him, a man like Jesus'. At the end of 1925, she was still writing of her desire for the dentist, grateful for help 'to cast all thought of him out of my mind and I ask how soon for there he seems to have a grip'. She and her husband continued to have sex (presumably with 'precaution') in the clean time, though she now wrote of it as a 'sin' and felt that if they were able to be 'separate' they would both gain by it. They talked about this frequently but could not quite take the step, even with the help of the water.[23]

The Panacea Society was presenting its own radical, utopian solution to 'the marriage question' and changing nature of gender relations that obsessed much of the rest of society. The Panaceans, for their solution, turned back to the Book of Genesis in which they perceived that the relationship between men and women had been distorted by the Fall, so that man had gained the upper hand and created an imbalance of power. The implication was that heterosexual intercourse epitomised that imbalance, though Octavia never went as far as a radical feminist like Frances Swiney who advocated the superiority of women, not least because she saw a role for marriage and children for ordinary people, and she had conventional ideas about what marriage was. Octavia's answer was the ascendancy of Woman, and ultimately the renunciation of sexual relations for all of the chosen. Only this would enable the necessary adjustment of relations between the sexes that would bring about the Second Coming of Christ, the millennium, and thus the reign of God on earth. While the world offered solutions to the marriage question by rethinking marriage as an institution, for Octavia the solution lay in bypassing the old world and its institutions altogether; in this case, the institution of marriage.

Those who had a head start in the Panacean utopian experiment were the single, either unmarried or widowed. They had the answer in their hands: they need never marry. Any sign of any intimate relationship or liaison amongst those at the Bedford headquarters was quickly squashed. Evelyn Gillett and George Goodwin (son of Emily, and a non-resident member) had struck up a friendship in the summer of 1923. Evelyn shared with George a love of gardening and working on motor cars. Her mother Mary Gillett had felt fine with the two of them spending time together: 'she is *absolutely* free of any falling in love with him'; though admitted 'her [Evelyn's] going to London for a week with him was a bit queer from the world's point of view but felt it must be all right or else you [Emily Goodwin] or Octavia would not have allowed it'. But Mrs Goodwin was less keen on the friendship. One evening when she went over to the Gilletts' garden and saw Evelyn holding a piece of wood for George to nail up, it looked to her as if she needed to take steps to stop their being together. Evelyn protested, saying that George had up until then been working in different parts of the garden, and she had only just gone to help hold the wood when Mrs Goodwin arrived.

Mrs Goodwin moved to discourage the couple – or rather, to push Evelyn away from her son – while Mrs Gillett questioned the apparent ban on their sharing company: 'If he is *really* very much in love ought he not to go to his sister's for a while and be away from . . . E.? Or does he realise what the Visitation means and is willing to just see E. as a sister?' Mrs Gillett thought if he could accept the latter, then Mrs Goodwin should permit them to see each other. George needed a congenial companion and Evelyn, being close in age and sharing his interests, was still the best person to provide it.[24] The incident shows not only how quickly Mrs Goodwin and Octavia reacted to a potential relationship amongst the Society's few young people, but also the confusion, in this case, of her role as mother of her son and her new role as Divine Mother in the community exercising control over all members' lives.

In the 1925 Sex Paper, Octavia expressed an understanding that not all would feel called to celibacy and the single life: 'if any are still attracted to the ideas of the old "flirting" and love-making (to which however, we take no special exception in the world), they must make a statement to the effect that they prefer to join the circle which will now be provided in which they can marry if they wish, and in regard to which they would receive further instruction'. But those who chose to marry would form an outer circle, of lesser believers. Rachel Fox echoed this in more explicitly theological language when she wrote, 'Those called "aliens to the commonwealth of Israel" & "strangers to the covenant" will still through the millennium bear children, but under the laws of Lev. XV which they will keep; so that woman will only bear clean pure seed, & Satan being cast out, it will not be difficult for them to be good & law abiding. The test will be when at the end of the Millennium, he is to be let lose [*sic*] again to see if they have power over their bodies & love for the Divine Rule.'[25]

But for those who wished to be at the centre of the Visitation, only celibacy and a renunciation of interest in sex-relations would suffice. 'To attempt to remain in the Visitation as deceivers in this matter, using sex-attraction as an amusement, is now stated to be *impossible*.' Octavia continued in the 1925 Sex Paper, with the earnest belief that people could be freed from the desire for sexual relations:

> This could not be sent forth were it not that all who truly desire to be freed from the great dangers of sex-attraction can be freed. It will help many young persons to make a decision, to discover whether they are finding life in the Visitation dull, whether the idea of going to meetings or visiting the Centre, palls upon them, for where their treasure is, there will their heart be also . . .
>
> LET IT BE CLEARLY UNDERSTOOD FROM HENCEFORTH THAT EVERY MAN, WOMAN OR GIRL IN THE VISITATION WHO PUTS FORTH REPORTS TO ATTRACT, IS DELIBERATELY WORKING AGAINST GOD, WHOSE PURPOSE IS TO DESTROY THIS VERY THING BY THIS VISITATION, IT BEING THE ACTUAL SACRIFICE OF THE BEAST.

Once again, the behaviour of those in the Visitation was seen as affecting the cosmic order: their sexual renunciation would slay 'the beast' (satanic influences). Conversely, events in the world, however minor, were regarded as signs to the Society. Octavia wrote that the 'removal of the Statue of Eros from the fountain in Piccadilly Circus (a fountain from which water has never been forthcoming) is a sign to the Visitation of the coming cessation of all old world attraction'.[26]

So what happened when members decided they *did* want to marry? It was not as straightforward as Octavia seemed to imply. In October 1925, seven months after the Sex Paper had been sent out to the non-resident 'inner circle', Olive Morris, daughter of Helen Morris (who had so many difficulties with her husband), wrote to Octavia suggesting that 'in the world to come, it does seem a very beautiful thing could be made of marriage. Strange as it may seem there is such a thing as "pure love" in this degraded world of ours.' Olive believed that she had found it with a twenty-four-year-old pilot in the Royal Air Force, Leslie Thorp, whom she had known since childhood, to whom she had been writing about Panacea beliefs, and who was about to return from Egypt to Britain. And so she asked Octavia: 'If for the sake of each others [sic] constant companionship we were to marry, would it make so much difference?' At this point, she declared: 'Mind you, nothing on earth would make me leave the inner circle, if I could. But it is a question which often arises in my mind & I know it is in his.'[27]

In her reply to Olive, Octavia seized upon the possibility of a new, young male follower, and focused her attention on getting Leslie to join the Society, praising him to Olive: 'a person who can approach the thing as seriously as your friend, and merely through correspondence, is likely to be one of the numbered multitude'. As to marriage, she wrote that for 6,000 years that was 'the only way out of the difficulties brought about by the Fall' but now the six thousand years were coming to an end, the Lord was coming again, and 'God has now held up his Hand to stop the traffic' so that 'even the idea of suitable, really happy marriages . . . would cease to be possible, because of the circumstances'. Never mind marriage: Olive and Leslie represented, for Octavia, the 'young men and maidens' who were catching hold of the Visitation's 'splendid help and cheery outlook'.[28]

Two months later, there was a much more acrimonious correspondence between Octavia and Olive and her mother Helen. In mid-December, Olive had visited Bedford with Leslie, and had taken Octavia an artificial flower arrangement. Afterwards, Octavia wrote to Olive, ostensibly apologising for not doing much for her and Leslie, and wondering whether they should have discussed the marriage question in greater detail. In reality, the letter was a sharp criticism of Olive's flower arrangement – 'though I admire the flowers, I am worried about the falsity of them – there is a danger in working in leather and shells and in making things which belong to one world fit and imitate another' – and her style of dress, which she considered too old for her.[29] Octavia sent the letter to Helen Morris, with a note in which she criticised both mother and daughter: 'I do feel strongly, and have always felt that your life should be simplified. You look too well off, you do too much . . . and I feel that the time has come for you to face this.' All of these things she felt to be 'dangerously on the artificial tawdry side of life – and do not fit in with our ideal of the children of the kingdom of heaven'.[30]

As Panaceans, both Helen and Olive should have realised that they could be criticised, and sharply, by Octavia at any time. The right response was to fall into line. But both were shocked and rose to their own defence in spirited letters. Indeed, Olive made an acutely perceptive comment about the dynamics of the Panacea leadership when she said, 'I think you must be changing your views a great deal and we are left to discover our new positions as best as possible. Up till now you have told us to go on exactly the same as usual leading our normal lives, doing nothing abnormal, attending to our social duties, and to do everything possible to please Daddy. Now it appears this is all to be reversed.'[31] In fact, in the Panacea Society things did often change, as Octavia and Emily Goodwin declared themselves ever open to God's directions and revelations (not least through the Instrument of the Divine Mother) so that new ideas and new rules could be declared at any time, either for the whole community or for individuals, often leaving members bewildered but unable to question the new edicts. Helen Morris wrote eleven pages in her own and her daughter's defence and asked, 'Why is it I wonder that this should happen just now of all times?'[32] One possible answer was that Olive was moving, against Octavia's wishes, towards marriage. Another possibility was that Octavia often needled those members who were wealthy and of higher social status than she was, especially if they showed any independence of spirit. And then there was always an underlying antagonism between Octavia and Helen, because of Helen's involvement in the Edgar Peissart saga, and at various times Octavia felt the need to assert her authority over this independent-minded woman.

Helen stayed in the Society, but her daughter dropped out. As Olive wrote rather wistfully in her December 1925 reply to Octavia: 'I was so thoroughly "in the Visitation". I have been able to think and talk of nothing else for ages – & with Leslie in it too, there seemed absolutely nothing wanting. (Leslie & I never talk of anything else but Bedford.)' Eight months later, on 15 September 1926, she and Leslie were married.

A month after the wedding, she wrote to Octavia: 'I have gone directly against your wishes by marrying, but it was done with the confirmed knowledge that I was obeying God. It was a command from Him to both of us, & therefore nothing could stop us.' In the Panacea Society, obedience to the Centre, and not to one's own perceived messages from God, was mandatory. Olive and Leslie had gone against that, believing that 'we *know* for a fact that from babyhood we have been Divinely led – towards each other' and, as Olive put it, 'If I find through disobedience I have been cast right out, it will surprise, but not hurt me, nothing can do that now, because I know I have obeyed the *direct* commands of my God.' But they, especially Olive, *had* been hurt by Octavia: 'the instructions and messages we received from the Centre cut us like a whip', and this left them with 'mixed feelings towards the Faith'. But some aspects of the Panacea teaching remained central for them, not least the quest for perfection and immortality, now refashioned by Olive and Leslie in their own image. Olive wrote that they were pioneering a celibate marriage, hoping to 'perfect themselves up to the point where we may create by the power of Thought and Prayer alone'. As to the Levitical laws, which Octavia had instructed them to keep, 'If we were to lower ourselves, even to the Levitical Laws, we should expect to die on the instant! But as we do not intend to die & we have proved there is no sex in our natures, we really have no fear.'[33] Ironically, Olive claimed to have achieved what her mother had so long desired: freedom from sexual intercourse in marriage. Olive closed the letter by asking what position she now held in the Panacea Society; Octavia replied that she could at least keep on taking the water, for 'to do that you need not believe in what I say'.[34]

The exchange between Olive Morris and Octavia represented in microcosm a much bigger conflict that was to arise over questions of marriage, also shot through with questions of obedience and jealousy, just a few months later. At just the moment when Octavia and the Divine Mother were focused on the non-resident members and the many letters they were writing about their 'sex-relations', the community was unexpectedly rocked from within. In 1926, Octavia's best friend, one of the founding members of the community and an apostle, Kate Firth, fell in love.

IO

Don't Fall in Love

In November 1925, at just the moment when Emily Carew-Hunt was writing to Octavia about the 'sex question', a man with the unlikely name of Leonard Squire Tucker arrived at the Society. He had been taking the healing water for his kidney trouble and rheumatism since July that year, and had visited in September. He moved into 24 Rothsay Road, one of the recently acquired community houses, on 19 November, rather inauspiciously a couple of weeks after kissing had been forbidden in the community. He described himself as an 'artist, student, psychologist, occultist', the grandson of a well-known healer, Mrs Bertha Squires, drawn to practise healing himself. He was the son of a spiritualist medium, also named Bertha, and a 'chemical' or manure merchant named George.[1] He had been born and grown up in Edmonton, north-east London, which was not a rich part of town.[2] By his early twenties, he was working as a clerk, like his older brothers,[3] and before the war, he had run a photography business, the Connaught Studio, in Connaught House at Marble Arch in London, trading under the name S. Leo.[4] After fighting in the war, he had lost his business and had been reduced to working night shifts in a menial job. He was 'daily contacting the God consciousness for guidance & direction in my affairs in order that I may be ready for the immense events upon which this world is entering'. He had read widely in esoteric and heterodox religious writings, as well as psychology. In short, he was a religious seeker of just the sort drawn to the Society, and his daily life and work were unsatisfactory to him: he wanted a better life. He sought it in the Bedford community, and shared their belief in the Second Coming of Christ.[5]

In early January 1926, a few weeks after he had arrived, Octavia asked him to sing at the Society's party later that month, and he had to practise the music with Kate Firth, the pianist for the evening. Kate soon fell for him, recording in her diary that he had a beautiful voice and it was a great treat. He also recited for her – ' he must have been wonderful before the War,' she wrote poignantly[6] – and stayed until 11 p.m. talking with her, after the others in the house had gone to bed. He was of average height, good looking, with thick blond hair, and he was a rarity in the Panacea Society: an eligible, middle-aged man – he was forty-six when he met Kate, thirteen years her junior. At one level, this was the story of a fifty-nine-year-old widow finding love in later life. In the world, it would have been a matter for rejoicing; in the Society, it was a serious problem. At another level, it was a story of one member's simmering jealousy and suppressed doubts finally emerging, seven years after Octavia's identity as Shiloh had been confirmed. It is a story that reveals the ways in which members were encouraged to spy on one another, and the ways in which that broke trust in the community. And finally, it is a story that tells us how the Society appeared to a sceptical newcomer entering it.

A few days after the January party, Octavia received news that the London address which the Society had used since its inception for initial enquirers – so that the Society's location would remain secret unless someone were serious about joining – could no longer be used for any of their correspondence. She did not want to use her own address, preferring to keep her anonymity. Worried about what to do, she went to discuss the matter with her old friend Kate, who immediately offered not only her own address for all the Society's correspondence, but also several rooms in the house itself for the Society's activities. Handily, the Lord confirmed this decision in the Script that Octavia received that night. Hitherto, Octavia's own home had been used as the headquarters. Kate's home, The Haven, which she had bought in 1923, was large and substantially grander than Octavia's and was located on Newnham Road, which ran parallel to Albany Road, where Octavia lived. Octavia's garden and the Garden Room (chapel) backed on to The Haven's garden, so that the two were connected, and members would sometimes gather in The Haven garden for informal social occasions.

The use of The Haven for society business was to have several consequences over the next few months. The first was that Leonard Squire Tucker was put to work in one of the rooms set aside as an office there almost immediately, so that he and Kate began to have daily contact. They also began to see each other socially, singing and playing the piano together in the evenings, and going to cultural events in the town, such as the opera *Faust*. Within a couple of weeks, this was causing comment. In an interview with the Divine Mother on 24 January Kate was instructed not to go out with him alone, as it might cause comment. Four days later, the Divine Mother told her off for making arrangements for Mr Squire Tucker's working conditions in The Haven without consulting her. Kate noted in her diary that she 'felt tearful about it all' but this did not stop her from inviting Mr Squire Tucker over to supper two days later when her son Geoff, an audit clerk with a London accountancy firm, was home for the weekend; they sang songs together and 'Geoff did some of his comic things'. The consequence, the next day, was that she received another scolding from the Divine Mother. She wrote in her diary, 'I know she is right, but O it is difficult to overcome my weakness etc, and it will be another fight.'[7]

It was indeed to be a fight and, very quickly, Kate's doubts about the whole Visitation enterprise – first expressed in her sceptical reply to Ellen Oliver seven years earlier, when Ellen had suggested Mabel might be Shiloh – began to re-emerge. It was one thing to be scolded by the Divine Mother; quite another to be told off by Octavia who was, at some level, still her old friend Mabel. When she and Octavia had the first of several arguments about Mr Squire Tucker in early February, Kate wrote in her diary: 'It is all very upsetting and it brought back some of the old antagonistic and contrary thoughts.' Meanwhile, the Divine Mother and Octavia were also warning Mr Squire Tucker not to have favourites amongst the members.

The result of the Divine Mother's and Octavia's warnings was, of course, that Kate and Leonard were thrown together as co-conspirators, rather in the way that young people, whose parents disapprove of their romance, become more determined to proceed with it. Precisely because of this interference, the relationship hurtled along, flourishing with surprising speed. Kate and Leonard would sit next to each other in the chapel services and exchange news on what had been said to them, or they would meet furtively in a café in town. For by now, they felt they were being watched. Already by early February Kate was writing in her diary, 'Felt very nervy [in the chapel service] as I know Octavia had her eye on me and was on the strain, also on Mr S. It is a wretched state of affairs and so awkward for us both and it makes us feel so unnatural.' And then, a few days later: 'I am having a miserable time as I feel there is some spying going on and it makes me un-natural.' The Divine Mother claimed to be omniscient: in reality, Emily Goodwin required all members to spy on each other and report to her about what they observed was going on in the community. Out for a walk one afternoon together, Kate and Leonard bumped into Alice Jones; Kate wrote that she feared 'the worst now' and felt under great strain in the chapel service that evening.[8] She also felt that her servant, Amy Smart, was being asked to report on her activities, and this was especially galling as there was a long history of tension between the two of them.

Intertwined with Kate and Leonard's mutual attraction was Leonard's scepticism about the Society's claims, and his ability to tap into Kate's doubts, which had lain dormant for several years. In mid-February, about six weeks after their initial meeting, they had a conversation in a café in town in which Leonard confided his views of the Visitation to Kate. At that point, she was still confident enough in her own beliefs to write in her diary: 'He told me much that surprised me about his views of the Visitation and I see he will have to change them considerably if he remains here.' A few days later, in another café conversation, Leonard's articulation of his doubts began to unsettle her, raising 'all the old fears etc' and the next day she wrote, 'I fear he will go out of the Visitation as he cannot accept much that he is told. I wonder what will be the end!' Kate could 'feel a storm brewing'. The question was: when the storm broke, what would her position be and what would she do? Would she stay with the Society of which she had been a founding member and in which she had lived for seven years, or would she go with the man to whom she was becoming closer, not least because of the atmosphere of spying and suspicion that was unwittingly throwing them together?

The choice was not straightforward for Kate, torn between old loyalties and new romance; between the comfort of the familiar and old doubts that her new friend was stirring up again. She was anxious and unsettled, sleeping badly and fearful about the future. 'O how I pray that God will hear our prayers and prove quickly the truth or error of this great work,' she wrote in her diary at the end of February.[9] She also missed her sister, Hettie, who had died just four days before Leonard came into the Society, on 15 November 1925. And as she grieved, she remembered that Hettie had largely broken free of the Society, finding happiness in a second marriage. Hettie had been a founding member and apostle, but while travelling around the country to various spas for her health, at the middle-class seaside resort of Southport in Lancashire she had met Charles Ashton. In late 1923, she had married him in Wharfedale, Yorkshire, close to the area where she and Kate had grown up, and had 'moved away from Bedford permanently.[10]

Leonard was much more sure about what he was doing: within weeks of arriving in Bedford he had decided the whole Visitation was nonsense, and he was out to prove it. His particular target was Emily Goodwin in her guise as the Divine Mother. He began to tell all sorts of lies to the Divine Mother to catch her out, confessing things that he had not done, and omitting things which he had, and she 'took it all in'.[11] Shortly after his arrival he had decided that she was a fraud, relying on others for all her knowledge: 'The weakest feature in the "Divinity" claim is that the Divine Mother never appears to be cognisant of the thoughts and desires in the minds of her followers & has to rely entirely upon what she is told audibly & every thing therefore has to be *voiced* before her.'[12] But for Leonard, with his spiritualist background, the Divine Mother was not just a fraud but also, he believed, controlled by an evil spirit. In focusing on the Divine Mother, Leonard appealed to Kate's dislike of the Divine Mother whom she found terrifying, and who persecuted her – 'I did not know what I had done wrong to be so severely treated'.[13] Kate felt the harshness of the Divine Mother particularly at that time when she was still grieving the loss of her sister. Furthermore, the Divine Mother would not allow her to see a doctor for her eye, which was giving her daily, acute pain.

In his criticism of the Society, Leonard was supported by Kate's son, Geoffrey, who was often in Bedford at weekends; he had become a sealed member in 1921 but had had his suspicions about the Society for a while, though had gone along with it for his mother's sake. Exactly a year earlier, Geoffrey had encountered his own problems with love, sex and the Society. He had been boarding in London in the house of a Mrs Isa Agate, an unhappily married woman whose husband – an alcoholic and a spendthrift – was living in Morocco. She had poured her heart out to Geoffrey – 'having reached the limit of human endurance and suffering' – who had introduced her to Panacea teachings, which she had embraced enthusiastically.[14] The inevitable happened and they fell in love. For a while, they had tried to keep it from both the Divine Mother and Octavia and believed they could manage their feelings for each other, but they eventually gave into their desire and felt compelled to confess it. Octavia and the Divine Mother made it clear that the sexual relationship could not go on, and the question was whether Geoffrey and Isa would be allowed to remain friends. Geoffrey was intensely worried that, if such a continuing friendship were not permitted, Mrs Agate would have to go out of the Visitation and lose all contact with those who had been supporting her. Both he and Mrs Agate wrote a spirited defence of their capacity to give up their 'intimate affections' and responsibly remain friends. Isa Agate wrote to Octavia, 'Now I ask you once more to leave it to us. I have never yet failed to see a thing done, that I was determined to be done, and I am jolly well going to see this affair through.' At that point in her writing of the letter she dramatically fainted, and Geoffrey had to finish the letter for her hurriedly in pencil.[15] Geoffrey and Isa were, in the end, allowed to remain friends but the episode was a reminder to Geoffrey that obedience was always required and, further, that Octavia could make anything relate back to her and her suffering. Struggling with their feelings for each other, they were compelled to take account of Octavia's feelings too. Isa Agate wrote to Octavia: 'it was only our anxiety to save you suffering that made us refrain from coming to you some little time ago, but we thrashed the matter out ourselves and undertook to put our backs into the big fight'. She also tried to wrest back the role of the suffering one from Octavia. 'I am deeply grieved that you have had this additional trouble on account of Geoffrey and I, I would have done anything to have spared you this and since knowing how worried you have been, I seem to have gone right back to where I was, and can neither eat nor sleep. I am dreadfully unhappy.'[16]

Geoffrey therefore had real compassion for what his mother was going through and he was worried about her. He had had his faith in the Panacea Society's doctrines and practices shaken by Leonard too. One day, he went into a church in London, and prayed: 'O God I demand a proof whether this thing is evil.'[17] By the end of February, Geoffrey, Kate and Leonard were engaged in long conversations about what to do. Kate felt that 'everything is known and that the D.M. is waiting for me to make a move'. The only question now was *when* the crisis would come. A relatively new member, Miss Emma Craig, who had come up for a visit from Eastbourne, had been told by another resident member that Kate 'had to be watched'; on 2 March she came over to Kate's house to give her a singing lesson and confirmed to Kate, who she saw was troubled, that the community was spying on her.[18] Believing it was unsafe to venture out, and compelled to stay in her house the next day, Kate felt it was all 'simply hateful and could not go on much longer'. Leonard sent a telegram to Geoffrey who arrived the next morning, clutching a letter from his old friend Adrian Barltrop in India, who had decided the whole Visitation was wrong. After a disastrous visit to Bedford in 1924, Adrian was now giving up any last vestiges of belief in the Visitation. He, like Leonard, was particularly suspicious of the claims that Emily Goodwin was the Instrument of the Divine Mother. This letter was, for Kate, 'wonderful proof that this Visitation is not what we think it' and the final impetus for her to speak out at the worship meeting that night, supported by Leonard, Geoffrey and Miss Craig, 'a little brick and a staunch friend.'[19]

So nervous about the inevitable conflict that she feared she might die suddenly, and yet determined to speak up and break the terrible tension of the preceding days, Kate went over to the Garden Room for the worship service and, before Octavia read the daily script, stood up to speak. It was significant that Kate took the initiative. Three years earlier, Octavia had tricked Edgar Peissart into going to the Garden Room, where she and the Divine Mother had confronted him. On this occasion, Octavia and the Divine Mother were not in control. Kate, agitated but determined to continue with her speech, said that she could not go on bearing things; that she had tried to Overcome and it was too hard for her and she had been terrified; and she had decided to leave the Visitation. When Kate denounced the Society and announced her decision to leave, a terrible scene ensued in which Octavia wept, and the Divine Mother seemed bereft of her usual power. One member, Irene Mellor, writing an account of the evening's events, said that Kate's speech 'came as a bombshell to everyone' and that 'the whole affair was so rapid in movement' and everyone present was 'thunderstruck & appalled by what had happened'. After Kate had spoken, Geoffrey also announced his decision to leave the

Visitation, and Leonard got up, 'white with passion' and 'very dramatic', to state that 'he had no time for the Visitation, and it was utterly untrue in every way'. Irene Mellor wrote that 'he levelled all his terrible railing at the Divine Mother' and demanded that she show her power. All three declared that they had no quarrel with Octavia, but it was '"that entity" behind her . . . of whom they were terrified'.[20]

Afterwards, Octavia asked to speak to Kate alone, 'for the sake of a long friendship', while Geoffrey and Leonard went back to The Haven. Octavia gave her a cup of the Blessed Water to drink and prayed for her repentance. According to Irene Mellor's account, Kate was finally constrained to state that 'she hoped the Visitation was true'. It was, for Kate, 'the most strenuous day of my life' and, after the confrontation, she felt her brain was dead. She arrived home exhausted but stayed up talking until after midnight with Leonard and Geoffrey about what they should do next.[21]

Two agonised and agonising sleepless nights later, Kate got up early in the morning, full of joy. The scales had completely fallen from her eyes: the Visitation *was* 'awful', and she now believed that her deliverance from it was great. She had made the choice to be with Leonard: 'It is heavenly to be with him and to know that we shall continue to be together, and my heart and soul simply shout with praise and thanksgiving.' She returned her seal, the sign of her Society membership, to Miss Green, who was very frosty. That night, free from the dietary strictures of the community, as a symbol of their liberation from community life, they had 'ham – the first for 3 years, we all enjoyed it thoroughly and I feel fed'. Their sense of release was palpable. Geoffrey spoke of how free he felt at last, and how happy he was that 'once more I have a personality of my own'.[22]

She and Leonard had decided that their new mission was to stop the Visitation, and to rescue those who had been trapped by it. And they began to have seances to get in touch with Mrs Tucker (Leonard's mother), Hettie (Kate's sister) and Harry (Kate's first husband who had died in 1905) who 'are going to help us in the great work of stopping the visitation, so we shall be guided'. But before embarking on that 'great work', they felt they needed to get away from Bedford for a holiday, and so they went off to London for a few days, where they dined well, went to the theatre every evening, and visited a famous medium named Mr Vango. Kate went to see an eye specialist, who told her that she had permanently lost the sight in her eye and that it might have to be removed to save her further suffering. While this was distressing news, it was also a vindication of her decision to leave the Society, which had prevented her from seeking the medical help that might have saved her sight much earlier. Finally, freed from the constraints of the inward-looking and ever-vigilant Bedford community, Leonard at last kissed Kate 'in the most lovely way', and she recorded in her diary, 'I feel sure he sees now where we must end and that we cannot do our great work without being united.'[23]

But things remained uncertain for some time. Was his primary interest in getting her out of the Bedford community or did he (also) love her? He might have kissed her but he had not proposed. She was certainly in love with him but was uncertain about how he felt, and her daily diary entries often ended with phrases such as 'I wish he would say something definite' and 'Oh how I love him'. Eventually, she decided to trust God, and her intuition told her that when the right time came she would have to take things into her own hands and steer the course she wanted. There was, however, the awkward question of money: he had none; she had some. She had inherited some money from Hettie, and when that came through in April, it was more than she expected and she was able to give Leonard £30 to start a bank account. This seems to have helped, and her diary entry for that evening notes, 'L. came to say good night, and was especially loving. Bless him!'[24] Her diary ends in early August so we do not know whether she took the unconventional path and proposed to him, or whether he finally proposed to her, but they were married in Putney in London at the end of the year.[25]

While Kate was feeling liberated and was enjoying the early stages of being in love (even if it was sometimes agonising as well as blissful, as the first throes of love can so often be), for Octavia, back in Bedford, the agony had only just begun. Her best friend had betrayed her; she had been publicly humiliated in her chapel; and she had lost the large house that had so recently been put at her disposal for the Society's work. The practical matter had to be dealt with first. Kate's first act, after making her resignation speech in the worship meeting on 4 March, was to write to Octavia asking her to clear The Haven of all Society papers and books in one month's time. This was done immediately, long before the deadline – a ton of books was moved in two days –

and the Panacea office workers continued their daily duties at small tables in corners of other, smaller community houses owned by members (numbers 5 and 8 Albany Road). Yet more upsetting to Octavia was the request from Kate, sent via a lawyer's letter, that the openings between the Society's property and The Haven were to be bricked up. For Octavia, who never went more than 77 paces from her house, this represented a serious loss of space (and view), and the loss of part of the Garden of Eden, and it was thus a very severe blow. In May, the faithful Peter Rasmussen duly bricked up the openings, using cement made with the blessed water. For good measure, the assembled members threw a spider (a sign of poison) into The Haven's garden and gathered in the Garden Room (now bricked up on one side) to sing the hymn 'Jerusalem the Golden'.[26]

Octavia made theological sense of what had happened in the way she knew best: by casting the figures that surrounded her back into the biblical narrative, and giving the happenings in the community cosmic significance. The scriptures had to be enacted there and then. The events of 4 March were interpreted as a replaying of the Fall. Kate had been tempted by the 'beast' or Antichrist (Leonard), as only 'the most foolish, vain, ambitious & most unscrupulous woman' would have been. In contrast with the Daughter (Octavia) 'who knows practically nothing – but has the gift for you all', Kate who was an apostle in the Society had 'the highest opportunities to learn wisdom' and threw it all away. Having set up their paradise in Bedford, having rediscovered the Garden of Eden (Genesis 1), the Panaceans now *had* to experience the Fall (Genesis 2); so it all had to be, just as the episode with Edgar Peissart had to be, in that case so that the Divine Mother could emerge.[27] March 4, the day when Kate Firth stood up in chapel and announced that she was leaving, therefore marked the beginning of War in Heaven, which meant 'contentions and fallings away in the Society itself'.[28] The events that followed were, as Rachel Fox put it, 'ravages in her [Octavia's] paradise, caused by the unfaithfulness of one whom she had trusted implicitly'. But the Divine Mother reassured Octavia that her Jerusalem had to experience desolation, just as the ancient city of Jerusalem had.

In the face of this, members were exhorted to remain firm in their belief and be more obedient than ever before. As Octavia put it in the preface to one of the scripts: 'Now I ask that all of the sixty-six [the inner circle] will stand firm and unmovable. Neither prayer nor sympathy are any good. All you can do is be loyal, contented and obedient.' Members were to 'consolidate under the *Most Highest*'. They were to realise fully their part in the cosmically significant events that were taking place daily in their midst. 'You are not to be any longer as merely people "following the Woman" or "on Octavia's side." No, that is too small. You are the children of the Great I AM, sent down to form the Kingdom, THE Garden, Paradise on Earth – and I, the Daughter, am with you on the side of the Great Father and Mother.' In a telling phrase, Octavia commanded members to 'Think Imperially'.[29]

Later in that year, 1926, Octavia drew a parallel between recent national and community events as she so often did. Deeply opposed to the General Strike, which began just two months after Kate's dramatic exit from the Society, Octavia believed that standing firm was essential in both cases, and that the Panaceans' actions could affect the nation's welfare. A week into the General Strike she wrote, 'I am more than ever convinced that our warfare and the nation's warfare must go on side by side, that all depends upon our standing firm and immovable – not truckling to intimidation and exhortation – and . . . I want all here to examine themselves on the matter of firmness and firmlessness.'[30]

The Panaceans were commanded to examine themselves often, and to confess more frequently, just as they had been exhorted to do three years earlier, after the Edgar Peissart episode. There was a drive to make members pure. 'Voice and voice and voice again your remaining frailties at your bedside and use the Power to overcome them.'[31] In particular, members were urged to confess their sexual past and their current desires. One confession in particular threw light on Kate's behaviour and reiterated that her questions about the Society and Octavia's leadership went back to its beginnings. A confession made by Alice Jones suggests that Kate used Alice's 'crush' on her, when Alice first arrived in 1920, to try and take some of the authority for herself. Alice confessed 'an entirely sensual affection' for Kate, drawn to her 'wonderful gift of prayer'. At a little tea that Kate had hosted for Ellen Oliver, Alice Jones and Gertrude Searson, Kate suggested that Octavia was making a mistake by not letting her exercise this gift more fully in the Society's worship, and that they would not be doing

right by Octavia herself if they did not tell her so. Alice, as a consequence, spoke to Octavia about Kate's wish to exercise this gift, and ✓
this seems to have been manipulated by Kate. Horrified, and with the
benefit of hindsight, Alice stated that at no time had it ever entered
into her head to compare Kate with Octavia 'as possibly being equal
to or any thing in opposition to her' or imagine that Kate was anything
other than 'one of us helping Octavia'.[32] Reading this confession of
events that had happened in 1920 reminds us of Kate Firth's negative
reply to Ellen Oliver's Valentine's Day 1919 letter, and Kate's resistance to Mabel's leadership from the very beginning, especially to the
idea of her as Shiloh.

Was Kate Firth seething with jealousy and resentment for years
after Mabel had been named Shiloh? Or did she make a bid for power
in 1919–20, fail in her bid, and then accept the situation? Did her resentments only re-emerge when she met a person with whom she could
be truly intimate – Leonard – who also perceived her doubts and fed
them or, at the least, encouraged her to voice them? Certainly, after
she had left the Society, her resentments against Octavia all came
tumbling out: that the Visitation was practically started with her
money; that Octavia admitted being jealous of her; that Octavia was
at heart mean and admitted it; that Kate had difficulty in accepting
Octavia's claim to be Shiloh; that Octavia 'in anything she was interested in, must take the lead and be top or nothing at all'. And she had
another set of resentments about how little she was allowed to do in
the Society. Although she was a good chairwoman, she was told her
capacities were useless; she was not allowed to arrange flowers
although she had a natural gift for it; she had taken over addressing
a very tricky audience at the Church Congress in Bournemouth (a
Church of England meeting) from Alice Jones, at Alice's request, and
had done a good job of it, but had been reprimanded for doing so by
the Divine Mother on her return to Bedford; the amount of money
she was allowed to spend on housekeeping was not enough; she was
scolded for things she had not done and was constantly told that the
things she did or said were wrong. All of these resentments were
stored up over seven years, the put-downs – and thus the resentments
– becoming worse from 1923, after Emily Goodwin's manifestation as
the Divine Mother. Kate drew a picture of community life in which
members were constantly denigrated.[33]

In Leonard, Kate met someone who also wanted a role, and who would not stand for being put down; certainly he wanted to do far more than either Octavia or Emily Goodwin would let him do in the Panacea Society. In his early correspondence with the Society, before going to Bedford, he had written: 'For a very long time I have felt intuitively that I had been spared through the 4 years of war for "*Something*" but I have not been able to discover what', though he spent much time exploring many different religious and moral traditions, believing that he was thus developing his spiritual wisdom. He was, therefore, shocked, and felt conflicted when he read in *The Panacea* editorials 'a condemnation of the whole gamut of my past studies and spiritualist experiences'. He felt that his family had received much help and 'heaven sent advice' via his mother, a spiritualist medium; and he believed that his grandmother's healing ministry had been in the tradition of Jesus' own healing mission. Both his mother and grandmother had healed through breathing on pieces of flannel (strangely prefiguring Octavia's own healing method) and he believed the healing gift had been passed on to him. Furthermore, psychology was 'being taught and understood & used to benefit and uplift the human race causing them to "think" & think rightly, & consequently "DO" rightly'. Octavia renounced all other religious groups, healing ministries and the role of psychology in modern life, and she commanded her followers to do likewise. Just over a month after writing of his own call and spiritual knowledge, Leonard was testifying to the success of the healing water, and was willing to be signed up to the Panacea Society 'as a very solid Brick in the Tower of Refuge'.[34] But he came to Bedford with the hope of being able to assist with the healing, and that was never to be.

Leonard could not and did not permanently give up all past teachings and competing religious beliefs, as Panacea members were told to do. In fact, he used his past spiritual experiences as the means by which to measure and judge the Society. It was not just that he thought the Panacea Society was wrong or fraudulent in its claims; he also thought it was being influenced by evil spirits. After returning to The Haven from their holiday in London, Leonard and Kate planned to set up a healing ministry, not least to free the inner circle of Panaceans from the satanic grip holding them in Bedford. Leonard took to wearing a clerical garment – a black cassock – around the place, and built an altar in his bedroom at The Haven, at which he prayed that all might be shown the truth. Mixed with their desire for a more significant role were Kate's resentments, not least that she had unnecessarily lost her sight in one eye. In discussion with Rachel Fox she said that she had told the London specialist about the Panacea treatment, and that 'I should never rest day or night till the Society was rooted up & would willingly suffer the loss of an eye & disfigurement possibly if I could bring the 33 [one of the inner circles at the Panacea Society] out of this sink of iniquity.' She told Rachel that she [Kate] was the greatest danger to the Panacea Society 'because God has through it all kept a little bit of me which was not completely under Octavia'. She went on: 'I, as you know, helped to found it and I shall work to turn it over. All my plans are made and in six months you won't hear any more of the Panacea Society!'[35]

Octavia was perfectly aware that Kate and Leonard represented a danger. They had already gathered around them others who were discontented: Miss Craig and a married couple, Mr and Mrs Gardner. All three left after Kate resigned from the Society, and Kate and Leonard claimed that there were others who wanted to leave but could not afford to do so, such as Mr Boddington, the head of the Protection Department, who 'if he had a hundred pounds to his name would not put up with it a day longer'.[36] Leonard described the Society as a place for 'old people and cripples and feeble-minded'. He was sharply observant, rather cruelly perceiving Octavia's snobbery by commenting to Amy Smart, Kate's servant at The Haven: 'O, dear no, it takes a good income and some position to be adopted by *this* God.' Leonard focused on the absurdity of the Society's claims, regarding it at some level as 'a perfect scream'.[37] In 1927 he wrote up some notes for a newspaper article that would expose the Society, though the article was never written. The thrust of his criticism was that the Society was making blasphemous claims when it said that Emily Goodwin was the Divine Mother; that Octavia – who was simply mad, having been in a lunatic asylum – was the daughter of God; and that Arthur Barltrop had been, as a priest, one of the three manifestations of Christ. His greatest wrath was reserved for the Divine Mother, who at times 'becomes fierce and even abusive when annoyed & frequently issues commands for people to do the very thing they most dislike, in order to enforce absolute & slavish obedience'.[38]

Kate and Leonard's claims that they would bring down the Society came to naught. It was deeply uncomfortable living in Bedford so close to the Society's headquarters, especially bumping into the Panaceans – Kate's old friends – who would bow and then walk on, which, as Geoffrey put it, 'gives the impression that they are acting under instruction'. They loved having the house to themselves once again, and Geoffrey wrote of having 'a real home once more', but they did not stay there long.[39] In early August 1926 they moved to London. Using a London agent, the Society bought The Haven that very same month. The Panaceans seemed to think that Kate had no idea what was going on; but Kate's diary makes it clear that she was well aware that Octavia wanted to buy it, and – with what may have been a residual nostalgic affection for the Society – she was not displeased about it. The bricks came down, and the gardens were re-joined. The Haven was once again used for the Society's work; its Blue Room – a lovely, light-filled room looking out on to the gardens – became the main meeting room for the Society, and the gardens were used for tea parties and other more informal social gatherings. Eden was restored to the Panaceans. They had 'entered into possession of the Estate of Jerusalem'. The first person to be sealed in the newly restored Blue Room was Helen Shepstone's son, and it was felt to be 'a striking event'.[40] Helen Shepstone was, of course, accepted by the Panacea Society as their seventh prophet.

Octavia still feared the threat of Kate, who was out there in the world. She made it clear to members that they were to have no communication with either Kate or Leonard – and to report to her if either of them made any contact. When she found out that Mr and Mrs Gardner – recently sealed, but regarded as potentially important members because Mr Gardner was an Anglican priest – had heard from Kate Firth and had not reported it to her, she wrote them a furious letter berating them for their disloyalty. She also noted that they were not progressing in the healing, and should therefore pay attention 'to their inner life and to their relations with the Centre'. Mrs Gardner wrote a spirited defence, saying that she regretted Octavia's presumption that she and her husband were disloyal and that she had made it a rule for many years never to show her correspondence to a third person. She also stated that she sympathised with Kate Firth, but 'certainly not with the man who has been her undoing'. By mid-July both she and her husband had decided to leave. Mr Gardner wrote to Miss Green: 'since my visit to Bedford in Jan. last I have had grave doubts about the authority which you recognise as speaking through Mrs Goodwin, and I have found it increasingly difficult to swallow much of the teaching which you at Headquarters seem able to accept so readily'. Mrs Gardner went for a further visit to Bedford on 11 July where she had an interview with the Divine Mother, and then wrote to say that she had made her decision to leave during that interview. They received a very cutting reply from Miss Green: 'One naturally regrets the amount of time and sympathy spent over such a case, but of course in an enormous affair like this, it is unavoidable that there should be some occasional waste.'[41]

No disloyalty could be countenanced. Any last remaining vestiges of friendship with Kate were to cease. To this end Octavia provided a new interpretation of Jesus' edict to forgive your enemies: no forgiveness should be given if they were *God's* enemies. And clearly Kate and Leonard were that for the Panaceans. Octavia and Emily Goodwin remained obsessed with Kate's fate. In August – coincidentally, just as they were buying The Haven – they sent Kate a message from the 'Divine Mother' trying to get her back into the Society by playing on her fears. Geoffrey Firth replied on Kate's behalf reminding Octavia – now significantly addressed as Mrs Barltrop – that it was a serious legal offence to threaten a person, and simply stating of the message itself that 'it would be an insult to God to dare to imagine for one moment that it is of divine origin'.[42] The fact was that Kate's dramatic resignation had got under the skin of Octavia; it rankled with her, and she could not let it go. For seven years after they had left the Society, Emily Goodwin paid a member who lived in London, Geoffrey Reinli, to befriend and spy on them, sending in frequent reports. This he dutifully did until 1933.

Leonard wrote in again for the healing water in November 1927, and Kate followed in January 1928, writing that she had 'every faith in it both spiritually and physically'.[43] They never returned to Bedford but took the water sporadically, writing in to report on their health. We do not know what caused the change of heart. But the same month that Leonard wrote to ask for the Panacea healing, there was an article about his own healing ministry in *The Rally*, a Higher Thought magazine. Leonard ran his healing ministry at the Higher Thought centre, the Rendo, on Denmark Street, near Tottenham Court Road in London, every Monday afternoon. He claimed to be a natural healer – healing being one of the gifts of the Spirit – and to heal through blessing people and the laying on of hands, and he had written two small booklets on the subject: *Healing through Divine Laws* and *God's Divine Method of Healing*.[44]

How much was this a story of romance? It began with the emotional pull of an eligible man meeting an attractive widow when they were asked to sing together. They soon began to enjoy each other's company, but by that time Leonard had decided that the Panacea Society's claims were all a delusion: his scepticism quickly melded with Kate's long stored-up resentments. The attempt to control their behaviour, by both Octavia and the Divine Mother, merely drew them closer together. Kate found a confidant; someone to rescue her from a society about which she had always had some underlying doubts. She also found a companion after the death of her sister. In return, Leonard got himself a widow of some means. He had gone to Bedford to escape his menial job and find a better life. He managed just that. It was a story of love, especially on Kate's part, but also one of old jealousies, new doubts and the power of money. It was, most of all, a story of the tension between the inward-looking and intense life of the community and the pull of the world, a tension that Octavia's children felt more acutely than perhaps any of the other Panaceans, as we shall see.

II

Family Problems

At the height of Kate Firth's crisis of faith in 1926, it was a letter from Adrian Barltrop to Geoffrey Firth, quite out of the blue, that proved to be a turning point. Kate and Geoffrey regarded it as an answer to prayer. Adrian's news – that he had decided the whole Visitation was wrong and he could no longer accept it – gave them encouragement that, by leaving the Panacea Society, they were on the right path. Adrian had lost his faith in the Panacea beliefs when he visited Bedford in 1924, on leave from the army in India, and had found the revelations of 1923 too much to bear. He could not accept the idea of Emily Goodwin as the instrument of the Divine Mother – a stalling point for others too; but nor could he accept 'the Family Business', as he put it. This was an allusion to the other extraordinary idea that Octavia and her followers had come to accept as true in 1923: namely, that Arthur Barltrop, Adrian's father, had been Jesus. These revelations caused Adrian's loss of faith. If these two tenets were not true, he decided, 'the whole thing is not authentic'.[1] By May 1926, he had come to the certain decision that he no longer believed.

For a while after leaving, Adrian maintained that he had no hard feelings. He was not one of those members who had gone off 'in a huff', as he wrote to one Panacean in 1926.[2] This was, in fact, an allusion to Kate and Geoffrey, from whom he was keen to distance himself. Adrian, still loyal to his mother, told her that he thought Kate and Geoffrey Firth 'queer people' and 'when I found that they were attempting to start a campaign against the Visitation from without by means of a Press Campaign, assisted by some "gentleman" (a word they love!), I wrote an extremely strong letter to Geoffrey Firth telling him very nearly exactly what I thought of him & his mother'. Adrian nevertheless still believed he had to resign his Panacea membership, even during the General Strike when industrial unrest was at its worst, revolution seemed probable and the millennium just around the corner to the politically conservative Adrian who still retained a millenarian mindset, believing that 'things will come to a climax in our time'. But he could not change his mind.[3] He continued to maintain that if he could believe, he would do so, because 'to take it just from a selfish point of view alone, look at the advantage it holds out'.[4] He considered the whole thing marvellous, but he had simply lost faith. He needed some proof to believe and, in the absence of any, he found he could not do so. Two years later, he had much more than a crisis of faith. He had a nervous breakdown. All of his feelings about his mother's peculiar religion came tumbling out.

In April 1928 Octavia received a letter from Adrian, announcing his impending marriage to Marjorie Ramsay, a twenty-three-year-old who had grown up in Australia, spent time in England and whom he had met when she was visiting her aunt in India. It was a difficult letter for Adrian to write. He had composed and torn up five other versions over the previous couple of months, and even now wondered whether he had done the right thing in posting it. The problem was that Panacea people did not marry. Adrian's news was a rude shock to his mother – not even the fact that he was marrying the daughter of *Sir* Herbert Ramsay made it all right. And as Adrian was, in the Panacea theological scheme, the grandson of God, his marriage was a very serious disappointment, not just to his mother, but also to the whole community.

Adrian had been away from home since the Panacea Society had started. After attending St John's Leatherhead, the school for clergy sons where his father had taught in the early 1880s before being ordained, at the age of eighteen in the middle of the war, in 1916, he had gone straight into the Indian army and received his commission in Queen Alexandra's Own Gurkha Rifles in 1918. He was awarded the Military Cross for leading his company forward with great dash under heavy artillery and machine-gun fire. Rather than come home, he remained in the Indian army, perhaps because he liked it, perhaps because it was the career he wanted, perhaps because it offered him a way of avoiding the religious society that was emerging from the parlour of his family home. Nevertheless, he became a Panacea member and even converted one of his colleagues, the enthusiastic Captain Richard Maguire at the Army Signal School in Kakul, Abbottabad. He believed he was a protected person, part of a chosen group, and so he put aside ideas of marriage and eagerly awaited the millennium.

In 1928, when he broke down emotionally and psychologically, he realised the extent to which his mother's new religion had affected his life, thoughts and outlook, despite his absence from Bedford. And he resented it. He wrote to his sister Dilys, 'I'm awfully sorry to have to say it but I've grown to simply hate the Visitation, because it has completely broken up our family life.' He wrote to his mother, more bitterly, 'I have had no mother & no religion to all intents & purposes . . . since I left school.' He rued the day that she had heard of Joanna Southcott 'because it deprived us both of our mother & our home'.[5] He begged his mother, if she had any doubts at all about the Visitation, 'to stop it all at once & get our dear little *home* going once more'. The very fact that he asked that shows how out of touch he was with his mother's daily life; how little he realised that she lived and breathed Panacea all day and every day, that her world was the community that she had formed. But he still longed for a home. 'For a man to have a *real* "home" to turn to is the best thing to keep him straight.' The difficulty of having lost his father at the age of ten, and having an absent or religiously absorbed (one might say obsessed) mother – who had been in a lunatic asylum during his last year at school and as he entered the army – began to dawn on him. He saw that without a mother or father when he was a teenager, he had been left too much to himself at an impressionable age, had got into the habit of intro-spection and had ever since been prone to worry.[6]

As the founding members enthused about how wonderful their new community was in 1919, they spared little thought for the family at 12 Albany Road who had to deal with their home becoming its headquarters. The Panacea members, in thrall to Octavia, simply marvelled at how she coped with it all. For the younger children, Dilys and Adrian, family life was especially difficult. The older boys, Eric and Ivan, largely avoided it. The oldest, Eric, did not live to see his mother declare herself the daughter of God. He was away at boarding school (also St John's Leatherhead) when their father died. He went to Queens' College, Cambridge after school – where he made his mark in rowing rather than scholastic achievements though was granted a BA degree after he left, in 1915 – and then entered the East Anglian Royal Signallers, went to fight in the war in November 1914, and was made lieutenant in 1915. He fought at Gallipoli, went to Egypt and got typhoid and was sent home – though at this time his mother was still in St Andrew's – and then volunteered for the Royal Flying Corps, which desperately needed officers. He received his pilot's certificate and was shot through the head and died instantly in April 1917, aged twenty-seven, during an engagement with a German aeroplane.

Ivan went to Bedford Grammar School, not to boarding school, but then followed Eric to Queens' College, Cambridge, where he too rowed enthusiastically and also managed to get a BA degree. Like Eric, he seems to have had no particular enthusiasm for religion in college: the Queens' College magazine of this period mentions neither of the young men in its reports of Christian Union activities, theology discussion groups or missions to the college's settlement house in London. Graduating in 1914, Ivan went into the Royal Engineers and straight to war where he was eventually made a major. He stayed in the army until February 1920 when he was twenty-eight years old. On leaving the army, he married Violet Schvener in St Oswald's Church in Edinburgh on 20 February, and they moved to Canada in March.[7] They lived first in Medicine Hat, Alberta, where their son John was born in 1922, and then in British Columbia where Ivan worked for the government as an assistant superintendent in the Public Utilities Commission. He solved the problem of his mother's religion by getting away as fast as he could and never coming back to England.[8]

Adrian and Dilys were the ones who had to bear the psychological burden of their mother's religion. Adrian, although he was far away for much of the time, remained consistently agonised by it. In 1928, his discomfort and grief about his robbed childhood and teenage years came to a head when he met and fell in love with Marjorie Ramsay and realised he had no real family home to take her back to, and that his mother would have no pride in his marriage and little if any interest in her daughter-in-law. He implored his mother to 'take a motherly interest in a son's marriage & tell me how proud you are that in spite of all my difficulties I have captured such a charming girl & how pleased you are that I am to be married'.[9] Both Octavia and Dilys did write to Marjorie, but they did not take the interest that Adrian so desperately wanted. Several months later, he wrote to Major Carew-Hunt, now a resident member of the Society: 'The fact that one's people do not want one to get married makes it all seem rather an unnatural business, whereas it is the most natural thing imaginable.'[10]

It is no surprise that deciding to marry Marjorie brought things to a head. How do you tell your fiancée that your mother thinks she is the daughter of God? Sensibly, Adrian did not tell her, at least not until they were married and about to visit England. He merely mentioned that his mother was the head of a religious movement. To Marjorie's aunt in Lansdowne in northern India, he felt obliged to explain 'that Mother is really a religious maniac in a sense, but that she is otherwise quite normal', though he did not explain who his mother thought she was nor the doctrines of the Visitation. He saw no purpose in saying more than he thought was required.[11]

Meeting Marjorie also made him rue much of what he had done in his youth, and he blamed the Panacea religion for it. He felt that he had run riot for thirteen years, living a very much more sinful life than the average man, though he spared his mother the details in his letter. Believing that the millennium would come and he would never reach the age of thirty, he had lived on the principle of eat, drink and be merry, with little regard for his body or fitness and certainly no interest in saving money for marriage and a family. If he sinned, he could simply confess it when he got home, and he could even believe that his sin was the devil's fault. While the strict Panacea practices made most members strive for perfection, Adrian saw the frequent confessions as an escape clause for high living.

Initially thinking he had heart trouble, he took leave in Kashmir with a friend and collapsed. A sensible doctor told him there was nothing wrong and he should not worry. His complaint was merely a nervous one, his activities as a young man normal and not dissolute. Gradually he recovered, and made his way back to the army base and to Marjorie, realising 'to the full what an exceedingly lucky man I am to be getting married to a girl like Marjorie'. He felt 'like a man who started drowning in 1920 and got deeper and deeper into the mire, and who has suddenly been rescued'.[12] Having someone else to think about lessened his introspection, but he was still profoundly anxious about what was going on in Bedford. Reading through his letters in the Panacea archive for the first time in 2006, his daughter Anna shrewdly observed that he was fighting wars on two fronts: not only in India in the army but also on the home front.

Adrian did not give up wanting a relationship with his mother. He wrote, 'Please never think you have lost me, mother dear, this is impossible & you can always rely on me for help.' He persisted in hoping that she might show some real interest in his life as he had chosen to live it, and he enthused to her about how wonderful Marjorie was and how happy he was to be marrying her, but he came to recognise that his mother was 'so completely wrapt in the Visitation & thinks of little else'.[13] It was hard to get through to her, especially when there were so many dutiful Panaceans willing to intercept her post to prevent her from being upset by an 'unpleasant' letter. He had himself been dogged by concern for her mental health since his childhood (he was just eight when she first went into a lunatic asylum) and now he worried that the news of his impending marriage and total rejection of the Visitation would cause her to have another mental breakdown. Sometimes, when writing about his marriage plans, he sent letters to Dilys and asked her to judge whether they should be passed on to their mother. And then there was Mrs Goodwin, the Divine Mother, presiding over everyone, giving reasons for everything. Her role as intermediary distressed Adrian, as it had upset others before and would upset others in the future. As he expressed it to his mother, 'You will go straight to the D.M. with this letter, she will smile comfortably & say that she knew all about my sins. She will say that it had to be, I as the son *had* to go through this. For God's sake don't believe it.' On another occasion he wrote, 'She uses the same old platitudes as she has always used e.g. "all will come right." He pleaded with his mother to think for herself and stop being ruled 'by an old woman who hasn't the brains of a louse'.[14]

Adrian and Marjorie were married at St Mary's Church in Lansdowne in the autumn of 1928. Soon after, they spent six months on leave in Australia visiting Marjorie's family, and then arrived in Bedford in July 1929 for a six-month visit to England. Adrian was anxious ahead of time, and wrote several letters to Dilys about their mother's behaviour, which speak to his wish to impress Marjorie and his embarrassment about his mother, as well as his having inherited from his mother a rather nervous sense of social status combined with a keen wish to follow proper etiquette to offset that social anxiety. He had no qualms about his mother *socially* because 'I know she knows (after all; she taught us!) what to do.' But, he wrote to Dilys, there was one thing – 'an extremely small matter but a matter on which people often remark': she called a 'table napkin' a 'serviette', but this 'simply isn't done', as he had discovered when he went to India. If Mother still called it a 'serviette' might Dilys have a quiet word about it with her without mentioning him or his letter on the topic? He need not have worried: the injunction to call the item a napkin rather than a serviette was in the Society's Manners Paper. He was also hoping that he might be able to eat meat, as the Panacean vegetarian diet did not suit him. In another letter he asked Dilys to make sure Mother was 'natural' about everything as she was 'inclined to overdo things rather i.e. to apologise for things etc.', perhaps because 'she tried to create a good impression i.e. make things seem rather grand etc.' And then, finally, a third letter, a few days before they set sail, with 'just one more thing'. He asked Dilys to 'try and get mother not to talk too much about the House & how well she has furnished it etc etc.' When people talk about it, they 'take all the gilt of [sic] it. Far better to let people notice how nice it is & to let them take it more as a matter of course.' He claimed that 'nothing really matters as far as Marjorie is concerned' and he was not going to be 'nervous of what mother will say' but his letters suggest otherwise. Perhaps, having spent time with Marjorie's family in Australia, he was keenly aware not just of the religious peculiarities of his own surviving parent, but also of his very ordinary middle-class background. One can detect in between the lines the nervous son, bringing his new bride home.[15]

On 12 June 1929 they sailed on the *Chitial* from Sydney to London via Marseilles. On arrival they were, in Octavia's diary, 'two best beloved children' but six days into the trip 'dear Dady [Adrian]' was being 'so trying', wanting her to break up the Panacea Society. 'I will not do it,' she wrote in her diary, and underlined it.[16] Conversations continued to be difficult, the atmosphere tense, and one day when Adrian came over to talk to her she avoided him altogether by hiding in Miss Tweedie's room in The Haven. In November, as he and Marjorie packed for a visit to other relatives and friends, he said to his mother, 'You have not done one single thing I asked you.' He met with other members, including Rachel Fox and even Emily Goodwin, but all to no avail. Octavia began her diary for 1930 with the words: 'After a difficult year of awful trials with my children I give thanks for all blessings & for being brought through such Turbulence. Now I ask for sight for Adrian.'[17] On 14 January 1930, Adrian and Marjorie left. They had not had the homecoming that Adrian so dearly wanted. His mother had eaten no meals with them, not even tea in the afternoon, and their time in Bedford had been full of conflict and difficulty. He had hoped 'to bring my sweet wife back to a nice home in which you were naturally mistress & I find that I have come home to what is nothing more than a Boarding House with a most unpleasant and soured landlady, & one or two boarders of a type which I am not accustomed to associating with'. On several occasions during the visit, Octavia had said to Adrian: 'Honour thy father and mother', but he asked: 'how can I honour anyone who has turned me out of my home, and filled it with strangers?'[18] As they parted, Adrian said to his mother, 'I am sorry things have to be so uncomfortable.' Marjorie, practical and full of common sense, simply said, 'Better luck next time.'[19]

And then there was Dilys, the daughter who never married, who stayed in the Panacea Society for her whole life, who ran around after her mother, especially as Octavia grew increasingly stout with untreated diabetes. Adrian was deeply worried about Dilys. Close in age, they had always stuck together, especially in the bad times of their childhood. He was concerned about her future. 'Do not forget your responsibilities towards your daughter,' he chided his mother; 'she is a charming girl & should have been married ages ago. Why should she remain an old maid?'[20] He wrote to Dilys: 'I hate to think of you being unhappy & I do so *long* to dig you out of all this.'[21] He was anxious that his marriage should not drive them apart, and he repeatedly invited her to come and stay with them in India, but she never did.

When Octavia wrote at the end of 1929 that she had had awful trials with her children, it was not only Adrian who had been causing her anxiety, but Dilys too. For Dilys had inherited her mother's tendency towards melancholia and propensity for mental illness, and in the summer of 1929 she was seriously mentally ill, but this fact Octavia found hard to face. Dilys had been to stay with her cousin Rita in May, and Rita had been horrified at how unwell she had found Dilys, 'both in health and mind'. Dilys wrote to Emily Goodwin from her cousin's house during this period, and her letter demonstrates how distraught she was. It swings dramatically between rational discussions of how long she might stay with Rita and her husband Earl, descriptions of visits to the beach, comments on how nice the animals and dogs are there, and agonised regret about her past behaviour along with expressions of the wish to die. She feared going home and seeing the misery on her mother's face and having to deal with people that she believed she had insulted. She imagined everyone was talking about her. Even more, she feared living with her own ghastly misery for millions of years: immortality seemed no prize to her. She wanted Emily to petition the Divine Mother to allow her to die. 'Oh my dear, my dear, pray unceasingly that I may die: I cannot live.' She also had suicidal thoughts: 'I must take every step to try and get rid of myself: no one could live in such a hell of remorse.' For Dilys, this was not only a suicidal plea in the midst of deep depression and mental illness, it was also a longing for a normal life – away from prying eyes and gossiping community members – and, even more, a normal life span.[22]

Rita had hoped to be able to nurse Dilys back to health away from the Panacea Society, but Octavia ordered Dilys to return home. Major Carew-Hunt was dispatched to collect her and bring her back to Bedford. Rita was furious that Octavia seemed unwilling to do anything to help her daughter, and a couple of weeks later wrote an angry letter, demanding that Dilys be sent to a recognised nursing home. Knowing that mail often did not get through to Octavia, she copied her letter to resident member Jessie Tweedie, and the police (who must have wondered what it was all about).

On the afternoon of 17 June, the day that Rita sent her letter to her Aunt Mabel about Dilys, Panacea apostle Mildred Hollingworth was washing the dishes at her kitchen sink after tea and saw an angry woman talking to Evelyn Gillett, gesticulating and dancing from one foot to the other on the garden path, 'in a way that only a highly excited person would act'. It was Lennie Bull, Rita's mother and Octavia's sister-in-law who had had her sectioned in 1915 and who now shared her daughter's fury about the neglect of Dilys's mental health. She spent the afternoon and evening storming around the Panacea community houses trying to find Dilys, demanding answers and venting her anger about Octavia and the Panacea Society, which she loathed. At about teatime, she tried the Gilletts, knowing that they were friendly with Dilys. She met Evelyn Gillett at the gate and launched into her torrent. Dilys was going out of her mind, was half-starved and was ill treated by the Society. Octavia had hypnotic powers and was using them on poor Dilys, and Octavia was herself out of her mind. Getting no answers from Evelyn Gillett, Lennie moved on to Evelyn Peck's house. Evelyn Peck, having been married and had children and, living a couple of streets away from the central community houses and therefore not quite in the middle of things, was regarded as more sensible by outsiders such as Lennie and Adrian, who corresponded with her several times during his 1928 nervous breakdown. Lennie even remarked that she was surprised that a woman of such sound common sense, whom she admired as a mother, should have allowed herself to be persuaded into the Panacea Society. She was vitriolic about Mabel (still Mabel to her, of course, not Octavia), who 'must be top dog', saying that if the Panaceans turned her down as leader they 'should soon find out the sort of person Mabel Barltrop is, and that she would not stand being anything but leader' – a comment that was not necessarily untrue.

At last Lennie found Dilys at The Haven, where she was peacefully playing the piano before dinner, and quite resistant to going with her aunt. Failing in her mission to rescue Dilys, Lennie was determined to see Mabel and berate her, but the Panaceans were good at protecting their leader from this kind of onslaught, so Lennie carried on charging around various community houses that evening, eventually ending up back at the Gilletts', at 9 p.m. where she had a half-hour conversation at the gate, this time with Muriel Gillett. Having no more success in persuading Muriel of her point of view than she had had with any of the other Panaceans that night, she turned on her heel and 'tripped on her feet in a curiously excited manner', as Mildred Hollingworth, who just happened once again to be looking out of the window at the right moment, noted with glee.

Adrian arrived in July, in the middle of this drama. Dilys and Major Carew-Hunt met him and Marjorie at the railway station, and Adrian saw at once that Dilys was not herself. He and Marjorie were staying in The Haven with her, and often found her walking around the house in a nightdress. He was determined that she should see a specialist, but when he had arranged it Dilys refused to comply, so he took her away to stay on a Quaker farm about fifty miles away from Bedford, accompanied by Evelyn Gillett, Marjorie and himself, and got the specialist to visit her there. To Dilys, the doctor said nothing about her deteriorating mental state. (Informing patients themselves about their health or diagnosis is a more recent phenomenon.) To Adrian, he said that he could not be responsible for her mind if she remained in the religious atmosphere of the Panacea Society. Dilys, driven back to Bedford by Evelyn Gillett, gave a positive report of her health to her mother, the Divine Mother and other Panaceans.

Adrian wrote to his mother with the true report on Dilys's health from the doctor, noting that she was unbalanced though could not be certified insane, had been suicidal and was likely to be again. Her case was urgent, she should be removed from the religious atmosphere immediately, and it would take about six months to cure her. This had no effect on his mother or others in the tight inner circle of Panaceans who would have undoubtedly read the letter. Adrian realised that letters were not getting through to his mother and he ended this one with the words: 'If mother is not allowed to see this letter, I hold you, who is reading it, entirely responsible. I have witnesses to the effect that I have written this letter.'[23] Writing a week later, he demanded that she reply to him immediately so that he would know she had read his letter 'for up to the present you have only received 50% of the letters that have been addressed to you' and he suggested that she issue an order that no one tamper with her correspondence.[24]

The issue of Dilys's health became entwined with Adrian's distrust and dislike of the Society, and his anger towards his mother. While in England in 1929, staying with Marjorie's relatives and other friends, he wrote a series of letters to his mother. The displacement of their family unit by the Panacea community rankled with Adrian and hurt him enormously. 'Both Dilys & I feel & know that we are quite secondary considerations in your life; complete outsiders seem to have first place in what should be our home & in your estimation. Ivan says the same thing.' It was the 'wretched religion' that had 'split up what otherwise would have been a happy family'.[25] How much the might-have-been family life was wishful thinking on Adrian's part is hard to know. Certainly, Octavia was obsessed with the Panacea Society but they had not had an easy family life before its foundation. Arthur had been ill throughout Adrian and Dilys's childhood and had even left home and gone to spend some time in South Africa. He had died when they were young, while their mother was in an asylum. Dilys had been largely brought up – at least in her teenage years – by her Aunt Lennie, and Adrian had spent barely any time at home after he went to boarding school. There had been very little family life, except perhaps when they were very young, but the Panacea Society was an easy target to blame.

If Adrian was furious that their family home had been largely taken over by strangers, Dilys tried to adapt. She gives a rather sad account of the difficulties of living with strangers, of one head of a community house banging doors to wake her in the mornings. She tried to make herself the least bother possible. 'Always living in other people's houses – though I have worked hard to repay them – I have neglected my food for fear of taking the last bit that did not belong to me.' It is no surprise that Adrian found her looking thin and haggard when he arrived in 1929. As one of the youngest Panaceans, Dilys found herself especially caught between community life and the casual speed of modern life as lived by her friends of old. She was often invited to stay with a friend in town, and she went there 'with old-fashioned manners and a great dignity, which did not suit their modern haste'. And so 'with fatal adaptability, I tried to alter myself to suit them, for fear of being a discredit to them', but this interfered with her religious way of life and thus she believed she lessened herself. Coming from the Panacea community, she had little to talk about with those outside, except literature, which she loved, but her friends had no particular interest in books. 'And so I shrank within myself once more and took on a little of their superficiality to my shame.'[26]

Adrian was acutely aware of the ways in which religious groups could destroy families and individuals. He wrote to Dilys that he was grateful that most of the Panacea members were single, 'which means that children are spared such unhappiness as you have had'.[27] During his visit to England that year, he was constantly combing the newspapers for cases of heterodox religious groups causing unhappiness or being implicated in suicides, and mentioning them to his mother, even when they did not quite back up his argument. One case, for example, was that of a woman jumping from a window of a care home in Barnes, London, owned and run by a Christian Scientist, put there by her Christian Scientist brother when she was mentally ill because he thought it preferable to an asylum. When the case went to court, the jury declared it a case of suicide during temporary insanity, though the foreman noted that the proprietress was guilty of neglect and deserving of censure, but the Coroner noted that the fact that it happened in a Christian Science home was irrelevant, as it could have happened in any home.[28] Every night, Adrian told his mother, he 'listened IN DREAD to the S.O.S on the wireless for fear that Dilys's name will be amongst them'.[29]

With Adrian demanding action and the possibility of public embarrassment, the Panaceans decided that they had to do something about Dilys, but Dilys herself was fearful of going into a nursing home. They managed it in their own way, ignoring Adrian's demands that Dilys seek medical help. They decided to send her away, though whether that was to remove her from the religious influence of Bedford, as Adrian requested, or from the 'devilish' influence of Adrian (as they would have seen it) is open to question. They sent her to France with Evelyn Gillett as her companion and minder. The two of them arrived in Paris, where they stayed for a while in the Paris apartment of 'Madame', Charlotte Twemlow-Allen, a Panacean and the Tower for France, and then went to stay in Fontainebleau, the headquarters of La Panacée CSS.[30]

From France, Dilys wrote to her mother and Adrian, mostly reassuring them that she was fine, reserving her true feelings and agonies for her letters to Emily Goodwin and the Divine Mother – and she did send separate letters to these two personae. Even though all her letters were passed through the filter of Evelyn Gillett, they were long, rambling and endlessly self-analysing. The woman who emerges from them is someone who is clearly mentally ill, desperately trying to get to grips with that illness, inclined always to blame herself rather than others, and intensely sensitive. While earlier Dilys had been embarrassed about her (mis)behaviour – though vague about the details – she nevertheless began to defend herself. When the mind has brain fever and is affected by worry, she wrote, then 'the tongue becomes unwise & says things that are absolutely foreign to the nature'. So, she argued, those members who had been disillusioned by her behaviour, such as Major and Mrs Carew-Hunt, needed to understand that. She therefore petitioned the Divine Mother to 'clear me in their eyes'. Indeed, 'In Justice's NAME, Divine Mother, *clear my good name.*'[31]

If the Visitation had caused Adrian to be rather careless about his behaviour, living the high life in the knowledge that he could simply confess his sins and carry on, then Dilys went to the other extreme and was over-scrupulous. She wrote that she 'knew every shade of the overcoming for my own self – did as far as possible everything the Scripts taught, never had a thought that was hidden. Exhausted myself in penitence, prayer, thankfulness – loved tribulation'. She had thought herself very wicked, but had now come to know that 'no one could very well have done less wrong, for I could look the whole world in the face – was scrupulously honest and truthful – austere and dignified and calm – my only aim the elimination of self to be ready for Our Lord's Coming'. She had even come to feel that she had responsibility for '60 people's health, death, relations as well as my own' – that is, all the resident members. The religious atmosphere in which she was living, with its constant attention to the self and the erasure of self, seems to have had a deleterious effect on her health. In that, Adrian was right.

Dilys's continued scrupulousness about the behaviour of others – which all Panacea members were commanded to report on – did not cease even in France, despite her mental illness. With Evelyn she discussed the ways in which Major Carew-Hunt 'uses his eyes too much. Nothing escapes him & it makes me very uncomfortable.' When she had a spot on her dress once, he saw it before she had had a chance to change, and 'his eye fastened on to it *at once*'. Writing to the Divine Mother, Dilys said that she and Evelyn thought 'he should learn the custody of the eye'. Dilys noted wryly: 'Of course he has to look at soldiers: but not at ladies so penetratingly.'[32] When they left Madame Twemlow-Allen's house after staying with her for several months, they filed a report on her, for 'she needs a great deal of help for her character'.[33] Dilys even reported on Evelyn, who was looking after her, and whose tomboy behaviour and unsuitable dress had always caused her pain. 'Evelyn is a different person,' she wrote to Mrs Goodwin. 'I have corrected many most peculiar habits she had formed through not being normal & through being personally lazy. She is very industrious in other ways but very lazy in speech, movement & being gracious: I let *nothing* pass.'[34] Later she wrote: 'Evelyn is improving – but she *did* need it . . . I have worked *hard* with her. Let us hope you will find a difference.'[35]

In France, Dilys managed to have a sedate and peaceful life, taking music lessons, singing, learning French, with the ease of awareness that no one knew her or knew about her mental illness. In that sense she had got away from Bedford and the intense scrutiny of community life. By the beginning of the new year, when she had been resting and recuperating in France for several months, albeit with Panacea members, she was writing to Emily Goodwin that she could no longer be in the Visitation and planned to move back to Britain and live in Aspley Guise or Woburn Sands, attractive villages near Bedford, with Evelyn. To the Divine Mother she wrote: 'As I have left the Visitation, I cannot very well come home, nor do I desire to see those people any more – after the shame & degradation.'[36] Adrian hoped she would go to stay with Ivan in Canada. Nothing came of these plans. She and Evelyn returned to England in the spring and spent two months there. Dilys went to stay with Mary Warry, the non-resident member of her own age who lived in Somerset, and then went to Bath accompanied once again by Evelyn Gillett, and sometimes Jessie Tweedie. But Dilys was soon again writing anguished, suicidal letters to the Divine Mother, and so the decision was taken to send her back to France, again accompanied by Evelyn. Charlotte Twemlow-Allen met the boat, and then Evelyn and Dilys made their way back to Fontainebleau where they now stayed in an apartment in the home of one Madame Joyeux. France seems to have suited Dilys. By the autumn of that year, she was writing letters that were not only rational and straightforward but also witty and sharply intelligent. To her mother, she wrote of going to concerts, giving singing lessons, how much she liked the French people, the delights of their flat, which she had painted and decorated, of her busyness.[37] Dilys enjoyed a sense of purpose and independence in France, but by January 1931 she had decided to return home to Bedford.

Both Dilys and Adrian found themselves struggling with their place in relation to the religious community that consumed their mother. Adrian's response manifested itself in intense worry; later, in anger; and throughout the rest of his life, physical distance from it. Dilys's response emerged through her mental illness. This is not to deny that mental illness ran through the Andrews and Barltrop family lines. It did, and Dilys might have suffered from her illness whatever she did with her life, but undoubtedly the Society's focus on self-scrutiny, confession of sins, and the aim of becoming 'zero' had a profoundly negative effect on this acutely sensitive young woman. She found herself in a largely older community with no real friends, living in community houses where she always felt obligated to the head of the house, rather than in her own home, with her needs largely neglected by her mother. Octavia might have been wise about other people's family dynamics – sorting out how the Gillett sisters related to each other and their mother, for example – but she was not so wise about her own. Where her children were concerned, she largely buried her head in the sand. Octavia had not had a strong relationship with her own mother, and after her father died she had turned to the other (older) woman in the household, her Aunt Fanny, for sustenance and support. This pattern was reproduced in the next generation with Dilys. With an emotionally absent mother and (like her mother) no father from an early age, Dilys turned to the older woman in her mother's household, Emily Goodwin, for emotional support. While Aunt Fanny was, for the young and middle-aged Mabel, wholly benign and generous by all accounts, Emily Goodwin, both as herself and as the Divine Mother, was an infinitely more complex character. She was so entwined with the community that caused Dilys so much agony that the relationship was neither healthy nor helpful to Dilys in the long term. In other words, Dilys turned for help to the one person who most symbolised the problems of the community with which she was battling.

Dilys's anger at and ambivalence about the Panacea Society is expressed in her letters to this pivotal figure. To Emily Goodwin, she wrote (in early 1930 after seven months in France): 'Why didn't you warn me? . . . Why didn't you do something?' She continued: 'Why in God's name did you say "Do everything with out a thought?"' And referring to the Society's endless rules about everything, she asked: 'If it was wrong to open a window or drink a glass of water – then what about real wrong sins of the tongue? Why in Heaven's name didn't you warn me?'[38] Two weeks later she wrote the same things to the Divine Mother, showing how fused the two personae were for her: 'If to open a window or to drink a glass of water be wrong – or to have a thought be wrong – what about real wrong? You told me to do everything without a thought.' She continued to berate the Divine Mother and thereby criticise Panacea practices: 'You have lead [sic] me into wrong-doing thereby because you caused me to alter my whole character – which is impulsive, generous & active. I have always obeyed you therefore, doing everything without a thought made life intoler-able. I only care to die.' The Panaceans always emphasised that Emily

Goodwin was merely the *Instrument* of the Divine Mother, the person through whom the feminine aspect of God spoke (unlike Octavia who was believed to be literally the daughter of God), but here we can see how easy the slippage between the two was.

For Dilys, the Divine Mother was the person upon whom she could vent her greatest anger: 'my illness can be put on your head as I obeyed you & got into trouble'. She also blamed her embarrassment and humiliation on her: 'I cannot go back to Bedford, where that kidney trouble I told you of caused me to have accidents in the street. I am disgraced there for ever. But I have been perfectly open: I told you of that – you did nothing to advise or help me.' But paradoxically the Divine Mother was also the person from whom Dilys sought both permission and help. In the same letter, she veered between asking for permission (as Panaceans had to do) and asserting her independence: 'Please can you cable "yes" to Aspley Guise . . . If not, I go *without* permission as I am no longer under the Visitation.'[39] Similarly, letters to Emily Goodwin went with rapid speed from 'Why didn't you do something?' to 'Your Xmas card was *so* sweet'; from a discussion about the French love of cats to 'For God's sake get me out of this hellish mess. I must put the blame on the one who said "do everything without thought." I mean the Mother.'[40] She longed to get away from the Society and the double maternal influence there – her real mother and Emily Goodwin/the Divine Mother – yet at the same time the only emotional resource and support she knew was in Bedford.

The correspondence opens a window on to how Emily Goodwin operated as the Divine Mother. She wrote frequently to Dilys during this period (much to Adrian's irritation) and, just as Dilys confused the two personae, so Emily Goodwin seems to have made little distinction between her own voice and that of the Divine Mother. Reading through these letters, one is left wondering how on earth the Panaceans ever believed that this rather ordinary woman was actually channelling the divine. The rather bland and repetitive letters, all written in the same voice whether from Emily Goodwin or the Divine Mother, express the wish that Dilys is having a nice time in France, with a change of scene (as if she were merely on holiday) and urge her not to blame herself or, indeed, the Divine Mother who made things happen for a reason and is in control of what will happen. Emily Goodwin wrote to her: 'everything depended upon you dear having to pass through the furnace of suffering', while the Divine Mother wrote: 'you have accomplished by your suffering and sacrifice a work for Me, and it was the only way Penitence could be brought upon the earth'. What the Divine Mother offered, which Emily Goodwin could not, was a new brain. 'I will perform my promise (a definite promise & no conditions) to take away the brain of torture & put a new mind or spirit or brain, which will only know & remember joy, peace & rest & blot out all remembrances of torture soon.'[41] Just as Octavia and her followers interpreted her mental illness as suffering for the redemption of humankind, so now Dilys's mental illness – also called suffering – was given a theological gloss. This meant that the Panaceans could avoid the real issue: that Dilys was mentally ill. About this evasion Adrian was incandescent with rage. He wrote to his mother: Dilys 'laughs at the idea of being given a new brain (& well may she laugh) as promised by that wicked old woman, yet she clings to some vague hope of getting one. She says she's waited for months & has had no luck so far. Of course the whole idea is preposterous & childish.'[42]

In the face of external pressure from Adrian and others, the Society closed ranks. Their first instinct was to protect Octavia – precisely because of her mental illness – and so they kept Adrian's letters from her, colluded with her wish not to have confrontations with her son or her sister-in-law, and withheld information from her. At the top of one letter from Adrian to his mother, Emily Goodwin has written 'Parts underlined I read to Octavia'.[43] Not many sentences are underlined. Whenever Adrian asked members why his mother did not know about something, 'their shamefaced excuse' was that it might worry her.[44] The daughter, Dilys, was sacrificed in order to save the mother, Octavia. As Emily Goodwin wrote to Dilys (with a distinct lack of punctuation): 'Octavia does not know how long you are staying she would rather not then she does not have to think about the end of time, she was very pleased with the map & letter & will write soon her time is so full now.'[45] How odd it must have been to hear her mother spoken of as Octavia; how peculiar to have someone else say how busy her mother was and therefore would write when she had time; and how very sad to know that her mother could not cope with the details of her absence because it raised unsettling theological questions. Octavia gave over all the negotiations about Dilys to the Divine

Mother, and it is hard therefore to know how much she knew or indeed cared about Dilys's condition.

The one person who knew everything that was going on was Emily Goodwin, though her theological views, with her strong sense of evil spirits and the activity of Satan in the world, may have prevented her from realising or understanding that Dilys was seriously ill. As the Panaceans closed ranks against the outsiders who questioned their wisdom and their activities, members relentlessly spied and reported to the Divine Mother on these 'enemies of the Lord'. They knew not to open their front door to Lennie, Octavia's sister-in-law, precisely because everyone watched and reported her every move whenever she came over to the community houses to try to find out what was happening to her niece. As Jessie Tweedie – who lived at The Haven – put it, 'We can see who comes through the glass, but they cannot see us.'[46] How much they would have loved the speed of texting, alerting members to the danger coming to the doorstep. But without even telephones in the community houses, they did a remarkably good job of keeping each other informed about what was going on. Extremely detailed reports of all sightings of and conversations with the 'enemies' were regularly filed. This meant that Emily Goodwin, as always, had a very powerful position, and she was constantly looking to protect the Society rather than individual members; to prove her omniscience and retain her power rather than understand what was really happening to people. Anyone who showed any signs of cracking and sympathising with Adrian or with other members of the family such as Lennie and Rita, who were opposed to the Society, were immediately cast into the outer darkness or pulled into line. When Dilys was at one of her most distressed points, in January 1930, Emily Goodwin wrote, in her guise as the Divine Mother, to tell her that 'the enemies have failed'. The Panaceans had made the Society 'more secure – if it could be – than ever by being able to stand against the biggest charges that have ever been made against it, & it has brought out who are your mother's friends – true & who are the enemies'. Mr and Mrs Bevan, non-resident members who had met with Adrian, 'have not proved friends', she wrote. 'They are carriers to the enemys [sic] camp under the disguise of having such an interest in you, but they leave your Mother & me out of the question.'[47] The fact that Mr and Mrs Bevan, as well as Adrian, were genuinely concerned about

Dilys's health could not be faced. Dilys's acute illness was ignored and explained away in theological terms. The Divine Mother's task was to keep the Society secure even at the expense of the divine granddaughter's health.

Adrian, Lennie and Rita all made threats against the Society. As he was about to leave Bedford at the end of 1930, Adrian told Rachel Fox that he had a doctor, a lawyer, a clergyman, the Chief of Police as well as his cousin supporting him, and if necessary he would call upon the Home Secretary to order an investigation into what went on there.[48] Lennie made similar threats to the Panacea members she managed to corner: not only would she cable for Ivan to come home, but she would also tell Kate Firth, she would tell the bishops, she had already told the police, she would expose the whole Society publicly. 'Nothing she could do to put an end to the Society and its practices, should be left undone.' If anything happened to Dilys, she would take the matter to court. Adrian and Lennie both felt there were grounds for investigation, not only because of what was happening with Dilys, but because of other bits of scandalous information they picked up here and there, whether true or not. Because Lennie lived – literally – around the corner from the Society she was plugged into the town's perceptions of the Society and passed all information on to her nephew. Adrian claimed the Panaceans were known throughout the town as 'The Bedford Loonies'. The fact that unmarried members of the opposite sex lived together in community houses was a cause of rumour. Adrian was especially worried that Octavia and Peter lived in the same house and he believed he had 'very strong proof' that they engaged in various erotic and sexual practices.[49] Anna, his daughter, repeated the rumour to me nearly eighty years later. 'Religious mania and sex are closely related,' he wrote didactically to his mother. Of course, the opposite is also true: that those who live rigorous and secluded lives as religiously committed people are often accused of irregular sexual practices. Where there is a lack of real knowledge, rumour will always fill in the blanks. And the Panacea Society was mysterious to the townspeople of Bedford. One man who grew up in Bedford spoke to me of all the schoolboys running to the top of the bus when it went down Albany Road so they could look into the garden of the secret society and try and see someone there.[50]

Adrian carried out none of his threats, perhaps because it would reflect badly on himself as much as anything else. He was certainly embarrassed by the Panacea Society and his family connection to it. He said he was ashamed of the name Barltrop, and he asked his mother to order the Divine Mother not to mention him in her letters. She had, apparently, been telling people that he had been treated like a prince while at home. Fearing that this was related to the claim that he was the grandson of God, he wrote: 'this would make me a laughing stock and ruin my career if it got out'.[51] He made his mother promise that if his wife's aunt from India came to England and asked to see her, she would on no account meet her. Adrian was worried that Mrs Bateman Champain 'would soon size up the state of affairs & the result for me might be great unhappiness'.[52] The tension with the Society and his mother remained for Adrian, but he stopped trying to do anything for Dilys. He had been proven powerless in the face of the Society and he did not try to exert the family's influence again with any great energy.

Dilys never left Bedford after she returned in early 1931. She remained unmarried, living with a group of people who were almost all much older than her. She was treated with respect because she was the divine granddaughter, but she was deeply alone. Some of the older married men had crushes on her. Members speculated that Major Carew-Hunt was in love with her. Canon Russell Payne confessed to the Divine Mother that he constantly tried to win Dilys's affection, would find excuses to bump into her in the garden and go for walks with her, longing to touch her and sometimes succeeding with a brush of her hair, or the chance to take her arm as they climbed over a stile. In the face of this rather creepy attention, Dilys seems to have created an imaginary boyfriend for herself in the 1940s, writing a sequence of letters to him which remain in the Panacea Society archives (with no replies!). Adrian's daughter, Anna, remembers visiting Dilys in the 1950s and '60s, when she was living alone in a little art deco house that the Society had built on The Grove, a nearby street, but not at the heart of community activities. The great treat of Dilys's day was to walk down to the river and eat an ice cream. She was sad and lonely, and had a sense that life had passed her by.

Adrian and Marjorie made one last visit to Bedford. They came for another six months of leave in 1933, bringing their baby Anna and her nurse with them. Octavia's diary is much less fraught this time. She went to great trouble to prepare suitable accommodation for her family, and her diary pages this time are filled with notes about tennis, picnics, and altogether more pleasant events. She often played with Anna in the garden, and on Anna's second birthday, she gave her a brush, comb and cheque. They left in October and Adrian never saw his mother again.

III
The World

Negotiating the World

Falling in love, using birth control, having sexual desire, difficulties with family members getting married – that all of these human experiences and activities created tensions in a tightly knit community advocating celibacy is unsurprising, but for the Panaceans there were myriad other ways in which their beliefs and experiences rubbed up against the values of the world. Non-resident members, living and working in society, had to negotiate this tension every day. As Mary Warry put it:

> Living in a sea of Panacea unbelief as one does in the world, one learns to a hair's breadth how much can be said on these matters to ones so called friends before they come to the point of regarding one merely as a crank. Wholesale Panacea truths nearly always produce that polite smile, (having eaten your good lunch) which one knows denotes complete inability to follow with comprehension.[1]

Mary Warry's cousin whom she had brought into the Panacea fold, Lt. Harold Dolphin, trained at Sandhurst as an army officer and, now serving in Lucknow in India, faced the daily navigation of life as a Panacean in the officers' mess. In particular there was the problem of the Panacea ban on drinking spirits. As an officer it would have been difficult to obey this without seeming 'peculiar', he wrote in an anxious letter to Miss Green. 'After a game or on guest nights, it is thought more or less unsociable not to partake of a whisky and soda.' Prone to being over-conscientious – for which Octavia had already gently chided him – he found himself in a complete dilemma about this, as well as the question of playing bridge for money. His solution, never to buy a spirit from the bar but to accept a drink when offered one by others, and never to propose playing bridge but agree to make up a foursome if he were needed, brought approbation from Octavia, showing that certain delicate compromises were from time to time possible.[2]

Resident members living in Bedford also experienced this tension, in some ways more acutely, because they were under scrutiny from their fellow Panaceans and the watchful eye of the Divine Mother every minute of the day, as Kate Firth learned to her cost. Muriel Gillett, struggling with the practice of Overcoming and fighting back tears as she received criticism from Octavia, made it clear that she loved being in the community but that it was 'the things of the old life' that made her unhappy. Adjusting to obedience in the ways they offered hospitality was one difficulty that both she and her sister faced. They were wealthy and had bought a large house in Bedford, a block away from Octavia and headquarters, and they often had Panacea visitors to stay, but they had been commanded not to be extravagant in their hospitality, as was their former custom. Muriel wrote plaintively to Octavia: 'we have the money to give them [visitors and members] pleasure with & have liked to take one and another with us when there is anything special to go to.' But Octavia was determined that they should not deviate from the community rules of hospitality.[3]

As they negotiated the demands of the world, the Panaceans were, like everyone else, trying to come to grips with the devastation of the war, and the losses they had sustained. Several of the women – Octavia herself, Frances Wright – had lost sons; some of the men who joined the Society, such as Cyril Carew-Hunt, were scarred for life by their time in the trenches. The institution of Armistice Day was a national attempt to deal corporately with that grief. In 1919, with the country still mourning the loss of so many in the war, and with no clear idea how to express their grief communally, an Australian soldier and journalist, Edward Honey, had written to the *London Evening News*, suggesting that there should be a national five-minute silence to remember the five million men who had died in the war. The Prime Minister, Lloyd George, took up the idea and suggested it to the King who, after initial reluctance, took it up enthusiastically. The country observed silence for two minutes at eleven o'clock on 11 November, the moment that the armistice had been signed a year before. As the rest of the country stopped working, as cars, trains and the underground came to a halt, as horses were steered to the side of the road, as conversation ceased, as men took their caps and hats off, as Big

Ben chimed and as the Prime Minister laid his wreath of orchids and white roses at the still makeshift cenotaph in Whitehall, Octavia and her followers gathered together in Bedford – but they did not mark Armistice Day in the same way as the rest of the nation. They declared that they were assembled against Satan. They repudiated his hidden evils, which had the appearance of being good, and refused to accept as final, satisfactory or of any permanent value, all the apparent good which Satan instigated. This included commonly accepted religion; ancient and modern cults; imperial and municipal politics, and civil and social ethics. As they all knelt, Octavia prayed that they might empty themselves of Man's teaching. Armistice Day – that emotionally charged moment when the whole nation was, for two minutes, united – was rejected by this little band to indicate that Man's peace was illusory, and only God's peace was real peace.

By rejecting the ritual as the nation commemorated it, they were declaring that they would play no part in improving a world they regarded as Satan's kingdom. It was a ritual that they repeated annually. It was a radically counter-cultural move.

To reject what the world thinks is for the good – in this case, a united moment of mourning – is contentious. The Panaceans did it because they believed human solutions were futile, but their actions could seem heartless. As so many men – and some women – returned from the war with limbs missing, sight gone, faces burnt, and psychological damage, they needed care and nursing. They wanted to work but often could not find employment, or they dared not leave the house because they thought they looked unsightly, or could not hold a job because of their trauma. All of this meant that the call for charity was greater than ever, in a period before the welfare state was established in England. Many of the Panacea women had given years of their life to philanthropic causes, and their instinct was to go on helping. But Octavia now taught them that 'philanthropy had been tried, had had a long innings and had proven inadequate to do more than patch up the broken fragments of Society, that it must be regarded as man's best work for man, not in any way as a work of God'. Philanthropy had been a makeshift until God could come on earth Himself, 'and by his perfect work do away with all need for philanthropy which is only the love of man by man'.[4] Mary Beedell, a non-resident member who lived in Eastbourne, reflected

the Society's attitudes to traditional charitable giving when she wrote
to Octavia:

> I have been today to help count at the presenting of purses to Princess
> Helena, on behalf of the YWCA (I might add that neither my husband
> or myself gave any contribution to it) & I thought as I stood watching
> the well-dressed crowd: I wonder if when our King of Kings comes if
> the crowd will throng like this. It seems so empty when there is so
> much to be done for the Kingdom.[5]

The Panacean answer was to trust only divine solutions, which they
believed they knew from their direct hotline to God, and if that meant
rejecting what society thought to be good, then so be it.

In other ways, the Panaceans' rejection of worldly values reflected
the ambivalence that many others in society felt about the innovations of modernity. The Hollywood stars of the talking pictures
presented new models of femininity that many young women loved
to copy, painting on bright red 'Clara Bow' lips (even, daringly, in
public, with the new twist-up lipstick tubes), and it was easy for them
to do so with the advent of stores such as Woolworth's selling glamour
at an affordable price to anyone. For the really fashionable woman, a
pot of Unwin & Albert's kohl gave her the desired Egyptian look. To
those with one foot in the Victorian era, lipstick was, like rouge, what
prostitutes and actresses used, and it was scandalous. The hierarchi-
cally minded Duke of Portland wrote: 'It is neither becoming or
attractive for an otherwise pretty or charming young woman to appear
with a half-smoked cigarette hanging from her vividly painted lips.'[6]
To others, cosmetics helped them follow the popular song, 'Keep young
and beautiful' and represented the fun they wanted to have in the
wake of a devastating war.

Octavia did not even consider the use of lipstick, forbidding Panacea
members to use any make-up at all. Wella Bauer wrote from
Independence, Missouri, to ask whether she could use cleansing cream
on her face. The reply came back that the Water was enough: 'The
object of the divine water is to keep us nice without any use of these
things like cream.' Finest oatmeal was to be used for face powder,
plain fuller's earth for any chafing, and only salt for cleaning teeth,
the latter of particular interest perhaps to Mrs Bauer who so intensely

desired her dentist.[7] Not all members appreciated Octavia's injunctions against the use of such face creams. The upper-class Madeline Smith, an English non-resident member, wrote to the Confidential Department asking that the Divine Mother be informed of her grief that Octavia had forbidden her to use cold cream and Vaseline on her face, and glycerine and cucumber on her hands. She had very dry skin, believed that wrinkled skin would be torture, and wanted to make the most of her appearance for her children. She played what she thought was her trump card, appealing to the Panacea Society's wish for more young people to get involved. 'I have seen many young people disgusted with religion because their mother did not care what she looked like and took no pains to make herself look nice – all in the cause of religion – and it was very distressing.' She was perhaps speaking more of her own attitudes than those of her children: 'When I was young, I used to think that a shiny skin – and a dowdy appearance – went hand in hand with religion, but I have not thought so since I saw more of the world.' In the end it all came down to obedience: 'It is so difficult to be obedient as it is, so I dare not promise to give up any of these things or not to make the most of my appearance.'[8] But obedience was necessary if members were really to join in the 'way of life' and destroy the mortal soul. As the Divine Mother put it, 'Some of you are not in the way with her [Octavia] and there is danger lest they lose the road to life because they are unwilling to give up some trifle such as cosmetics.'[9]

It was not that Octavia did not care how people looked: she cared very much and had very definite views that had to be heeded. She disliked women following the fashion of wearing short skirts, which by 1925 had risen just above the knee. When she saw members, she was in the habit of adjusting their hat to a different angle, telling them what colours suited them best, scolding older women for wearing outfits that were too young for them, and – as in the case of Olive Morris – berating younger members for wearing clothes that she regarded as too old for them. All of this was done because people in the community might otherwise have had the temerity to 'dress as they chose', as Rachel Fox commented. The younger members gradually began to bring their outfits for Octavia's approval ahead of time, learning from experience perhaps that new fashions had to be checked. Octavia did not discount everything in modern clothing, approving what was 'pretty and useful'. Wearing lighter-weight fabrics, discarding whalebone corsets and starched petticoats in favour of less oppressive underwear, and choosing silk rather than wool stockings – Octavia did not forbid any of these innovations even if she did not embrace them herself. The Panaceans never had a specific dress code, as some other religious communities such as the Amish or Shakers or Christian Israelites did, but Octavia cared that people were well dressed, and in 1929 she issued her one and only codified injunction about dress: members were not to wear or buy crocodile or snakeskin handbags or shoes, or anything made of material that looked like the skin of reptiles. The reason was theological: just as they rejected the serpent in spirit, so they must reject it in material things, for she did not want them wearing a symbol of their damnation.[10]

Other products of the new consumer culture largely bypassed the resident members, given their relatively simple communal lifestyle. The Gilletts, being wealthy, had a good camera and took home movies of community life, as well as a car that was frequently put to the service of other members. The craze for drives in the country and even foreign travel were not indulgences that the resident Panaceans usually allowed themselves, and of course after 1919 Octavia never left her home or the grounds around it. No Panaceans would go up in a plane, at least in the 1920s and '30s, or take a trip on an ocean liner for a vacation. They enjoyed simpler and more local pleasures: cycling trips in the countryside, visits to cafés in town, and the talking pictures. Two cinema visits a week were allowed to members – which was the average attendance in England – though the Divine Mother forbade them to visit one particular cinema hall in town. She did not explain why, simply declaring: 'you must keep yourselves "unspotted from the world" and you must not take pleasure in the things it enjoys'. Here she diverged from Octavia who believed in pleasure in moderation. Octavia never saw a talking picture – the cinema was too far from her home – but she acquired a wireless in 1923 and loved it and the connection it gave her to the outside world. She also had a gramophone player, inherited from her older sons, but stuck to classical music, which she loved. While the bright young things of London were dancing to the jazz music imported from America until the early hours of the morning in the rapidly opening West End nightclubs, the Panaceans preferred more old-fashioned musical entertainments. They still liked to gather and play the piano and sing in the evenings, and at their garden party in 1928, twelve members dressed up in smocks and 'panier' dresses and performed country dances.

One shimmering, gleaming sign of the new technology often appeared just above their heads in Bedford in 1929. The new airship R101 was being developed at the Royal Airship Works in nearby Cardington, and when it was taken out for its test trials, the Panaceans would leave their desks, rush out from their offices and watch fascinated as this marvellous production of the human brain and hand floated above, gleaming gold in the sunshine, silver in the shade. The inside of the airship was like a luxury floating hotel, with a dining room to seat sixty, a smoking room for twenty and space for walking around. Airship travel promised to surpass aeroplanes, which were cramped, noisy and smelly, and ocean liners, which were slow. But the Panaceans received knowledge of divine disapproval of this glittering symbol of modernity. They were told that Englishmen could not rely on safety in the air because of the capriciousness of the weather and atmospheric conditions, and that as the air was still the territory of the Prince of the power of the air, he was able to take his toll of those who were not protected by the Water. Octavia and the Divine Mother issued statements against the increasing speed of travel, which they regarded as unnatural. Man, in his desire to emulate the birds of the air, was preparing the methods of his own destruction. The craze for speed was condemned and Octavia declared: 'In this mission we have the truth about everything, and we maintain that man does not fly – it is the machine that flies!'[11]

On the evening of Saturday 4 October 1930, the R101 sailed once again in all its beauty over the Panacea community as it circled the town. Members stood at the healing room door and watched it pass, 'lighted up and presenting the most beautiful appearance, almost of a spiritual kind'. It was on its maiden voyage to Ismailia in Egypt. Although Octavia believed that flying was not allowed in the divine scheme, she could not help praying, 'O God, take care of them.' Six hours later, in the early hours of Sunday morning, the airship crashed near Beauvais in northern France, killing forty-eight people. The Panacea views on air travel were vindicated but Octavia was 'stricken to the heart at the thought of how the relatives of the unfortunate victims of the disaster would suffer'. Because the Panaceans had gazed up into the sky at the glittering floating ship so many times over the last year, they felt an odd affinity with this symbol of change while at the same time disapproving of it so deeply. Indeed they felt it was *their* airship because it was built nearby, within the Royal Domain that had been so carefully staked out with linen sections and blessed water in the Protection scheme five years earlier, in October 1925. Octavia had had an odd foreboding about the voyage and when she had heard details of the banquet the passengers were to enjoy in Ismailia when they arrived, she said to herself, '*If* they get there.' She therefore felt the Panaceans must learn something from the episode, and at the worship meeting that Sunday evening she instructed the members that none should even wish to go into an aeroplane, let alone actually fly in one. They had to be content with primitive conditions: 'you have legs and arms and can walk about, even if horses and ships are taken away,' she told the assembled company. After all, for thirteen years she had not been beyond the Panacea garden, and had had to trust to her feet only, and she did not feel she was much the worse for it. (Others might, of course, privately have disagreed.) The airship was 'the top note of human self-sufficiency, foolishness and pride in achievement' whereas the Panaceans must have 'the top note of common sense and of surrender of our own ideas'.[12] Perhaps the fact that her son Eric had died in a plane crash in the war influenced her feelings.

Many of the rapid changes were associated with America and 'Americanisation' became a code for modernity. America was glamorous – the movies showed that – and it represented speed and technology, hallmarks of the time, but many people felt ambivalent about America and what it symbolised. Noël Coward's 1924 play, *Easy Virtue* (which opened in London in 1926), in which a young American woman marries into a down-at-heel English gentry family, explored the inevitable culture clash. Octavia always felt ambivalent about Americans, and that was reinforced by the Edgar Peissart debacle. Early on in the Society's history, she commanded American members and enquirers not to come to Bedford because there were no jobs and no houses for them.

In the face of the speed of change and the uncertainties it provoked, the Panacea Society's appeal to a nostalgic English identity was one of its attractions. The articles and illustrations in *The Panacea*, deliberately appealing to the middle-class members' innate conservatism and desire for a domestic sense of 'Englishness', gave readers the reassurance that amidst all the changes of modernity, there existed a haven of the familiar and the orderly. This was especially designed to appeal to the members around the world, the vast majority of whom lived in the dominions (which Octavia still called the colonies) and parts of the Empire such as India. The Panaceans believed that the Empire was an entirely good thing and, like other Britons, many of them had strong ties to it. Octavia's brother had gone to live in South Africa. One son, Ivan, lived in Canada, and the other, Adrian, served in the army in India and had very definite views about the excellence of the British Empire. As he wrote in 1927, 'The Hindus and Mohammedans will never see eye to eye and it is for this reason that India belongs to the British Empire.'[13] Cyril Carew-Hunt had spent time in Australia as a young man and had Australian relatives. Mildred Hollingworth, the apostle in charge of the healing ministry, and her husband William in charge of the printing, had been missionaries in Africa. Frances Wright had lived in India. These countries were part of their identity; they were Greater Britain. As the notion of empire was gradually challenged, and imperial power weakened, a secure and indeed mythical notion of England – home – kept spirits up. That link between empire and home was a vital one to the Panaceans, on both sides. The enthusiastic Harold Dolphin, in the army in India, sent Octavia a piece of the Union Jack flag that flew on the residency in Lucknow, 'the only flag in the world that is never taken down', he claimed. Walking in the Lucknow residency grounds on Easter Sunday he had found part of the flag's seam, which had come off when the flag was flapping in the wind and fluttered to the ground where he had found it. Octavia was thrilled and wrote back to say that the flag had, appropriately, arrived on Empire Day, and coincidentally, on the same day, another flag had arrived from someone in Liverpool. That flag represented England, his the Empire, and she was delighted.[14]

Watercolours of country cottages, abbeys, country churches and gardens by artists such as William Ball (who painted Sussex scenes) were reproduced in *The Panacea*, and presented a 'timeless' version of England at a time when the country was changing rapidly. These were stock items, also used in other magazines and publications that were targeted at a conservative, middle-class readership. Such images represented a partial view of England, one very much based on the rural south. They offered a nostalgic look back into a time before the disruption of the war, and the possibility of escape from the uncertainties of modern life. Articles such as 'Merrie England' by non-resident member, Colonel Sullivan, appealed to those who were 'wearied by the world's inability to secure a lasting peace' or were 'oppressed by the anxieties and fears so common to-day'. Anyone who felt like this was encouraged to write in for the healing for a lasting solution, but also to respond more generally 'by the preparation of himself and then by the influencing of a home where the hearth, around which the family gathers, is the Altar, not of sacrifice, but of Incense – the incense of fragrant domesticity'.[15]

The Panacea Society, with its deliberately domestic religiosity tended by the female apostles and its carefully preserved hierarchies, especially appealed to this nostalgic view of England. And it was very much about *England* for the most part, rather than Britain. Their view could be found throughout the wider society, which in the interwar years embraced an inward-looking and domestically focused sense of national identity and character. Stanley Baldwin, the sometime Conservative Prime Minister whom the Panaceans especially liked, offered such a perspective in his 1924 address 'On England' to the Royal Society of St George. What epitomised England for him were its rural sounds and sights: 'the tinkle of the hammer on the anvil in the country smithy, the corncrake on a dewy morning, the sound of the scythe against the whetstone, and the sight of a plough team coming over the brow of a hill, the sight that has been seen in England since England became a land'. England was to be found in the 'wild anemones in the woods in April, the last load at night of hay being drawn down a lane as the twilight comes on' and 'the smell of woodsmoke coming up in an autumn evening'. Baldwin represented all of this as timeless: 'These things strike down into the very depths of our nature, and touch chords that go back to the beginning of time and the human race, but they are chords that with every year of our life sound a deeper note in our innermost being.' Baldwin was, too, nostalgic about all of this in a rapidly changing, suburbanised world. 'These are the things that make England, and I grieve for it that they are not the childish inheritance of the majority of people to-day in our country.' When he wrote that they 'ought to be the inheritance of every child born into this country' he seemed to regret the realities of the industrialised north upon which so much of the nation's economy depended. This was especially ironic given that the address was published in a book of essays in April 1926, on the eve of the General Strike. His piece ended with an appeal to the domestic and a link to empire. The love of these things made 'for that love of home, one of the strongest features of our race, and it is that that makes our race seek its new home in the Dominions overseas, where they have room to see things like this that they can no longer see at home'.[16] It was a view that appealed to a supposed 'golden age' when everyone knew their place under the squire, and workers ploughed the fields and were happy.

Undoubtedly, one of the changes in society that made the middle classes anxious and vulnerable, and long for the good old days, was the post-war shortage of domestic servants. Books about the 'servant shortage' abounded, such as Harold Begbie's *Life Without Servants* (1916 and 1930) and Randal Phillips's *The Servantless House* (1922). Young women who had experienced freedom from domestic service in the war now sought other employment. They did not always find it but when they did enter domestic service, they were now often more resentful of the poor conditions and less inclined to be deferential. Life as the sole domestic servant in a small middle-class household – such as the community houses of the Panacea Society – could be hard: getting up early and cleaning the grates, laying the fires, getting water for householders to wash, making breakfast, scrubbing the steps, and after all that there was still a day's work to be done. Gladys Powell, a surviving member of the Panacea Society who worked as a domestic servant there in the 1940s and '50s, describes breaking the ice on the bowl of water to have a wash early in the morning before making her way downstairs to heat the water for the middle-class members, which she would then carry upstairs to their bedrooms so that they could wash themselves.

The Panacea Society addressed the 'servant problem' by ensuring that the domestic servants they did have were entirely deferential and knew their place. Panacea servants were believers who had little or no money and therefore paid their way by working for the households. Even though they were Panacea believers, they were not allowed to imagine that they were the equals of the middle-class householders whom they served. Amy Smart, Kate Firth's servant until Kate left in 1926, was reprimanded by Octavia on numerous occasions for crossing the boundaries of social status. She was told off for not calling Dilys Barltrop 'Miss Dilys'. She had slipped into calling her Dilys as everyone else did, and wrote a grovelling apology for being 'weak enough to do it myself. This is not, I know a sufficient excuse, as Miss Dilys's gracious ways & manners should have been a better example to me.'[17] In 1922, she had to have a meeting with Octavia and Kate Firth because she had complained about Kate's treatment of her, but the meeting resulted in her being told not to criticise Kate again. 'Kate was entirely exonerated,' wrote Octavia to Hettie Leach, Kate's sister, when she returned from one of her visits to a spa.[18] Again, Amy sent letters of deep penitence to Octavia. On another occasion, Amy asked Octavia if she could go to the chapel meeting every evening of the week, as other members did, not just on the evenings to which she had been assigned. As an aside, she noted, 'Mrs Firth owes me the time, as I have lived with her for more than 4 years and during that time have had only 12 days holiday, and have many, many times given up my half-day to nurse her when she had a headache', giving an insight into how hard Panacea servants worked. The answer came back: it was a clear no. Amy Smart wrote back, apologetic that her request might have caused Octavia distress, and noting: 'I am sorry I am such a poor Overcomer as I do wish to be a thorough one.'[19] Amy Smart may have been a difficult character – the letters do not reveal enough for us to know – but the capacity of the older, more powerful women to make everything her fault was quite remarkable. Gladys Powell, explaining that servants were not allowed to the chapel meetings for those who were most far along in the Overcoming, gave as the reason not social status, but that all the servants were young and therefore bound to be less far along in the practice of Overcoming. In fact, Amy Smart was in her early forties in the early 1920s, and nearly a couple of decades older than Dilys. There were people with different attitudes in the Society: the down-to-earth Hodgkinson sisters, founding apostles, made it clear before they even moved to Bedford that they did not have a servant and they did all their own housework, but their attitude was the exception.

Gladys Powell tells how life for servants continued to be hard and strict into the 1940s and '50s. Having been brought up with Panacea beliefs, she joined the Society when she was sixteen, the minimum age for membership, and went to live in the community in 1942. She was paid a weekly allowance of ten shillings as she had no money of her own. She had one half-day off a week – from 2 to 9 p.m. – and occasionally she was allowed to go out with another community servant, Phyllis Wood, and they would cycle into the country with a picnic if the weather were good enough. Gladys's aunt, Miss Vann, who had begun to take the blessed water and then joined the Society along with Gladys's mother in 1930, went to live in the community when she retired in 1938. She worked as a servant there but because she had a state pension was paid nothing for her work. The Panacea Society's structure of membership enabled them to maintain a middle-class servant system long after most middle-class householders had come to terms with the reality of servantless homes and had come to rely on labour-saving devices such as washing machines, refrigerators, electric cookers and vacuum cleaners. The Panacea kitchens retained an Edwardian feel to them, even into the twenty-first century when I first saw them, with ranges rather than modern stoves, and few modern appliances, suggesting not only the Panaceans' frugality – they were, after all, saving for Christ's return to earth – but also their unwillingness to come to terms with the technology and social equalities of modernity.

In creating their identity, the Panaceans appealed to widespread images of Englishness that indicated the tension between modernity and nostalgia at large in society, but they also had more eccentric ideas about their own special role in England and the distinctive place of Britons in the created order altogether. The view that England was special permeated the Society's theological beliefs, not least in the idea that the community's garden was the Garden of Eden, right there in England. When the Society regained The Haven after Kate Firth had left in 1926, Octavia wrote an editorial in The Panacea saying 'Paradise being regained for us, it will go on to be regained for the world.'[20] The restoration of God's kingdom was beginning in Bedford: the epicentre. It would spread to the rest of England and thence around the world. The Panaceans also accepted the notion, current for a long time and widely propagated in the Middle Ages, that Christianity had some of its earliest origins in England. They thought that the conventional story – that Christianity was brought to England by Augustine in 596 – was mistaken. Rather, they believed that Christianity had been founded in England long before that in Glastonbury, when St Joseph had visited 'apparently accompanied by Mary Magdalene, Martha, Lazarus and eight other believers' in the year 36. Joseph had struck his staff into the ground and it had grown into the distinctive 'Glastonbury thorn' plant. Accepting this story of alternative origins gave the Panaceans evidence, they believed, for their claim that the English Church was 'the premier Church in the world'.[21]

The Panaceans also adopted British Israelite ideas for their own purposes. Drawing on the notion that the Lost Tribes of Israel settled in Britain, British Israelites believed Anglo-Saxons to be the blood descendants of the Israelites, with Great Britain and her Empire as the inheritors of the covenant blessings given to Abraham. These ideas had been around for several centuries, but coalesced in the nineteenth century, and in 1919, the same year that the Panacea Society was founded, the British-Israel-World Federation was formed (it still exists). Octavia had been given a British Israelite pamphlet by a piano tuner at her house in the summer of 1914, a few months before she read Southcott's writings. British Israelite ideas therefore became fused with her theology as she subsequently developed it. British Israelism, with its literal reading of carefully selected passages of the Bible, its reliance on the Book of Common Prayer, its random appeals to philology, archaeology, heraldry and genealogical charts, along with its deeply royalist and patriotic fervour, combined to form a body of work which had the trappings of scholarship and appealed to the same sorts of conservative, middle-class and largely uncritical autodidacts who were attracted to the Panacea Society. While the Panaceans saw no need to join the British Israelite fellowship (which claimed it had two million adherents in the early twentieth century), they nevertheless assumed many of the movement's ideas.[22]

Similarly, they took an interest in the contemporary craze for pyramidology. In the nineteenth century the Astronomer Royal for Scotland, one C. Piazzi Smyth, took up an older idea that the Pyramids in Egypt were expressions of divine guidance, containing within them not only spiritual but also mathematical knowledge, indeed knowledge of the whole of human civilisation. Piazzi Smyth proposed in particular, in his 1864 book *Our Inheritance in the Great Pyramid*, that from the measurements of the Pyramids it could be deduced that the English were descended from the Ten Tribes of Israel. All kinds of esoteric groups were fascinated by pyramidology, and after the discovery of Tutankhamun's tomb in November 1922 by Howard Carter there was a renewed interest in it. The Panaceans went so far as to reproduce some articles by the Pyramid Group in *The Panacea*, but they 'did not make exhaustive studies of the Pyramid because we are too much engaged with the Healing work, and with preparing everything for which the Pyramid stands'. They borrowed what they needed and they were relentlessly interested in a range of eccentric ideas, but 'if there was no Pyramid and no British-Israelism we should not be affected by a hair's breadth', declared a *Panacea* article.[23]

The Panaceans did, however, take up wholesale another peculiar and, for more recent members, embarrassing idea about their identity and the categorisation of people. They divided human beings into three races: the Anthropoids, the Aliens (meaning others), and the Immortals. The Anthropoids were the ungodly or godless, striving to pull down all that is good, and their end was to be annihilation. The Aliens were persons with 'living souls' who would not enjoy immortal life but would go to heaven. They were subdivided into the penitent and the impenitent. The penitent would go straight to heaven on their death and they had a chance of becoming Immortal after the return of Christ. The impenitent probably believed in God but kept putting the matter to the back of their minds and therefore opposed their own salvation. They would have to wait until the thousand years of the millennium were over to get into heaven. The Immortals were those who would live for ever on earth under the reign of Christ, the 144,000, perfected through the process of Overcoming. They were, of course, the Panaceans. This schematisation relied on the notion that human beings had dual origins, namely that there existed people before Adam and Eve, an idea that had been around since the seventeenth century – when it was regarded as highly unorthodox – and had been particularly developed in the nineteenth century.[24] It was these 'pre-Adamites' whom the Panaceans called Anthropoids, harking back to the Greek (*anthropoeides*), which suggests 'resembling a human', or, in more modern usage, a higher order of primate.

The nineteenth century's twin obsessions with race and evolution meant that this idea was used by various religious groups, not just the Panaceans in the early twentieth century, to shore up orthodox belief in the face of Darwin's theories and infuse prevailing ideas of racial hierarchy with theological meaning. An Arabic scholar and lexicographer, Edward W. Lane, came to the conclusion that the 'black race' constituted the initial form of the human species, in the Upper Nile Valley and then spreading through Africa and Asia. There developed the notion that the 'inferior' races were older than the 'superior' races. This meant that Adam could, in this scheme, become the father of the Caucasians. And far from seeming unscriptural, the idea was now used to explain the two creation narratives. Genesis 1 and 2 were taken as accounts of the creation of two entirely different human species at different times. By the early twentieth century this formerly heretical idea of the pre-Adamites had gained a certain degree of respectability amongst some evangelical and fundamentalist Protestant groups, largely in America where racial politics remained fraught in the wake of the Civil War. Even the Theosophists, who prided themselves on promoting the peaceful brotherhood and sisterhood of all people, believed in multiple origins for human beings. The founder of Theosophy, Madame Blavatsky, proposed in her book *Isis Unveiled* (and expounded in detail in *The Secret Doctrine*) that there had been the simultaneous evolution of seven human groups on seven different portions of the planet.[25]

For the Panaceans, the notion of Adamic man was fused with their ideas about the Lost Tribes of Israel and the special nature of 'British Israel'. They were concerned with gathering the progeny of the Adamic line, who had been saved in the Ark, had received the promises made to Abraham, and from whom the Tribes of Israel had descended. These people, the Immortals, would form the 'Israel of God', delivered of the mortal soul and the mortal mind, ready to be filled with a new spirit. The Panaceans believed these Immortals were Aryan and that they were primarily British. Conversely, they believed that the Anthropoids were black, with mere mortal souls and minds. There had, they thought, been millions of Anthropoids before Adam, and they continued to coexist with the Adamic race. In coming up with this scheme, they took that rather odd, pre-Adamite theory of human origins – which nevertheless could be found in a variety of other religious groups, including some which regarded themselves as entirely orthodox – and melded it with a cultural opinion that was not uncommon in their day and justified Britain's Empire, namely the superiority of white people. This racist view of human nature was part of the Panacea theology, but in practice they treated sealed members who were not white, such as Ernest Gideon in India, equally, and they made no comment at all on his race. Maybe Gideon's English education saved him, or maybe the Panaceans were like so many other religious people who propound unpleasant and condemnatory doctrines about those they wish to exclude from their inner circle – or could not even imagine including as part of their inner circle: when faced with the reality of those persons, they treat them as they would treat anyone else, with courtesy and respect, allowing individuals to be exceptions to the rule.

The Panaceans' ambivalence towards Americans related to this cluster of ideas. Were the Americans British or not? That was the question. The British Israelites believed that America was Britain's offspring, and marked it as 'Manasseh', one of the Israelite tribes, but the Panaceans thought differently. Octavia noted that 'Manasseh' in America amounted only to a small number of survivors of the *Mayflower* emigration, who were few and hard to find. This remark came at the end of Rachel Fox's review of a book on America by a French intellectual, André Siegfried's *America Comes of Age*, in *The Panacea*. Siegfried noted that the fundamentally English America of his youth, the late nineteenth century, had been transformed by the immigration patterns of 1880 to 1914. Rachel Fox noted that by the 1920s, of the 95 million white people in the USA only 58 million had been born in the USA of American parents. She interpreted evidence of the changing ethnicity of the population in America to mean that 'non-British life' was 'undermining the sturdy stock from which our brethren over-seas originally sprang'. This illustrated 'the danger that American civilisation is in', she concluded. For the Panaceans, it meant that America could not claim superiority over, or even equality with, Britain as it was increasingly doing. Octavia commented with British smugness: 'Nothing could be further from the facts than for America to suppose that she will be the premier continent.' As for the Americans' ultimate salvation or immortality, 'All that will happen is that some Americans who are direct descendants of our countrymen who went over in 1620 will be members of the Lord's Kingdom. For the rest, America will simply fade away!'[26]

The Panacea Society had not only a racialised theology of humankind; they also had a politicised one. As popular democracy expanded in England, and they perceived the threat of communism to be spreading across the globe, the Panaceans decided that the Bolsheviks were Anthropoids, and they needed to do something about it. Just as their rejection of so many aspects of modernity struck a chord with those who felt the world was changing too fast and in directions they did not like, so their paranoia about the 'Bolshevik menace' was shared by many of their contemporaries.

13

Defeating the Bolshevik Menace

On 1 May 1926 the British Trades Union Congress (TUC) announced that there would be a General Strike starting in two days, in support of coal miners who were being forced to work longer hours for lower wages. The country prepared. The police and army were mobilised, and tanks could be seen on the streets of London as the Conservative government feared violence and revolutionary activity. The government's main response was resistance, and it got ready to mobilise its Organisation of National Supplies, designed to keep the country moving and distribute anti-strike propaganda. The volunteers who sided with the government got ready to drive buses, trams and trains, deliver milk and mail and take up the jobs that would keep Britain running. Supporters of the strikers also got ready to turn out in force. The Panacea Society prepared in the way they knew best: with linen sections. Rachel Fox gives a wonderful description of the protection work she undertook in Cornwall.

> I shall never forget the strange furtive feeling which possessed me lest I should be observed, when I fixed the sections for Protection on the underside of the woodwork of a few bridges and stations. No volunteer for laying bombs with intent to blow up railways could have felt more anxious not to be noticed than I, though my object was the reverse! Like an ant under a granite wall I stood under the great viaduct which spans the ravine at Truro station and affixed my sections, in full faith that the bridge would be preserved from assault in any form.[1]

In those first few days of May, Panacea Wardens for the Protection Ministry and their bands of workers in counties all over England were, like Rachel Fox, affixing sections to public buildings across the country. The Panacea Society had been getting ready for this industrial unrest for some time. Not only had they been sprinkling

buildings and dropping and sticking linen sections here, there and
everywhere, but they had also been preparing for the possibility of a
breakdown of communications. The Wardens received papers from
headquarters teaching them how to be local centres for the healing
and sealing. Any national emergency might signify the beginning of
the end times, and thus the 144,000 would need to be sealed. The
Wardens were to put their signature on the seal and keep careful
numbered lists, which they would later send to headquarters.[2] 'Saviours
of your country!' wrote Octavia, 'preserve and study all instructions
we send you. If you do your best, it is a Divine Promise that you shall
not make a mistake.'[3] Practical instructions were given to Panacea
members and water-takers. All Panaceans were to be economical with
light, heat, fuel and food, and they were instructed that if they drank
the blessed water with small portions of food in times of scarcity, then
their hunger would be appeased. The Divine Mother taught that they
could live on the divine water alone if necessary. In June 1926, as the
miners continued to strike – when others had returned to work – and
there was the possibility of a coal shortage at a time when most homes
needed fuel for heating water, all water-takers were instructed that,
should it be difficult to get hot water, Water B should be rubbed
vigorously into the skin, letting the friction supply the heat.

Affixing linen sections to bridges may not seem a very effective
response to a General Strike to most people – regardless of political
leaning – but it made sense to the Panaceans who regarded any human
solution to the world's problems as entirely useless. Only their God-
given (as they believed) answer to the world's difficulties – their teachings, the healing water and protection work, and the practice of
Overcoming – would be effective as the world reached its cataclysmic
end. The Panaceans were always ready for events such as the General
Strike, given that their whole purpose was to prepare for the Second
Coming of Christ and all that would follow in its wake. Rachel Fox
wrote in her diary that they believed the coal strike would be 'the
beginning of "the End"'.[4]

The General Strike had been brewing for several months as a result
of several volatile issues: the country's economic instability, the role
of the unions, and Britain's poor trade in exports. In particular, coal
and the conditions of miners' work had been long-running issues. The
heavy domestic use of coal in the war meant that Britain had, in that

period, exported less coal, and other countries had filled the gap. Coal exports remained low, and took a further knock when Churchill reinstated the Gold Standard in 1925, making the pound too strong for exports to be affordable. Mine owners proposed to recoup their profits and to do so they wanted to reduce miners' wages and lengthen their hours. Not only in the mining of coal, but throughout British industry, the costs of production were becoming less and less competitive. At the same time there was a rise in wages and in the standard of living, while the cost of living remained low. All of this resulted in low exports and unemployment, which was at about 10 per cent in the mid-1920s. The General Strike was a test of the power of the unions, and raised fears in many quarters both about Britain coming to a standstill and about the possibility that the government would be made to submit to organised labour. Meanwhile, both the Labour Party and the TUC itself worried that the strike would unleash revolutionary forces that were not under their control.

The Panaceans were therefore not the only ones who saw the General Strike as a potential doomsday moment, when, on 3 May, one and a half million workers went on strike in support of the miners. In the end, the General Strike lasted only nine days and did not, as many people – including the Panaceans – feared, break out into class warfare, paralyse the economy or bring down Stanley Baldwin's Conservative government. After much pressure from many sides, including the Churches, the government and TUC forged a compromise agreement, and on 12 May, the TUC called off the strike. Everyone went back to work except the miners, who remained on strike for another six months, but they were ultimately broken and returned to work on the mine owners' terms. Rachel Fox's comment on the General Strike reminds us whose side the Panaceans were on. 'On Tuesday, May 4, 1926, the anticipated General Strike began; transport, press and post office were disorganised, but there was a magnificent response from volunteers from all classes of men and women to fill up places vacated by the men on strike, and to undertake the responsibility of unaccustomed duties.' Even more striking is the Panaceans' belief that their 'divinely led' work had affected the largely peaceable course of the strike, and its early ending. Rachel Fox commented: 'It will be seen that our work to protect England preceded and ran parallel with the human efforts to bring about peace by means of law and order.'[5]

A central feature of the Panacea Society's attitude to national politics was their simultaneous distancing from, and obsession with, them. In particular, the Panaceans constantly sought parallels and correspondences between life in the community and events outside it, and they continued to be convinced that what they did in the Society influenced what happened on the national political stage. Theoretically, they regarded politics as offering futile human solutions when only divine answers would solve the world's problems, but in reality they took an avid interest in politics, had decided political opinions and, as with everything else, interpreted political events in terms of the cosmic battle between good and evil, with Bedford as the epicentre of all activity. These parallel and often contradictory approaches meant that they were not above changing their attitude to political involvement when they needed to do so, and at the end of the 1920s and into the early 1930s, the Society took a decided turn towards political engagement as the forces of evil seemed to be advancing at ever greater speed.

From the very beginnings of the Society, Octavia declared that voting in elections was forbidden, precisely because it meant colluding with the world and its human solutions to society's problems. Mary Beedell, a non-resident member, wrote to the Society about voting in 1923: 'Eastbourne tonight is very excited about the Election. What a farce it all seems to us. Needless to say I have not voted this year and my husband did not mind a bit.'[6] The injunction against voting was, of course, ironic given that some of the founding members were former suffragettes and suffragists. They joined the Society just as women were given the vote, and thus never had the chance to exercise their new right. Octavia reiterated the views on women's rights to suffrage that she had held as the young Mabel, but with some Panacea teaching thrown in. In an article in *The Panacea*, she wrote that there 'should be no contest between the sexes and no "Woman's Rights" because both men and women need a new rule, and in a world like this, there are no rights that are worth having'.[7] Even voting for a party of which they approved was useless for it would merely 'keep the evil of the world in abeyance for a little longer'.[8] Reform was useless, for it was merely forming again and again on the old pattern, as one of Octavia's *Panacea* editorials put it. The state was composed of dying men in a dying world.[9] Until Jesus came again, the divine daughter's rule was what counted for the Panaceans, and on the days of General Elections the Society held their own election in which Octavia was always elected as 'the woman to rule'. Commanded by the Divine Mother, members signed a sheet of paper that stated:

> In conformity with this command, I definitely sign my name to my desire to elect Octavia, to continue the temporal and visible Rule in the Kingdom coming on earth until such time as a more definite Divine Rule comes into operation, and I quite understand that this election includes implicit obedience to the commands of the Divine Mother.[10]

The Panaceans' absence from the ballot box did not, however, curb their enthusiasm for believing that they wielded influence in other ways. When the Conservatives – their favoured political party – won the general election in October 1924, Octavia wrote a circular instruction to sealed members (marked 'private and confidential' and not to be shown to others) saying 'The Conservatives are returned to power because Mr Baldwin represents the via media, which is the God-like way of dealing with things. Neither Aristocracy nor Labour would be permitted to rule, as rule in the country must go alongside the rule here.' The reasons for Conservative rule in the country were equivalent to Octavia's rule: 'steady perseverance in the middle course, therefore, on behalf of all joined with Octavia, is the bulwark behind Mr Baldwin to-day and will secure that his party will retain the reins of government'. The Society's members, she wrote, 'shall have ways and means of supporting the Conservative Government and of protecting the King, whatever transpires'.[11]

The Conservatives dominated British politics in the 1920s. The Liberal Party was a largely spent force, having lost popular support. The new political contender was the Labour Party, growing in popularity in tandem with the rise of trade unions. After the 1924 election, the Conservatives remained in power, with Stanley Baldwin as Prime Minister, until 1929. The second half of the 1920s, with its economic uncertainty, unemployment and signs of a declining British Empire, gave rise to a steadily growing sense of national crisis that was fully expressed in the early 1930s by intellectuals and opinion-makers on both the Left and the Right. Combined with these national concerns was a sense that the axes of power in the world were shifting, and

the fundamentals of the modern state were being shifted and challenged in the wake of the Russian Revolution, and in both the growth
of popular democracy and serious challenges to democracy.
International events therefore impinged on national discussions, as the
opposing forces of communism and fascism began to shape world
politics.

The Panaceans held a right-wing, pessimistic view of the inevitability
of class conflict, not only – or even necessarily – because of class
discontent in Britain but because of international forces that they
believed were at work in sinister ways to unsettle all that was precious
about English life. An article in *The Panacea* described the General
Strike as 'one of the biggest Bolshevik blows against Civilisation that
has ever been delivered, but at present the mailed fist still wears the
soft glove of humanity, and desire for fairness and justice to miners
and other industrial workers'.[12] The Panaceans regarded the communist uprising in China in 1927 as dangerous (even though it was ultimately suppressed by the nationalists) because it signalled 'the influence
of Bolshevik strategy'. In that, their interpretation was not unusual,
for Soviet hopes for revolution in China were high – but for the
Panaceans the events also indicated that 'the Luciferian power of
Russia shall be successful through China'.[13]

Many people believed that communism was advancing through the
world, taking advantage of economic instability and weak political
regimes. What marked out the Panacean perspective was the theological spin they put on political events. In the Panacean view of the
world, where everything was a battle between God and Satan,
Bolshevism was regarded as Satanic or Luciferian. In the late 1920s
and early 1930s, the Society increasingly monitored and commented
on what it regarded as the dangerous advance of Bolshevism, and thus
of Satan's rule and the spiritual war on earth. They believed Satan
was making his way through the world via communism. For them,
the General Strike was merely the devil's first attack; the devil had
withdrawn for a while but, they believed, would launch fresh, worse
attacks – for which the Panacea Society was ready! By 1934, Rachel
Fox was writing: 'it is obvious that we are on the very edge of the
revolutionary effort so long and so carefully fostered by Russia and
the "Friends of Russia" in Great Britain'.[14]

There were plenty of Britons who shared the Panaceans' fear of the 'Bolshevik Menace'. Octavia's statements and Rachel Fox's accounts repeat the rhetoric of contemporary right-wing propaganda, with the idea of sinister outside influences – notably Bolsheviks and Jews – acting in the background to unleash class warfare in Britain. Indeed, the Panaceans were profoundly informed in their political views by the conservative newspapers they read, such as the middle-brow *Daily Mail* and the *Daily Express*, and the ultra-conservative broadsheet, the *Morning Post*. Each community house was expected to take at least one newspaper in order to keep informed about political events of importance, and to bring to Octavia any items of interest. In 1928, the Divine Mother commanded that they should focus their reading, in part to save time and in part to avoid articles on murder, trials and divorces (which, it was feared, would blunt their feelings).[15] Their focus was to be the political news. While Octavia maintained that the Panaceans should not allow their opinions to be formed by newspapers, she still offered guidance on which newspapers were sound and which were not. In a *Panacea* editorial in 1934, she put at the top of the list the *Morning Post*: 'sound, independent, loyal, and patriotic' especially on the monarchy and British Empire. Also solid was the tabloid *Daily Express*: 'a strong champion in the cause of Empire and Free Trade within it'. The *Daily Mail*, a firm favourite in the early days of the Panacea Society, was now liked less because it took up and dropped causes too quickly: it 'violently espoused fascism, especially Sir Oswald Mosley's variety, then fell out with him' and it urged its readers to vote socialist in 1929. Then there was a sort of middle band of papers. *The Times* had 'no very decided views' and was consequently 'dull'. The *Daily Telegraph* was excellent in its general news but not necessarily sound on the India question (home rule was anathema to the Panaceans) or the League of Nations. Absolutely bottom of the list were the *News Chronicle* and the *Daily Herald*. The *News Chronicle* was 'the chief liberal organ' which 'toadies to the Socialist party and is constantly being rebuffed by it', was in favour of the despised League of Nations, and 'a whole-hearted advocate of throwing India to the wolves (Gandhi's party)'. The *Daily Herald* was 'Labour's Own' and represented everything Octavia despised: internationalist, in favour of the League of Nations, anti-fascist, admiring of Gandhi 'and most impatient to give away India – and in fact, the whole Empire' and in 'full sympathy with Soviet Russia, with which it advocates closer relations'.[16] The Society had a special relationship with the *Morning Post*, which Octavia considered, of all newspapers, 'the least affected by modern ideas'.[17] The Panaceans even made a scrapbook of newspaper clippings from the *Morning Post* demonstrating how it stopped Bolshevism and the world's decline.

Socialism was the thin end of the wedge and it was dangerous, said Octavia, because it was the root of Bolshevism. 'Where the devil could not get people wicked enough to become Bolsheviks he made them Socialists, and where he could not get them to be Socialists, he tacked on the name "Christian" and produced "Christian Socialists", it is the tiny bud of the fruit Bolshevism.'[18] The Panaceans supported their views with scripture, interpreting socialism as un-biblical. They took texts such as Paul's statement about slaves, in his letter to Titus – 'Put them in mind to be in subjection to rulers, to authorities, to be obedient' – to reflect the God-given order of society. Octavia repeatedly emphasised that servants must not rule, quoting the Gospel of Matthew (10: 24) that a servant is not above his Lord, and she made sure the servants in her own community got no ideas above their station. An article in *The Panacea* reiterated the Society's paternalistic attitude. It argued that because much had been done in England 'for the bettering of the conditions of the employees', as for example at Cadbury's chocolate factory in Bournville and Port Sunlight where soap was made, the 'employees should work all the harder in order to recompense employers who do so much for them'.[19] Octavia, writing under the pseudonym of 'Mark Proctor', did not deny that workers needed to have their material welfare protected, but she believed that socialism and communism had got the order of matters wrong by putting the interests of labour before the interests of capital. She maintained that socialism would 'destroy all existing institutions, is careless of religion apart from humanitarianism, is international, loves every country better than its own, but has no foreign policy'. Most of all, she hated the way socialism would rule – via democracy.[20]

Democracy was anathema to Octavia. The most perfect form of government was absolute monarchy and this was how God would rule the earth. 'Is it likely,' she asked, 'that God will much longer allow His great country of England, His New Jerusalem, to be ruled by the system which prevails now, a system which takes count of the opinions of irresponsible persons and of boys and girls hardly out of their teens?'[21] Octavia proclaimed that the most perfect form of absolute monarchy was absolute kingship, given by God; and the divinely appointed king was the British king. 'The world must be ruled and the world must be ruled by a man who is kin to David, and that man is King George V,' wrote Octavia. She continued: 'Britain is God's Holy Mountain, so its Throne is the one and only Throne ever established by God.'[22] Only the divinely appointed monarchy was good enough for England. The Panaceans therefore closely monitored the activities of the royal family, and were most distressed when the King was taken ill in 1928, not least because the blessed water could not be taken to his bedside. When he recovered in July the following year, the community said prayers of thanksgiving, the Divine Mother declared that the Spirit had been carried to him in the Divine Breath (quite how was not clarified) and Octavia proclaimed increased loyalty to the throne, to the man who was neither servant nor friend of his country but ruler. 'He will not do what the people want,' she said, 'but what he knows to be good for them.'[23] Octavia believed that England stood at the centre of the world and was divinely chosen: 'England is the new Jerusalem, our throne is the throne of David, for King George is descended from Zedekiah, King of Judah.'[24] The notion that the English royal family was descended from the House of David was an old British Israelite idea that had been around since the nineteenth century,[25] here adapted by the Panaceans to suggest that when Christ came, his chosen human ruler on earth would be the English king.

In her own Society, Octavia insisted on divine rule and obedience to it, foreshadowing the perfect rule that would come one day to all the world. 'Your duty in the present,' she told members, 'is to obey the Divine Mother's Rule very carefully.' Otherwise, she argued, with her conviction that what the Panaceans did affected the rest of the country, 'there would be a danger of a Socialist Government coming into Power in this country'. For her it was simple: 'Those who are meant to be ruled will be perfectly happy, being ruled. Somebody must rule, and some be ruled.' She later wrote, 'The chief thing in Bolshevism is to dislike to be ruled, so if you have a dislike to be ruled you cannot be in this Mission.'[26]

Octavia was completely opposed to the Labour Party. She declared, 'I stand for the absolute repudiation of Socialism in all its forms. You must not allow for a moment the belief that it will rule in England.' This she stated in February 1929. Unfortunately for her, three months later, a Labour government was voted in.[27]

At the 1929 general election there was, for the first time in Britain, a fully democratic franchise. Popular democracy had arrived. Since 1918, when women over the age of thirty had been given the vote even though the voting age for men was twenty-one, the inequality between male and female voters had been contentious. In July 1928, legislation was passed that allowed women to vote at the age of twenty-one too. Even if a few former suffragettes privately cheered, most Panaceans did not regard this favourably. Rachel Fox commented: 'This opened the way for a great change in the political situation for masses of new voters who had no stake in the country, and particularly no knowledge of political matters; this extension doubled the forces of irresponsible and inexperienced voters.'[28] There is no evidence that the younger female vote particularly biased the election results in favour of Labour, but it was convenient to think so. The Society was full of forebodings and noted the thunderstorms in election week, as if the heavy rain were a sign of what was to come. The general election of 1929 resulted in a hung Parliament, with Labour having 27 more seats than the Conservatives, though the Conservatives in fact had 300,000 more votes. Labour formed a government, a minority administration in coalition with the Liberal Party. Octavia was horrified. Her response was to declare that Labour must not rule. The Society needed to repudiate the Labour government – just as they had repudiated the Treaty of Versailles in 1919. She therefore decided that the Society would elect in its place a Spiritual Cabinet with Mr Baldwin at its head. The Divine Mother gave her assent. Resident member Major Carew-Hunt, one of the most right-wing and politically active of all the Panaceans, was charged with drawing up a list of members of this Spiritual Cabinet, wholesome Conservatives, and this list was 'submitted to The Great Divine Father and the Son for Their Approval'. Handily for the Panaceans, the Great Divine Father, through the Son, was said to have assented to this cabinet and 'promised to work his Will through these men so elected'. It became the Divine Mother's custom thereafter to refer to Mr Baldwin as 'My Prime Minister', even though he was not in power.[29]

It was of course rather awkward that Labour remained in power for two years after this but the Panacea Society found themselves able to justify it on theological grounds. 'A great point to get hold of . . . is the ACTUAL REASON WHY A LABOUR GOVERNMENT IS RULING. It is an anomaly and quite opposed to Divine ordinance, which forbids rule by servants and only delegates it to kings, but it is part of the Divine strategy, whereby the enemy is being lured into our country; so that it is all to the good and according to plan, and the "earth" is acting up to the prophetic declaration and is properly "disquieted", as it should be when servants reign.'[30] An explanation could always be given. In an editorial in *The Panacea*, Octavia wrote 'Asked if we are sorry Labour has got into power, we answer "Quite the reverse, for it will give the Lord the opportunity to show how disquieting it is to the Earth for servants to rule".'[31]

Octavia assiduously monitored and commented on political events both at home and abroad in her own distinctive way. The spread of communist ideas – whether in Cape Town, Germany or China – was always regarded as troublesome. The persecution of Christians by the Soviet government became a particular topic of concern. In Britain the Christian Protest Movement (CPM) was founded in December 1929 for 'the support of religion and morality against the menace of Bolshevik communism' and it protested against the suppression of religion in Russia. It attracted the support of many clergy, including three bishops and an archbishop (of Armagh in Northern Ireland) as well as many members of the aristocracy. The movement held a mass protest in the Albert Hall on 19 December 1929, which James Hancock, the Panacea Society's man in London, attended. The Society gave it £100 at its outset, though Octavia felt that the movement was doomed because it was 'run upon clerical lines' and would therefore fail to have any impact on the actions of the Russian government. Nevertheless, when the CPM shifted its focus in 1932 to combat anti-religious teaching in Britain, and began to expound the view that those conducting the anti-religious campaign in Russia were now extending their activities throughout the civilised world, Octavia became more interested. The Panacea Society responded to their circular that called for co-ordination of all religious bodies in resisting 'the anti-God campaign now being conducted by Bolshevik-Communist propaganda in this country'. The Society received further literature, including the *CPM News*, and Rachel Fox commented from time to time on their activities in her histories of the Society, but the Panaceans did not become otherwise involved.[32]

Octavia began to pontificate more and more on the Soviet Union's aims, interpreting these as the destruction of family life and individualism, which would remove the foundations of civilisation in order to produce a 'slave state'. This sounded in some ways like the aims of Panacea life: despite her instinctive belief that the family was a foundational institution of society, she ruled over a celibate community; and what was the practice of Overcoming if not in some way the destruction of individualism? In 1931, studying the Russian five-year plan for the rapid development of that country's economy, which by then was in its third year, Octavia began to see parallels between the aims of her own Society and the aims of Soviet life. They were both striving for utopia. Both believed that active benefit must accrue here and now. Russia demanded, as they did, that change must take place. And, Octavia continued, 'What about the Russian determination to make all people alike and to have but one aim!' This, she said, was 'reminiscent of the Panacea demand that we must all think on the same lines and eventually become alike by possession of one spirit – the spirit to think and do rightfully'. So what was the difference? First, the Panaceans did this not as slaves of the state but as sons and daughters of God. And secondly, and most importantly, while there was divine power behind the Panacean plan, devilish and Satanic influences were behind the Russian scheme. Thus, as the Panaceans were told in a script, 'The race between good and evil is neck and neck.' It was a theme she returned to. 'There is a terrible correspondence in the Russian ideas and in our own mission too,' she wrote.

Octavia was perceptive: she understood that she was living in an era of political utopias; that what looked like opposing dreams ran on parallel lines. But her insistence on making the Panacea Society a major world-player appears to the outside observer odd to say the least, and a part of her realised that would be the case. While retaining her belief that the Panacea Society was of world significance, she acknowledged that it was numerically small and relatively unknown. 'Thus the Bolshevist plans to obtain world dominion and to destroy all faith in God and his Son are being put into effect *side by side* with the great Divine Purpose, which is being quietly carried out unknown to the world, to save a remnant and to organise it for use in the troubles to come.'[33]

Meanwhile, the country's economic difficulties deepened along with much of the rest of the world's, as banks crashed in America and around Europe, causing the Great Depression. England was deeply in debt, the demand for British products kept falling, and by the end of 1930 unemployment had risen to 20 per cent of the population, higher in the north of England, cities such as Glasgow in Scotland and the mining towns of Wales, those places where the traditional industries of coal mining, steel, textiles and shipbuilding were badly hit. The Panaceans blamed the Labour Party. Writing in 1931, Rachel Fox declared: 'owing to democratic and socialistic rule we are within visible danger of national bankruptcy,' provoked by what she described as Labour's policy of 'dole without work'.[34] As it turned out the Labour Party was irrevocably split on the solutions to the country's economic woes, deadlocked about how to deal with the deep recession that Britain was now in. The Prime Minister Ramsay Macdonald briefly headed up a National Government in the summer of 1931 to manage the crisis, and when Britain left the Gold Standard in September, there was restoration of confidence and the hope of economic recovery. Nevertheless, a general election was called for 27 October 1931.

With the chance of ridding Britain of Labour's rule, Octavia was taking no risks. She was so worried about Labour being re-elected that she broke her own rules and allowed community members to vote in the general election, 'which meant votes for Mr Baldwin'.[35] Dissent was not allowed. All Panaceans were commanded to think alike. Octavia had told a member who was a Labour supporter in 1924, when there was briefly a Labour government, that if they continued to think like that then they must leave the community. On election night, Octavia, Emily Goodwin and Peter Rasmussen sat by the wireless from 9.30 p.m. until four in the morning listening to the results. The National Government (with a Conservative majority – 473 Members of Parliament out of 615) was returned, and this was regarded as a great divine work, miraculous; indeed, more than a miracle. Panacean activity was seen to have influenced national events once again. As Octavia put it, 'It appears that our voting at this Election has surprised the devils, who thought we should not vote, as we have been stopped voting before.' God had done a wonderful thing, but how? 'The answer is,' she wrote, 'that He first secured that there should be a little body of people here who laid down their self opinion and wanted right-minded men to rule and then He got the country to do the same.'[36] Indeed, she believed that 'the people were moved upon Divinely to vote in such a manner as to secure a Conservative rule for the country because it is a safe rule.'[37]

The Panaceans breathed a sigh of relief. Major Carew-Hunt, by now honorary secretary of the Panacea Society and therefore a key figure in the Society's dealing with the outside world, wrote to the editor of the *Morning Post* on 4 November in prophetic vein. 'The earth was so disquieted "for a servant when he reigneth" (Proverbs 30: 21–22), that the rule of Labour WILL NEVER COME AGAIN.' He predicted that 'When belief in success and prosperity apart from the Only Giver of all good things has vanished, our country, the "glorious land" of Scripture, will enter a peaceful millennium of security, prosperity, health and happiness under King George V and his Committee of Experts in every department.' He continued: 'These devilish absurdities, Democratic rule, Universal Franchise and Internationalism, will have no place in the coming administration.'

Cyril Carew-Hunt had something of the Little Englander in his mentality. Along with his Conservative politics he shared the deep-seated patriotism of all in the Panacea Society. The Panaceans monitored world politics, but so far as they entered the political fray, it was as English men and women. Events in Europe might impinge on their thinking, especially as the clouds of war gathered in the 1930s, but they were clear that they were not part of Europe. Internationalism was a dangerous trend; indeed it was regarded as 'not in the divine purpose'[38] – not just in politics but more specifically in trade.

It was Cyril Carew-Hunt who spearheaded the 'Buy British' campaign in the Society. In 1931, Panacea members were instructed to buy British. It was a 'spiritual command' in part because it came through the Prince of Wales, son of King George V, who had inaugurated the campaign in November that year, and in part because God's kingdom could only be established in a prosperous country. As God's kingdom was going to be established in Britain, Britain needed all the economic support it could get. The Panaceans actively had to help build Jerusalem in England's green and pleasant land by boosting the country's trade, not just by singing a hymn. England was, after all, the motherland of the world (*pace* Hitler) as two *Panacea* articles expressed it, 'the country in which Divine Rule under George V is beginning, slowly but surely, to operate'.[39] Britain of course included her Empire: the injunction to buy British included not only British-made goods but also dominion and colonial produce.

Panaceans were not allowed to join other societies and movements but once again Octavia bent her rules to support a cause dear to her heart, urging members at headquarters and readers of *The Panacea* to join the Tudor Rose League, an employer-sponsored, popular movement for protectionism to circumvent the free-trade position of the British government.[40] Octavia herself was in touch with the head of the Tudor Rose League, Admiral Mark Kerr, in November 1931, answering his questions about the Panacea Society. She wrote to him: 'in days when Internationalism is becoming a positive religion, and the idea of a United States of Europe is projected with such amazing seriousness, it is very necessary that Great Britain should take her place as the premier power of the world, because she is the Divine Battle-Axe against all that opposes her destiny to govern a world redeemed from all distressing circumstances'.[41]

Supporters of the movement wore a badge to show their intention to buy only British goods, the Tudor Rose, an 'historical emblem which does not savour of jingoism and which is not associated with "partisanship" being made up of both the red and white roses of Lancaster and York', and thus 'symbolic of unity and cooperation'. There were also badges for shop windows, factories and restaurants, denoting that those places sold British-only goods. There was an implicit understanding that the price of British goods might be higher, but supporters were willing to pay in order to overcome the undermining of British labour and industry by 'unfair competition from overseas'.[42] Cyril Carew-Hunt was in correspondence with a member of the League and ordered two guineas' worth of badges to sell to resident and non-resident members. This was done through the Society's Publication Department, and there was a strong response from members, but the market eventually dried up: the number of badges that could be sold to members was limited – no one needed more than one badge – so by April 1934, the account for badges was closed and the unsold badges and brooches were put away in a drawer to gather dust where I tumbled across them one day nearly eighty years later.

Octavia acknowledged that in allowing members to vote and join the Tudor Rose League, she was breaking down the barriers between religion and everyday life.[43] Political activity increased in the Society, especially as God's kingdom did not come, as the international situation became more grave and the economic crisis deepened. This greater involvement was given divine sanction. In the wake of the October general election in 1931, a script from the Lord in November declared that religion could not be separated from the material affairs of the world. Whilst in heaven they might be separate, on earth the two were united; and as the Immortals, the Panaceans were preparing to live on earth for ever.

The Panaceans were not alone in their anxiety about the world. The perceived crisis in civilisation was at the centre of public debate, discussed not only in the newspapers and Parliament but also in bookshops, societies, homes, and on the lecture circuit, whether from the perspective of the Left or the Right. The journalist and former editor of *The Times* Wickham Steed wrote in 1931, 'there is no precedent . . . It is a chaos of ideas'. As Steed suggested, theories and solutions came from all quarters, whether from Sigmund Freud in his 1930 *Civilisation and its Discontents* or the lesser known Scottish cleric, Norman Maclean, on how to avoid war, in his book *How Shall We Escape? Learn or Perish*.[44] Within this melange of ideas, Fascism began to rise as a potentially serious force in British politics.

Mussolini had come to power in Italy in the early 1920s. Conservatives in Britain responded positively to his regime. Newspapers such as the *Daily Mail* and *Morning Post* thought Italian Fascism an experiment worthy of success: Lord Rothermere, the proprietor of the *Daily Mail*, was one of its greatest proponents in Britain. Fear of the advance of Bolshevism, economic instability, labour and trade union militancy: balanced against all that, the retreat from democracy not only in Italy but also in Spain, Greece, Bulgaria, and Hungary and Turkey in the 1920s did not seem such a bad thing to many conservative Britons. Irene Mellor, a resident member, had seen the nascent Fascist movement when visiting Florence in 1921, and had been impressed by it. She wrote in *The Panacea* in 1923 (by which time Mussolini had assumed power in Italy): 'The Fascisti movement must and will spread and its supporters must give their lives, martyrs to the preservation of all that is best in the civilised world, but it needs man's

Edgar Peissart as a young man. On seeing this photograph, Kate Firth said he looked like 'the devil himself'.

Edgar Peissart at about the time he came to Bedford (1922).

The poster Edgar had made up of his image fading out of Cyrus Teed's to show that he was Teed's natural successor in the Koreshan community in Estero, Florida. Edgar's distinctive, florid handwriting is on the poster.

Donald Ricketts, the Cambridge undergraduate and Panacea member with whom Edgar fell in love.

Jesse Green, Edgar Peissart'
sometime lover, after he had
returned to America, with hi
children. Note that a photo
of his wife, Marie, has been
pasted onto the scene

Helen Morris, non-resident
member and confidante
of Edgar Peissart.

Emily Goodwin, whose alter-ego as the Instrument of the Divine Mother wielded such power in the Society after 1923.

Leonard Squire Tucker in a cassock outside The Haven, just after he and Kate Firth had dramatically left the Society in March 1926.

Peter Rasmussen and another member knock down the wall between Octavia's garden and The Haven after the Society had bought Kate's house in the summer of 1926.

Octavia in the Blue Room at
The Haven with the cot made for
Joanna Southcott's anticipated child,
Shiloh, in 1814. The Panacea Society
acquired it on permanent loan
from the Salford Museum.

Brigadier Adrian
Barltrop, 1946.
This painting
hangs in the
Chetwode
Building of the
Indian Military
Academy in
Dehradun, India.

Dilys Barltrop in the Panacea
gardens late 1920s.

Anna Barltrop,
as a child, in the
Panacea gardens
in 1933.

Joanna Southcott, the late eighteenth- and early nineteenth-century prophet whose writings inspired Mabel Barltrop.

(*Above right*) Posters for the Box campaign laid out on the lawn in the Panacea gardens.

Panacea member handing out leaflets in front of a Box poster, Regent Street, London.

Advertisements to open the Box were displayed on the side of London buses in 1932. The Panaceans carefully documented which bus routes carried the ads.

Public Petition to the Bishops to open Joanna Southcott's Box

To the Archbishops and Bishops of the Church of England,

WE, the undersigned, and 28,757 others, do petition the Bishops of the Church of England, that 24 of their number do send for and open Joanna Southcott's Box of Sealed Manuscripts, as we are of the opinion that anything purporting to be a Divine Revelation laid up for the world at this critical period should be examined by the Heads of the Church, whose duty it is to look into such matters. And your Petitioners will ever pray for the advancement of the Kingdom of Christ under your jurisdiction.

The Sheets bearing the signatures to the Public Petition to all the Bishops of the Church of England having Sees are delivered to His Grace, The Lord Archbishop of Canterbury, as Primate of all England, on this day, 23rd April 1935, in trust for his and their consideration.

The Public Petition is sent also to the Lord Archbishop of York, as Primate of England, and to all the Bishops having Sees, together with the information that the names of the 28,000 petitioners lie at Lambeth Palace, and that there is power to add thousands upon thousands to their number, but that the Lists are called in and presented at the beginning of the period—May to November—when the Box can be delivered up, because it appears wasteful of time and of effort to proceed beyond a number that is sufficiently representative of all classes in the North, South, East, and West of Great Britain.

Right Reverend Bishops who are willing to accede to this Petition are requested to communicate with

C. Carew-Hunt
Major R.A. (ret.)
Honorary Secretary, THE PANACEA SOCIETY.

Rachel J. Fox
(President)

Russell Vague
(Canon)

Petition to open Joanna Southcott's Box of Prophecies delivered to the Archbishop of Canterbury on 23 April 1935.

The Daily Courier—MARCH 20, 1925.

JOHANNA SOUTHCOTT CHURCHILL.

BUDGET BOX O' TRICKS

It is reported that Johanna Southcott's Mystery Box is to be opened this year.

Cartoon with Winston Churchill portrayed as Joanna Southcott, 1925.

Joanna Southcott's Box of Prophecies.

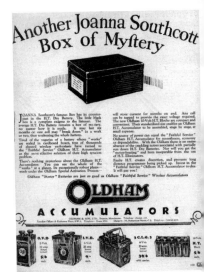

Another Joanna Southcott Box of Mystery

OLDHAM
ACCUMULATORS

Advertisement showing how much Joanna Southcott's Box had entered into the public consciousness as a result of the Panacea Society's campaigning.

Octavia at a garden party
in the early 1930s.

Octavia and Dilys reading at home,
early 1930s.

Octavia towards the end of her life,
now heavy and suffering from diabetes,
with the Jackdaw she kept as a pet.

(*Above left*) Advertisement for the Panacea Society's Healing.

(*Above*) The linen squares used in the healing water. Octavia breathed on large supplies of the linen to bless it.

Peter Rasmussen and John Coghill in the 1950s on Albany Road.

Aerial view of the community in the 1970s. The Panacea garden can be seen in the middle.

highest devotion to save the world today.'[45] Her view was not out of kilter with the beliefs of a sizeable segment of the population. Later in the 1920s, British views on Italian fascism became increasingly polarised, as liberal newspapers carried less favourable accounts of Italian politics, and even Rothermere conceded that it was a system more suited to Italy than to Britain.

For the Panaceans, dictators such as Mussolini were 'on monarchical lines', more desirable than democracy, and perfectly acceptable for other countries. Octavia believed that the Fascist movement in Italy was 'the struggle of right-minded men and women against the totally evil intentions of Bolshevik Red shirts' and claimed that she had received teachings from the Lord saying so. Indeed the Bolsheviks and Fascists were seen to fit rather neatly into the Panacea categories of different sorts of human beings. The Bolshevists, communists and socialists, the redshirts, were Anthropoids, with no immortal souls. They were enemies of God and of good; they were destroying angels. The Fascists or blackshirts were Aliens. They were persons who expressed 'belief in law, order, goodness, justice, equity, who will die fighting on the side of God and good'. The Immortals were, as ever, the Panaceans, who 'will form the great Church of the Realm and will be the nucleus of the new kingdom'. They would be identified by their white robes, as a bride adorned for her bridegroom worn in the Book of Revelation 21: 2.[46] In the war in heaven, described in Revelation 12: 4, there were three groups of combatants; and so in the final war on earth there would be three contending groups once again: communists, fascists and Panaceans. This still meant that the fascists offered only a human solution, albeit a good one according to the Panaceans. Rachel Fox commented that the rise of fascism in Italy brought a welcome return of law and order in the country, and 'the Dictatorship of Mussolini was permitted to show to the world the *highest human effort*, by force and by the power of the Law, to control devils in human guise' [my italics].

By the early 1930s, after the political and economic crisis of 1931, Britons of an anti-democratic persuasion were now more convinced than ever that firm government was required. Some combination of fascism and the British monarchy might, some people thought, provide a solution. Oswald Mosley had been a junior minister in the 1931 Labour government. When his economic solution – including tariffs to protect the home market, control of the banks to promote investment, and plans for boosting industry, agriculture and employment – was rejected, he left the government. In February 1931 he formed the New Party, which met with little success. In October 1932, he launched the British Union of Fascists (BUF), the most prominent and most violent of the various home-grown fascist groups that had been cropping up since the 1920s.

Octavia was uninterested in Mosley and disliked the BUF. It was too anti-Semitic, for one thing. Nevertheless, the Panaceans briefly flirted with a minor fascist group, but with no lasting affiliation. Both Octavia and Major Carew-Hunt had some dealings with the Unity Band, which was run out of a London fascist publishing house, Boswell Printing and Publishing. The group was linked to the proto-fascist monthly journal *The Patriot*, which had a circulation of about 3,000 and had been founded by the Duke of Northumberland in 1922. The Duke, supported by his income from coal and steel, spent his time peddling right-wing conspiracy theories about movements threatening the safety and welfare of the British Empire, both in his own journal and by subsidising the Panacea Society's favourite newspaper, the *Morning Post*. The key figure in the Unity Band was one Colonel Oscar Boulton, who was the uncle of Panacea member, Lieutenant Commander W. S. Galpin. It was Galpin who brought the Society's attention to his uncle's 'big scheme . . . for doing away with politicians . . . . His ideas seem very similar to the Panacea Society's in many ways and I wish he would join as I feel sure the Water would help him.'[47] The Unity Band's ideas that Galpin felt were similar to those of the Panacea Society included re-establishing the Empire, resuming British government of India, rigidly restricting the admission of aliens to Britain while also creating a well-devised scheme of emigration for the young of both sexes, a drastic reduction in taxation, and the preservation and protection of the 'true womanly ideal'. Boulton also wanted to abolish parliamentary government and replace it with a directing council and a House of Commons based on merit and capacity. But what the Panacea Society really liked was the centrality of religion to the Unity Band. Oscar Boulton believed not just that religion was important for fascism but that the survival of civilisation itself was dependent on Christian virtues, over and against the materialistic basis of the utopias proposed by the revolutionaries whom he so deeply despised and opposed. The Unity Band stressed the need to recall the nation to God, and described itself as an association of Christian men and women. Boulton published a poem in *The Patriot*, called 'The Coming of Lucifer', which Octavia read out in one of the Society's worship meetings. All the members commented on the poem's 'amazing grasp of the conditions which the Panacea Society is out to combat', wrote Octavia to Boulton.[48] Cyril Carew-Hunt remained in touch with the secretary of the Unity Band and seems to have been a member and subscriber for at least a year – from March 1931 to April 1932 – receiving the group's own magazine, *The British Lion*, but when he was asked to circulate a petition asking the King to 'dismiss Ministers who are unworthy of his confidence' Carew-Hunt declined, saying that he did not think anyone would sign it.[49] In the end, the Society was interested in other groups only to the extent that those groups' interests supported what the Panaceans believed to be the true solution to the world's problems.

Octavia liked running her own show, not joining other people's groups. She decided to form her own movement for change, urging the nation to turn to God and recover its greatness. In December 1932, she launched the Realities campaign and National Petition, conducted through the *Morning Post*. Its purpose was to 'deliver Great Britain from the Godless menace and from the present distress and perplexity'. She wrote in a briefing paper to members: 'This is a very serious affair, because it is given to us to initiate the first step in National Recovery – which is to turn the face of the Nation to God – but it must be done, and can only be done, without a grain of sectarian religion of any sort including itself; this means that even the Panacea teaching must not be included.'[50] When the materials arrived at the *Morning Post* offices for the National Petition to be launched, she noted that it was three years to the day that the Christian Protest Movement had been launched. Octavia commented in her daily late afternoon conversation with God: 'The great difference between the two appeals is that one is to man, asking for means with which to project a human attack on this terrible enemy, and the other is an effort to set people to work to appeal to God alone for aid in our national trials as well as in regard to the godless menace.' God replied: 'This is the crux of the whole matter – to realise that man cannot fight the spirit of Evil; and this is why it says in the Lord's Prayer "Deliver us from Evil".'[51] The Society calculated that the National Petition had gathered 43,000 signatures by the end of 1934; bundles of signed petitions in the archives suggest that the final total was 47,240.[52]

More important, however, than the Realities campaign and National Petition was the Society's longest-running campaign for change, the one that had put Mabel Barltrop (as she was then) in an asylum with exhaustion, the one that had galvanised so many women in the war years and had brought the founders of the Panacea Society together. This was the campaign to get the bishops to open Southcott's Box of Prophecies, which, the Panaceans believed, contained God-given solutions to the world's problems. They put up posters all over the London underground which declared: 'Moscow will be London's doom, unless the Bishops open Joanna Southcott's Box'. Surely if the Box were opened, the Bolshevik menace would truly recede?

14

Open the Box!

On a (literally) dark and stormy night, 11 July 1927, in front of a crowd of 400 at Church Hall in Westminster, Harry Price, the infamous exposer of fraudulent mediums, opened what he claimed was Joanna Southcott's Box of Prophecies. In fact he knew perfectly well that this was not *the* Box – the one in which prophecies had been placed 'year by year as ordered, sealed in bundles with seven seals'[1] – which was to be opened by twenty-four bishops. Price had intimated as much in a letter to Rachel Fox at the Panacea Society the previous month.[2] He even knew what was inside, as he had X-rayed the box in May, but he could not resist the laughs of the crowd and the attention the stunt attracted as, with the help of the one bishop present, the Bishop of Grantham, he pulled out of the box, as the storm raged outside: a pistol; a lottery ticket for 1796; a nightcap; two earrings; a dice-box; a metal puzzle; a calendar of the French court for 1793; a bead purse and some coins; a picture of the River Thames, dated 1814; some medals and several writings – but nothing by Joanna Southcott.

Meanwhile, seven members of the Panacea Society stood outside in the rain getting drenched as they handed out leaflets. The tube stations had been flooded and so they had already got their feet soaked walking through deep puddles to Westminster. They handed out leaflets that confidently proclaimed 'The Box of Sealed Writings of Joanna Southcott, prophetess, which the 24 bishops will open, remains and will remain in safe custody until circumstances force the bishops to do what they refuse to do.' These were illustrated with a photograph of the real Box.

What Harry Price did not know was that the real Box was underneath a bed in a bungalow in Morecambe, with a cover on it, hidden by a valence around the base of the bed. No one would have imagined that Southcott's Box was hidden in a modest house – albeit, one named 'Southcot' – in a northern English seaside town, but the Box's custodian, an old Southcottian named Emily Jowett, was taking no chances. She wrote to Octavia, as publicity about the Harry Price event was splashed across the newspapers, that 'We do not talk or appear to take any interest in the matter for fear someone might come to see us . . . The quieter we are about it the better, I think, & you know where it is when called for.'[3]

In fact the old Southcottians had always kept rather quiet about the Box, and it was only with the revival of interest in Southcott in the early twentieth century that there was a concerted effort to make the opening of the Box a public cause. The letter-writing campaign of the war years to the Archbishop of Canterbury, Randall Davidson, and other bishops was what had brought together the founders of the Panacea Society.[4] Even before the Society was formally founded in 1919, the campaign to get the Box opened had continued, with Rachel Fox as the central agitator. In 1915, as a result of their interview with Davidson, Rachel Fox and her cousin Lady Portsmouth had sent out letters and one of Fox's books to all forty diocesan bishops. On the basis of the replies they received, in 1916 Rachel Fox reckoned that the bishops of Gloucester, Lichfield, Chichester, Hereford, Worcester, Sodor and Man, and Exeter were willing to have the Box opened 'in order to settle the minds of many good people, and not because they themselves believe that it will yield anything of value'. The Bishop of Wakefield desired it 'to expose the fraud whom he believes J.S. to be'; the Bishop of Southampton was interested, as was Bishop Boyd-Carpenter.[5] It was Boyd-Carpenter who turned out to be the ladies' best hope: their letter-writing campaign culminated in an offer from him to open the Box.

Boyd-Carpenter had been Bishop of Ripon, in Yorkshire, until 1911 when he had become a canon of Westminster Abbey in London. Throughout the summer months of 1917 he and Rachel Fox were in constant communication by letter about the conditions under which the bishops might be persuaded to open the Box. Rachel Fox understood the difficulty of 'how to convince the Bishops that it is the "will of the Lord" and not only the fuss of a deluded woman – for nothing but close investigation which they will not give to the published writings [of Southcott] can convince them of this'. Boyd-Carpenter was nervous that Rachel Fox spoke of 'the opening of the Box as an "act of faith"'. He continued, 'I can quite understand that you should so regard it; but the bishops would hardly be asked to let their action in opening the box be so regarded.'[6] Once that little misunderstanding had been cleared up, Rachel Fox now saw Boyd-Carpenter as their best bet, and did her utmost to convince him that he should persuade his brother bishops to open the Box.

She urged him that the time was right – in what was now the third year of the war: '"time is waxing late" for this action if we would save the country, the church & our army from further disasters,' she wrote, urging him to gather the names of bishops or their proxies who would agree to be involved. In turn, the Bishop wrote seriously of the practical considerations, requesting a lawyer and other experts: 'the box ought to be examined before opening & the witnesses should be satisfied by expert examination that it has not been tampered with since it was sealed & fastened. It is important therefore that experienced men should give their assistance in this way.' Presumably the 'experienced men' would also counteract his fear that this was merely the delusion of some inexperienced women.[7]

In 1918, Bishop Boyd-Carpenter declared that he had the names of twenty-four bishops who were willing to request the opening of the Box. Whether the Box would ever have been opened is not known because Alice Seymour, the Custodian of the Box (though she did not own it), declared that the time was not right for its opening after all. She wrecked the best chance of having the Box opened, and a rift developed between her and the Panacea Society that was never healed. When Bishop Boyd-Carpenter died the following year, so did the ladies' main hope of help amongst that generation of bishops. This did not stop them writing to others with influence. Rachel Fox wrote to Queen Mary and received a curt and rather wry reply from her private secretary stating that 'Her Majesty, while fully appreciating the kind thought which has prompted the offer, regrets that she is unable to avail herself of the book "England's Way of Escape from the Power of Evil" as it is not usual for The Queen to accept works of this nature.'[8] Despite this, Rachel Fox wrote to the King in 1920, and again in 1930, encouraged by the support she had received from Princess Louise in 1918, and Lady Paget, who had been an intimate friend of Queen Victoria and was a woman of progressive views, a vegetarian, anti-vivisectionist, Theosophist, and author of the introduction to a sex-education manual for girls in 1909, who had no problem in adding Southcott's Box to her range of interests. But even dropping their names failed to attract any flicker of interest from Buckingham Palace.

While Boyd-Carpenter's offer to open the Box in the end came to nothing, it made the potential of the Box being opened seem very real to the women gathered around Octavia. The ladies even began to consider what they would wear to its opening. In March 1919, Ellen Oliver – who at that point had not yet moved to Bedford – sent Octavia a blouse and coat made from a shawl that her father had acquired in China, which was originally made into a dress and then 'made up like this for the opening of the Box'. She no longer felt it was right for her, and wanted Octavia to have it. The description gives a good sense of the make-do-and-mend mentality of the post-war middle classes, as well as the seriousness with which the women regarded the potential Box event. Octavia replied, 'it is absolutely *lovely* – a raiment of needlework indeed!' She continued, 'I never saw such embroidery . . . lilies . . . a kind of cross on the back! And yet not a cross – a bow really but it gives the effect of the cope which the clergy so dearly love. The shape is ecclesiastical and yet present ladies' fashion – wonderful! We have positively gloated over its beauty.' And she added her own little sketch of the garment. But she worried: 'what will *you* do for the Box opening?' She then proceeded to offer various suggestions: 'If it be summer; I have two lovely embroidered Indian skirts – (washing ones) you will have to have one of them and a blouse can easily be got to match. This would please me greatly.' Later that year, Ellen, who was always lavishing gifts on Octavia, gave her a bag made of embroidered fabric which she had had made up for her. Octavia wrote back: 'I do love the beautiful Bag . . . Shall I carry it to the Box-opening, think you?? It would be very nice for my papers and my Bible – because I should want one to look up texts for the Bishops.' The women were, as ever, thinking domestically and practically as well as spiritually and aesthetically.[9]

Once the Society was formed in 1919, the members began their own relentless campaign to get the bishops to open the Box. It was based on frequent advertising in national and local newspapers; posters on the London tube, buses and buildings; speaking at Hyde Park Corner; petitions that were circulated to the public and presented to the bishops at various intervals; and frequent letter-writing to the bishops and other clergy.

Advertisements were placed in national and local newspapers stating: 'War, disease, crime and banditry, distress of nations and perplexity will increase until the Bishops open Joanna Southcott's box' or, more modestly, 'England's Troubles will continue until the Bishops open Joanna Southcott's Box'. The Society particularly advertised in the papers of their own choice and sympathy: right-wing papers such as the *Daily Mail* and national broadsheets such as the *Morning Post*, and they showed their political sympathies in the wording of their newspaper advertisements as well as in the huge posters that were put up on the underground and in railway stations, giving seven days' warning that 'Moscow's Fate will be London's Doom unless the Bishops open Joanna Southcott's Box'. An even more alarmist form of wording, referring to 'England's Peril' had been rejected by the commercial advertising agent of the Metropolitan, London Electric, City and South London, and Central London railway companies as being 'rather too strong, and we must make allowance for some of our nervous passengers'. The Panacea Society was asked to alter the wording and 'arrange for something a little less terrifying than the new bill which you have sent'.[10]

On Sunday afternoons in the summer of 1923, Alice Jones, one of the apostles, would travel up to London and speak at Hyde Park Corner, that well-known forum of free speech. She would set up her stand, which was about two feet high, unfurl her banner and begin an informal conversation with those around her. Then she would get up on the stand and hold forth on Southcott, the bishops and the Box. She found it taxing: 'few people would realise what it costs in the way of strength and nerves, for a quiet, ordinary woman to enter Hyde Park on a Sunday, set up, all alone on her little stand, without one friendly spirit to support her.' Every Sunday, she fought the same battle with herself, wishing she could slink away, but when she began to speak the fear would vanish. Her 'unveiled scorn of the Bishops . . . held the people enthralled' and many stayed for the full three hours of her talk. One man came every Sunday and remarked to her, 'Well, miss, I must say you handle them well, and you are always pleasant with them.'[11]

A petition to get the bishops to open the Box was launched in 1923, and energy was focused on gathering as many names as possible. Joanna Southcott had petitioned God for the destruction of Satan, and also understood one of her missions to be petitioning Christ on behalf of humankind.[12] Petitions, the idea of collecting names to exert pressure for something, had a long pedigree within English democracy. The Panaceans fused the two traditions together, ironically seeking to make democracy work for them on this occasion. Non-resident members – not only in Britain but also in the dominions of Canada, Australia and New Zealand – were vital in the exercise and they were always on the lookout for potential signatories. Mary Beedell, one of the prominent non-resident members in Eastbourne, wrote that she 'gave a Joanna petition to my window cleaner to sign and he said he could get me a lot of signatures and so of course I let him take it'.[13] James Hancock, originally a New and Latter House member, who undertook evangelistic work for the Panaceans, went door-to-door soliciting signatures and sympathy for the cause. By May 1924, 10,000 signatures had been collected. It was felt that this was a sufficient number to gain the attention of the bishops, and so the petition was sent by registered post to Lambeth Palace on 29 May by Rachel Fox and another member, Francis Medd. The petition was addressed to 'The Archbishops and Bishops of the Church of England . . . that 24 of their number shall send for, and open Joanna Southcott's Box of Sealed manuscripts, as we are of the opinion that anything purporting to be a Divine Revelation, laid up for the World, at this critical period, should be examined by the Heads of the Church, whose duty it is to look into such matters.'[14] By this time, Rachel Fox had been publicly named as the leader of the Joanna Southcott movement, and the newspapers reported that she was 'a middle-aged Quakeress who has spent a good deal of her private income in supporting the movement'.[15]

All of this activism was backed up with a relentless barrage of letters from the Society to individual bishops and the two archbishops. In 1920, the bishops were sent several of Octavia's scripts; in 1921 rural deans were warned about the dangers of Bolshevism, which could be prevented in England, said the Panaceans, if the bishops opened the Box; in 1922, the bishops were told about the Divine Motherhood; in 1923, they were warned, in a series of letters, about the foolishness of their not attending to Southcott's prophecy, the dangers of aerial warfare, and the earthquakes in Japan, and were informed of the Panacea Society's healing ministry; and at the end of that year they (along with 2,000 rectors and vicars) were sent a special publication called *A Lifeboat to the Rescue of the Sinking Church*. Individual members, such as Gertrude Hill, who was of course a vicar's wife, sent letters like this one to all the bishops: 'I am constantly being asked "Why do not the Bishops open Joanna Southcott's Box?" As a churchwoman, I should be glad to know what is the reply to this question.' This rather one-sided correspondence from the Panaceans to the bishops continued over the years. None produced much reaction beyond cursory replies which stated that they had no interest in the Joanna Southcott movement or merely acknowledged receipt of the papers. Much to Octavia's chagrin, these replies were often written by the bishops' chaplains, which she realised could mean that the bishops never saw the letter or the materials in the first place.[16]

The Archbishop of Canterbury, until 1928 still Randall Davidson, the man Rachel Fox and Beatrice Pease had met and with whom they had had an extended correspondence in the previous decade, refused to take action on the Southcottians' terms. After the submission of the petition in 1924, Davidson wrote an exasperated reply to Rachel Fox saying that he thought the Box should be opened in order to end the controversy, but he 'refused to summon 24 Bishops to sit around and watch the procedure', a point he had made 'at least twenty times'. He reminded her that he could produce 'scores of letters' to show that he had done his part to meet their wishes, 'short of acting in a way which I should regard as partly profane and partly fanatic'.[17] He invited her to publish his letter, which the Society did widely, using Reuter as well as their own press agent. They used the letter to their advantage, regarding it as 'an excellent advertisement of the fact of the Box of sealed Writings and of the obstinate attitude of the bishops'.[18]

While the Panaceans were frustrated in achieving the ends they sought, the result of all this publicity was that the Box became a public phenomenon. It was a nationally recognised icon, even though only a handful of people had seen it and even fewer knew where it was. A 1922 article in *The Nation and Athenaeum* (which included amongst its contributors in the 1920s Aldous and Julian Huxley, Roger Fry, Virginia and Leonard Woolf and many others from the literary intelligentsia, and was politically, religiously and culturally far removed from the Panacean world) commented on the many advertisements in the tube that declared 'London is doomed!' The article adopted a light, ironic tone but its chief target was not the Box or those who believed in its significance, but rather the bishops and their hypocrisy in pointedly refusing to open the Box while at the same time failing to condemn other 'superstitions' such as the Cottingley Fairies episode, in which Arthur Conan Doyle had publicly championed the belief that two young girls had photographed fairies at the bottom of their garden; and had written a book about it, *The Coming of the Fairies*, published just that year.[19]

> Have the bishops reproved the little Yorkshire girls who photographed fairies, or the applauding spectators who swallowed the fairies, camera and all? Do they laugh at the absurdity of men who refuse to light three cigarettes from a single match; . . . or at those who will not sit down thirteen at table, or walk under a ladder, or look at a new moon through glass? Are the men and women who spend money in advertising the Doom of London unless the Bishops open the box any more to be despised than all those others who long to be deceived, and deceived they are?

The author had a sneaking appreciation of 'the delight in the irrational' and 'man's longing for a fairyland to transcend the common laws of nature', not least because it presented established religion with a problem. The article ended with a challenge to the bishops: 'Here is another manifestation of that longing, and what are the bishops going to do about it?'[20]

A cartoon in the *Daily Courier* on 20 March 1925 played on the mystery of the Box's contents, when it portrayed Winston Churchill, then Chancellor of the Exchequer, as Joanna Southcott, sitting on a box marked 'Budget Box o' Tricks'. At that point, there was much speculation about Churchill's budget, the details of which were regarded as being as mysterious and unknown as the contents of Joanna Southcott's Box. He did not make his budget speech until 28 April, when he announced that England would return to the Gold Standard, which, in retrospect, was not a good economic move and caused many problems: the General Strike happened the next year. In its visual imagery, the cartoon recalled a similar cartoon in the London evening newspaper, the *Star*, eighteen months earlier, in November 1923, in which Stanley Baldwin, the Conservative Prime Minister, was dressed as Joanna Southcott, again sitting on a box, this one marked 'Tariff Details'; the cartoon's heading was 'The Empire Doomed unless Johanna's Box is opened'. Baldwin was pushing for the reintroduction of trade tariffs – and therefore protectionism – but he stood by his predecessor's pledge that it would not happen without another general election, which was duly called.

Another result of all this publicity was that Alice Seymour desperately sought to distance herself from the Panacea Society and their campaign. In August 1923, she wrote a letter to her old Southcottian followers stating that the large poster in the London railway stations and carriages, giving seven days' warning that London was doomed, and that Moscow's fate awaited it unless the bishops opened the Box of Sealed Writings, 'was not issued by us but by the Bedford group of so-called followers of Joanna Southcott'. This was just the latest evidence for her that Octavia had gone far beyond the 'true' Southcott remit, 'teaching many things which are quite contrary to the Bible and also to the Southcott works with regard to "Shiloh" and other strange doctrines'. She went on to say that she agreed with one who had been a member of the Bedford community but had left, who said that it was 'full of fads and superstitions – a mixture of Theosophy, Spiritualism and High Church Ritual'.[21] She took the quarrel public, writing letters to newspapers that had given the Panacea Society publicity: 'I beg on behalf of the hundreds of Southcottians both in England and abroad, to state that we have no connection with this small colony of about 30 or more, men and women in the well-known secret place in the Midlands, except at one time they were joined with us, but now are under the leadership of one they regard, and obey, as their High Priestess!'[22]

In her private correspondence she was much ruder. To Rachel Fox, in a letter she presumed Octavia would see, she wrote: 'the declaration of a female personal Shiloh, or one spiritually embodied in a female today, is preposterous and foolish – contrary to the Bible and contrary to the whole teaching of Joanna's writings'.[23] To one of 'her' group of followers, she wrote that she would 'far rather persons remained as they are in their churches and chapels, than have this garbled version of Joanna's beautiful and simple teaching'. She hated the ways in which the Panaceans exalted Woman over Man and forbade marriage, and as for their gendered theology, 'Baptising in the name of the Father-Mother-God', she regarded it as 'revolting'.[24] She had numerous other criticisms: not least that Octavia received messages via automatic writing, which for her stank of spiritualism, and she thought that the claim of immortality was displeasing to God. In particular, she would not allow anyone who wished to be sealed in the Panacea Society to be also sealed by her in Southcott's name, and asked her devoted followers to return their Panacea seals to the Society, as one A. Garnham did, writing that she had heard that those 'that have joined with the "Woman" at Bedford' were engaged in spiritualism.[25]

Octavia remained remarkably serene in the face of such vitriol, courteously and repeatedly asking Alice Seymour not to judge them on hearsay, but to come and see the community for herself. The invitation was never taken up. But other Panaceans felt able to write to Miss Seymour rather more smugly: 'While you are waiting for the answer . . . Yes, dear Miss Seymour, the Deliverance from Satan's power promised to the Believers first is given at last and we are the first to receive it.'[26] The open rift about Southcott's teachings as a whole meant that there was now no co-ordinated effort to get the bishops to open the Box, and the Panacea Society, with its greater resources, made the louder noise and very much the greater effort from the 1920s onwards.

The Panacea Society's long campaign to get the bishops to open the Box so captured the public's imagination that others who brought sealed boxes to light with the claim that they were Southcott's Box could be assured of good publicity and inquisitive audiences. Several sealed boxes were circulating as Southcott's Box. Two rival boxes of this sort were opened in early April 1925. The first was known as the 'Hammersmith Box' and contained a leather-bound copy of the Bible dating from 1702, with a wisp of grey hair in it and a prophecy about monsters written on a piece of parchment apparently signed by Southcott. The actor and theatre manager W. J. MacKay was in charge of the opening of this box at his home in Hammersmith in London. Readers of national and local newspapers woke up to colourful headlines on 5 April: 'Eerie scene in a London room' (The People), 'A Southcott Box opened – Monsters from the Lost World' (Daily Express)

'Joanna Southcott – one of her boxes opened and very little in it!' (*Daily Mail*). The box had apparently been left in the cellar of Mr MacKay's house by a mysterious Miss Morristown who had foretold that whoever opened it would be cursed. MacKay took the risk anyway. But when Alice Seymour dispatched a follower to Mackay's house to verify Southcott's handwriting, the box had disappeared as suddenly as it had appeared; and two Americans who tried to buy the Box were consequently disappointed.[27]

A second box, the 'Doctor's Box', was opened later in April in Bournemouth, and was found to contain many original manuscripts, including prophecies and dreams recorded by Southcott that were already known to followers and a letter addressed to the Southcottian Lavinia Jones in 1839, which verified its origins as Southcottian – but later than Southcott (who had died in 1814).[28] The doctor reported that he and his family 'felt a little nervous' opening it because they had 'always believed that it was the great box that should only be opened in the presence of 24 bishops. But we decided to take the risk of seeing what it was.' Even though there was 'a tense moment as the cover was lifted' they were 'quickly disappointed' as the box contained eight and a half pounds of manuscript which was, in the doctor's words 'jargon, written in scriptural language'. The doctor found it all 'totally unintelligible'.[29] These various boxes often had Southcottian items in them, and a provenance that took them back to Southcott or old Southcottian families, though none of them contained the thus far unseen sealed prophecies. The box that Harry Price opened on that stormy night in 1927 had been entrusted, he claimed, to a follower – Mrs Rebecca Morgan – by Southcott at her death, and it had been passed down the Morgan family, though the letter may have been a forgery by Price to obtain further publicity and credibility for his box.[30]

The opening of all these boxes provided more free publicity for the Panacean cause. After Harry Price had X-rayed his Southcottian box in May 1927 at the National Laboratory of Psychical Research, a couple of months before he opened it, and pictures of the X-rays had been published in the *Graphic* on 14 May, the X-ray theme quickly became incorporated into advertisements and cartoons that made allusions to the Box. The London menswear store, Austin Reed's in Regent Street, ran an advertisement for its foot X-raying machine –

designed to make sure you bought shoes that fitted well – with a
narrator asking whether the 'mysterious-looking cabinet' into which
a man was gazing was Joanna Southcott's Box. A political cartoon in
the *Evening News* in the same month was titled 'Joanna's Box X-rayed'
and showed two figures in the box called 'Dilly' dealing with the
economy, and 'Dally' dealing with pledges. A portrait labelled Joanna,
hanging above the Box, shows an old woman in a bonnet with the
face of the Prime Minister Stanley Baldwin smoking a pipe. Two days
after the opening of the Price box, the *Daily Chronicle* ran a cartoon
– 'Another wonder box opened' – that once again portrayed Stanley
Baldwin dressed up as Southcott in a portrait. This cartoon was the
vehicle for a generic criticism of the Conservative government, three
years into its term of office: the opened Box is called 'Joanna Tory's
Wonder Box', contains 'Legislation rubbish' and is marked with a
label: – 'Ye chest contains ye wondrous election promises to be opened
at ye time of national stress!'

Perhaps the best bit of publicity came from the Cambridge
University student Rag event in June 1927. Male undergraduates
dressed up as twenty-four bishops and gave themselves spoof titles
close to the names of real diocesan bishops in England, such as Bishop
of Swear and Wells (for Bath and Wells) and Bishop of St Alebuns
(for St Albans), while the 'Archbishop of Gota-Beret' (for Canterbury)
wore mauve garters decked with bells and carried a golf club for a
staff. They solemnly processed to a box, surrounded by other male
undergraduates dressed as women (they had borrowed their land-
ladies' clothes, so the newspapers reported), and opened the box
which contained such items as exam papers (which they shredded),
a woman's leg, and a bottle of beer marked 'JS'. What is remarkable
about this episode is that it was fully reported in national newspapers, albeit the popular papers, such as the *Daily Mail*, *Daily Mirror*
and *Daily Chronicle*, showing not only that Southcott's Box was a
subject of endless public comment but also that the frivolous activities of undergraduates at the ancient universities such as Cambridge
were a matter of much greater public interest than they would be
today.

By the mid- to late 1920s, the Box was therefore once again at the
forefront of the news. It had become such a recognisable cultural icon,
while at the same time retaining an air of mystery, that it was evoked

in just this spirit in an advertisement for Oldham's radio accumulators in the *Radio Times* in 1928. Batteries were 'mysterious' – you never knew when they might not work, and you could not see inside them, so they were 'a complete enigma to the listener' – which made them just like Southcott's Box. The Oldham H.T. accumulator was reliable: 'you could see the whole of the "works" at a glance', and it would keep your radio going longer.[31]

The Society's response to the Harry Price box of 1927 and all the hoopla surrounding it was to capitalise on the public's interest and increase their own publicity. As Octavia wrote to the Society's solicitor, Cecil Goodhall, 'We are about to put up Posters in the Tubes again and are printing a quarter of a million handbills, as now is the time to strike, the interest aroused by that ridiculous meeting in London on Monday, 11th July, being considerable.'[32] Ironically, just in the years when the Panacea Society was making the greatest push in their campaign, the Church of England officially asserted that the Box had now been opened – by Harry Price in 1927. This position was stated in George Bell's biography of Randall Davidson, and the Church refused to deviate from it. As late as 1960, the then Archbishop of Canterbury (Geoffrey Fisher) received a letter from one Roger Garth Hooper, who claimed that he held an office known as the 'Grand Serjeante', having been 'initiated . . . as the custodian of an archive known as "Joanna Southcott's box"' in the 1920s. He did not state whether he had a box or not. But the reply he received from the Archbishop's office confirmed the Church of England's official position: that the authentic box had been opened in 1927.[33] Another Southcottian group called the Fishers of Men, seeking the opening of the Box, relaxed the rule that it had to be twenty-four bishops, and said it only needed to be twenty-four clergy. They were sometimes confused with the Panaceans in the public mind, much to the chagrin of the Society. An attempt by the Fishers of Men to publicise their position on this clergy concession in 1935 provoked a demand from the Panacea Society that the two organisations be clearly distinguished from each other in papers like the *Evening Standard*. *The Patriot*, a fascist journal, notably confused them in an article on the Box.[34]

Regardless of the attitudes of the archbishops and bishops, regardless of confusion with other groups with different demands, the

Panaceans always believed that the opening of the Box by twenty-four bishops was imminent, and they were constantly getting ready for it. In 1929 they began to prepare in a new way, opening negotiations to buy a large house called Castleside next to The Haven (Kate Firth's old house) and behind Octavia's, which could be used as a suitable place for the bishops to meet when they gathered as the Panaceans inevitably believed they would to open the Box. It was a boarding house for boys from Bedford School throughout the 1920s, and the piano practising and the noise of servants and boys caused the ever-sensitive Octavia great misery. What could be better for the Panaceans than to rid themselves of that troublesome noise and, at the same time, acquire a house in which the opening of the Box could be staged? They negotiated the purchase of the house for £8,000 at the end of 1929, with money scraped together by the resident members and one non-resident member, Willoughby Rokeby, a single, elderly man of considerable means. The school moved out a year later, and Octavia got the keys to Castleside on 31 December 1930. Ever searching for deeper meaning in every event in the community's life, Octavia interpreted the possession of the key as symbolic: 'the key with which to open a house is only a sign of our much greater need to have the House of the Mind opened and cleansed and purified, to entertain the Guest we desire'.[35] The Divine Mother declared Castleside to be (God) the Father's house, and said: 'the Daughter will rule it till He sees fit for the Son to come'.[36]

On that same New Year's Eve, they had a special ceremony, pregnant with meaning, in which the Instrument of the Divine Mother spoke to twenty-four especially selected resident members, who promised (yet again) to obey the Divine Mother and Octavia in all things, and report their own and other people's failings daily until they became faultless and could be presented 'before the Throne of the Great Divine Father'. And God the Father was reported – through the Instrument of the Divine Mother – as saying that he would 'make the Bishops tremble until they bend their stubborn hearts and seek for refuge under my Words'. His next promise was to his Daughter (Octavia) who would 'reap the world that she has sown – and in power'.[37]

If we want to understand why the community would invest £8,000 (a large sum in 1930) in a house and prepare it for twenty-four bishops who might one day come to open a box of prophecies, leaving the house empty (which it still is) until they came, when the odds seemed high that those bishops never would arrive, then we have to remember that they believed they were receiving messages of this sort from God on a daily basis. They believed they were absolutely right, they were chosen and they were obeying God's commands. In that they had absolute faith.

The Panaceans therefore set about refurbishing the house to make it fit for the visit of the bishops. By the end of that year, Octavia was writing to Mr Rokeby that they had panelled what had been the boys' dining hall in oak, putting a blue frieze above it. This room was furnished for the opening of the Box, with 'a long handsome carved table and 24 rather handsome chairs' and the floor-covering and curtains were 'of a beautiful blue'. Octavia wrote, with her usual wish to impress, 'One feels that the Bishops could hardly fail to think it was worthy of their presence, when they come to open the Box, but of course this is all *entre nous.*'[38] The Panaceans even had a special oak chest made for the Box to stand on. In August 1931, the furniture was moved into the rest of the house. The thirty-odd rooms were furnished mostly as bedrooms for the twenty-four bishops, and there was a fine sitting room, heavily cluttered with furniture in the late-Victorian style, and two bathrooms. On the top floor there was a museum, or treasury, where the Society's valuables – many of them gifts to Octavia – could be displayed. In particular, this provided an excellent display area for the elaborate cot made in 1814 for Joanna Southcott's child Shiloh, which the Society had acquired on permanent loan from Salford Museum in May 1924.[39] Peter Rasmussen created a fish pond and built a conservatory at the side of Castleside and set about joining the gardens of Octavia's house, The Haven and Castleside together to form a large and beautiful garden (the Garden of Eden, of course) in which members could enjoy their garden parties, as they did on 11 July 1931, the first such party to use the newly created large garden. The thirty members who came played tennis and other games, acted out scenes from *Cranford* and enjoyed tea on the lawn.[40]

Octavia's attention to detail in the arrangement of the rooms was obsessive, as ever, and she made constant notes about exactly what would happen when the bishops came for the opening of the Box and thus the trial of Southcott's writings, which would compare 'for importance with the Trial of Christ before the Sanhedrin'.[41] The provision of a suitable house was one of the conditions for the opening of the Box, along with the presence of twenty-four bishops, an attorney, the appropriate writings and witnesses. Who should sit where? Should Castleside be turned into a small hotel, with 'our people acting as chambermaids, kitchen and scullerymaids etc?' Where would the press and visitors be? And could there be an overflow meeting in The Haven garden? What about the heating? And surely microphones and better lights would be needed. She even drew a diagram outlining who would sit where, and noting that on the long table there should be a blotter, a silver inkwell, a gong and a bowl of flowers.[42] She wrote to Cecil Jowett, one of the old Southcottians, about all these practical matters: in 'this Divine work we must recognise that the material arrangements must play a great part'. And she could not resist a dig at Alice Seymour, even though she had the grace to allot her a good seat for the event herself. 'To such a person as Miss Seymour, for instance, who supposes that Joanna herself will rise out of the tomb with the child in her arms, arriving at some house in Paddington where the Box will be found – no one having the smallest idea of how the Box got there or she got there – is very different to your idea and ours.'[43]

With the house ready for the bishops, the early 1930s saw a great push in publicity. Huge posters appeared all over London in the summer of 1932. They were above shops and on billboards in Piccadilly, on Regent Street, at Vauxhall Bridge, Trafalgar Square, Kensington High Street and Finchley Road as well as further afield in places like Hackney, Stamford Hill and Newington Green Road. In November, one was posted strategically opposite Lambeth Palace, on the Albert Embankment. Double-decker London buses carried posters announcing that England's troubles would not cease until the bishops opened Joanna Southcott's Box, and the Panaceans typically kept a meticulous record of the routes on which their message would appear: routes 9, 25, 29, 59 and 73 in July 1932, and routes 14, 18, 27, 88 and 153 in August, and told readers of The Panacea exactly where they could see them.

Two further petitions to open the Box were organised. The first was the Petition of the Jews, drawn up from September 1932, which had gathered 3,000 names by 1934. Much was made of the fact that Southcott had addressed many of her writings to the Hebrews. On the basis of this interest, Octavia allotted 'the Jews' six front-row seats at the opening of the Box. The second petition was prepared in 1933; Octavia died before the signature-gathering had been completed, but the Society soldiered on with the task, and by 23 April 1935, 28,757 people had signed. On that day – St George's Day – Canon Russell Payne, a Church of England clergyman who was now a resident member of the Panacea community, delivered it to Lambeth Palace along with an Address to the Archbishop of Canterbury, a covering letter and a copy of the Panacea publication, *Transactions of the Panacea Society with the Archbishops and Bishops of the Church of England*. The Archbishop – now Cosmo Lang – sent a perfunctory letter stating that he was 'sorry that so many people thought it right to sign the Petition' because he was 'unable to review the decision which was made after much thought many years ago'. Forty-six diocesan bishops and the other Archbishops in Britain were sent a copy of the Address, covering letter and *Transactions*. Of these, only two acknowledged receipt; the Bishop of Peterborough returned the materials; and the Archbishop of Wales sent his back unopened, perhaps warned by his English counterpart about what the parcel contained.[44] This was the last major petition asking for the Box to be opened by the bishops.

The Panacea Society never owned the Box in Octavia's lifetime. It was always in the hands of old Southcottians. It was only in 1957 that they finally acquired the Box. Cecil Jowett, its custodian, had died and his widow asked the Panacea Society to collect the Box personally, it being the wish of her father-in-law, Edwin Jowett, that they should acquire it. Two members collected it by train, thinking that driving it in a personally owned car was not safe enough! Owning the Box made no difference to what the Society did, and few knew of the Box's new whereabouts. The campaign to get the bishops to open it continued, with advertisements being placed in newspapers into the 1990s, and members writing to bishops and other dignitaries from time to time. The Box remains a cultural icon, though one redolent of a different time, in which the authority of English bishops mattered enough that they should be present as a condition of its opening. It even featured in a *Monty Python* sketch in 1969, as part of a furniture race at Epsom racecourse in Surrey:

RACE COMMENTATOR: Well, here at Epsom we take up the running with fifty yards of this mile and a half race to go and it's the wash basin in the lead from W C pedestal. Tucked in nicely there is the sofa going very well with Joanna Southcott's box making a good run from hat stand on the rails, and the standard lamp is failing fast but it's wash basin definitely taking up the running now being strongly pressed by . . . At the post it's the wash basin from WC then sofa, hat stand, standard lamp and lastly Joanna Southcott's box.

Cut to three bishops shouting from actual studio audience.

BISHOPS: Open the Box! Open the Box! Open the Box! Open the Box! Open the Box!

For the Society, the Box contains a promise – that one day, their prophecies will be fulfilled. Sociologically speaking, the Box fulfils an important role. As Christ does not return, so that can be explained by an event that is virtually impossible: getting twenty-four bishops of the Church of England to open the Box. To the wider world, the Box remains an object of fascination, like the Lost Ark of the Covenant, because everyone loves a mystery. But while, in the film *Raiders of the Lost Ark*, that box or ark when opened causes destruction, in this case the opening of the Box promises the opposite: the solution to the world's, or at least England's, trials and tribulations, the fantasy of everything finally being all right.

15

The Church

The Society's campaign to get the bishops to open the Box illustrates, in microcosm, its paradoxical relationship to the Church of England. The Panaceans at one level scorned the bishops and yet, at another, they had a traditional respect for them and *needed* them to open the Box. Likewise, they thought the Church of England was entirely wrong about almost everything, but they also believed it was the true Church. While the preparation for Christ's coming had to take place outside the Church of England – because the clergy and bishops had so stubbornly refused to do anything – when Christ came, he would use the Church of England 'as the Home of the new beginnings'.[1] It was also important to them that it was Joanna Southcott's Church. Hilda Green wrote about the significance of the Church of England in her notebook, under the heading 'Things to Remember' (being the chief correspondent with the public, she needed to remember what to tell them).

> The Church of England is the Standard Church, Joanna belonged to it[,] Octavia has been born and brought up in it, and from the *altar* of the Church the Truth will burst. The Prayer-book is inspired by the Lord Himself, He having told Joanna that this was the case. Believers should possess 'Daily Light' (Bagster) can be obtained at any bookseller 3/6 – Morning and Evening. A Church of England Prayer Book should be at hand for the Daily Psalms and the Collects and Lessons are most valuable at Services.

All those who wished to become sealed members had to be baptised Anglican, even if they had been baptised before. Hilda Green wrote: 'All who apply for the Royal Seal must have been Baptised (not necessarily immersed). The Lord told Joanna the cross was to be marked in the *Forehead*.'[2] The irony here was that the Church of England (along with most other churches) did not believe in re-baptism (following the ancient creedal statement 'one baptism for the remission of sins') but Octavia blithely ignored that, such was her belief in baptism in the *Anglican* Church. Early on in the community's history, she made the point by instructing the lifelong prominent Quaker, Rachel Fox, to get baptised and confirmed in the Church of England.

In one sense, the Panaceans were like other contemporary heterodox groups (such as the Spiritualists or the Theosophists) in their scepticism about the institutional churches' capacity to provide spiritual nourishment. The Society's appeal can be understood as part of a more pervasive desire in the wider society for spiritual *authenticity* – which the churches seemed increasingly unable to offer. But in one sense they were completely different from those contemporary groups: they had a paradoxical reverence for the Church because it was the state Church, headed by the monarch, and they were royalists and patriots. To that end, the Church of England was the true Church but, in a twist, they believed that the Panacea Society was the true development of it. In 1921, the Society declared: 'the purpose of the Lord is to set up within the Church, and by the hands of Churchwomen, His own Church, which will have powers that the Bishops will not be able to gainsay.'[3] Six years later, Hilda Green (the daughter of an Anglican priest) wrote in her diary, at the time when the revised Prayer Book was causing dissension within the Church of England: 'The Ch[urch] of E[ngland] is at variance within. The Panacea Society has *become* the C of E – as might be expected.'[4] The Panaceans believed that the Church kept missing its way, especially when the bishops would not open Southcott's Box, and they were forever trying to steer them on to the right course. Hence they bombarded bishops and clergy with their materials and writings, and maintained a lively and vigilant interest in what the Church was doing.

Anglican clergy were scolded in publications such as *The Lifeboat to the Rescue of the Sinking Church*, for ignoring all that the Panacea Society taught: eternal life on this earth; the doctrine of the Divine Family of four; the Second Coming of Christ and paradise on this earth. They were berated for the foolishness of their preaching; for their refusal to deal with 'sex-difficulties' – despite hearing so many confessions about them; for ignoring modern prophecy (Southcott, the nineteenth-century Southcottian prophets and Octavia herself, of course) and the Second Coming. They were exhorted to alter their views: 'teach your people about the new Heaven coming on earth – not a clerical heaven of a Universal Church, Heaven forbid – but the Heaven of Life with Jesus, the Healer and Helper, the Bishop and Priest, the Prophet and King. A Life which will be undying, unending, free from sin, sorrow, affliction, pain, controversy, war – a life described by the angels as "peace *on Earth*"'.[5]

The Panaceans grasped every opportunity to spread their message to the Church of England. They went to the annual Church Congresses armed with their pamphlets, ready to tell the gathered clergy and laity about the Box and their own healing ministry. At the Church Congress in Oxford in 1924, Alice Jones and several others stood in the pouring rain giving out 5,000 leaflets titled 'Deliverance'. Their presence at such events was becoming well known, and the *Church Times* reported: 'Of course the Panacea Society and Joanna's Box were represented!'[6] Eight members went to the 1925 Church Congress, that year held in Eastbourne, where they not only distributed tracts but also held open-air meetings at which Rachel Fox, Alice Jones and Kate Firth all spoke, and sprinkled the holy water around so that any opposition would be defeated by its power.[7] In 1927 members went to the Church Congress in Ipswich, this time distributing a leaflet on Darwinian theory in the light of Panacean teaching, along with pictures of the Box. As Rachel Fox put it, they used the Box as 'a sort of stalking-horse which anyone can see and follow' as an introduction to Panacea teachings. She reported that at the Ipswich congress, 'all our efforts were smilingly accepted, much as one accepts the repetition of an old joke', but despite the fact that church people may have been humouring them, Panacean literature went home in people's suitcases and the Panaceans firmly held that numbers of applications for the healing and Panacea books increased after these events.[8] In 1930, at the Lambeth Conference, specially bound copies of a month's worth of the scripts, the *Writings of the Holy Ghost*, were placed in the bishops' mailboxes.

Individual members also sought opportunities to speak to clergy about the Society's beliefs. Non-resident member Mary Warry told her parson about the healing, and 'my heart thumped so hard, because he's not a person I've ever spoken to about things that matter & you never know how the clergy are going to take things'. She had introduced the topic by way of the Society's healing ministry, which had given the vicar pause for thought and he replied to Mrs Warry: 'hard facts of people being healed had to be explained somehow!'[9]

What the Panaceans wanted, of course, was some public sign from the Church that it was taking notice of them. They scoured the newspapers for any evidence. Occasionally they got a mention in a sermon, and even if it was negative they were pleased that they were making some kind of impact. The national broadsheet newspaper, the *Guardian*, reprinted a sermon preached by the Archdeacon of Worcester on Pentecost in 1925, in which he mentioned that he had received the Panacea booklet, *The Coming of Shiloh*, through the post. 'The school of Joanna Southcott is not so completely dead,' he wrote. 'It has more than an antiquarian interest as is shown by our pamphlet, and by notices which have appeared lately in newspapers', but, he continued, 'I think one may say without intolerable condescension that it is not taken seriously by the majority of thinking and educated Christians.' Despite this damning comment, for the Panaceans the important point was that a clergyman had taken notice of their literature and their advertisements. One member has written in the margins of the newspaper cutting in the Society's archives: 'They do see them!! This is an unsolicited testimonial!'[10] And at the top of the page: 'Sermons now!' All publicity was good publicity.

Most of all, the Panaceans wanted to attract the allegiance of the clergy, and early on in their community life they had one significant success. In 1921 they hit the jackpot with a mailing to all rural deans, who had been targeted because they were responsible for gathering groups of clergy in their area, and thus might disseminate Panacean ideas.[11] One relatively local clergyman, Lawrence Iggulden, vicar of the small village of Caxton in Cambridgeshire (population 398 in 1928),[12] about twenty miles from Bedford, replied. He asked for the Society's literature, read it and maintained a correspondence with Kate Firth and Rachel Fox for several months. His engagement with the Society's ideas was serious: he did not dismiss them out of hand, but nor did he jump at them immediately. He assessed them in relation to his reading of the Bible, other contemporary movements such as Spiritualism, Christian Science and Theosophy, and the evidence of what was happening all around. He described himself as being 'an inquirer & seeker after knowledge & understanding' all his life, and was open to 'spiritual communication' though as far as he was aware had not personally received any yet.[13] He was an open-minded, serious and practical man who wanted to see the reality of the Gospel at work in the world – in this sense he was not unlike Octavia – but he was also a self-styled modern man who took science seriously, and he wanted and needed facts. And while he was open to the possibility of modern prophecy, he wanted facts to indicate the truth of it. 'Words are not enough without acts or things done.' After some correspondence with the Society in the summer and autumn of 1921, he was not convinced enough of the factual basis of the Panacea claims to take them on. 'My faith I hold fast. If anything comes to break that and wishes to take me away, it must be stronger & clearer & give more power.'[14] He therefore ended his correspondence with them in November 1921, six months after he had first received their materials.

And then, a year and a half later, in June 1923, there was a knock on his door and it was the Panacea evangelist, James Hancock, asking him to sign the petition for the Box to be opened. Still a little embarrassed that he had dismissed the group, this time he signed up – not only to the petition but also to membership. He had been thinking about the Panaceans and their beliefs in the interval, attracted to the 'feminine' aspect of their theology, the promise of the redemption of the body and the possibility of something only accomplished in part, now being completed (in the Second Coming of Christ). 'I do not mind adventuring,' he said, but he reminded them that he was 'a definite Churchman and true to my Church and orders'.[15] Therein lay the tension with which he would live for the rest of his life, as a priest of the Church of England and an active member of the Panacea Society. For the Panaceans, in the wake of the Edgar Peissart scandal that had rocked the community earlier that year, the addition of a respectable clergyman to their growing membership was marvellous.

In early August 1923, Mr Iggulden visited Bedford for the first time and met Octavia. He was undoubtedly attracted to the Society's theology, wanting to 'get the world back to life & health again' as the Panaceans promised was possible.[16] And like other Panaceans, he felt there was something lacking in the Church that he served so obediently; he wanted his knowledge 'to be 1st hand and personal' and he wrote to Octavia, 'All the Teaching in your letter I have realised more or less vaguely, as being the Reality I wanted but could not quite reach.'[17] But it was his relationship with Octavia that became central to his spiritual life and ministry as a priest for the next decade. They corresponded regularly and, in letter after letter, we see him asking her advice, and Octavia providing common-sense answers. Here she emerges as a woman with real spiritual wisdom, as someone who, in another time, might herself have been an Anglican priest or the abbess of a convent. In that sense, she functioned as a spiritual director to him, and he accepted her direction, usually without question.

Iggulden's affection for Octavia was apparent in his frequent gifts of butter, made from the milk of his three cows, and flowers from his garden, sent to her throughout the summer months. He sent his parcels of butter through the post – though never if it were too hot – reminding us how quickly the mail worked in those days: such a parcel would arrive at its destination on the same day. In turn the Panacea Society helped him, even on one occasion with a small gift of money when he had mentioned that he was hard up. He felt awkward about this, because he had 'joined to help you all I could, and not to take, so much as to give all the strength I could to further a cause, which attracted me and which I wanted to come into action in every way. I did not want anyone to say "Look what you have got out of it!"' But in the end he accepted the gift graciously, saying 'Let me know all I can do and I will try & do it.'[18] The episode is interesting for the insight it gives into Octavia's generosity when she trusted someone, and into the genuine affection and mutual respect that existed between Mr Iggulden and the Panaceans. They were friends.

The simple fact was that, before he joined the Panacea Society, he was lonely. 'Of course up to my entering into correspondence with Mrs Fox and my coming to see you, I have been on my own and sometimes have felt very isolated, no one about me or that I was in touch with was able to help or sympathise much with me.' His letters reveal how isolated the life of an intelligent, questioning country vicar could be. He was married and had three daughters but there is little sense that his wife and daughters provided much intellectual or spiritual stimulation for him; rather, he spent much of his time caring for his wife who had suffered from 'nerve attacks' ever since the war. Meeting Octavia was a revelation to him, providing emotional support and spiritual sustenance where formerly he had none: 'You have evidently hit upon my own feelings & inclination in quite a remarkable way,' he wrote after meeting her for the first time.[19] For the next few years, Iggulden sought Octavia's advice on many facets of his life and ministry, whether it was his campaign to save church schools, the health of his wife and his youngest daughter Laura, or the problems he was facing in his own parish.

Iggulden was a conscientious parish priest, concerned to do right by his parishioners. Sometimes he sought advice from Octavia about specific pastoral cases, and his letters often mention individual people and their problems. In mid-August 1923, soon after joining, he wrote to her about one Ada Baxter, a thirty-year-old woman in the local workhouse, Caxton Union House,[20] who was unable to do anything, spoke only childish language, and spent most of her time just sitting. Iggulden regarded this not as mental illness nor as a severe learning disability but as her having been 'possessed from her earliest days', or 'devil afflicted'. He regarded her state as 'a kind of idiotic control, which can do things when it likes occasionally and gazes about as if it sees things'. This was his description of her 'possessed' state of being. But he also ascribed some agency to her actions: he described her as knowing 'her brother & others when she likes, if they give her things like sweets, but is generally wilfully obstinate & hysterical when she is wanted to be sensible'.[21] Octavia – despite her knowledge of medical explanations for such behaviour and her own time in two asylums – accepted Iggulden's explanation for the woman's behaviour. By this time, the Divine Mother had been relentlessly 'casting controls' and driving out devils for several months, after the expulsion of Edgar Peissart earlier that year, and thus the notion of 'possession' had come to have some pre-eminence in the Society's understanding of the world. So Octavia sanctioned Iggulden to perform a sort of low-key exorcism, gave him a form of prayer to use with the woman and suggested that he use blessed milk rather than blessed water on this occasion.

The incident is revealing both of the culture and attitudes of the time – the survival of a nineteenth-century workhouse into the 1920s in a rural community and the continued belief in possession by evil spirits as a cause of madness – and of the relationship between Octavia and Iggulden. She had quickly and undoubtedly been cast as his spiritual superior, and he sought to obey her instructions. Earlier that month, he had written of using the blessed water with his parishioners, 'I did not want to do anything without asking.'[22] Now, the prayer which Octavia sent for his use made clear that she, the Divine Daughter, was petitioning 'the Divine Parents and their Son our Blessed Lord Jesus Christ' on behalf of 'Lawrence Iggulden Priest, who is humbly accepting the new Revelation'. And she was able to do that 'according to the promise made by the Lord Jesus Christ' that she should bring relief to those who suffered – both the Overcomers, and others, such as Ada Baxter, 'who cannot attain to the Glory of the Sun'. It was Octavia who had the power to bless the milk and ask that 'this daughter be filled with the Grace of our Lord Jesus Christ and abide in his peace for ever'. Moreover, Iggulden was not attempting to perform this healing alone. At the hour that he was visiting Ada Baxter, Octavia would be praying, reading scripture (Mark 1: 23–25, about Jesus commanding an unclean spirit out of a man) and 'casting the controls' back at the Panacean headquarters. She warned Iggulden: 'there may be no sudden change; in every case here it has been gradual, because the mind is so scared by & the muscles so accustomed to the control that what one may call reflex-action has to be allowed for.'[23]

Iggulden reported that he carried out the instructions exactly, and after some giggling and silly behaviour 'the girl' (despite her age, her disabilities made her still a girl to him) 'gave a deep sigh & stopped for a while and looked serious'. Although she initially refused to drink the blessed milk, once Iggulden assured her she was 'all right now', she drank it all. Two days later, he reported that he had visited her again and the nurse had noted a difference in her. She listened and took notice of the clock ticking, which she had not done before, came when he called her, and seemed older and more sensible.[24] Two weeks later he reported that she came to a worship service and looked at a book and stood for the creed, and 'she would never do quiet simple things like this for me before'.[25]

Iggulden, like other Anglican clergymen of the time such as Percy Dearmer, was interested in spiritual healing. The Panacea Society's healing ministry was one of its main attractions for him. His interest came out of his practical experience in ministry. In the parish of Eversden in Cambridgeshire, where he had served for five years before becoming Rector of Caxton in 1906, there had been no doctor for seven miles. Iggulden therefore took on the role of healer as much as vicar, and when he had left the parish, the people said: 'Oh we shan't miss you so much as a parson, but we shall as a doctor.' In

Caxton there were two active doctors, as well as a retired physician, but people still went to him for healing.[26] This may have been in part because his treatment was free whereas the doctors – in the days before the National Health Service – charged a fee, but it was also because he seemed to have a genuine gift of healing. About this he was, as in other things, deeply humble, ascribing all power to the divine. Speaking of two nurses who were in contact with him and wanted to help in his pastoral work, he wrote that 'they have known of things which have happened through my agency before I got into correspondence with you, and which made people give me a kind of respectful reverence which almost shocked me, but I passed it onto my Master, as it was His, not mine'.[27] By using the Panacea healing water in conjunction with his own gifts, simple medicines and prayer, he continued his healing ministry in Caxton, though always in concert with Octavia and the Society. He would give her names and details of others who needed the Panacea Society's prayers for healing or 'casting' of their controls. This included his youngest daughter Laura, who broke one knee in 1923 and then fractured her other hip in an accident in 1924. He listed the names of those who needed healing in a 'book of remembrance', then put it on the altar and asked for help for them. Just as he was keen not to overstep the boundary between his priesthood and Panacea membership, so he recognised the need not to worry or seem to oppose the doctors of the village.[28] He emerges from the pages of his letters as a scrupulous, careful and kind man.

In 1924, Iggulden was instructed in a message from the Divine Mother to use the divine water in his communion wine at the Eucharist in Caxton parish church. It began with the amazing statement that 'one [i.e. one Anglican clergyman] with God is now a majority' and went on to give an explicit direction to him:

God will dispense from the Altar of the Church of England what the Church has refused. God has now a foothold in the Church. Thus Lawrence Iggulden becomes an apostle sent by God to do this work in the Church, and he shall use the 'mixed chalice', adding the blessed water to the wine, and fulfilling the word, 'out of his side came forth blood and water'.

(I John v. 6; John xix 34)

The Panacea Society was therefore instructed to 'Send him the linen section; he is to use the mixed chalice, with the blessed water and the wine, and he can put a few drops into the baptismal water.' At one level this was just about the parishioners of first Caxton and later Elsworth unknowingly receiving drops of Panacean water in their communion wine. But of course in Panacean terms it had cosmic significance. The message from the Divine Mother declared: 'though the Church has refused the healing water, and though the world has refused it, YET God has overruled the world and the Church and has secured that the Healing Water shall come "from the altar of the *Church*"'. This meant that in the cosmic battle between good and evil, in which they were the frontline troops, 'There shall be nothing that Lucifer can say is his. Lucifer can have the majority – *one* is sufficient with the Lord for Him to work.'[29] Iggulden did as instructed and wrote back to the Society to say that he had used some of the blessed water from the altar in the font for a baptism and he 'was much struck by the way the little baby smiled at me immediately after I had baptised her'.[30]

Iggulden was an ambassador for the Society within the Church, and he was its chaplain, though in both roles he was local in his operations. In the first role, he distributed literature to those who he thought might be sympathetic and attempted to get other clergymen interested, though in this he was never very successful. One meeting, which he organised for clergy of his rural deanery area to discuss the Society's ideas, was thwarted by a thunderstorm.[31] Occasionally he would have hopes that clergymen – such as the Revd Walter Simons, Rector of Croxton, a village of about 300 close to his own – were getting keen, but their interest would wane. He read the literature that Octavia wrote specifically for the clergy, and offered her comments, and he used it in his attempts to interest other clergy but often to no avail. At least one clergyman wrote to complain. Edward Woollard, from the nearby parish of Elsworth (where Lawrence Iggulden went as his successor several years later), wrote: 'the Southcott business may be new to you, but to most it is a very old subject unworthy of consideration'. Iggulden's discussion of the Panacea Society had not gone down well at the August meeting of the rural deanery, where he had dared to mention it: 'what alarmed several . . . was the awful blasphemy on [*sic*] reputed daughter of this woman was destined to be the Bride of CHRIST!!!' As a result of this, Mr Woollard had determined not to attend the next meeting.[32]

Iggulden knew when to back off. He continued to support the Society's efforts to reach out to other clergy, but he did less of it himself, concentrating more on his healing ministry in his parish and his own significant role in the Society as their chaplain. In this capacity, he baptised all their members as Anglicans and he must have done this knowing that many of them had been baptised before. In this regard, his obedience was to Octavia and the Divine Mother rather than to his Church, which taught that there should be no re-baptism. For this reason, he did not record the baptism of Panacea members in his parish's baptismal records book; Hilda Green recorded them at the Society in a Panacea baptism book. The first baptisms he performed were in the Garden Room at the Society on 8 April 1925 when he baptised thirteen people, including Peter Rasmussen, Emily Goodwin, Gertrude Searson, Kate Firth, and Muriel and Evelyn Gillett, but later members went over to his church to be baptised. And oddly, six of that original thirteen were baptised yet again (for some, a third baptism), as the act in the Garden Room was 'shown later to be in shadow only'.[33] John Coghill described being driven over to Elsworth Church (where Lawrence Iggulden was now rector) by Evelyn Gillett, in her car one afternoon, and being baptised by Mr Iggulden privately in the parish church with Evelyn Gillett acting as his godmother. She wanted to take him to tea afterwards, but he was to have his first ever interview with the Divine Mother and he did not want to be late for it. This was in 1935 and it was his first visit to Bedford (he had become a member in late October 1934). He confirmed that Iggulden baptised many of the Panaceans, including re-baptising some such as John Coghill himself who had already been baptised in the Presbyterian Church of Scotland.[34]

Iggulden's dual allegiance to both the church and the Panacea Society meant that he sometimes faced a conflict of interests. Early on in his relationship with the Society, he was asked to participate in the casting of controls, and although he had asked it for others, he was less willing to participate in it himself, not wishing 'to do anything which would make me untrue to my church. To that in my vows and my work I am pledged.' Nevertheless, he was willing to make his confession, and do the spiritual and practical inventory required by

the Society, such as going through his possessions and making sure
he had nothing belonging to anyone else, and the payment of his bills
was up to date. And, on balance, he was often on the side of the
Panaceans. He clearly had a sense of critical edge about the Church
and the clergy. He wrote to Miss Green in 1925 that he thought that
the Archbishop of Canterbury's address at the Church Congress held
in Eastbourne that year, should be called 'The Life and Death of an
Earwig'.[35]

After the initial flurry of enthusiasm – in 1923 and 1924 he was, on
average, writing once a week to Octavia – the letters became rather
less frequent, but he continued to ask Octavia and, as the Divine
Mother's position crystallised, the Divine Mother's advice on his
pastoral cases and on major personal decisions, such as whether he
should take the nearby parish of Elsworth, which would give him a
larger salary. The Divine Mother gave her assent to this move, as long
as it would not prevent him working with the healing water, and in
December 1926 he wrote to say that he had been offered the parish
of Elsworth by its patron, the Duke of Portland, and had accepted it.
His diocesan bishop, the Bishop of Ely, had not objected to his appoint-
ment, even though Iggulden had written to him in 1923 about Joanna
Southcott's Box, but perhaps that was because a new bishop had been
appointed in 1924. There are fewer letters about his life in Elsworth
but he continued to obey Octavia's and the Divine Mother's instructions about the conduct of liturgy and the integration of the healing
water into his pastoral ministry.

One reason why he wrote fewer letters was that in the summer of
1925 he had acquired a car so – no longer reliant on just a bicycle or
pony and trap or the train – he was now able to drive to Bedford more
frequently. The car had been bought in part with a gift of £21 collected
by the clergy of his rural deanery, who obviously held him in affection. At this time, an Austin Seven, a small mass-produced car that
enabled far more of the population to become motor owners, cost
£165, while a Morris Cowley cost £225. These lower prices meant that
by 1930 over a million Britons were car owners.[36] Iggulden was thrilled
with his new car (we do not know what make it was), and he bathed
it in the Panacea water and asked for a blessing on it before he took
it out for its first drive. This was in the days before the driving test
and he wrote of driving to Bedford and then the towns of Ely and

King's Lynn – a journey of about four hours then, when the speed limit (not always observed) was twenty miles an hour. He described the journey as a sort of self-given driving lesson – 'a good experience for sitting at the steering wheel'.[37]

1927, the year when Harry Price opened the fake box, and Lawrence Iggulden was tootling around the countryside in his recently acquired car, serving his new parish of Elsworth, proved a particularly taxing one for the Church of England. There was internal fighting about the revised Prayer Book, and the Panaceans took a keen interest in what was going on for they believed the 1662 Book of Common Prayer, which they used, to be 'inspired' – just as the King James Version of the Bible was.[38] For several decades there had been arguments in the Church of England about the extent to which Anglo-Catholic liturgical innovations should be accommodated in the rites of the whole Church. At the heart of the changes in the new Prayer Book was a long-running debate about the sacrament of Holy Communion or the Eucharist. The new Prayer Book was a compromise with the Anglo-Catholics, offering a different form of words at the moment of consecrating the bread and wine, and also providing the opportunity for the reservation of the consecrated sacrament. All of this suggested that something happened when the priest consecrated the bread and wine; the service was not a mere memorial of Jesus' Last Supper. This issue – a divisive one amongst the sixteenth-century Protestant Reformers in Europe – had been fudged at the English Reformation. The new Eucharistic prayers leaned towards the more Catholic understanding that some change occurred in the elements. For the Anglo-Catholics, once you believed in that change, then it was meaningful to reserve the Sacrament after it had been consecrated (usually in the sanctuary close to the altar, with a lamp by it). Many people in the Church believed in reserving the Sacrament so it could be taken to the sick, but balked at the idea of reserving it on display in the Sanctuary as an object of devotion.

The new Prayer Book passed with a good majority in the Church Assembly, the Church's main decision-making body (34 to four in the House of Bishops; 253 to 37 in the House of Clergy and 230 to 92 in the House of Laity). As the Church of England was the state church, and a new Prayer Book represented a change in the law, it required an Act of Parliament to be implemented. It was a shock when, in

December 1927, the House of Commons threw out the revised Prayer Book. Fear of 'Romanism' largely dealt the death-blow to the new Prayer Book, and the papers were full of assertions about proper English Protestantism, though the lukewarm attitude of Randall Davidson – still Archbishop of Canterbury, aged eighty – did not help its fate in Parliament. The Church did not give up. In 1928 it brought forward an amended version of what was known as 'the Deposited Book' and again the Church Assembly passed it, and again the House of Commons rejected it, on 14 June 1928.

Back at the Panacea Society, Octavia and her followers were acting out their own drama about the 'Deposited' Prayer Book and finding meaning in small events and coincidences. As Parliament was preparing to vote, and the weather turned boisterous 'just as it has always been when we undertake some fresh move,' wrote Rachel Fox, Octavia prepared a leaflet for the bishops, *How we Endeavoured to Rouse the Bishops*, and brushed each of the leaflets with the blessed water before they were posted. The next day, she put her foot accidentally upon a book and found it to be the Archbishop of Canterbury's book on the Prayer Book, and saw that the Church was thus symbolically 'under her feet'. On 12 June, she took both prayer books to the chapel meeting and threw the 'Deposited' Prayer Book to the floor, saying 'We here have rejected this book by 33 votes to none.' She gave the 'Deposited' Book to a member to dispose of and declared: 'We shall use the old Prayer Book, as the Bishops have given permission to the people that they can do as they like about it.' She then took the 1662 Book of Common Prayer to all the members present and 'each put it to their lips in token of affection and devotion to it'. When she asked the Divine Mother if they had safeguarded the Prayer Book for the Established Church, there came the dramatic reply from Mrs Goodwin, in Divine Mother trance: 'You *are* the Church of England, The Established Church, Established by the Father, by Me, and by the Son.' On the day of voting, 14 June, Octavia, Emily Goodwin, Peter Rasmussen and Hilda Green huddled around the wireless waiting for Parliament's decision to come through, just as they would listen for the 1929 general election results two years later. The Commons voted against it, by 46 votes. The next day in chapel before the evening meeting, the Divine Mother declared (with useful hindsight): 'The result is exactly as the Divine Family intended it to be . . . The clergy were led in their own wisdom in seeking this revision of the decision of the previous voting. They have never mentioned God in this matter.'[39]

What is striking about this episode is how keenly the Panaceans followed the activities of the Church and yet with what disparagement too, exhibiting a paradoxical obsession with the Church's activities, all the time disavowing their importance. This was in many ways like their attitude to politics. The fact is that the Church of England formed a constant backdrop to everything they did, though we should remember that this was truer for the population at large then in a way that is hard to imagine now. The Prayer Book controversy was never out of the newspapers. Nevertheless, the Panaceans had a distinctive investment in what the Church was doing. Octavia was always reading sermons and speeches, theological articles and books, constantly taking the temperature of the Church of England and keeping abreast of events. In November 1927, in face of the Church's continued non-response to the Society's efforts and in the midst of the Prayer Book controversy, she decided to make this reading a priority, giving résumés of recent theological books by men such as W.R. Inge, Dean of St Paul's Cathedral, and Bishop Barnes of Birmingham, to the members at their evening chapel meetings. Rachel Fox called this 'a controversial period between Octavia and a silent Church'.[40] Bishop Barnes had been one of the most fervent opponents of the new Prayer Book, intensely hostile to Anglo-Catholicism and to the Roman Catholic doctrine of transubstantiation, developed in the Middle Ages: that the bread and wine actually changed into the body and blood of Jesus in the Mass. Octavia used the controversy stirred up by the Prayer Book and Bishop Barnes's provocative comments about the mysteries of the sacrament of Communion to educate the Panaceans on the sacraments. She ran a series of clear, learned articles (demonstrating once again how much she knew about theology) in *The Panacea* on the meaning of Holy Communion, coming to the profoundly Anglican conclusion that it was neither a mere memorial nor transubstantiation, both of which were 'theologically unsound', but that the Church of England was broad enough to hold all opinions.[41] But the final article contained the Panacean punchline: what really mattered was the institution of the *new* Panacea sacrament, the blessed water, which led to the healing of body, mind and soul, and ultimately to immortality. This was the 'last and final Sacrament offered to man, a comprehensive sacrament offered for the Redemption of the Body'.[42]

It was the modernists – men like Barnes, a mathematician by training, who sought to historicise the Bible and make rational sense of the supernatural claims of Christianity – who came in for particular criticism. The modernists were, as Rachel Fox put it, 'practising how to preserve a living body while dismembering it leisurely on a dissecting table, that body being the Mother Church'.[43] What was so galling to the Panaceans was that the Church continued to ignore their answer to its problems, while the dissection continued apace.

One best-selling book particularly got under Octavia's skin: Dick Sheppard's *The Impatience of a Parson*, published and reprinted several times in the autumn of 1927, and selling 90,000 copies by the end of the year – which 'really shows how popular error is', wrote Rachel Fox.[44] Until 1926, he had been the charismatic vicar of St Martin-in-the-Fields in Trafalgar Square. In 1924, he had started to broadcast regularly from the church on (the newly formed) BBC Radio, becoming a public figure; he was perhaps the most well-known Anglican clergyman in Britain in the interwar years. At St Martin's, he created an environment in which anyone felt welcome, quickly growing the congregation from 11 to 1,200. He abolished the reserved pews, experimented with more informal services, and in the final years of World War I opened the church all night for members of the armed services, turned the crypt into an air-raid shelter and set up a hostel for the destitute. He believed that the Gospel message was simple: loving and serving others. 'I can more easily see our Lord sweeping the streets of London than issuing edicts from its cathedral,' was one much-quoted sentence from his book.[45]

While Octavia and Dick Sheppard were both appealing to ordinary people's sense of disillusionment with the Church – and therein lay their shared impatience with the Church – Sheppard's vision was the polar opposite of Octavia's. He was impatient with it as an institution because he believed in a radical Christianity that put the welfare of people, especially the poor, first. He embraced a form of Christian socialism and was an increasingly active pacifist. He even believed that the Church should seek to disestablish itself. While Sheppard's sense of dissatisfaction with the Church struck a chord with Octavia, his analysis and solution were anathema to her. As Rachel Fox put it, 'She felt the writer dishonoured Our Lord and threw dust into eyes that were wearying to see the real Man Who alone is worthy to be crowned with many crowns.' Octavia believed strongly in the Church's hierarchy and established status, detested any form of socialism and had no interest in 'the emotional outpourings of Mr Sheppard and other such priests who suggest the substitution of a pseudo-brotherhood for a Royal Kingdom of obedient and loyal priests and people'.[46] So angry did this make her that the community was directed to acclaim Christ as King in a special service designed as an act of reparation – by the Panaceans on behalf of the Church and all bodies of religion which had so gravely missed the point – on Sunday 4 December 1927.[47]

Octavia's response was to write a book, a vigorous reply to Sheppard's *The Impatience of the People*, under the pseudonym Mark Proctor (the one that she used frequently to write about political and theological issues in *The Panacea*). She may have chosen this male pseudonym deliberately for a book that was to target Anglicans, and especially Anglican clergy. For Octavia, Sheppard's mistake was to proffer a human solution to the problem, merely proposing 'to lead a weary flock from one human pasture – which he is among the first of the clergy to realise to be completely barren – to another human pasture which he hopes or thinks may be satisfactory'. No, what the weary flock really sought, Octavia (predictably) said was 'the cession of pain and sorrow and unending Life, here and now'.[48] In January 1928, copies of the book were sent to forty-two bishops and other selected clergy. Dick Sheppard wrote to the Society acknowledging receipt of it, but failing to engage with it: 'I could not possibly resent whatever you have felt called upon to say in *The Impatience of the People*,' he wrote. Rachel Fox commented that it was an example of how 'so-called Christians evade reproof and lose all benefit from it'.[49] As someone who frequently accepted reproof from Octavia, she was entitled to comment.

But the book prompted more engaged reactions from many of its readers, who wrote in, eager for knowledge of the Society. Letters arrived throughout 1928 from clergy and laity not only in Britain but also Ireland, Morocco, Australia and New Zealand. Many of the correspondents expressed just that dissatisfaction and impatience with the Church that the Society so often articulated. Miss M. Hayward, a twenty-seven-year-old nurse from Horsham in Sussex, wrote that although she was an Anglo-Catholic, 'the priests are strangers to us, they neither care whether we go or stay away from the Church'. She admitted to being lonely, wanting 'advice and sympathy', and she wrote, 'I attend the Church regular, but even then there is something *vital* missing.'[50] She was sent some leaflets about the Society (as were all enquirers, but the selection varied according to the correspondent) and was invited to apply for the healing. She applied for the healing but lapsed in her reporting two years later. The Society had more luck with Mrs Margaret Morton from Strathaven in Lanarkshire, a Presbyterian who for a long time had not been able to accept that Church's doctrines. She had found a good deal of help in psychology and metaphysics and kept 'an open mind for all the instruction I can get'. She had been sick with a badly damaged shoulder joint and tuberculosis. She had read *The Impatience of the People* with the keenest interest and reported that she had been thinking along those lines for a long time 'but when I mentioned them, I was looked upon as fully qualified for the place where queer folk are confined'. In their reply, the Society ordered her 'to leave the material and psychic behind and follow the beckoning hand of God, whose promise is that Water and the Spirit shall bring about the new birth – in fact without those one cannot enter the Kingdom on earth, though for entering the Kingdom of Heaven, the blood of Jesus is all sufficient.'[51] She applied for the Healing and reported in faithfully. A scribbled note on her letter says 'going on well'.

People of all classes and backgrounds wrote in response to the book. Sir Arthur Limpus was a retired admiral who had served with the navy in east Sudan, South Africa, northern China and as head of the naval mission in Turkey. During World War I, he had been the senior British naval officer in Malta and president of the Shell Committee at the British Admiralty, and had retired in 1919. In retirement he had the leisure and time to reflect on his life and ponder theological questions, and he wrote in 1928 from the Hotel Val d'Olivo in Alassio, on the Italian Riviera, after reading Mark Proctor's 'remarkable book'. He wrote that for the first fifty-five years of his life (he was now sixty-eight) he had not realised what Jesus meant by the words 'if you shall ask anything in my name I will do it' and 'Lo – I am with you always'. He was now trying to eradicate his bad habits of thought and what he felt he needed was a stronger, more confident faith. He was interested in healing, had seen examples of it in his 'wanderings in many lands', prayed for those who were sick, and said that 'sometimes I see clear answer to my prayer – sometimes not'. He responded to the invitation to take the water, and a note on his letter says: 'reporting steadily'.[52]

F.W. Lyons, a boot repairer from Ewshot in Hampshire, wrote in wishing for a fuller explanation of the Blessed Water and reporting his troubles, the worst of which was the separation from his wife 'which I thought could never have happened'. He wrote, 'I am a very hard worker working sometimes 12 or 14 hour a day at boot repairing to live respectably and to owe no man anything always seeking to do good and to do no one any harm,' and although he felt assured that he was 'living in the sunshine of God's affections' he was aware of troubles and sought help. He applied for the healing but lapsed in his reporting.[53] A fifty-year-old woman, (Miss?) A. Findell wrote in, describing herself as 'a working-class woman, C of E, High Church (but not Roman)' who said that for the last ten months material success had not come her way. 'I used to "follow the sea" but because I would not accept a post offered me, I lost the berth altogether & since then have been unable to obtain another ship, but feel it is all in God's Plan & get despondent sometimes but not very often.' She wrote in not so much for help but with endearing, theological curiosity. 'I love the dear old Church & have always thought, in my humble way that if we all followed the teaching of the Bible and the Church there would be an end to all this unrest. I haven't thought much about Christ's Second Coming, it always seemed such a long way off, & always antic-ipated the grave & "beyond", but now, since reading your book if I may I would love to stay & see Christ coming as King.' She did not apply for the healing after being sent the Panacea leaflets and books, so her desire to see Christ as King on this earth perhaps waned; but more to the point, the Society was probably not what she expected it to be. She wrote in her letter of enquiry that *The Impatience of the People*, lent to her by a friend, was 'wonderful reading, especially as the author & members of your Society belong to the Church of England'.[54] On receiving further Panacea leaflets she may have realised how far from the Church of England its members were in their beliefs and practices. But Octavia's canny sense of marketing got people to respond in the first place.

This realisation of the Society's actual distance from the Church of England may be the reason why many of the correspondents did not apply for the healing or quickly lapsed in their reporting. The book led them to imagine this was a rather more orthodox group than it was. This may have been the case for Miss J. Searby from Cricklewood in London, who was 'high Church in her views' and had 'great faith in the Sacraments', whose chief problem was deafness which she tried to bear patiently as she had been taught to 'bear the Cross willingly, as Christ did, and so hereafter receive the Crown'. But 'your teaching seems different altogether' – she wanted to know about it but when she learned more, she did not get back in touch. Some wrote with outright hostility, such as Mrs A.K. Woodward, from west London, who had greatly admired Sheppard's book and for that reason read *The Impatience of the People*. Writing did 'in no way betoken sympathy' for the Panacea Society but she wanted more information 'as to how such extraordinary confidence can be felt by any human creature'. She was sceptical about 'blessed water [that] can charm away air attack etc!! It sounds as if we were – according to your Society – to revert to medieval times of superstition.'[55] Hilda Green (who did not reply for a month, knowing this was not a promising possibility) eventually wrote back, asserting: 'the confidence that you speak of is due to our having proved, and to thousands having proved, the Power of the Water and the Spirit'.[56]

Yet others corresponded about their own agenda. A letter from Miss A.F. Smith of Loughborough gives a flavour of the concerns of the day and the kinds of issues to which Hilda Green found herself responding. She wrote to ask the Society's views on 'the iniquitous practice of vivisection' which many of the 'so-called Christian churches' refused to condemn, even though it was an 'un Christian practice'. Hilda Green wrote back, putting Miss Smith and her obsession firmly in her place: 'The rejection of your efforts on behalf of anti-vivisection would not be sufficient evidence against the Church, as it is too specialised a subject to make it a test of any person's morality or general efficiency . . . It would be useless to try and test The Panacea Society in the same way – indeed you might spend your life testing Churches and Societies, your friends and neighbours, by a specialised matter of this sort and find that the Bridegroom had come and the guests had sat down to the wedding feast and that you were left outside hugging your particular opinion on *one* subject!' Miss Smith replied with a four-page letter, again rehearsing the evils of vivisection; there is no record of any further reply from the Panacea Society.

A number of clergy wrote in, several with some personal difficulties or questions and possibly no one else to turn to about them. One Revd E. W. Freeman in Wargrave, Berkshire, enquired about the Second Advent, but his real concern was whether he might find a parish in the Church in England or would need to return to Australia to serve again there. He asked for advice 'as to the best way to present "the Message"' – to which Hilda Green replied, writing of 'the need to come to the help of the Lord, by getting yourself right first . . . all done by the Power of the Water'.[57] He did not apply for the Healing. H.E.L. Russell, a Lay Reader in the Church of England for thirty years, who lived in Ladbroke Grove in west London, was in good health but had recently lost his capital and his income. He was so keen that he went to the London postal address of the Panacea Society only to be disappointed to find no one he could talk to. He did apply for the healing but lapsed in his reporting a couple of years later.[58] Barrington Philpots was a disillusioned rural vicar from Bletchley in Buckinghamshire. He had 'laboured in this small country parish 35 years with scant success & I might style myself a disappointed parson, supremely disappointed with myself and my work'. Like the Panacea Society, he had a vision of death being conquered. He had 'studied spiritual healing for 40 years' and was sure that 'in the near future it will supplant either physical or mental healing & the Lord will be glorified as King'. Despite the perceived resonances between his own theology and Panacean beliefs and his interest in their healing ministry, he did not apply for the Water.[59]

In *The Impatience of the People* Octavia had without doubt tapped into a rich vein of discontent and disappointment with the Church of England, but once correspondents received the Panacean literature, they rarely went further with their enquiries. The Panacea Society's distinctive and heterodox answer was not for most who wrote in, with one great exception. A copy of the book made its way to Calcutta, and there an honorary canon of the cathedral and chaplain of Kharagpur in West Bengal, Russell Payne, found it, read it, and was instantly captivated. The Panacea Society had another clergy member.

Russell Payne first wrote into the Panacea Society in the spring of

1928 and soon thereafter began taking the water. He was told, as Lawrence Iggulden had been, that he must 'drop the altruistic side of things and be helped yourself first'. The Society had come, by this time, to the notion of predestination: 'If you are one of the numbered flock you will be bound to get it and you will be bound to tell those who have got to hear it,' Canon Payne was told, in answer to his question as to how he could be helpful.[60]

Canon Payne became an enthusiastic sealed member, worked hard at the Overcoming, was never shy about making detailed confessions and found the Panacea teachings a comfort, especially the Divine Mother because he missed his earthly mother so much. At every phase of his life he had wished he could tell his own mother what he was doing, for her to be proud of him. He was 'only a little village boy, born in a tiny cottage in Norfolk' but his mother had always wanted him to be a priest, although nothing seemed more improbable at the time. In the absence of his real mother, he hoped the Divine Mother would know and understand what he was feeling. He was also – like Lawrence Iggulden – willing to be obedient and accept what Octavia or the Divine Mother told him to do. When the Bishop of Calcutta, Foss Westcott, told him to go to the clerical society meetings in the diocese, a sort of debating society from which he rather shrank, he was resistant. When Octavia told him to attend, because it would be an excellent opportunity for speaking on 'the purely scriptural points which the clergy miss but which no one can take any exception to any Christian believing', he did so, drinking the water before he went and wearing the linen section for protection. She reminded him that there was 'so much of the Visitation, even without our revelation on it, in the Bible, that it is perfectly safe for any clergyman to speak of the many things we stand for'.

Canon Payne found this to be entirely the case and he began writing a series of articles on Christian theology, delicately infused with the Panacea perspective without getting into the Society's distinctive beliefs, for the Calcutta diocesan magazine. The first of these was on empty pews, and the articles continued to be on thoroughly orthodox topics such as the Eucharist, the way of life, righteousness, the nature of humankind, the immaculate conception, the Church, baptism and atonement. Octavia was thrilled. After reading the first of these articles, she wrote to him: 'It would be difficult to give you any real understanding of its effect upon me.' He had put into practice what she felt was necessary: that she had to teach the teachers, like Russell Payne, so that *they* would reach the multitudes. Canon Payne was 'the very first to show the capacity to do what is absolutely essential for the time being, namely to introduce the Truth in a completely normal manner'. His writing was 'very clever' and he had the 'necessary "pulpit style"'. What this came down to was that 'the traps must and can be laid for the Church by Her own sons' and this gave Octavia 'an extraordinarily welcome sense of how glorious the rest will be when it is all in working order'. She had read Canon Payne's article at the Sunday worship meeting and 'all alike felt it was very wonderful to hear our truths dressed in such ecclesiastically correct garments!'[61]

Basking in Octavia's approval – in his confessions he revealed how much he sought praise – Canon Payne set to work, producing some fourteen such articles. Octavia warned him not to sacrifice himself, not to do anything to imperil his position or cause friction, not least because this would stop him being able to do what was so useful to the Society. She wrote: 'I think your metier is to get in the thin edge of the wedge and not to spoil such a good opportunity by anything precipitate.'[62] But he was disobedient – as he later confessed to the Divine Mother – talking and preaching about the Visitation, and eventually the Bishop got to hear of it and took steps to remove him from the diocese.

Canon Payne and his wife Mary came to live in Bedford in April 1932. He was fifty-nine and she was sixty-two. They had been longing to get back to England for some time. They were sick of the climate in India, the nine months of intense, sticky heat every year. Back in 1929, Mrs Payne had written to the Panacea Society asking whether there would be any possibility of work in Bedford for her husband, and whether they could come to live there. They were asked – as all prospective residents were – to list their assets and their gifts. Mrs Payne had no savings, but a house in the hill station of Kalimpong, which she hoped to sell, and some silver. She would have no pension but she had no debts. She was unable to type but could do housekeeping. Canon Payne listed his assets very methodically: he had his salary but no private means; twelve bookshelves, a dressing table, five writing tables, a dining table, an upright piano, a gramophone player and hundreds of records, six record cabinets, a clothes *almirah* (a Hindi word for cupboard), two typewriting tables and two typewriters. He had a Ford motor car that was ten years old and some crockery.

He would have no pension and he had few savings. He could type and offered his services to the Society in 'literary secretarial work'. The Paynes had dependants: Mary's widowed daughter and her twelve-year-old daughter, Babs, and Mary's son. Canon Payne clearly felt responsible for his stepchildren and after he had returned to England with his wife, he remained financially responsible for his stepdaughter and step-granddaughter.[63]

The Paynes sincerely believed in Panacea theology and rigorously followed the practices of Overcoming and taking the water. But it is also true that the Panacea Society was the means by which they could return to England, when no other route seemed possible. It is quite obvious from the listing of their assets that they did not have the financial resources to return to England in any other way. Like many English people who had gone out to the colonies, they did not intend spending their whole lives out there – Canon Payne had been there for thirty-three years – but they found they could not afford to do otherwise. The Panacea Society allowed them to return when the Church of England would have had little use for a fifty-nine-year-old priest with eccentric views. The Society gave them a home – they lived in a community-owned house with the wealthy resident member, Margaret Conde-Williams – which allowed them to live inexpensively as part of the community in return for typing and work in the gardens. Canon Payne acted as chaplain to the community and occasionally helped in churches around Bedford.

While the Panacea Society (paradoxically) needed the Church of England and expended a lot of energy in trying to get the Church to take notice of them, it is revealing that the two clergy who became seriously committed members (there were one or two others who were marginally affiliated) needed the Society just as much as the Society needed the prestige of their membership. Lawrence Iggulden, lonely as a rural vicar, found in Octavia a spiritual director, and in the Society companionship and friendship, while Russell Payne, sick of India and longing to return to England, found an English home in the Bedford community that would otherwise have eluded him. However, his services in the community's chapel would soon be needed, for Octavia would no longer be able to take services in the chapel, and Canon Payne stepped in to fill the breach.

16

Death, after all

Octavia died on 16 October 1934. Although she had been feeling ill for a while, and suffered from diabetes, the doctor who examined her the day before said that she was only experiencing a 'slight block of undigested food'. This was put down to some pears she had eaten. That night she was weak but still took down the daily script and read it in the chapel service. As usual, she had hot milk in bed, and said goodnight with a smile to Emily Goodwin at midnight. The next morning it was thought that she was sleeping late. Peter Rasmussen went in at 11.20 a.m. to light a fire in her bedroom and discovered that she was dead. As he wrote in his diary: 'Our dreadful loss, the worst that has ever been or can ever be. Oh how cruel Death, Cold & Still.'[1] The shock was not just that of discovering a dead body; it was the horror of discovering that the beloved divine daughter had actually died in a community that promised immortality. As Mrs Goodwin later wrote in a letter to the non-resident members: 'You may be sure what a shock it was to us, because we never thought about Octavia having to die in the body, we thought her deliverance would be from all her sufferings and to go on with the work in freedom.'[2]

Their first reaction, on discovering her cold, still body, was disbelief. In their agony of mind, the little group called to the scene tried to revive her with hot-water bottles, blankets, massage, brandy and the blessed water, but nothing could rouse her. It was, after all, possible that she was still just alive – in a diabetic coma – and even the doctor, when he arrived, gave her an injection to try and start up her heart again, but with no success. At ten past two, the doctor pronounced her dead. Mildred Hollingworth, trained as a nurse, changed her nightdress and the bed linen, and tidied the room. A vigil by Octavia's bedside began.

The Panaceans kept the body for as long as they could, in the hope that Octavia might be resurrected, just as members had kept watch with Joanna Southcott's body after her death in 1814 for the same reason. Two of the original apostles always kept the night-time watch: Hilda Green and Gertrude Searson. On the third day – which would be the expected day for a resurrection following the pattern of Jesus – Octavia was still very much dead, and Hilda Green and Dilys were obliged to see the undertaker. Four days later, the coffin arrived, and the body was put inside it. Because of the body's decaying condition, the coffin lid had to be fastened on. By the sixth day, reality had set in, and flowers were being ordered for the funeral. Still, the apostles sat with her.

The glaring absence of Octavia was most obvious at the evening chapel meetings where her chair was empty, the wit and charisma of her leadership were missing and, for the first time in fifteen years, there was no script. Members gathered at the usual time on the evening of Tuesday 16 October, the day she died, and read chapter 14 of John's Gospel, part of Jesus' great speech before he was crucified, in which he tells his disciples that he has to leave the world but he will not abandon them: 'I will not leave you comfortless: I will come to you. Yet a little while the world seeth me no more, but ye see me; because I live, ye shall live also.' In fact, most of the members did not yet have any idea that Octavia was dead. Mrs Goodwin, in her guise as the Divine Mother, simply declared that there was no script because her daughter had not been able to take one. The moment when the charismatic leader of a group dies is a delicate one. Mrs Goodwin wanted to pave the way for a smooth leadership succession. She wanted to prepare the others to be obedient to her, to ensure there was no power vacuum, and to prevent panic. So in the chapel that night, she did not tell them of Octavia's death but instead asked them: 'I want you to say whether, whatever happens, you will trust Me, The Great Divine Mother – your faith may be greatly tried: it rests with each one of you whether you have that faith.' Only the next day, after they had answered this question in their hearts, as commanded, did Mrs Goodwin gather the resident Panaceans and tell them that Octavia's 'spirit took flight and there remains nothing but the shell'. She reassured them that 'no doubt she knows all that you are doing' and promised that 'We do not feel that she has gone away to stay' while at the same time assuming their obedience to her: 'The Divine Mother hopes that you will give yourselves up to the work with your whole heart.'[3]

Canon Payne now took the evening services, and the Divine Mother spoke at them from time to time. Everyone tried to carry on as usual, as they believed Octavia would have wished, but the light at the centre of their world had gone and everything seemed lifeless. As Hilda Green put it, 'We listen for her step and her voice – not there.'

Each of them coped with the grief in the ways that they knew how. Hilda Green, ever the efficient secretary who had served Octavia faithfully in that capacity for so many years, listed all the tasks that had been completed before Octavia's death, noting what remained to be done and what Octavia had been planning as new initiatives. Mildred Hollingworth, as she quietly kept vigil in Octavia's bedroom, took comfort in her medical background and observed the changes in the gradually decomposing body of the woman to whom she had been an apostle for fifteen years. The day after Octavia's death, she noted that the face and fingernails grew very dark, and two days later the limbs were becoming more supple and the mouth was haemorrhaging a little. Rachel Fox, at heart a theologian, began to look for an explanation for what had happened. Away from the community at her home in Falmouth, she had to try and come to terms with this loss without the comfort of other Panacean companions, and she spent her days and nights combing through Octavia's writings for signs that this death was, after all, 'part of the Divine drama that she the daughter – the woman – had to pass through'. She listed the various passages that seemed to offer a clue and sent them to resident member Irene Mellor for study. She found that many texts could now be understood in the light of the present. 'One cannot but wonder and expect that all is come to time and that the best is yet to come, but how to face the Centre without her!!'[4] But face it she did: eventually she could not bear to be away from the community any longer, and she made the long train journey up to Bedford to be with her friends there just in time for Octavia's funeral.

Dilys, about whom everyone was so worried, rallied and arranged the funeral, telling her brothers the news and organising her mother's finances. As the closest family member present in Bedford, she had to take charge of all the bureaucratic and personal matters associated with her mother's death, and her resilience and efficiency surprised everyone. As Hilda Green put it, 'Dilys is so brave. What a lesson to everyone.' Octavia left all her property to her children, never having updated her will from the one she made in 1910. Dilys organised it all with the solicitor and her mother's executor. Number 12 Albany Road, Octavia's home, which was indispensable to the Society and such a central part of its life and history, was sold by the Barltrop children to the Society for £1,000 – the same price that Octavia had paid for it in 1921. With the brothers abroad, and the Society wanting the house so much, it was a convenient arrangement. Dilys was also given a £120 annuity for life, presumably to make up for her loss of potential income from renting it out, and this may have been the condition on which the brothers sold the house to the Society, especially at such a favourable rate. Octavia's Aunt Fanny's house in Croydon, from which Octavia had usefully been receiving rent for so many years, was now sold for £700. All in all, Octavia's estate came to nearly £3,000, so each child received nearly £900 in total, and as neither brother returned home for the funeral or to deal with any of this, it was Dilys who managed it all.

The person who was patently struck down with grief was Peter Rasmussen, who had devotedly served Octavia since the day he arrived in 1920. Now he wandered the community houses, utterly lost. Five days after her death he wrote bleakly in his diary: 'Nothing in the big hall & no Octavia.' Peter was the first person Rachel thought of: 'Poor Peter,' she wrote to Irene Mellor, knowing how distraught he would be. On the day of Octavia's funeral, he wrote, 'O – she has gone, "my only hope" is past, is gone, "don't be long O."' Without Octavia, he was alone. 'Oh this grief I cannot get away from, no where, nothing can help, no one to speak to about this matter, not one is of any use – human or divine.'[5]

The day of Octavia's funeral, exactly a week after her death, was gloriously sunny, with the golden brown autumn leaves shining in the sunlight. Members noticed the stillness of the atmosphere, an almost Sabbath-like quietude, which had descended on the neighbourhood, with only the birds singing softly. Peter was up early preparing the chapel. In front of the altar he placed white chrysanthemums, Octavia's attaché case, her bible and prayer book. On the altar he put a pot of winter cherries alongside bound volumes of Octavia's writings, *The Panacea*, Rachel Fox's volumes about the Society and other key publications. This was all for the private Panacean service, prior to the funeral. At this they could say what they wished and express their beliefs freely. As that service ended, Octavia's body was carried down from her bedroom and through the garden – the Garden of Eden, as they believed – and to Castleside, the large house set aside for the bishops when they opened the Box. As the coffin was put into the hearse it was covered in flowers, and a cortège of three cars followed, with just a small group of Panacea members: some long-standing apostles, some newer resident members, and two of the community servants. The formal funeral service in the Bedford cemetery chapel was not a Panacea occasion; it had been organised by the family and was attended by Lennie Bull and her daughter Rita who had always been so hostile to the Society. The Panaceans had said their goodbyes privately behind the closed door of their chapel. As Octavia's coffin was slowly driven to the cemetery, men and boys reverently doffed their caps, as was the custom of the day, and the Panaceans thought: little did those men and boys know to whom they were paying respect. After a brief funeral service, Octavia was buried high on the hill with an extensive view over the town. There is a minimalist inscription on her tombstone, giving no clue to the passer-by of what she had stood for, or who she had claimed to be. It simply says: 'In Loving Memory of M.B. Oct 16 1934. I am the Resurrection and the Life.'

Octavia had, in fact, been ill for a couple of years before she died. In the spring of 1932, she had complained that she was feeling badly, and that she could not see properly. Despite their faith in the water, a doctor was called. Emily Goodwin anticipated the criticism this might receive, for surely Octavia, of all people, should depend on the blessed water alone. But Mrs Goodwin justified the action, saying that 'our work has to be proved by man on the earth, and we have to have a doctor to prove the human side of our Leader – the suffering body'.[6] The doctor diagnosed a broken blood vessel at the back of the eye, but also said that her general health needed attention. Once again, Octavia was shielded from the truth by Emily Goodwin and those at the centre of the community, this time the truth of her own health, and she was not told that she had the symptoms of diabetes. As she was a short, heavy woman, over eleven stone in weight, the doctor's injunction that she had to be put on a diet, with no pastry, white bread or other starches and using saccharine instead of sugar, could be easily explained. Mildred Hollingworth was put in charge of her health and kept a regular diary of their leader's bodily condition. Urine samples were taken once a week to check for sugar. Throughout 1933, Octavia's health gradually improved, but early in 1934 Mildred Hollingworth's regular reports show that she had taken a downturn and was being carefully monitored. Her feet were sore, her eyes were still not good, she had shingles on her chest though it cleared up fairly rapidly, and her diet became stricter. The doctor visited regularly. She seemed to be getting worn out. In the days before her death, more sugar was found in her urine, she had chest pains, she did not feel like eating much, she was sleeping badly and was utterly exhausted, finding it difficult to take the script and lead the meeting.[7]

Even those in the know about her health were shocked to the core when Octavia died. How were they to make sense of it? In retrospect, the followers explained her death by believing that she would indeed come again, this time with Christ himself. Emily Goodwin wrote, 'We know her and will wait patiently for her return.' The parallel with Christ was drawn clearly, so that her death could be made explicable. Peter Rasmussen wrote in his diary, 'Octavia . . . bore all her suffering & then she had to die – that we should live.'[8] Octavia's words were examined for meaning. Emily Goodwin recalled the conversation they had the night before her death, in which Octavia seemed to have some sense that she had to go through something more, that something would happen to her to try the Panaceans' faith and put them to the test. When Mrs Goodwin talked of the great work of ingathering that Octavia would yet do, Octavia replied that she could not do it now, for she was worn out. The Panaceans now believed that Octavia was doing that work of ingathering after her death: she was thought to be mysteriously busy in the world, preparing for the day when she would return with Christ.

Panaceans had died before, and each death had prompted consternation amongst the followers and ridicule from outsiders. The first to die was Ellen Oliver on 8 July 1921, two and a half years after she had identified Mabel Barltrop as Shiloh. Like all the Panaceans she did not believe that she could or would die. Going for a routine visit to the doctor some time before she became terminally ill, she said to the doctor that she now meant to grow younger and had no idea of dying. After the apostles had been through the marriage ceremony to the Lord in 1919, she had written to Octavia: 'The dear Lord would not let me die, would He? Now that I am married to him.'[9] But in May 1921, she was diagnosed with cancer with not long to live. As she rapidly declined, Mildred Hollingworth nursed her. In the last days, as it became obvious that she would soon die, the Panaceans kept a careful notebook of her passing, not only of memorable events such as the moment when Kate Firth broke the news to Octavia that Ellen would never recover, Ellen's last Communion and her last conversation with Octavia, but also (typically) of signs and coincidences that might be seen as a key to the reason for her dying – white gloves, a black dog, the number 8 – but which in the end did not add up to much. Finally, it was decided that Ellen represented the eighth angel of the Book of Revelation (chapter 8) who sends the prayers of the saints up to God with clouds of incense from the golden censer. Before she died, Ellen recited the names of the 144 people already sealed as Panaceans at that time in prayer to God. As she lay on her deathbed, she agreed that the prayers of those she was leaving could be deposited in a silver bowl on the table near her bed, so that she might present them before the throne of God. The answers to these prayers were, Rachel Fox reported, remarkable. As they contemplated the end times, always so close for them, the Panaceans decided that Ellen had to die in order to be their intercessor in heaven. As Octavia wrote to Rachel: 'we are a little Kingdom, now sufficiently a Power, to be permitted to send an ambassador to the Highest Realm'. On the evening before Ellen died, Mildred Hollingworth was kneeling by Ellen's bed and looked up out of the window to see the sky full of dancing angels. Coincidentally, not knowing that Ellen was dying nor of Mildred's vision, Octavia looked out of the window of her own house and saw a circle of cherubs and angels heading in Ellen's direction. Or so they believed.[10]

The decade after Ellen had died in fact saw very few deaths. Nevertheless, Octavia felt the need to clarify that she had never said that Panaceans would not die. She merely held out the promise and possibility of immortality. She would tell members: 'You can never be sure of not dying. In any case you can only prove you will not die by not dying!' She stated that the Society aimed for two things: the better resurrection and not to die. No Panacea person could be sure of which would be his or her fate. So, if a person died, it must be assumed that they went to the better resurrection, and that should make no difference to any of the living Panaceans' hopes for themselves or others.[11]

In other words, speculation as to one's own fate – or that of anyone else – was discouraged in just the way that Calvin discouraged the sixteenth-century Genevans from speculating whether they were the elect or not. When the popular non-resident member Colonel Sullivan died in 1928, it was a blow, but what they learned from it was that not everyone who had been through the ritual of destroying the mortal soul would necessarily achieve immortality, as they had assumed would happen.

In the months before Octavia's death a number of prominent Panaceans died. This is no surprise, given that many of them were of Octavia's generation, now in their sixties and seventies. Hilda Green began to keep a register of members who had died, called *The Flock*, each entry containing a little note about the person's life and character, in some cases offering an explanation for their mortality, usually by way of a feature of their character that they had not yet overcome. Resident member Emily Carew-Hunt died just a year before Octavia. Hilda Green wrote: 'She had gone through every Act and received long instruction but illustrating the inability of the Mortal Mind to say "I will not" she was a witness to the powers of that mind in not submitting to the ruling of the Divine Mother.' Brenda Greig, another resident member, died in March 1934 after being ill for seven months. Although during that illness she was 'nursed and cared for entirely at our expense, she on no occasion offered thanks for the same', noted Miss Green. James Hancock, the roving Panacea evangelist, who distributed pamphlets and gathered names for the petition, died in August 1934. He was 'discontented with money affairs though we gave him £104 yearly and all expenses' and was afflicted with 'spiritual ingratitude'. In September 1934, just a month before Octavia's death, Kate Firth, her former best friend, died. 'Ambition caused her downfall,' wrote Miss Green, with some bitterness, recalling the traumatic events of 1926. Ethel Cooke-Yarborough died a year later, in September 1935. She had become a resident member after the death of her husband in 1933, but 'she was unable to overcome discontent with her surroundings & home & was in consequence unhappy'. The Panaceans had to suffer criticism of their faults and failings even in death.

But then, awkwardly, there were those who died of whom nothing negative could be said. They were faithful Panaceans, women like Gertrude Hill, one of the original apostles, who died in April 1934 'after twenty years faithful devotion to the cause' and Frances Wright, the former Theosophist, who died just a month after Octavia's death, in November 1934. They were the ones who might have been expected to achieve immortality. No reasonable explanation could be given for their deaths. If they had died, what hope was there for others?[12] A script received from the Holy Spirit by Octavia on 19 June 1920 was seen, retrospectively, to hold the answer: there were Immortal Beings on the planet Uranus.[13] The community came to believe that their members would go, after death, to Uranus and wait for the next Coming of Christ and Octavia, when they would return to earth in their radiant, resurrected bodies.

Despite these explanations, people still had doubts, even someone as central as Peter Rasmussen. His intense grief mingled with his creeping theological doubts. A month after Octavia's death, lonely and desperate, he wrote in his diary, 'It said in Gal. VI. 7 "Be not deceived; God is not mocked". If God be not mocked, He must reveal Octavia to us in *living reality* with flesh and bones, or men & *woman* must be mocked also in believing on The Word & in all the promises to *Octavia and us*.' Emily Goodwin sternly told him not to dwell in the past, but he wrote, 'the past is the present & future to me, & the past I don't forget, therefore it has become my present. Day by day I live in the present, rather, only exist. Got nothing, got no one, God has departed, I did believe in Octavia . . . No one can fill her place & I know it.'[14]

Work at the Society settled back into the old routine but, without Octavia's energy and enthusiasm, there was no spark. Emily Goodwin tried to assert control and rein in any doubt or dissent. Soon after Octavia's death, she wrote a letter to all non-resident members describing what had happened, and she ended it by encouraging everyone to go on with the work. As the Divine Mother, she told them that she would guide and direct them until Shiloh (Octavia) returned. Although there were no new scripts, people were commanded to read through the scripts from the beginning again. The letter ended 'We [resident members] are all under the Divine Mother and hope to hear you will be firm.' At the chapel meeting five days after Octavia's death, the Divine Mother reiterated the message of obedience: 'Hasten, hasten, let nothing stand in your way. Do not cling to anything – money, possessions, relatives – nothing; but only cling to the Divine Family – the Great Foursquare.' And she emphasised unity: 'I want you all to band yourselves in one body, so that not all the powers of hell can break even one link or one strand.'

The unity held to a degree. Most did remain firm, but some left, disillusioned by the Divine Mother and her endless rules. Most dramatically, the Scottish branch, which had only been formed as a distinctive branch just before Octavia's death, seceded. A year after her death, in October 1935, the six members wrote a letter to the Bedford headquarters declaring that they had full faith in the Visitation to England – all the prophets right up to and including Octavia. They affirmed their acceptance of Bedford as the Centre, were grateful for all the spiritual work that had been done for them there, and even accepted the death of Octavia as a necessary step in that work. But they rejected the Divine Mother. They had become convinced that 'the Voice now endeavouring to lead Israel is not always THE VOICE of the Shepherd and God of Israel'. They had been startled and had become anxious and uneasy under its uncertain guidance. They thought that Lucifer was leading at Bedford, claiming to rule as the Divine Mother, exacting unquestioning obedience and even deceiving the elect. They dedicated themselves to God and to the continued practice of Overcoming but they could no longer accept the Divine Mother's rule.[15]

The response to such dissent was, ironically, more exacting rules. The only way that Emily Goodwin knew how to try and foster unity was to demand obedience. The year 1936 saw endless new rules, especially for the resident members. Mrs Goodwin made self-opinion the target – after the self-opinions of the Scottish branch had led to their rejection of her authority – and she gave a series of addresses on the subject. Resident members and others in the inner circle now had to write their reports daily rather than weekly. Everything in their mind was shown to be self-opinion. Emily Goodwin began to meet each resident member weekly to help them get rid of the dreaded self-opinion. In 1937, resident members were instructed to eat all food that they were given, regardless of their likes and dislikes. The Sabbath was now to be kept strictly with no work, not even letter-writing or sewing, to be done on Sundays. By 1938 resident members were signing a document asking the Divine Mother to rule over them. In 1942, there was an injunction against smoking. The commands to obey were relentless, and ultimately became thoroughly routinised without the charismatic leader at the helm.

The offices remained busy, and the resident Panaceans continued to do the usual work of sealing, healing and engaging in correspondence with enquirers, members and all those who wrote in to the Confidential Department with their problems. They delivered the petition to Lambeth Palace, as planned, in 1935. They sent letters, pamphlets and booklets to the King and to the bishops, as they had always done. They put advertisements in the newspapers asking the bishops to open the Box. They distributed leaflets within Bedford, and got non-resident members all around the country to put leaflets through people's mailboxes in their neighbourhood. This was how John Coghill – who became a member just after Octavia's death – came to know about the Society. They even allowed some interviews in the newspapers. Their innovations were few, though in 1938 they did build a smart new printing press – The Garden Press – to replace the little printing press they had housed in a caravan. Occasionally they tailored leaflets to the political circumstances of the day, such as the Spanish Civil War (which they called the Spanish Revolution) in 1936.

In fact, for several years after Octavia's death, the Society continued to grow. The resident community grew from fifty-four at the time of her death in 1934 (with six-non-communal members living in the town of Bedford) to sixty-six at its height in June 1939, with a further fifteen non-communal members living in Bedford. The membership as a whole also continued to grow, by about 700 sealed members in the nine years between Octavia's death and that of Emily Goodwin. When Octavia died in October 1934, there were 1,285 sealed members, the majority non-resident of course; in 1943, when Emily Goodwin died, there were 1,978 sealed members altogether. Usually any group that relies on the authority of its charismatic leader begins to decline quickly after that leader's death. In this case, the presence of the Divine Mother contributed to the maintenance of the Society's growth for a while, despite her unpopularity with some members.

The healing ministry continued to grow long after that, needing no charismatic leader to maintain it, but merely regular newspaper advertisements and conscientious workers in the CSS department. By the time of Octavia's death, 32,742 people had applied for the healing since it had started in 1923. By the time of Emily Goodwin's death, that figure had more than doubled, reaching 72,806. Of course not everyone who applied continued to report regularly. Some did not respond, some only reported for a while before lapsing. But the Society was undoubtedly dealing with the case papers and reporting the letters of tens of thousands of water-takers on an annual basis in their healing ministry. Even after the advent of the National Health Service in England interest continued, and in countries that have poor health care to this day, such as parts of the West Indies, there are still keen water-takers. To date there have been – at a conservative estimate – 130,000 applications for the healing water.

After Emily Goodwin's death in 1943, with the change in values in post-war Britain and the emergence of a different, less religiously inclined culture, the Society gradually went into decline. Members continued to live in the community. The number of resident members declined only gradually in the 1940s and '50s because non-resident members came to live there in old age when their spouses had died or other responsibilities had ceased. Rachel Fox, for example, after so many years of taking the long train journey up for visits from Cornwall, moved to the Society in 1938 after the death of her husband. The Society effectively became a retirement community and younger members like Gladys Powell, who worked as a servant there in the 1940s and 50s, spent most of her time looking after the ageing members and their ageing possessions. When she wasn't cooking for the elderly members, she was treating their furniture for woodworm. By 1965 (when accurate records stop) there were twenty-one members living in the community, with a further six living around Bedford and partic- ipating in chapel services and other activities at headquarters. But the glory days of tea parties and packed chapels were by then long gone. As members died, their rooms, with all their possessions, were left untouched for the day when they would return from Uranus to join Christ and Octavia in their Garden of Eden. It was those intact rooms that I just missed seeing in 2001.

Epilogue

In 2001, the year of the auction and the year I first visited them, the last few surviving Panaceans made the decision not to seal any further members. They had had no new members for many years: the decision was the recognition of how things were. This did not stop them believing in their original purpose and awaiting the Second Coming of the Lord and Octavia, and they made preparations for that event. In 2003, Ruth Klein said: 'The Lord has promised through Octavia and in the writings – we have it in black and white – he's promised to come here.' She went on to explain that the Panaceans are ready for the event. 'Everyone needs a home. How many people have prepared a home for the Lord? That is what we've done. We've prepared Number 18 [Albany Road] and in fact he's told us that is the house for him.' Number 18 is another Victorian villa exactly like Octavia's, and just three doors away, so Jesus and Octavia will be close neighbours, with the Panacea Society headquarters in between them for efficient organising of the millennium's activities. Happily the attention to domestic details of previous generations of Panacean ladies has not been lost. Just as Octavia took great pains to furnish Castleside perfectly, so Ruth Klein has ensured that Jesus will be comfortable. 'We've had it completely refurbished, new carpets and curtains. You may well say, "Will he need a shower?" He will have a radiant body so I don't think he will but we've prepared it as a normal house anyway and we've called it The Ark. So we're really looking forward to that.'

There is one tiny difficulty: because there are so few members left, most of the community houses have been rented out, so Jesus might find his house occupied when he returns. 'There's some people living in there at the moment,' reported Ruth. 'Little do they know and little have we told them what a special house it is.' But the Panaceans have prepared for the eventuality of Jesus coming. As Ruth summed up: 'They're on two months' notice.'[1]

Should Octavia return, she will find her house unoccupied and
ready for her, restored to its original condition with her furnishings
intact and the accumulated rubbish of the last few decades since her
death thrown out. Her furniture, books, china and pictures are all in
place. The kitchen and bathroom remain as they were in the 1930s,
with few modern conveniences, but the whole house has been painted
and the place swept, dusted and cleaned, and some very discreet under-
floor heating has been installed. She should be comfortable.

As I write at the end of the first decade of the twenty-first century,
the Panacea Society 'campus' is being prepared for visitors. Now that
the Society will no longer be attracting new members, the major buildings are being renovated (with the aid of architectural historians and
sympathetic builders) for educational purposes: so that the outside
world can see what went on there for nearly a century. While the
Society began with few resources in 1919, and was run on a shoestring
for some time, the generous tithing and legacies of so many members
over the years gives the Society today the income and capital to set
about such a project. The chapel and wireless room are being restored
to their original condition. The large house Castleside has been put
aside for the bishops since the 1930s. But in the last few years, John
Coghill and Ruth Klein came to the decision that Castleside was no
longer suitable for the bishops to stay in, having only two bathrooms
to be shared by twenty-four of them and a rather primitive kitchen
with an Edwardian range and lead-lined sinks. The local Swan Hotel,
they felt, might be more comfortable. Mr Coghill, an architect, nevertheless drew up many plans for how and where the bishops would
meet on the Panacea campus, and what space would be needed for
the journalists and others of the curious as the bishops opened the
Box. Freed from its role as a house for visiting bishops, Castleside is
now being made into an exhibition centre, with displays on the whole
Visitation (all the Southcottian prophets, and the communities some
of them formed). This will draw together the complete history of
Southcott and her successors. The work of the Panacea Society's
printing press and the healing ministry – including the squares of linen
on which Octavia breathed – will be displayed. The room set aside
for the bishops to gather in to open the Box, the drawing room
prepared by Octavia for the bishops to relax in, a sample bishop's
bedroom and the (shared) bathroom will be shown in their original

condition. The Haven, Kate Firth's old house, bought by the Panacea Society after her departure, and the site of many important meetings in the Society's history, will be recreated to show what a community house looked like, and give a glimpse into Panacea life. Thus this little slice of England's social, cultural and religious history will be preserved, both in its buildings and grounds, and in its remarkable archive now catalogued.

The Panacea Society stands as a testimony to great faith on the part of many and Octavia's indomitable spirit. What has struck me over and over again is Octavia's remarkable capacity in founding what was, essentially, a new religion. The Panacea Society is a period piece, very much of the 1920s and '30s. Its history is a window into the broader history of the interwar years in Britain and beyond, and people's lives, hopes and fears. But it also has resonances with new religious groups in all times and places, not least the utopian groups, communes and offbeat religious communities of the 1960s, through which the Panacea Society itself gently lived. Its history is at once unique and yet also charts the drive and enthusiasm, the squabbles and difficulties, the shift from charismatic and loose beginnings to tightened and bureaucratic structures, the sheer faith and obedience of all such religions.

The Panacea Society illustrates that the boundary between established religion and new religions is less firm than many would like to think. Many people hold allegiances to both the heterodox and the orthodox at the same time. There is always conversation between the official and the marginal, the orthodox and the upstart. Furthermore, one person's orthodoxy is another's heresy, and as long as people seek truth and purity of belief, new religious groups will arise claiming that they alone know the intentions and purposes of God. As long as people yearn for an unmediated, personal experience of the divine, regarding that as more fundamental than anything the institutional churches can offer, as Octavia and her followers did, then new religious communities and movements will emerge. But as they grow and develop, they will face questions about how to maintain order, organisation and uniformity of belief, just as the mainstream churches do.

The Society is also a testimony to the sheer force of Octavia's personality. Charismatic, testy, opinionated, humorous, autocratic, perceptive, snobbish, intelligent, narcissistic, faithful, conservative, innovative: she was all of this. But most of all it was her drive, and her conviction that she was right, that led to the foundation and growth of the Society. Octavia drew together a disparate group of women and men, taught them, chided them, encouraged them, disciplined them, created a community with them and led them to a life of faith. Whatever we may think of her ideas and the community's beliefs, her capacity to organise, manage, dream up new ideas, and lead people was extraordinary.

In 2005 I met Octavia's only surviving granddaughter, Anna Thomas, almost as far away from Bedford as one could possibly get, in her home city of Sydney, Australia. An attractive woman, then in her mid-seventies, she was rather less stout than her grandmother but nevertheless reminded me of Octavia in many positive ways – yet she knew very little about the Panacea Society. Her father, Adrian, had been so badly scarred by it, and had felt so abandoned by his mother because of it, that he rarely spoke of it as she was growing up. She visited only once during Octavia's lifetime, in 1933, as a baby. She has no memory of her grandmother, though Octavia's diaries reveal that she played with Anna in the Panacea gardens most afternoons during the family's visit. After their earlier, intensely difficult visit of 1929, Adrian and his wife Marjorie were concerned to have a more peaceful time with his mother, and Anna was an important catalyst in that, a baby over whom everyone could happily coo and fuss.

Anna went back once or twice in the 1950s to visit her Aunt Dilys, by then ageing and lonely in the declining community, but Anna had had little to do with the Society. In the summer of 2006, seventy-three years after her first visit, Anna and her husband Evan visited Bedford with me and spent time talking with Ruth Klein and John Coghill, reading the documents about the Barltrop family in the archives and looking at the family photographs. Anna caught up on this gap in her history, read about her father's conflicted relationship with his mother, and learned about the deeply heterodox nature of her grandmother's beliefs. Not surprisingly, the visit evoked mixed emotions in her. Although her father had rarely spoken of his mother's religion, Anna now realised how agonised he had been by it, why going back to live in England, even after Octavia's death, had been so difficult for her parents in the late 1940s, and why they finally made Australia their home.

If one of Octavia's legacies is the Panacea Society as it is today, its campus, buildings and rich archive, then another is Anna and her daughters. For in Anna I see some of the very best of Octavia's qualities: her strength and force of personality, her charisma, her perception and wit. In Anna's three daughters, the strong female line continues. Whilst they live on the other side of the world and know very little about what their great-grandmother did, they have inherited her drive and intelligence.

A third legacy is the international healing ministry, which is still thriving. Ruth Klein, who now runs the healing, receives two to three reports every week, and the occasional new applicant. She replies to each letter, and continues to maintain the files of each patient with enormous care. After the showing of a documentary about the Panacea Society on British television in 2003, there were many enquiries about the healing ministry and this led to 206 new applicants in that year alone, though most did not continue after an initial flush of enthusiasm.[2] In the nearly ninety years since the healing ministry began, it has reached over 130,000 people around the world: the British West Indies, the USA, the UK,[3] many parts of Africa, most European countries, Australia and New Zealand, India, the Baltic states, Russia, Canada and Brazil. The healing ministry has reached people of all ages, ethnicities, classes and backgrounds, though its primary appeal these days is to the elderly and to those who live where health care remains inadequate.

In 2005, I stepped into my fieldwork and presided at the funeral of Panacea member Madeline Tregunna, who had been living in a Bedford residential home for the elderly with dementia. The funeral service was to be conducted according to the Book of Common Prayer, something I could easily do as an Anglican priest. As we stood at the edge of her grave, the surviving Panaceans and I threw earth on her coffin and I recited the familiar words, 'From dust you have come and to dust you shall return.' As I did so, I felt the poignancy of burying a woman who believed, like several thousand others, that she really would live for ever. Three years later, when the much-beloved and still actively involved John Coghill died at the age of ninety-six, I led a simple memorial service at the Society's headquarters in Bedford for the little community of surviving members and workers, and those who had known him. Mr Coghill had done little to prepare for his death: having got to his late nineties, he really did hope that he would never die.

After nearly a decade of working with the community, I have become enormously fond of the Panaceans, though I still have the capacity to be astounded by their beliefs, and a clear line stands between my own faith and theirs. I am grateful and delighted to have been invited into their world. I have long been interested in 'lived religion' – what people actually believe and do, rather than official church doctrine – and the Panacea Society provides a rich and compelling example of that. My aim has been to write an account of their communal life that is fair, sympathetic and analytical, neither apologetic nor unnecessarily critical. I have written this book as the archives have been 'excavated' and catalogued, and I have been astounded by the ways in which the Panaceans have given up their secrets to me as I have needed them.

One day, I wondered aloud to myself what the Anglican clergyman Lawrence Iggulden looked like and, absent-mindedly opening a random drawer half an hour later, I found a folder of photographs of him and his family. There have been many such serendipitous findings. And at the end of many long days of research, when the light has been fading and my eyes have been tired from reading hundreds of pages of handwriting, it has seemed to me that in the shadows I have caught a glimpse of Octavia flitting about the headquarters, keeping an eye on me. I hope she would be pleased with this account of the community she built, but I now know her well enough to realise she would want to edit it.

List of Abbreviations

Brushes: Besma [Mabel Baltrop], *Brushes with the Bishops* (London: Cecil Palmer & Hayward, 1919)

F of S: Rachel J. Fox, *The Finding of Shiloh, Or The Mystery of God 'Finished'* (London: Cecil Palmer, 1921)

SASJ: Rachel J. Fox, *The Suffering and Acts of Shiloh-Jerusalem* (London: Cecil Palmer, 1927)

HWBJ Part 1   Rachel J. Fox, *How We Built Jerusalem in England's Green and Pleasant Land* Part I (London: Cecil Palmer, 1931)

HWBJ Part II   Rachel J. Fox, *How We Built Jerusalem in England's Green and Pleasant Land* Part II (Bedford; The Garden Press, 1934)

HWBJ Part III   Rachel J. Fox, *How We Built Jerusalem in England's Green and Pleasant Land* Part III (Bedford; The Garden Press, 1937)

HWBJ Part IV   Rachel J. Fox, *How We Built Jerusalem in England's Green and Pleasant Land* Part IV (Bedford; The Garden Press, 1938)

WHG   [Octavia] *The Writings of the Holy Ghost* Volumes 1–16 (Bedford: The Panacea Society)

Notes

Preface

1. Mabel Barltrop to Ellen Oliver, 27 April 1919 PS 4.2/3
2. Panacea Society Staff Meeting minutes, 29 May 1930 PS 3.1/7
3. Notes from Gladys Powell on life in the Society, 2001 (in author's possession)
4. Rachel J. Fox to Gertrude Hill, 15 August 1918 PS F 4.4/11
5. Martin Pugh, *We Danced All Night. A Social History of Britain Between the Wars* (London: The Bodley Head, 2008)
6. Richard Overy, *The Morbid Age, Britain Between the Wars* (London: Allen Lane, 2009) p. 7

Chapter 1: Seeking

1. Besma [Mabel Barltrop], *Brushes with the Bishops* (London: Cecil Palmer & Hayward, 1919) p. 25
2. *Brushes* pp. 25–26
3. Arthur Barltrop to Mabel Andrews, undated PS A 3.2/6
4. *Brushes* pp. 21, 19, 21
5. Octavia, *Octavia's Early Years* (published for private circulation by James H. Keys, Plymouth, no date) pp. 33, 34
6. Case notes No. 9972 for Mabel Barltrop, Three Counties Asylum (Bedfordshire County Archives); On the Three Counties Asylum, see Judith Pettigrew, Rory W. Reynolds and Sandra Rouse, *A Place in the County: Three Counties Asylum* (Bedford: Bedfordshire Community Health Care, 1998).
7. *Octavia's Early Years* p. 33
8. *Octavia's Early Years* p. 33
9. *Brushes with the Bishops* p.33
10. Alice Seymour, 'Introduction' to *The Voice in the Wilderness* (Ashford, Middlesex: Clockhouse Press, 1933) pp. x–xi
11. See Philip J. Lockley, *Millenarian Religion and Radical Politics in Britain 1815–1835: A Study of Southcottians after Southcott* (D.Phil. thesis, University of Oxford, 2009)

12. George Turner, Zion Ward, Mary Boon, William Shaw, Joseph Allman (who called himself Zebulun) were some of the immediate claimants.
13. Gordon Allan, 'Southcottian Sects from 1790 to the Present Day' in *Expecting the End. Millennialism in Social and Historical Context*. Eds. Kenneth G.C. Newport & Cranford Gribben (Waco, TX: Baylor UP 2006)
14. Rachel J. Fox, *SASJ* (London: Cecil Palmer, 1927) pp. 73, 96
15. Davidson papers, Volume 485, f. 242, Lambeth Palace Archives
16. Davidson papers, Vol. 485, ff. 253–4
17. Davidson papers, Vol. 485, f. 262
18. Davidson papers, Vol. 485, ff. 264–266
19. See Davidson papers, Vol. 485, ff. 229–50, for the range of letters the Archbishop received on Southcott's Box before Mabel Barltrop's letter, and ff. 251–252 for her letter.
20. *Brushes* p. 26
21. He remained un-named in her published account of these years, *Brushes*.
22. G.B. Hardy to Mabel Barltrop, 16 December 1910 PS F 6.1/6
23. G.B. Hardy to Mabel Barltrop, 31 October 1914 PS F 6.1/6
24. G.B. Hardy to Mabel Barltrop, 9 January 1915 PS F 6.1/6
25. G.B. Hardy to Mabel Barltrop, 9 January 1915 PS F 6.1/6
26. *Brushes* p. 36
27. *Brushes* p. 37

Chapter 2: Listening to God

1. Case notes No. 7586, for Mabel Barltrop, St Andrew's Hospital Archives
2. *Brushes* pp. 41–42
3. Janet Oppenheimer, *'Shattered Nerves': Doctors, Patients and Depression in Victorian England* (Oxford University Press, 1991), especially the Introduction, and Hermione Lee, *Virginia Woolf* (London: Vintage, 1997), chapter 10
4. *Brushes* p. 43
5. The Lunacy Commission, a government department, was set up in 1845 by the Lunacy Act, and was designed to monitor asylum provisions and activities. There were eleven lunacy commissioners, of whom six were paid (medical) professionals, and seven honorary commissioners. It became the Board of Control in 1913, with extended powers with regard to mental deficiency.
6. *Brushes* pp. 58–59
7. *Brushes* pp. 54–55

8. For a discussion of Georgina Weldon's case and the hostility of certain doctors towards spiritualism, see Judith R. Walkowitz, *City of Dreadful Delight: Narratives of Sexual Danger in Late-Victorian London* (Chicago: The University of Chicago Press, 1992), chapter 6

9. See Alex Owen, *The Darkened Room: Women, Power and Spiritualism in Late Nineteenth-century England* (London: Virago Press, 1989). See also Owen's discussion of the case of Louisa Lowe in chapter 7.

10. She died in 1919, after thirteen years in St Andrew's, and having been in the Leicester Borough Asylum for some time before that. Case notes No. 6846 for Minnie Oppenheim, p. 9, St Andrew's Hospital Archives.

11. Case notes for Mabel Barltrop, No. 9972, Three Counties Asylum (Bedford County Archives)

12. Case notes for Mabel Barltrop, No. 9972, Three Counties Asylum.

13. Mabel Barltrop to Kate Firth, 4 November 1915 PS 4.1/1

14. Case notes for Mabel Barltrop, No. 7586 St Andrew's Hospital

15. Entry for 18 April 1925. Diary by Peter Rasmussen of life at Number 12 Albany Road (marked II) PS C.3.1./28

16. Jeffrey Smith, *Where the Roots Meet for Water: A Personal and Natural History of Melancholia* (New York: North Point Press) p. 156

17. Mabel Barltrop to Kate Firth written from the infirmary in St Andrew's Hospital, 3 June 1916 PS F4.1/1

18. Mabel copied this out at the end of a letter to Kate Firth sent on 1 June 1916.

19. *Brushes* PS F4.1/1 p. 63

20. *Brushes* PS F4.1/1 p. 65

21. Mabel Barltrop to Kate Firth, 19 May 1916 PS F4.1/1.

22. Mabel Barltrop to Kate Firth, 20 May 1916 PS F4.1/1

23. Mabel Barltrop to Kate Firth, 3 June 1916 PS F4.1/1

24. Mabel Barltrop to Kate Firth, originally dated 3 June 1916, later corrected to 'after 3 June 1916' by Mabel Barltrop PS F4.1/1

25. Case notes No. 7586 for Mabel Barltrop, St Andrew's Hospital

26. Mabel Barltrop to Rachel Fox, 4 August 1916 PS F4.3/12

27. Author's conversation with David Laity, 9 January 2004.

28. A Watcher [Rachel Fox], *Rays of the Dawn: Fresh Teaching on New Testament Problems* (London: Kegan Paul, Trench, Trubner & Co, 1912) pp. vii–viii

29. Rachel Fox diary, January 1913 to December 1918 p. 148 PS C3.1/24

30. Draft of letter from Rachel Fox to Beatrice Pease, 26 August 1916 PS F6.1/8

31. For details of the Shepstone family in South Africa, see Ruth E. Gordon, *Shepstone: The Role of the Family in the History of South Africa, 1820–1900* (Capetown: A.A. Balkema, 1968)

32. Helen Shepstone to Rachel Fox, December 1913 PS F 4.3/4

33. Helen Shepstone to Rachel Fox, 22 December 1914 PS F 4.3/4

34. *F of S* pp. 76, 77

35. *F of S* pp. 84, 85

36. Quoted in *F of S* pp. 126, 128

37. Mabel Barltrop to Kate Firth, 26 May 1916 PS F4.1/1

38. Draft of letter from Rachel Fox to Beatrice Pease, 26 August 1916 PS F6.1/8

39. Mabel Barltrop to Rachel Fox, October 10, 1916, quoted in *F of S*, p. 143

40. Rachel Fox diary, 1913–1918, p. 150 PS C3.1/24

41. *F of S* pp. 137, 143.

Chapter 3: The Daughter of God

1. Rachel Fox gives the date of Mabel leaving the mental hospital as 18 September 1916. See *F of S* p. 137. A handwritten time note by a later member of the Society, gives the date of Mrs Barltrop arriving home as 25 October 1916. See 'The Records of Octavia's work and of the Panacea Society' p. 4. This later date matches that in the St Andrew's Hospital records.

2. Rachel Fox diary, 1913–1918, p. 157 PS C3.1/24

3. *Brushes* p. 129

4. See Roy Foster, *W. B. Yeats, A Life Vol II: the Arch Poet 1915–1939* (Oxford University Press, 2003) and Anne Saddlemyer, *Becoming George: The Life of Mrs W. B. Yeats* (Oxford University Press, 2002)

5. See Frederic W. H. Myers, 'Automatic Writing or the Rationale of Planchette' in *Contemporary Review*, 42 (1885)

6. Pamela E. Klassen, 'Radio Mind: Experimentalists on the Frontiers of Healing' in *Journal of the American Academy of Religion*, September 2007, Vol. 75, No. 3, pp. 651–683

7. Rachel Fox to Helen Shepstone, 2 November 1917, reproduced in *F of S* p. 167

8. *Brushes* p. 130

9. *Brushes* p. 131

10. The full text is in *Brushes*, pp. 134–139.

11. *F of S* pp. 167, 168.

12. *F of S* pp. 173 ff.

13. *SASJ* p. 22

14. Mabel Barltrop to Rachel Fox, 22 January 1918 PS F4.3/16

15. Mabel Barltrop to Ellen Oliver, 2 January 1919 PS F4.2/3

16. Rachel Fox to Gertrude Hill, 15 August 1918 PS F4.4/11

17. Mabel Barltrop to Ellen Oliver, 29 September 1918 PS F4.2/1

18. To protect her identity, she was named as Helen Exeter in all the Society's published writings. She had gone to live in Exeter, in Devon in England, in 1915, hence the choice of pseudonym.

19. Mabel Barltrop to Ellen Oliver, 17 January 1919 PS F4.2/3

20. An account of M.B.'s interview with J.C.J. (December 17, 1917) (typed ms, drawn up August 1918) PS F6.1/9

21. Mabel Barltrop to Rachel Fox, 28 January 1918 PS F4.3/16

22. Miss Johnson's (JCJ's) essay on the Millennium PS F6.1/9

23. Mabel Barltrop to Rachel Fox, 10 August 1918 PS F4.3/16

24. Gertrude Hill to Rachel Fox, 19 August 1918 PS F4.3/16

25. Ellen Oliver to Kate Firth, 15 February 1919 PS F4.2/4

26. Kate Firth to Ellen Oliver, 16 February 1919 PS F4.2/3

27. Kate Firth to Ellen Oliver, 26 February 1919 PS F4.2/3. In her volume on the Society in this period, Rachel Fox papered over Kate's initial hostility to the idea of Mabel as Shiloh, writing instead, 'It was at this time that K.E.F. had been going through a period of illness during which she also had written down her conviction that Octavia was 'Shiloh' and had had it witnessed by another person's signature.' *SASJ* p. 77

28. Kate Firth to Ellen Oliver, 26 February 1919 PS F4.2/3

29. Quoted in *F of S* p. 273. The last sentence here alludes to the fact that Mabel Barltrop had first read Southcott's writings in 1914, one hundred years after Southcott's death.

30. Mabel Barltrop to Ellen Oliver, 28 March 1919 PS F4.2/3

31. Mabel Barltrop to Ellen Oliver, 28 February 1919 PS F4.2/3

32. *F of S* p. 262

33. *F of S* pp. 263, 265.

34. Rachel Fox diary, 1919–1921, no page numbers, no dates PS C3.1/24

35. Mabel Barltrop to Rachel Fox, 22 October 1919 PS F4.3/18

36. This was based in a biblical verse: Genesis 3:15, that the seed of the woman should bruise the head of evil.

37. Mabel Barltrop to Rachel Fox, 16 September 1918, quoted in *SASJ* p. 20.

38. *Brushes* p. 174

39. *Brushes* pp. 174, 176, 175.

40. *SASJ* p. 139

41. *SASJ* p. 250

42. *SASJ* p. 151

43. Mabel Barltrop to Rachel Fox, 25 September 1925 PS F4.3/18

44. *SASJ* p. 24

45. *SASJ* p. 23

46. Mabel Andrews to Arthur Barltrop, undated letter, probably early February 1885 PS A3.2/6

47. Script number 4, 11 June 1919 in *The Writings of the Holy Ghost*, Volume 1, Part 1, p. 6

48. Ellen Oliver to Mabel Barltrop, 24 February 1919 PS F4.2/4

49. Ellen Oliver to Mabel Barltrop, 18 April 18 PS F4.2/4

50. She published two books that advocated a feminine God: *The Definition of the Godhead* (1928) and *Mysteries of Christianity* (1930).

51. See Joy Dixon, *Divine Feminine: Theosophy and Feminism in England* (Baltimore: The John Hopkins University Press, 2001), chapter 7. Christabel Pankhurst was converted to evangelical Christianity some time between 1918 and 1922 and became a well-known preacher, speaking on the Second Coming of Christ in Britain and the USA. She published books interpreting contemporary political and social problems in the light of biblical prophecy and God's impending judgment of the world. She did not embrace ideas of a 'feminine' aspect to God, but she remained convinced of the importance of female suffrage and carved out a role as a woman on the usually all-male fundamentalist preaching circuit. See Timothy Larsen, *Christabel Pankhurst. Fundamentalism and Feminism in Coalition* (Woodbridge, Suffolk: The Boydell Press, 2002).

52. See Jacqueline R. deVries, 'Transforming the Pulpit. Preaching and Prophecy in the British Women's Suffrage Movement' in *Women Preachers and Prophets through Two Millennia of Christianity* (University of California Press, 1998) pp. 318–333.

53. Ellen Oliver to Mabel Barltrop, 14 November 1918 PS F4.2/2

54. Swiney's books included not only *The Awakening of Women* (1905), but also *The Bar of Isis* (1907) and *The Cosmic Procession* (1906).

55. Mabel Barltrop to Ellen Oliver, dictated by Mabel Barltrop and in Gertrude Searson's handwriting, 28 February 1919 PS F4.2/3

56. Rachel Fox diary, February 1919, no page numbers PS C3.1/24

Chapter 4: Who was Mabel?

1. Croydon's population grew from 55,652 in 1871 to 79,615 in 1881.

2. An income survey from 1868 suggests that at this date 'those with about £100 or more a year probably corresponded fairly closely to the occupational groups . . . making up a large and inclusive middle class'. Those with an income 'near' or above £100 p.a. made up 20 per cent of the population; the remainder were below that. R.D. Baxter, *National Income: the United Kingdom* (London: 1868) and K. Theodore Hoppen, *The Mid-Victorian Generation* (Oxford: Oxford University Press, 1998) p.35. The middle-class 'mean' income at this point was very much closer to the £100 mark than £300 p.a. More than one source suggests that £150–160 is the best figure for the average middle-class income. J.A. Banks, *Prosperity and Parenthood: A Study of Family Planning Among the Victorian Middle Classes* (London: Routledge & Kegan Paul, 1954) p.107; Cynthia Curran, *When I First Began My Life Anew: Middle-Class Widows in Nineteenth-century Britain*, (Bristol, IN: Wyndham Hall Press, 2000) p.3.

3. Andrews family papers PS A3.1/1 and A3.1/2

4. Fanny Waldron diary, 1875 PS A3.1/3

5. *Octavia's Early Years* p. 18

6. Mabel Andrews diary, 19 September 1882, PS A3.2/2

7. This was rather like Virginia Woolf's father, Leslie Stephen, a distinguished man of letters of the same generation, who had rejected and yet remained haunted by his father's evangelical concerns.

8. Mabel Andrews diary PS A3.3/2

9. *Octavia's Early Years* p. 20

10. Mabel Andrews diary for 1885 PS A3.2/2

11. *Octavia's Early Years* p. 19

12. *Octavia's Early Years* p. 13

13. Mabel Andrews diary, 12 February 1889 A 3.2/2

14. *Octavia's Early Years* p. 15

15. Charles Andrews to Mabel Andrews, no date, probably March 1877 (written on board R.H.S. *Warwick* and on arrival in Cape Town) PS A3.2/1

16. Mabel Andrews diary, 24 January 1889; 15 March 1886 PS A3.2/2

17. Mabel Andrews diaries, 1885–89, passim. PS A3.2/2

18. Mabel Andrews diary, 1887 PS A3.2/2

19. Mabel Andrews to Arthur Barltrop, 1 February 1885 PS A3.2/6

20. Eliza and Charles Orme's granddaughter later wrote that Eliza was 'the presiding genius of the home' and 'a wonderful hostess – really interested

in hearing about other people's joys and sorrows. The names of the men and women of her day . . . who gathered around the hospitable dinner table, or walked on summer evenings in the Avenue Road garden, are names still remembered in this changed and changing world.' Flora Masson, *Victorians All* (London and Edinburgh: W & R Chambers, 1931) pp. 18, 19.

21. Their son Temple was a professor of science. Three daughters had married interesting men. Rosaline married David Masson, a literary scholar and expert on Milton, who had been introduced into the Orme literary salons by Patmore in 1847, and had married Rosaline in 1853 when she was eighteen; he was at that time Professor of English Language and Literature at University College, London, and then subsequently became Professor of Rhetoric and English Literature at Edinburgh University. See G.G. Smith, 'Masson, David Mather (1822–1907)' rev. Sondra Miley Clooney, *Oxford Dictionary of National Biography* (Oxford University Press, 2004). Blanche married Howard Fox, one of the well-known Fox family of Falmouth, who ran a shipping company and also became known for their exotic gardens: this made Blanche the sister-in-law of Rachel Fox. Julia was married to Charlton Bastian, a physician and neurologist whose views on spontaneous generation and the germ theory of disease were considered contentious by Darwin and others; he was, as Mabel put it, 'the great opponent of Professor Tyndale'. In fact, she meant John Tyndall, who argued that germs were the *cause* of disease, not the *result* (as Bastian thought). Mabel spent some time with the Bastians in 1885, and visited them in subsequent years at their home in Hanwell, becoming especially friendly with their daughter May. See Michael Woorboys, 'Bastian, (Henry) Charlton (1837–1915)' *Oxford Dictionary of National Biography* (Oxford University Press, 2004).

22. Leslie Howsam, "Orme, Eliza (1848–1937)" *Oxford Dictionary of National Biography* (Oxford University Press, 2004)

23. Mabel Andrews to Arthur Barltrop, 1 February 1885 PS A3.2/6

24. Mabel Andrews to Arthur Barltrop, undated letter (probably early February 1885) PS A3.2/6

25. Mabel Andrews to Arthur Barltrop, undated letter (probably early February 1885) PS A3.2/6

26. Mabel Andrews to Arthur Barltrop, 5 February 1885 PS A3.2/6

27. By 1879, one in six Anglican clergy had no degree, and this number increased to one in four during the 1880s (when Arthur was training). Owen Chadwick, *The Victorian Church, Volume II* (London: A & C Black, 1970) p. 247. There was an ongoing debate about whether the education

at these theological colleges should supplement or replace education at the universities. Revd E.B. Ottley, the Principal of Salisbury Theological College – a similar institution to that at Chichester – in 1881 argued that 'the main province of the theological college is to *supplement* the education given at the Universities, not to be a substitute for it' but he recognised the reality of the many persons who were without a university degree and 'whose admission to Holy Orders is on every account to be encouraged.' Indeed, the theological college education was indispensable to the non-university man, for 'how else can security be found for moral character, and intellectual and spiritual capacity?' Revd E.B. Ottley, 'Preface' to *Theological Colleges: their aim and spirit. Illustrated by two sermons . . . by the Revd R. C. Moberly and Rev. E. S. Talbot* (Salisbury, 1881).

28. *The Cisetrian* (1939) pp. 96–98, quoted in F.W. Bullock, *A History of the Training for the Ministry of the Church of England in England and Wales from 1875–1974* (London: Home Words, 1976) pp. 37

29. Mabel Andrews diary, 1889 PS A3.2/2

30. Arthur Barltrop, sermon text PS A3.2/10

31. *Octavia's Early Years* p. 30

32. Mabel Barltrop's Bible PS C3.3/4

33. Mabel Andrews diary, 1889 PS A3.2/2

34. *Octavia's Early Years* p. 30

35. *Octavia's Early Years* p. 6

36. *Octavia's Early Years* p. 6

37. *Octavia's Early Years* p. 13

38. *Octavia's Early Years* pp. 37–38

39. Conversation with John Coghill, 2004.

40. *Octavia's Early Years* p. 26

41. *Octavia's Early Years* p. 21

42. *Octavia's Early Years* pp. 10, 8, 11

43. *Octavia's Early Years* p. 21

Chapter 5: The Female Apostles

1. Mabel Barltrop to Ellen Oliver, 24 January 1919 PS F4.2/3

2. *SASJ* p. 70

3. Mabel Barltrop to Ellen Oliver, 16 April 1919 PS F4.2/3

4. *F of S* p. 291

5. Gertrude Hill to Mabel Barltrop, 14 June 1919 PS F4.2/9

6. Gertrude Hill to Mabel Barltrop, 14 October 1919 PS F4.2/9

7. Message given to Kate Firth re: marriage, 7 June 1919 3 p.m. PS F4.2/3

8. Gertrude Searson diary, Monday 9 June 1919 PS C3.1/2

9. Ellen Oliver to 'my very dear sisters' (probably Kate and Bessie Hodgkinson and Alice Jones), 17 June 1919 PS F4.2/4

10. Rachel Fox diary, 1919–1921 PS F4.2/4

11. Rachel Fox diary, 1919–1921 PS C3.1/24

12. *SASJ* p. 112

13. Ellen Oliver to Mrs Temple, 5 April 1919 PS F4.2/4

14. See Patrick Curry, *A Confusion of Prophets: Victorian and Edwardian Astrology* (London: Collins and Brown, 1992) and Ellic Howe, *Urania's Children: The Strange World of the Astrologers* (London: 1967)

15. *WHG* Volume 1, p. 176

16. Rachel Fox to Helen Shepstone, 1916 (no date) PS F4.3/7

17. She was born on 15 September 1865, four months before Mabel. *England and Wales, Free BMD Marriage Index: 1837–1983* (Oct–Dec 1865) 9b p. 537

18. They lived in a succession of houses in the relatively prosperous Leeds Road part of Dewsbury. 1861 Census, RG9/3411/47/10; 1881 Census TNA RG11/4806/18/29; 1891 Census TNA RG12/3731/74/1

19. *England & Wales, Free BMD Marriage Index: 1837–1983* (Apr-Jun 1894) p. 86

20. 1901 Census TNA RG13/4268/17/25

21. *England & Wales, Free BMD Death Index: 1837–1983* (Apr-Jun 1905) p. 100

22. Her first husband, Thomas Leach, died in late 1901: *England & Wales, Free BMD Death Index: 1837–1983* (Oct-Dec 1901) Vol. 2b, p. 423

23. *England & Wales, FreeBMD Marriage Index: 1837–1983* (Jan-Mar 1873) p. 835; 1891 Census, TNA RG12/3546/28/1; 1901 Census, TNA RG13/1041/41/15

24. Mabel Barltrop to Ellen Oliver, 5 November 1918 PS F4.2/1

25. Mabel Barltrop to Ellen Oliver, 23 June 1919 PS F4.2/3

26. Kate Firth to Ellen Oliver, 23 August 1919 PS F4.2/3

27. Kate Firth to Ellen Oliver, 25 January 1918 PS F4.2/1

28. Ellen Oliver to Mrs Temple, 14 June 1919 PS F4.2/4

29. *SASJ* pp. 95–97

30. *The Flock* entry for Alice Jones PS F2.2/29

31. *SASJ* p. 94

32. Ellen Oliver to Mrs Temple, 17 June 1919 PS F4.2/4

33. *SASJ* p. 70

34. Alex Owen, *The Darkened Room* chapter 7.

35. Gertrude Searson to Mabel Barltrop, 30 June 1919 PS F4.2/9

36. Gertrude Searson to Mabel Barltrop, 3 October 1919 PS F4.2/9

37. Kate Firth to Gertude Hill, 4 October 1919 PS F4.2/18

38. Gertrude Hill to Mabel Barltrop, 14 October 1919 PS F4.2/9

39. Gertrude Hill to Mabel Barltrop, 19 October 1919 PS F.4.2/9

40. Mabel Barltrop to Ellen Oliver, 5 November 1918 PS F.4.2/1

41. Ellen Oliver to Mabel Barltrop, 19 November 1918 PS F4.2/2

42. Ellen Oliver to Mabel Barltrop, 23 November 1918 PS F4.2/2

43. Ellen Oliver to Kate Firth, 17 February 1919 PS F4.2/4

44. Ellen Oliver to Mabel Barltrop, 14 November 1918 PS F4.2/2

45. Ellen Oliver to Mabel Barltrop, 24 February 1919 PS F4.2/4

46. Ellen Oliver to Mabel Barltrop, 19 November 1918 PS F4.2/4

47. Deborah Cohen, *Household Gods: The British and their Possessions* (New Haven and London: Yale University Press, 2006) pp. 105–108

48. Octavia to Rachel Fox, 21 January 1921 PS F4.4/6

49. Rachel J. Fox, *How We Built Jerusalem in England's Green and Pleasant Land Part I* (London: Cecil Palmer, 1931) p. 51

50. Gertrude Searson, diary, 23 July 1919 PS C3.1/2

51. Conversation with John Coghill, 6 September 2007

52. Gertrude Searson diary, 18 July 1918 PS C3.1/2, PS F4.2/3

53. *SASJ* p. 109

54. Letters from Mabel Barltrop to Ellen Oliver, 28 June 1919, 9 January 1919, and 23 September 1918 PS F4.2/3

55. SASJ p. 290

56. Author's conversation with John Coghill

57. *SASJ* p. 290

58. *SASJ* p. 289

59. Mabel Barltrop to Ellen Oliver, January 1918 PS F4.2/1

60. Kate Firth to Ellen Oliver, 25 January 1918 PS F4.2/1

61. Mabel Barltrop to Ellen Oliver, 23 June 1919 PS F4.2/3

62. Alice Jones, 'An Accusation Against Lucifer', 4 November 1925 PS F2.3/17

63. Mabel Barltrop to Ellen Oliver, 23 June 1919 PS F4.2/3

64. See Virginia Nicholson, *Singled Out: How Two Million Women Survived Without Men After the First World War* (London: Viking, 2007). Martin Pugh disagrees with Nicholson and other historians who have assumed that this was a generation of women condemned to spinsterhood. He argues instead that 'interwar British women by no means lacked husbands; despite contemporary fears, more of them got married than had before 1914, and by the 1930s the institution of marriage was reaching its heyday in this country'. *We Danced All Night* p. viii.

65. Evelyn Gillett to Octavia, 13 January 1925 PS F5.1/9
66. Gladys Powell, personal communication with the author
67. R.S. Sayers, *Gilletts in the London Money Market 1867–1967*, (Oxford: Clarendon, 1968) p. 198; Audrey M. Taylor, *Gilletts, Bankers at Banbury and Oxford: A Study in Local Economic History* (Oxford: Clarendon, 1964)
68. Octavia to Peter Rasmussen, 18 September 1919 PS F4.1/20
69. Octavia to Peter Rasmussen, no date, some time in 1923 PS F4.1/20
70. Octavia to Peter Rasmussen, 12 July 1921 PS F4.1/20
71. Hilda Green diary, 1922 PS C3.1/8
72. *SASJ* p. 129
73. Emily Goodwin to Octavia, 15 December 1920 C4.4/3
74. Emily Goodwin to Ellen Oliver, 27 October 1920 C4.4/3
75. *SASJ* p. 161
76. Emily Goodwin to Octavia, 15 December 1920 C4.4/3
77. *SASJ* p. 25
78. Mabel Barltrop to Gertrude Hill, 18 September 1918 PS F4.2/8
79. Gertrude Hill to Mabel Barltrop, 5 December 1919 PS F4.2/9
80. Mabel Barltrop to Rachel Fox, 3 February 1920 PS F4.3/20
81. *The Community Ordinances and Doctrines*, 1920, reprinted in numerous sheets and flyers, and also in *SASJ* pp. 119–123
82. *SASJ* p. 93
83. *Healing for All* p. 21
84. *SASJ* pp. 68–69
85. Rachel Fox to Beatrice Pease (Lady Portsmouth), 26 August 1916 PS F6.1/8
86. *SASJ* p. 67
87. Gladys Powell recounting Phyllis Wood's memory of chapel meetings which Octavia conducted. Notes from Gladys Powell on life in the Society, 2001 (in author's possession).
88. *SASJ* p. 127
89. *SASJ* pp. 127, 216.
90. *Healing for All* p. 23
91. Mabel Barltrop to Ellen Oliver, 5 April 1919 PS F4.2/3
92. Mabel Barltrop to Ellen Oliver, 9 January 1919 PS F4.2/3
93. *WHG* Vol. 1 p. 30

Chapter 6: How to Live For Ever

1. *The Panacea*, Volume 4, Number 41, p. 99
2. 'The Cleansing of the Sanctuary' 1933, ms. PS F3.4/3
3. *Healing for All* p. 88
4. 'Manners Paper' ms. PS F1.1/18
5. Ellen Oliver to Agnes Hilson, 28 January 1921 PS F5.1/14
6. *The Royal Sealing* (London: The Panacea Society, 1925) p. 11
7. 'Manners Paper', ms. PS F1.1/18
8. 'Notes on entertaining, cake-making etc.', ms. PS F2.4/37
9. 'The Cleansing of the Sanctuary' 1933, ms. PS F3.4/3
10. Point XXV in 'Residents Papers' Part 3 PS C1.1/3
11. *The Panacea*, Volume 7, pp. 132, 255
12. *SASJ* p. 356
13. *The Acts* (Bedford: The Panacea Society, 1925) Act III p. 3. See also *The Royal Sealing* (Panacea Publication 1925)
14. Ethel Castle to Octavia, 24 April 1927 PS F 6.2/7
15. Ethel Castle to Hilda Green, 10 October 1927 PS F6.2/7
16. Ethel Castle to Hilda Green, 29 October 29, 1927 PS F6.2/7
17. Mary Beedell to Octavia, 6 August 1923 PS F6.2/3
18. *Confession in Human Hands is Dangerous, in Divine Hands it is Safe* (Panacea pamphlet, republished from *The Panacea*, no date), p. 2 PS A5.3/5
19. Alexander Heriot Mackonochie lived from 1825 to 1887; for his biographical details, see Rosemary Mitchell, 'Mackonochie, Alexander Heriot (1825–1887)', *Oxford Dictionary of National Biography*, Oxford University Press, 2004 [http://www.oxforddnb.com/view/article/17627]. Arthur Henry Stanton was Mackonochie's younger colleague, and lived from 1839 to 1913. For his biographical details, see Roger T. Stearn, 'Stanton, Arthur Henry (1839–1913)', *Oxford Dictionary of National Biography*, Oxford University Press, Sept 2004; [http://www.oxforddnb.com/view/article/36254]
20. See Rene Kollar, 'Power and Control over Women in Victorian England: Male Opposition to Sacramental Confession in the Anglican Church', *Journal of Anglican Studies* 3.1 (2005) pp. 28–29
21. They also noted that confession was already allowed for in the Book of Common Prayer (albeit, in a limited way: at times of sickness, the priest should not deny the sick person the possibility of confession and absolution).
22. *Confession in Human Hands* p. 1
23. Percy Dearmer, *The Parson's Handbook* (London: Grant Richards, 1899) p. 203

24. J. Embry, *The Catholic Movement and the Society of the Holy Cross* (London: The Faith Press, 1931), Chapter V

25. See Alison Falby, 'The Modern Confessional: Anglo-American religious Groups and the Emergence of Lay Psychotherapy', *Journal of History of the Behavioural Sciences*, Vol. 39 (3) Summer 2003, pp. 251–267, and Matthew Thomson, *Psychological Subjects: Identity, Culture and Health in Twentieth-Century Britain* (Oxford University Press, 2006), especially Part I.

26. *Confession in Human Hands* p. 1

27. *The Royal Sealing* (London: The Panacea Society, 1925) p. 10

28. I am grateful for a conversation with Gene Lemcio with regard to this point.

29. Act VI in *The Acts* p. 3

30. Ethel Castle to Hilda Green, 8 November 1927 PS F 6.2/7

31. Octavia to Ethel Cooke-Yarborough, 31 March 1925 PS F 6.2/9

32. 'The Cleansing of the Sanctuary', ms. PS F3.4/3

33. *SASJ* p. 330

34. *The Panacea*, Volume 6, Number 71, p. 251

35. Muriel Gillett to Octavia, 12 January 1924; Muriel Gillett to Octavia, 4 May 1924; Mary Gillett to Muriel Gillett, March (no date), 1924; Muriel Gillett to Octavia, 30 March 1924 PS F5.1/10, F5.1/11

36. Muriel Gillett to Octavia, 11 July 1923 PS F5. 1/11

37. Muriel Gillett to Octavia, 30 May 1924; Mary Gillett to Octavia, May 21, 1924; Octavia to Mary Gillett, 22 May 1924 PS F5.1/10, F5.1/11

38. Muriel Gillett to Octavia, 13 January 1925, with annotations and notes by Octavia. Also: Evelyn Gillett to Octavia, January (no date) 1925. PS F5.1/11, F5.1/9

39. PS F5.3/11

40. Roy Hattersley, *Borrowed Time: The Story of Britain Between the Wars* (London: Little, Brown, 2007) p. 300

41. *HWBJ* Part II pp. 107–108

42. Hilda Green Diary 1927. PS C3.1/13

43. Octavia, ms entitled 'Buffet very bad on both occasions' no date, PS F1.1/13

44. *SASJ* p. 382

45. *HWBJ* Part II p. 107

46. M.S. Warry, 'A Visit to Headquarters', *The Panacea*, Volume 5, No. 54, pp. 130–1

47. M.S. Warry, 'A Visit to Headquarters', *The Panacea*, Volume 5, No. 54, p. 131

48. B.E. Greig and I.N. Mellor, 'The True Centre', *The Panacea*, Volume 6, No. 71, pp. 249–250

49. Josephine Low, 'A Weekly Meeting', *The Panacea*, Volume 5, No. 59, pp. 255–256

50. M.S. Warry to Octavia, 28 March 1924 PS F6.4/8

51. M.S. Warry to Miss Green, 22 March 1924 PS F6.4/8

52. M.S. Warry to Miss Green, 12 September 1924 PS F6.4/8

53. M.S. Warry to Octavia, 22 January 1925 PS F6.4/8

Chapter 7: Trouble in Paradise

1. *SASJ* p. 379

2. *SASJ* pp. 252–253

3. *SASJ* p. 252 and Prayer Request Book PS F.2.1/22

4. Edgar Peissart to Ellen Oliver, 27 January 1921; reply drafted by O and sent on 16 February 1921 PS F5.1/27

5. www.bfchistory.org/bethlehemclassbook.htm

6. Two-page timeline of EP's religious life, in Octavia's hand PS C4.5/2

7. Edgar Peissart and Margaret Webster to Octavia, no date but probably late 1921 F5. 1/27

8. See http://koreshan.mwweb.org/koreshan/gene/notes/nooooooy.htm 514

9. Another Koreshan, Mary Daniels, had successfully joined the Florida Shakers, so when Edgar showed interest in the Shaker community, he was given the Shaker novitiate covenant and invited to visit.

10. Quoted in Russell H. Anderson, 'The Shaker Community in Florida', *Florida Historical Quarterly*, Volume 38, Issue 1, July 1959, p. 37. Anderson dates this 1901 in the text; but the letter was clearly written in 1911, as Anderson's footnote indicates.

11. Edgar Peissart to Helen Morris, 13 September 1922 PS F5.4/10

12. Sara Weber Rea, *The Koreshan Story* (Estero, FL: Guiding Star Publishing House, 1994) p. 58

13. Octavia's notes and surviving correspondence PS C4.5/2

14. A Scribe [Edgar Peissart], *Verbum sat Sapienti!* (one-page flyer, not dated) PS C5.4/2

15. Edgar Peissart to Henry Rahn (with instructions for it to be sent on to Helena Lemke), 14 May 1922 PS C5.4/2

16. Rachel Fox diary, 1922 PS C3.1/24

17. There are echoes of the entirely contemporaneous spiritual group led by Georgi Gurdjieff in France at this time, famous for being the place where Katherine Mansfield died in January 1923. Gurdjieff developed

sacred dances and movements as part of 'The Work' that his disciples had (and still have) to do.

18. *SASJ* pp. 256–257
19. Octavia to Helen Lemke, 9 August 1922 PS F6.1/22
20. Edgar Peissart to Helen Morris, 20 August 1922 PS F5.4/10
21. Edgar Peissart to Helen Morris, 25 September 1922 PS F5.4/10
22. Edgar Peissart to Helen Morris, 13 September 1922 PS F5.4/10
23. SASJ pp. 307–309; Hilda Green diary for 1921–1925 PS C3.1/9
24. Thomas Charles Donald Ricketts was born in Greenhithe, Kent on 3 July 1896. He was admitted as an undergraduate at Trinity College, Cambridge, on 1 October 1921, as an ordinary undergraduate (a pensioner) not in receipt of any scholarship. He passed a qualifying examination in Forestry in 1921, and Parts I and II of the Diploma Examination in the same subject in 1922 and 1923 respectively, obtaining his diploma in the latter year. Presumably he was an older undergraduate because he had served in the war. Information given by A. C. Green, Asst Archivist, Trinity College Library, Cambridge.
25. Rachel Fox, diary 1922 (no page numbers) PS C3.1/24
26. 'Judicial statement taken down by KF from DR' (ms. typed) F5.1/27
27. *Celibacy: compiled from the writings of Koresh* PS C4.5/2
28. Edgar Peissart to Donald Ricketts, 9 January 1923 PS F5.1/27
29. Edgar Peissart to Helen Morris, 13 September 1922 PS F5.1/28
30. Helen Morris to Edgar Peissart, 30 November 1922 PS F5.1/28
31. Edgar Peissart to Helen Morris, 13 September 1922 PS F5.1/28
32. Quoted in Helen Morris to Edgar Peissart, 30 November 1922 PS F5.1/28
33. Edgar Peissart to Donald Ricketts, 9 January 1923 PS F5.1/27
34. Edgar Peissart to Helen Morris, 13 September 1922 PS F5.4/10
35. Octavia to Rachel Fox, 23 August 1922 PS F4.4/6
36. Helen Morris to Edgar Peissart, 7 February 1923. This is a transcription of a letter in Kate Firth's hand; members often transcribed people's letters in this way, so I assume it is genuine PS F5.1/28
37. Octavia to Adrian Barltrop, 18 February 1923 PS F3.5/6
38. Peter Rasmussen's diary of the activities of The Four PS C3.1/5
39. *SASJ*, pp. 311–312; Hilda Green's diary for 1921–1925; Peter Rasmussen's diary of the activities of The Four PS C3.1/9 & C3.1/7 & C3.1/5
40. In Genesis 4, Cain leads his brother Abel out into a field and kills him.
41. 'Trial and Condemnation of Satan. For the Offences committed against the Race of men'. (typed ms., 1923) PS F5.1/27

42. This was one of Augustine's three goods of marriage, and was enduring in the Christian tradition. Augustine, *De Bono conjugali* (410)

43. *SASJ* p. 331

44. *Trial and Condemnation of Satan*

45. John Tosh, *A Man's Place: Masculinity and the Middle-Class Home in Victorian England* (New Haven and London: Yale University Press, 1999), Chapter 8

46. Octavia to Henrietta Leach, 21 May 1923 PS F5.1/27

47. *SASJ* p. 331

48. *SASJ* pp. 338–339

49. 'Record of meeting between Octavia and Frederick Ibbotson and his mother,' 3 March 1923 (ms. in Rachel Fox's hand) PS F2.1/42

50. Letter addressed 'To Octavia and all' from Jesse Green, July 3, 1924. PS F6.4/26

51. Fannie Green to Hilda Green, no date, probably June 1928 PS F 6.4/26

52. Letters to Octavia from Jesse Green, 17 February, 11 May 1923; 31 January, 3 July, 1924; Marie Green to Miss Hilda Green, 3 January, 1925. PS F6.4/26

53. See Matt Houlbrook, *Queer London: Perils and Pleasures in the Sexual Metropolis, 1918–57* (University of Chicago Press, 2005)

54. Cf. Edward Carpenter's first great love, George Hukin, who followed his working-class societal expectation and married a woman, bringing his passionate affair with Carpenter to an end. See Sheila Rowbotham, *Edward Carpenter: A Life of Liberty and Love* (London & New York: Verso, 2008)

55. T. C. D. Ricketts Confession, 24 August 1924 PS F5.4/15

56. Ex inf. A. C. Green, Assistant Archivist, Trinity College Library, Cambridge. *The Times,* 28 June 1924 and 30 January 1943.

57. See Gregory Tillett, *The Elder Brother: A Biography of Charles Webster Leadbeater* (London: Routledge and Kegan Paul, 1982). The case of John Balcom Shaw, one of the authors of *The Fundamentals,* accused of sodomy, also provides an interesting example of religious arenas (the organ loft in the church, the YMCA) enabling homosocial (at the least) activity; see Kathryn Lofton, 'Queering Fundamentalism: John Balcom Shaw and the Sexuality of a Protestant Orthodoxy' in *Journal of the History of Sexuality* Vol. 17, No. 3, September 2008. On enclosed societies and homosexual activity, see also, for example, Paul Peucker, '"Inspired by flames of love": homosexuality, mysticism, and Moravian brothers around 1750' in *Journal of the History of Sexuality,* Volume 15, Number 1, 2006, pp. 30–64; Aaron Spencer Vogleman, *Jesus is Female: Moravians and Radical Religion in Early America* (University of

Pennsylvania Press, 2008) and Jonathan Yonan's forthcoming work on homo-sexuality and English Moravians in eighteenth-century Yorkshire.

58. *SASJ* pp. 345–346

59. 'Notes taken down of what passed when Octavia determined to share the great mystery which surrounded AHB with others, beside EG, PR and RJF' 30 May 1923, PS F 2.4/7

60. *Octavia's Early Years* pp. 33, 30, 41

61. Hilda Green's diary for 1921–1925 PS C3.1/9

62. Octavia to Peter Rasmussen, 21 July 1921; Peter Rasmussen to Octavia, 23 June 1921. PS F4.1/20

Chapter 8: Going Global

1. 'The History of the Healing' (ms.) PS F1.3/21

2. Papers of Rachel Fox November 1921; Octavia to Rachel Fox, 14 February 1922 PS C5.4/2

3. *SASJ* p. 400.

4. *SASJ* p. 400.

5. *HWBJ* Part I pp. 87, 90

6. Richard Maguire to Ellen Oliver, 5 December 1920 PS F 6.3/10

7. Mrs Louise Coventry to Octavia, 12 April 1923; Octavia to Mrs Coventry 26 June 1923 PS F5.2/34

8. Miss Jane Davidson to Ellen Oliver, 6 July 1920. PS F4.2/5

9. *SASJ* pp. 322–323

10. *HWBJ* Part I pp. 3–4

11. Files on the healing, PS F1.3/21 and PS F3.4/20

12. *HWBJ* Part I p.22

13. Frances Wright to Octavia, 25 April 1925. F6.4/16

14. Rachel Fox's diary, 1922–1926, PS C3.1/24

15. *Daily News* 24 April 1925

16. *Daily Mirror* 24 April 1925

17. *Daily Mail* 27 September 1924

18. *HWBJ Part I* p. 23

19. *Daily Sketch* 24 September 1924

20. *Western Morning News, Plymouth,* 12 October 1924

21. See, for example: *Truth,* 29 October 1924; *Western Morning News, Plymouth,* 30 October 1924; *Birmingham Gazette,* 26 November 1924; *Eastbourne Chronicle,* 7 November 1925. Alice Seymour also occasionally chipped in. See her letter to the *Royal Cornwall Gazette,* 10 December 1924

22. Early India Healing Files PS S6.1/8 and correspondence from Ernest Gideon at PS F5.2/34

23. *HWBJ* Part I p. 43

24. Early Australia Healing Files PS S6.1/7

25. JC Woodward to CSS, 1 May 1926. PS S6.1/7

26. Early India Healing Files PS S6.1/8

27. Early Australia Healing Files PS S6.1/7 Bertha Roberts to CSS, 12 July 1925; 31 December 1926, and correspondence in between PS S6.1/7

28. Mariane Winterton to CSS, September 15, 1924 PS S6.1/7

29. Early Australia Healing Files PS S6.1/7

30. Joseph Taylor to Emily Goodwin, 11 September 1929. PS F5.2/17

31. Elinor Partridge to CSS 5 February 1935 PS S6.1/7

32. Elinor Partridge to CSS 12 June 1935 PS S6.1/7

33. *HWBJ* Part I p. 70

34. Ethel Cooke-Yarborough to Miss Green, 18 June 1924 PS F6.2/9

35. Ethel Cooke-Yarborough to Miss Green, 15 September 1924 PS F6.2/9

36. Pamphlet 'What Membership of the Panacea Society Entails' (reprinted from *The Panacea*)

37. *HWBJ* Part I pp. 72–76

38. Instructions to Non-Resident Members, February 1924. See also *HWBJ* Part I pp. 31–32.

39. Early UK healing records. PS S1.7/1–7

40. Author's conversation with John Coghill

41. Gertrude Austin to Miss Green, 14 March 1928 PS F6.2/2

42. *HWBJ* Part I p. 220

43. Geraldine Bartup to Miss Green, 29 January 1932 PS F6.2/3

44. Elinor Partridge to CSS, 4 November 1935 PS S6.1/7

45. Mary Warry to Octavia, 17 June 1926 PS F6.4/8

46. Octavia to Mary Warry 20 June PS F5.4/22

47. See *HWBJ* Part I pp. 213–216; Rachel Fox diary 1922–1926, PS C3.1/26.

48. *HWBJ* Part I p. 40

49. Octavia, *Wrong at the Root, or the Bishop's Chaplain* (Bedford: The Panacea Society, 1929) and *The Rest House* (Bedford: The Panacea Society, 1934). On female domestic literature in this period, see Alison Light, *Forever England: Femininity, Literature and Conservatism Between the Wars* (London: Routledge, 1991)

50. Miss Absell to Miss Green, 3 November 1924; Gertrude Hallwood to Miss Green, 28 October 1924; CSS to Miss Absell, 8 November 1924 PS F 6.2/1

51. See *Theosophist Magazine*, October–December 1927, pp. 244–145; *Dawn* 2/14, 1 January 1924, pp. 3–7. Krishnamurti rejected that claim. Ironically, it was the magazine that the Panacea Society was advertising in so heavily, the *Herald of the Star*, that promoted that idea. See Joy Dixon, *Divine Feminine*, chapter 3.

52. Frances Wright, 'How I Came into the Panacea Society', *The Panacea* Volume 8, Number 39, p. 109

53. William Loftus Hare to Frances Wright, no date PS F6.4/13

54. Octavia to Frances Wright 19 June 1924 PS F6.4/5

55. Frances Wright to Annie Besant, 18 June 1924 (copy of letter) PS F6.4/14

56. *HWBJ* Part I p. 44

57. Frances Wright to Octavia, 15 November 1924 (copy of letter) PS F6.4/15

58. Frances Wright to Hilda Green, 18 December 1924 (copy of letter) PS F6.4/15

59. *HWBJ* Part I pp. 222–224

Chapter 9: Sex Difficulties

1. Mrs Carew-Hunt to Miss Green, 21 November 1925; Octavia to Mrs Carew-Hunt, 24 November 1925 (copy); Mrs Carew-Hunt to Miss Green, 30 April 1926 PS F5.3/6

2. *SASJ* p. 190

3. Sex Paper to non-resident members from headquarters, March 1925 PS F1.1/17

4. Mary Beedell to Octavia, 31 October 1923 PS F6.2/3

5. Helen Morris to Edgar Peissart, 1 September 1922; 26 September 1922; 13 October 1922; 30 November 1922 PS F5.1/28

6. Octavia to Helen Morris, 1 April 1923 PS F5.4/8

7. RJF diary 1922–26; PS C3.1/24

8. Wella Bauer to the Divine Mother, 14 April, 21 May 1925 PS F5.2/9

9. Hilda Abernathy to Octavia, 5 November 1928 PS F6.2/1

10. 'The Lambeth Conference' in *The Panacea*, Volume 7, Number 79, pp. 150–151. On the Lambeth Conference decision about contraception, see *Lambeth Conferences (1867–1930)* (London: SPCK, 1948) pp. 195–203.

11. See Caitriona Beaumont, 'Moral Dilemmas and Women's Rights: the attitude of the Mothers' Union and Catholic Women's League to divorce, birth control and abortion in England, 1928–1939', *Women's History Review*, 16: 4 (2007), pp. 463–485

12. Mrs A. H. Barltrop, 'To Mothers and Headmasters', *Mothers in Council* No. 95 (1914) pp. 133–144

13. Independence, Missouri, the Bauers' home town, is where Joseph Smith, founder of the Mormons, had originally planned to build the City of Zion or New Jerusalem, before he was killed in Carthage, Illinois in 1844 and his followers were chased out of the state, and moved on to Salt Lake City, Utah.

14. Wella Bauer to the Divine Mother, 5 August 1925 PS F5.2/9

15. Wella Bauer to the Divine Mother, 31 August 1925 PS F5.2/9

16. Wella Bauer to the Divine Mother, 6 October 1925 PS F5.2/9

17. Mrs E. L. Duncan to the Divine Mother, 19 July 1925 PS F5.2/9

18. Anna Summers to the Divine Mother, 5 September 1925 PS F5.2/9

19. James Hancock to the Divine Mother, 12 July 1925 PS F6.3/1

20. Norman Winckler to Divine Mother, 8 October 1929 PS F5.2/17

21. Sex Paper of March 1925 PS F1.1/17

22. Emily Carew-Hunt to Hilda Green, 21 November 1925 PS F5.3/6

23. Wella Bauer to the Divine Mother, 5 August 1925; 10 November 1925; 17 December 1925 PS F5.2/9

24. Mary Gillett to Emily Goodwin, 18 July 1923 PS F5.1/10

25. Sex Paper of March 1925, PS F1.1/17; Rachel Fox diary 1922–1926 PS C3.1/24

26. Sex Paper of March 1925 PS F1.1/17

27. Olive Morris to Octavia 17 October 1925 PS F5.4/8

28. Octavia to Olive Morris, 21 October 1925 PS F5.4/8

29. Octavia to Olive Morris, 17 December 1925 PS F5.4/8

30. Octavia to Helen Morris, 17 December 1925 PS F5.4/8

31. Olive Morris to Octavia, 19 December 1925 PS F5.4/8

32. Helen Morris to Octavia, 17 December 1925 PS F5.4/8

33. Olive Thorp [Morris] to Octavia, 13 October 1926 PS F5.4/8

34. Octavia to Olive Thorp, 19 October 1926 PS F5.4/8

Chapter 10: Don't Fall in Love

1. Leonard Squire Tucker to The Panacea Society, 22 July 1925 PS F3.4/30; 1891 Census, TNA RG12/24/17/78; 1901 Census, TNA RG13/26/10/50 F3.4/30

2. England & Wales, Free BMD Birth Index: 1837–1915, Vol. 3a, p. 542

3. 1891 Census, TNA RG12/24/17/78; 1901 Census, TNA RG13/26/10/50

4. Application for copyright, National Archives at Kew, 1912 http://www.nationalarchives.gov.uk/catalogue/displaycataloguedetails. asp?CATLN=7&CATID=-4711327&FullDetails=True&Gsm=2008-02-12

5. Leonard Squire Tucker to the Panacea Society, 22 July 1925 F3.4/30

6. Kate Firth diary 11 January 1926 PS F3.4/27

7. Kate Firth diary 25 February 1926 PS F3.4/27

8. Kate Firth diary 28, 30 and 31 January 1926 PS F3.4/27

9. Kate Firth diary 6, 11 and 26 February 1925 PS F3.4/27

10. England and Wales, *Free BMD* Marriage Index: 1837–1983 (Oct.–Dec. 1925) pp. 25 and 33

11. Geoffrey Reinli, 'Summary of Statements made [by Leonard Squire Tucker and Kate Firth] against the Visitation' (1927) PS F3.4/29

12. Leonard Squire Tucker, 'Some of the Blasphemous Claims made by "The Panacea Society"' (1927). This document was written after he left the community and was intended for the press as an exposé, though was never published. PS F3.4/30

13. Rachel Fox's interview with Kate Firth, 8 March 1926 PS F3.4/29

14. Geoffrey Firth to Octavia 25 January 1925. PS F6.1/23

15. Isa Agate to Octavia 23 April 1925. PS F6.1/23

16. Isa Agate to Octavia 5 February 1925 PS F6.1/23

17. Rachel Fox's interview with Kate Firth, 8 March 1926 PS F3.4/29

18. Kate Firth diary 2 March 1926; Rachel Fox's interview with Kate Firth, 8 March 1926 PS F3.4/27, PS F3.4/29

19. Kate Firth diary, 4 and 5 March 1926 PS F3.4/27

20. Irene Mellor, 'An Account of Thursday Evening', 4 March 1926, PS F3.4/26

21. Irene Mellor, 'An Account of Thursday Evening', 4 March 1926; Kate Firth diary 4 March 1926 PS F3.4/26, PS F3.4/27

22. Kate Firth diary 6 March 1926; Geoffrey Firth to Robert Temple 2 May 1926. PS F3.4/27, PS F6.1/23

23. Kate Firth diary 7, 15 March 1926; Rachel Fox's interview with Kate Firth p. 3 PS F3.4/27, PS F3.4/29

24. Kate Firth diary 12 April 1925. PS F3.4/27

25. *England and Wales, Marriage Index, 1837–1983* (Oct–Dec 1926) p. 288

26. *WHG* Vol 8, No. 5 18 May 1926 p. 110

27. Octavia, 'Statement' p. 2 PS F3.4/26

28. *WHG* Vol 8, No. 3 20 March 1926 p. 62

29. *WHG* Vol 8, No. 3 22 March 1926 p. 63

30. *WHG* Vol 8, No. 5 10 May 1926 pp. 103–4

31. *WHG* Vol 8, No. 3 22 March 1926 p. 63

32. Alice Jones, 'An Accusation Against Lucifer', 4 November 1925. PS F2.3/17

33. Summary of Statements made against the Visitation (interviews Geoffrey Reinli held with Kate and Leonard Squire Tucker from January to August 1927) PS F3.4/29

34. Leonard Squire Tucker to The Panacea Society 7 August 1925 & 17 September 1925 PS F3.4/30

35. Rachel Fox's interview with Kate Firth, 8 March 1926 PS F3.4/29

36. 'Summary of Statements made against the Visitation' (interviews Geoffrey Reinli held with Kate and Leonard Squire Tucker from January to August 1927) PS F3.4/29

37. Amy Smart diary, 7 March 1926 PS F3.4/39

38. Leonard Squire Tucker, 'Some of the Blasphemous Claims made by The Panacea Society' (1927) F3.4/30

39. Geoffrey Firth to Robert Temple 2 May 1926 PS F6.1/23

40. *WHG* Vol 8, No. 8, 10 August 1926 p. 180; *HWBJ* Part I pp. 276–282

41. Octavia to Mr and Mrs Gardner, 26 April 1926; Mrs May Gardner to Octavia 29 April 1926; Mr Gardner to Miss Green, 13 July 1926; Mrs Gardner to Miss Green 1 July 1926; Miss Green to Mr and Mrs Gardner, 16 July 1926 PS F3.3/24

42. Geoffrey Firth to Mrs Barltrop, 14 August 1926. PS F6.1/23

43. Kate and Leonard Tucker, Healing Applicants, PS A4.2/1

44. *The Rally*, No. 154, November 1927. pp. 7 and 9

Chapter 11: Family Problems

1. Adrian Barltrop to Mabel Barltrop, 24 May 1926 PS A3.5/8

2. Adrian Barltrop to Miss Mason (no date) PS A3.5/8

3. Adrian Barltrop to Mabel Barltrop 24 May 1926 PS A3.5/8

4. Adrian Barltrop to Mrs Peck, 29 July 1926 PS A3.5/8

5. Adrian Barltrop to Dilys Barltrop, 15 February 1928 PS A3.5/8

6. Adrian Barltrop to Octavia, 13 April 1928 PS A3.5/8

7. Marriage certificate for Ivan Barltrop and Violet Schvener, District of Morningside, Edinburgh. (Statutory marriages 685/070025) Violet's father was a minister; her mother had died. Her family had changed their name to Shannon, perhaps during the war.

8. Queens' College, Cambridge, archives (in possession of Chaplain)

9. Adrian Barltrop to Octavia, 13 April 1928 PS A3.5/8

10. Adrian Barltrop to Cyril Carew-Hunt, 26 June 1928 PS A3.5/7

11. Adrian Barltrop to Dilys Barltrop, 13 April 1928 PS A3.5/7

12. Adrian Barltrop to Major Carew-Hunt, 26 June 1928 PS A3.5/8

13. Adrian Barltrop to Mabel Barltrop with attached note to Dilys Barltrop, 14 June 1928 PS A3.5/7

14. Adrian Barltrop to Mabel Barltrop 10 August 1929 PS A3.5/7

15. Adrian Barltrop to Dilys Barltrop 21 May 1929, 28 May 1929 and 7 June 1929. PS A3.5/7

16. Octavia diary June 1929 PS C3.1/22

17. Octavia diary November 1929 & January 1930 PS C3.1/22

18. Adrian Barltrop to Mabel Barltrop 10 August 1929 PS A3.5/7

19. Octavia diary, 14 January 1930 PS C3.1/22

20. Adrian Barltrop to Mabel Barltrop 12 April 1928 PS A3.5/7

21. Adrian Barltrop to Dilys Barltrop 13 April 1928 PS A3.5/7

22. Dilys Barltrop to Emily Goodwin, 31 May 1929 PS A3.5/11

23. Adrian Barltrop to Mabel Barltrop 2 August 1929 PS A3.5/7

24. Adrian Barltrop to Mabel Barltrop 10 August 1929 PS A3.5/7

25. Adrian Barltrop to Octavia, 10 August 1929 PS A3.5/8

26. Six-page typescript to Major Carew-Hunt, no date PS A3.5/10

27. Adrian Barltrop to Dilys Barltrop 18 August 18 PS A3.5/7

28. 'Christian Science Home Censured' *The Times* 16 December 1929

29. Adrian Barltrop to Mabel Barltrop 29 November 1929 PS A3.5/7

30. La Panacée CSS was the healing headquarters of the first branch of the Panacea Society to be set up outside Britain. Madame Twemlow-Allen (the widow of a British soldier who had died in the war) and Monsieur Monard (a French engineer who had received the decoration of the Legion of Honor after the war) had both been Theosophists until they had become friendly with Rachel Fox and read Southcott's writings. In 1922 they arrived in Bedford and were resident in the Society until 1925 when they returned to France to set up the French 'Tower'.

31. Dilys Barltrop to the Divine Mother, August (no date) 1929 PS A3.5/13

32. Dilys Barltrop to the Divine Mother, 4 September 1929 PS A3.5/13

33. Dilys Barltrop to Emily Goodwin, 29 January 1930 PS A3.5/11

34. Dilys Barltrop to Emily Goodwin, 30 December 1929 PS A3.5/11

35. Dilys Barltrop to Emily Goodwin, 4 February 1930. PS A3.5/11

36. Dilys Barltrop to the Divine Mother, 25 January 1930 PS A3.5/13

37. Dilys Barltrop to Mabel Barltrop 11 September 1930, A3.5/11

38. Dilys Barltrop to Emily Goodwin 12 January 1930 PS A3.5/11

39. Dilys Barltrop to the Divine Mother 25 January 1930 PS A3.5/13

40. Dilys Barltrop to Emily Goodwin 12 January 1930; Dilys Barltrop to Emily Goodwin 30 December 1929 PS A3.5/11

41. Emily Goodwin to Dilys Barltrop, no date (1929); the Divine Mother to Dilys Barltrop, 5 December 1929 PS A3.5/9

42. Adrian Barltrop to Mabel Barltrop 21 January 1930 PS A3.5/17

43. Adrian Barltrop to Mabel Barltrop 21 January 1930 PS A3.5/17

44. Adrian Barltrop to Mabel Barltrop 16 August 1929 PS A3.5/17

45. Emily Goodwin to Dilys Barltrop, 28 August 1929 PS A3.5/9

46. Report to the Divine Mother, Jessie Tweedie, 21 June 1929 PS A3.5/10

47. Emily Goodwin to Dilys Barltrop, 23 January 1930 PS A3.5/9

48. Rachel Fox report of meeting with Adrian Barltrop 13 December 1929 PS F4.4/5

49. Adrian Barltrop to Octavia, 10 August 1929 PS A3.5/7

50. Author's conversation with Dennis Jones, 2002

51. Adrian Barltrop to Mabel Barltrop 21 January 1930 PS A3.5/7

52. Adrian Barltrop to Mabel Barltrop 16 August 1929 PS A3.5/17

Chapter 12: Negotiating the World

1. Mary Warry to Octavia, 12 March 1927 PS F6.4/8

2. Harold Dolphin to Miss Green, 3 May 1925 (Octavia's reply is scribbled on the back for Miss Green to type up and send) PS A3.5/11

3. Muriel Gillett to Octavia, 23 August and 1 December 1924 PS A3.5/11

4. *SASJ* pp. 27–28; and pp. 470–471. See also the Script for 16 November 1923, *WHG* Volume 5, p. 115

5. Mary Beedell to Octavia, 7 March 1923 PS F6.2/3

6. Quoted in Juliet Nicolson, *The Great Silence 1918–1920: Living in the Shadow of the Great War* (London: John Murray, 2009) p. 159

7. Wella Bauer to Panacea Society, 8 August 1924 PS F5.2/9

8. Mrs Madeline Smith to the Confidential Department, Panacea Society, 8 August 1928. F5.2/17

9. *HWBJ* Part II p. 124

10. *HWBJ* Part II pp. 469–470

11. *HWBJ* Part II pp. 455–456 and pp. 490–492

12. *HWBJ* Part III pp. 260–266

13. Adrian Barltrop to Miss Mason, 19 May 1927 PS A3.5/8

14. Lt Harold Dolphin to Octavia, 3 May 1925, and draft of reply on the back from Octavia PS F6.2/11

15. Colonel Sullivan M.B.E., 'Merrie England, *The Panacea*, Volume 2, Number 13, p.23

16. Stanley Baldwin, *On England* (London: Philip Allan & Co. Ltd, 1926) pp. 7–8. For further discussion of Englishness in this period, see Peter Mandler, *The English National Character: The History of an Idea from Edmund Burke to Tony Blair* (New Haven and London: Yale University Press, 2006), Chapter 5; and

on religion and Englishness in particular, Matthew Grimley, 'The Religion of Englishness: Puritanism, Providentialism, and "National Character," 1918–1945 *Journal of British Studies* 46 (October 2007) pp. 884–906

17. Amy Smart to Octavia, 27 April (no year) PS F5.1/30

18. Octavia to Henrietta Leach, 9 August 1922 PS F6.1/22

19. Two letters from Amy Smart to Octavia, one dated 21 March (no year), the other not dated PS F5.1/30

20. *The Panacea* Volume 3, Number 29, p. 100

21. Brenda Greig, 'The Church of England – The Premier Church of the World', *The Panacea*, Volume 2, Number 13, pp. 10–13

22. On British Israelism, see Tudor Parfitt, *The Lost Tribes of Israel, The History of a Myth* (London: Weidenfeld & Nicolson, 2002), Chapter 3

23. The Vice-President, 'The Pyramid', *The Panacea*, Volume 5, Number 50 p. 39

24. William Poole, 'Seventeenth-century Preadamism, and an Anonymous English Preadamist', *The Seventeenth Century*, Volume XIX, No. 1, Spring 2004 pp. 1–35; David N. Livingstone, 'Preadamites: The History of an Idea from Heresy to Orthodoxy', *Scottish Journal of Theology*, Vol. 40, pp. 41–66; Colin Kidd, *The Forging of Races: Race and Scripture in the Protestant Atlantic World, 1600–2000* (Cambridge University Press, 2006)

25. Kidd, *The Forging of Races* pp. 237–246

26. Rachel Fox, 'Reviews of Modern Books I' and Editor's Note [Octavia], *The Panacea*, Volume 7, Number 34, pp. 36–37

Chapter 13: Defeating the Bolshevik Menace

1. *HWBJ* Part I p. 255

2. Information on emergency sealing for Wardens, May 1926 (typescript) PS X–BOX

3. Emergency Note to the Wardens (typescript) PS X–BOX

4. Rachel Fox diary, 2 May 1926 PS C3.1/24

5. *HWBJ* Part I pp. 255, 256

6. Mary Beedell to Octavia, 6 December 1923. PS F6.2/3

7. 'Panacea Views on Legislation and on Women's Rights' in *The Panacea* Volume 2, Number 21, p. 201. Octavia wrote this under the pen name of 'Mr and Mrs Mark Proctor'.

8. *HWBJ* Part 1 p. 408

9. Editorial, *The Panacea*, Volume 1, Number 2, p. 30

10. *HWBJ* Part IV p. 297

11. Typescript circular to Panacea sealed members, October 1924 PS F2.4/18

12 'The Great Strike', *The Panacea*, Volume 3, Number 26, p. 33

13. *HWBJ* Part I pp. 368 & 369

14. *HWBJ* Part II pp. 558–559

15. *HWBJ* Part II p. 27

16. 'Newspaper Opinion must not Determine Our Opinion' *The Panacea* Volume 11, No. 126, pp. 129–130

17. *HWBJ* Part III p. 122

18. *HWBJ* Part III p. 35

19. *The Panacea*, Volume 4, Number 42, p. 139. The author was listed as R. A. Coote-Robinson.

20. Mark Proctor, *Socialism and Communism* [articles reprinted from *The Panacea*] (Bedford: The Panacea Society, no date) p. 12

21. 'Panacea Views on Legislation and on Women's Rights' pp. 198–199

22. 'What is Wrong?', *The Panacea*, Volume 3, Number 35 p. 250

23. *HWBJ* Part II p. 412

24. 'Panacea Protection from International Hypnotism', *The Panacea*, Volume 3,

25. See *England, the Remnant of Judah* (London, 1861) and J. C. Stevens, *Genealogical Chart Showing the Connection Between the House of David and the Royal Family of Britain* (Liverpool, 1877)

26. *HWBJ* Part IV p. 288

27. *HWBJ* Part I p. 286

28. *HWBJ* vol. 2 p. 380

29. List of Spiritual Cabinet Members PS F2.4/18

30. 'The Mission from a Political Standpoint: why a Labour Government is in Power', typescript paper written between 1929 and 1931 PS F2.4/18

31. *The Panacea* Volume 6, No. 64, p. 75

32. Circular Letter to supporters of the CPM, September 1932 PS F1.2/14

33. *HWBJ* Part III pp. 59–63 and 132

34. *HWBJ* Part II p. 42

35. *HWBJ* Part IV p. 298

36. *HWBJ* Part IV p. 301

37. *HWBJ* Part IV p. 313

38. *HWBJ* Part III p. 88

39. Mark Proctor, 'Buy British', *The Panacea* Volume 8, Number 93, p. 198 and 'Buy British' 'Be British' *The Panacea* Volume 8, Number 93, pp. 198–199

40. 'Buy British' 'Be British' The Tudor Rose League" *The Panacea* Volume 9, Number 99 p. 64

41. Octavia to Admiral Mark Kerr, 29 November 1931 (proof typescript letter) PS F2.4/33
42. *The Tudor Rose League: the Movement Explained.* Leaflet No. 1
43. 'Buy British', *The Panacea* Volume 8, Number 93, p. 198
44. See Richard Overy, *The Morbid Age* p. 369
45. Irene Mellor, 'Pen Pictures from Panacea People: Early Days of Fascismo', *The Panacea*, Volume 1, Number 8, p. 184
46. *HWBJ* Part I pp. 259 & 260, 261–2.
47. W S Galpin to Octavia, no date 1929 PS F1.12/15
48. Octavia to Col. Oscar Boulton, 26 November 1929, PS F.1.2/15
49. Cyril Carew-Hunt to Captain R. Smith, Secretary of the Unity Band, 28 April 28 1931 PS F1.2/15. On the Unity Band, see Thomas Linehan, *British Fascism, 1918–1939: Parties, Ideology and Culture* (Manchester University Press, 2000) especially pp. 133–136. On small fascist groups prior to Mosley's BUF, see Martin Pugh, *Hurrah for the Blackshirts. Fascists and Fascism in Britain Between the Wars* (London: Jonathan Cape, 2005) especially Chapter 5
50. Octavia, *Instruction*, December 1932, PS F1.2/10
51. *WHG* Volume 14, Number 2, December 8 and 9, 1932, pp. 328–329
52. PS F2.4/38

Chapter 14: Open the Box!

1. Alice Seymour, *Southcott Despatch*, 34, December 1921, pp. 2–3. The seven seals was a reference to Revelation 5: 1.
2. 'The Council of the National Laboratory are of the opinion that this will be a good opportunity of disposing of all existing Joanna Southcott Boxes and they therefore extend a cordial Invitation to your Association to have the so-called "Great Box" opened at the same time.' Harry Price to RJF 28 June 1927 PS C1.4/2.
3. Emily Jowett to Octavia, 6 July 1927 PS F2.2/21
4. Randall Davidson Papers 485ff. 229–277, Lambeth Palace Library
5. Copy of letter from Rachel Fox to Bishop of London, 1916 PS F6.1/8
6. Rachel Fox to Boyd-Carpenter, June 3, 1917; Boyd-Carpenter to Rachel Fox, 5 June 1917 PS F6.1/8
7. Rachel Fox to Boyd-Carpenter, 22 July 1917; Boyd-Carpenter to Rachel Fox, 27 July 1917 PS F6.1/8
8. Rachel Fox to Queen Mary, 4 August 1918; Edward Wallington, private secretary to H.M. the Queen, to Rachel Fox, 9 August 1918 PS F6.1/8
9. Ellen Oliver to Mabel Barltrop 19 March 1919; Mabel Barltrop to Ellen

Oliver, 22 March 1919; Mabel Barltrop to Ellen Oliver 28 June 1919 PS F4.2/4; PS F4.2/3

10. Commercial advertising agent for the Metropolitan District Railway Company, London Electric Railway Company, City & South London Railway Company, and Central London Railway Company to Kate Firth, 1 December 1923 PS F1.2/24

11. *The Panacea*, Vol. 2, Number 19, pp. 157–160

12. Joanna Southcott, *Second Book of Visions* (August 1803) pp. 33–34 and *An Explanation of the Parables* (1804) No, 34, pp. 48–9

13. Mary Beedell to Panacea Society, 9 October 1923 F6.2/3

14. See *Transactions of the Panacea Society with the Archbishops and Bishops of the Church of England* (London: The Panacea Society, n.d.) p. 53

15. *Daily Graphic*, 27 July 1923; *Evening Telegraph Dundee*, 28 July 1923

16. See *Transactions of the Panacea Society with the Archbishops and Bishops of the Church of England* (London: The Panacea Society, n.d.) passim

17. *Transactions* p. 54; also reprinted in Octavia, *Healing for All* p. 116

18. *Healing for All* p. 116

19. For an analysis of the Cottingley Fairies episode, see Alex Owen, "Borderland Forms"; Arthur Conan Doyle, Albion's Daughters, and the Politics of the Cottingley Fairies', *History Workshop Journal,* Issue 38, 1994, pp. 48–85

20. 'Life and Letters: O Bishops, Save Us!' in *The Nation and Athenaeum*, 21 October 1922, pp. 114–116

21. Printed letter from Alice Seymour to her followers, August 1923 PS F6.1/14

22. Alice Seymour, letter to the *Royal Cornwall Gazette*, 20 February 1924

23. Alice Seymour to Rachel Fox, 24 July 1920 PS F6.1/3

24. Alice Seymour to Miss Teasdale, 5 January 1922 PS F6.1/4

25. A. Garnham to Hilda Green, no year, PS F6.2/4

26. Christian Temple to Alice Seymour, no date PS F6.1/4

27. *The Southcott Express*, No. 4 December 1926, eds. Alice Seymour and Mary S. Robertson, pp. 93–94

28. *The Southcott Express*, No. 4, December 1926 p. 94

29. *Daily News*, 29 April 1925. The event was reported in national and local newspapers: see PS C2.1/1.

30. Harry Price, *Leaves from a Psychist's Case-Book* (London: Victor Gollancz, 1933) pp. 287–289. Trevor Hall argues that the letter making this claim was a forgery by Price to obtain publicity for the Box. Trevor A. Hall, *The Search for Harry Price* (London: Duckworth, 1978)

31. *Radio Times* 3 February 1928

32. Octavia to Cecil Goodhall, 28 July 1927 PS F1.2/16

33. Letter from Roger Garth Hooper of Whitchurch in Shropshire to the Archbishop of Canterbury, 29 July 1960, and reply from the Archbishop's office to Hooper, 30 July 1960. Lambeth Palace Library, Fisher Papers, Vol. 356, ff. 224–5. George K. A. Bell, *Randall Davidson, Archbishop of Canterbury*, 3 vols. (London: Oxford University Press, 1935) pp. 1193–1210

34. *The Patriot*, no. 705, Vol. xxxix, 15 August 1935, pp. 132–133

35. WHG Vol 12, Part 2, December 31, 1930, p. 318

36. HWBJ Part III p. 362

37. HWBJ Part III pp. 364–365

38. Octavia to Willoughby Rokeby, 21 December 1931. PS F2.4/25

39. See the correspondence in PS F1.3/1

40. HWBJ Part IV p. 159

41. Condition 14 in the list of 20 conditions, stated in *Healing for All*, pp. 117–118

42. PS F2.1/4

43. 'Information and Suggestions in Preparation for the Opening of the Box', typed ms. 1934, possibly but not necessarily sent to Cecil K. Jowett. PS F2.1/2

44. Addendum to the *Transactions* p. 129

Chapter 15: The Church

1. *Healing for All* p. 18

2. Hilda Green, notebook PS F2.1/11

3. 'The Progress of the Work', WHG, Vol. 2, Part 2, p. 383

4. Hilda Green, diary entry, November 21, 1927 PS C3.1/13

5. Octavia, *The Lifeboat to the Rescue of the Sinking Church* (PS booklet, 1923) p. 11

6. HWBJ Part I pp. 90–92

7. HWBJ Part I p. 210

8. HWBJ Part I pp. 435–6

9. M. S. Warry to Hilda Green 17 February 1925 PS F6.4/8

10. The Archdeacon of Worcester (the Ven. J. H. F. Peile), 'The Working of the Holy Spirit', *The Guardian*, June 5, 1925, p. 508

11. 'Important Communication Connected with Present Crisis (Addressed to the Rural Deans of the Church of England)', May 1921. PS pamphlet

12. Kelly's Directory Cambridgeshire, 1929

13. Lawrence Iggulden to the Panacea Society, 15 June 1921 PS F6.1/19

14. Lawrence Iggulden to the Panacea Society, 18 November 1921 PS F6.1/19

15. Lawrence Iggulden to the Panacea Society, 10 June 1923 PS F6.1/19

16. Lawrence Iggulden to Octavia, 30 July 1923 PS F6.1/19

17. Lawrence Iggulden to Octavia, 1 September 1923 PS F6.1/19

18. Lawrence Iggulden to Octavia, 17, April 1926 PS F6.1/19

19. Lawrence Iggulden to Octavia, 8 August 1923 PS F6.1/19

20. This was the Caxton and Arrington Union Workhouse, at the northern end of the village of Caxton. Built in 1836–7 it was designed to accommodate 160 people; it closed in 1932.

21. Lawrence Iggulden to Octavia 8 August 1923 & August 14, 1923. PS F6.1/19

22. Lawrence Iggulden to Octavia 8 August 1923 PS F6.1/19

23. Octavia to Lawrence Iggulden 15 August 1923, in Copy Book of Letters from Octavia, August 1923–April 1924 p. 18 PS F3.3/25

24. Lawrence Iggulden to Octavia 18 August 1923 PS F6.1/19

25. Lawrence Iggulden to Octavia 1 September 1923 PS F6.1/19

26. Lawrence Iggulden to Octavia 8 August 1923. PS F6.1/19

27. Lawrence Iggulden to Octavia 18 August 1923. PS F6.1/19

28. Lawrence Iggulden to Octavia December 1924 (no date) PS F6.1/19

29. Message commanded to be sent to the Revd L Iggulden. 14 November 1924 PS F6.1/19

30. Lawrence Iggulden to Octavia 18 November 1924 PS F6.1/19

31. Lawrence Iggulden to Octavia 23 August 1923 PS F6.1/19

32. Edward T. Woollard to Lawrence Iggulden, 3 December 1923 PS F6.1/19

33. Panacea Society Baptismal Register PS F3.3/15

34. Author's conversation with John Coghill, 13 February 2004

35. Lawrence Iggulden to Hilda Green 9 October 1925 PS F6.1/19

36. Martin Pugh, *We Danced All Night*, Chapter 12.

37. Lawrence Iggulden to Hilda Green, 22 June 1925 PS F 6.1/19

38. *SASJ* pp. 168–9

39. *HWBJ* Part II pp. 68–69, 75–77

40. *HWBJ* Part I p. 447

41. *The Panacea*, Vol. 4, No. 45, pp. 198–199; No. 46, pp. 224–227; No. 48, pp. 271–273

42. *The Panacea*, Vol. 4, No. 48, p. 273

43. *HWBJ* Part I p. 447

44. *HWBJ* Part I p. 477

45. H.R.L. Sheppard, *The Impatience of a Parson: A Plea for the Recovery of Vital Christianity* (London: Hodder and Stoughton, 1927) p. 156

46. *HWBJ* Part I p. 451

47. *HWBJ* Part I pp. 452–456

48. Mark Proctor [Octavia], *The Impatience of the People: A Reply to 'The Impatience of a Parson'* (London: Cecil Palmer, 1928) p. 10

49. *HWBJ* Part I p. 477

50. Miss M. Hayward to Panacea Society, 9 September 1928. PS F2.2/43

51. Mrs Margaret Morton to Panacea Society, 5 March 1928; PS to Mrs Margaret Morton, 10 March 1928. PS F2.2/43

52. Admiral Sir Arthur Limpus to 'Mark Proctor', 19 September 1928 PS F2.2/43

53. Mr F. W. Lyons to Panacea Society, 29 January 1928 PS F2.2/43

54. A. Findell to Panacea Society, 14 March 1928. PS F2.2/43

55. Mrs A. K. Woodward to Panacea Society, 7 February 1928 PS F2.2/43

56. Hilda Green to Mrs A. K. Woodward, 8 March 1928. PS F 2.2/43

57. Revd E. W. Freeman to Panacea Society, 23 March 1928 PS F2.2/43

58. H. E. L. Russell to Panacea Society, 23 February 1928 PS F2.2/43

59. Barrington Philpots to Panacea Society, 4 September 1928 PS F2.2/43

60. Hilda Green to Russell Payne, 7 May 1928 PS F5.1/24

61. Octavia to Russell Payne, 11 July 1929 PS F5.1/24

62. Octavia to Russell Payne, 11 July 1929 PS F5.1/24

63. Mary Payne to the Divine Mother 28 October and 26 December 1928; Russell Payne to the Divine Mother, 1 January 1930. For details of Russell Payne's life, see also his 'Reminiscences', 31 December 1933 PS F5.1/24

Chapter 16: Death, after all

1. Peter Rasmussen diary 1934 PS C4.5/2

2. Emily Goodwin, 'Letter written to the Scottish Branch', November 1934. PS F2.1/28

3. 'Some extracts from the words of the Divine Mother, spoken to those at HQ since 16 October' PS F2.1/28

4. Rachel Fox to Irene Mellor, 20 October 1934 PS F2.1/28

5. Rachel Fox to Irene Mellor, 20 October 1934, PS F2.1/28 and Peter Rasmussen diary 1934 PS C4.5/2

6. EG (Confidential Department) letter to Panacea non-resident members re: Octavia's death. No date – October 1934 PS F2.1/28

7. Mildred Hollingworth, 'Account of the final year of Octavia's life' (ms.) PS F3.5/2

8. Peter Rasmussen diary 1934 PS C4.5/2

9. Ellen Oliver to Octavia, 8 August 1919; Ellen Oliver to Octavia, 5 August 1919. PS F4.2/4 and F4.2/5

10. *SASJ* p. 172 and Chapter VII passim

11. *HWBJ* Part I p. 324

12. *The Flock* PS F2.2/29

13. *WHG* Volume 2, Number 1, 19 June 1920 pp. 33–34. Octavia had asked God whether Uranus represented the heavens, and the Lord replied: 'Uranus hath upon it Immortal Beings, but perplex not thy mind, simplicity is all I need.'

14. Peter Rasmussen diary 1934 PS C4.5/2

15. Secession letter, Scottish Branch, October 1935 PS F2.1/8

Epilogue

1. Interview with Ruth Klein in *Maidens of the Lost Ark* documentary, shown on Channel 4 television in Britain, 2003.

2. From 2003 to 2010, there have been 266 British applicants, twelve from the British West Indies and twenty from the USA.

3. The greatest number of applicants has come from the British West Indies – 41,510; the USA – 38,800; and the United Kingdom – 25,050.

Bibliography

Published Sources

Gordon Allan, 'Southcottian's Sects from 1790 to the Present Day' in *Expecting the End: Millennialism in Social and Historical context*. Eds. Kenneth G. Newport and Cranford Gribben (Waco, TX Baylor University Press, 2006)

Russell H. Anderson, 'The Shaker Community in Florida', *Florida Historical Quarterly*, Volume 38, Issue 1, July 1959

Stanley Baldwin, *On England* (London: Philip Allan, 1926)

J. A. Banks, *Prosperity and Parenthood: A Study of Family Planning Among the Victorian Middle Classes* (London, Routledge & Kegan Paul, 1954)

Mrs A. H. Barltrop, 'To Mothers and Headmasters', *Mothers in Council*, 95 (1914) p. 133–133

R. D. Baxter, *National Income: The United Kingdom* (London, 1868)

Caitriona Beaumont, 'Moral Dilemmas and Women's Rights: The Attitude of the Mothers' Union and Catholic Women's League to Divorce, Birth Control and Abortion in England, 1928–1939', *Women's History Review*, 16: 4 (2007) 463–465

George K. A. Bell, *Randall Davidson, Archbishop of Canterbury*, 3 vols (London: Oxford University Press, 1935)

Besma [Mabel Barltrop], *Brushes with the Bishops* (London: Cecil Palmer & Hayward, 1919)

Frances Brown, *Joanna Southcott's Box of Sealed Prophecies* (Cambridge: The Letterworth Press, 2006)

F. W. Bullock, *A History of the Training for the Ministry of the Church of England in England and Wales from 1875– 1974* (London: Home Words, 1976)

Owen Chadwick, *The Victorian Church, Volume II* (London: A. & C. Black, 1970)

Deborah Cohen, *Household Gods: The British and their Possessions* (New Haven and London: Yale University Press, 2006)

Cynthia Curran, *When I First Began my Life Anew: Middle-class Widows in Nineteenth-Century Britain* (Bristol, Indiana: Wyndham Hall Press, 2000)

Patrick Curry, *A Confusion of Prophets: Victorian and Edwardian Astrology* (London: Collins & Brown, 1992)

Percy Dearmer, *The Parson's Handbook* (London: Grant Richards, 1899)

Jacqueline R. deVries, 'Transforming the Pulpit: Preaching and Prophecy in the British Women's Suffrage Movement', in *Women Preachers and Prophets through Two Millennia of Christianity* (University of California Press, 1998)

Joy Dixon, *Divine Feminine: Theosophy and Feminism in England* (Baltimore: John Hopkins University Press, 2001)

J. Embry, *The Catholic Movement and the Society of the Holy Cross* (London, The Faith Press, 1931)

England Awake! (Bedford: The Panacea Society, 1935)

Alison Falby, 'The Modern Confessional: Anglo-American Religious Groups and the Emergence of Lay Psychotherapy', *Journal of History of the Behavioural Sciences*, Vol. 39 3 (Summer 2003), pp. 251–267

Roy Foster, *W. B Yeats, A Life Vol. II: The Arch Poet 1915–1939* (Oxford University Press, 2003)

Rachel J. Fox, *The Finding of Shiloh, Or the Mystery of God 'Finished'* (London: Cecil Palmer, 1921)

Rachel J. Fox, *The Sufferings and Acts of Shiloh-Jerusalem* (London: Cecil Palmer, 1927)

Rachel J. Fox, *How We Built Jerusalem in England's Green and Pleasant Land* (London: Cecil Palmer, 1931); Part II (Bedford: The Garden Press, 1934); Part III (Bedford: The Garden Press, 1937); Part IV (Bedford: The Garden Press, 1938)

Rachel J. Fox, *More Rays of the Dawn or Teachings on Some Old Testament Problems* (London: Keegan Paul, Trench, Timbner & Co. Ltd, 1918)

Rachel J. Fox, *Revelation on Revelation and these Latter Days* (London: Keegan Paul, Trench, Timbner & Co. and New York: EP Dutton & Co. 1916)

Rachel J. Fox, *Unexpected Tidings of the War and of the Future* (London: Keegan Paul, Trench, Timbner & Co. Ltd, 1918)

Ruth E. Gordon, *Shepstone: The Role of the Family in the History of South Africa, 1820 – 1900* (Cape Town: A.A. Balkema, 1968)

Matthew Grimley, 'The Religion of Englishness: Puritanism, Providentialism, and "National Character", 1918 – 1945, *Journal of British Studies*, 46 (October 2007) pp. 884 – 906

Trevor A. Hall, *The Search for Harry Price* (London: Duckworth, 1978)

Roy Hattersley, *Borrowed Time: The Story of Britain Between the Wars* (London: Little, Brown, 2007)

K. Theodore Hoppen, *The Mid-Victorian Generation* (Oxford University Press, 1998)

Matt Houlbrook, *Queer London: Perils and Pleasures in the Sexual Metropolis, 1918–57* (University of Chicago Press, 2005)

Ellic Howe, *Urania's Children: The Strange World of the Astrologers* (London, 1967)

Leslie Howsam, 'Orme, Eliza (1848 – 1937)', *Oxford Dictionary of National Biography* (Oxford University Press, 2004)

Ignatius and Candida (Octavia), *Letters from Angel-Land* (London: Cecil Palmer, 1919)

Colin Kidd, *The Forging of Races. Race and Scripture in the Protestant Atlantic World, 1600–2000* (Cambridge: Cambridge University Press, 2006)

Pamela E. Klassen, 'Radio Mind: Experimentalists on the Frontiers of Healing' in *Journal of the American Academy of Religion*, 75, No. 3 (September 2007), pp. 651 – 683

Rene Kollar, 'Power and Control over Women in Victorian England: Male Opposition to Sacramental Confession in the Anglican Church', *Journal of Anglican Studies*, 3, no. 1 (2005) pp. 11– 32

Timothy Larsen, *Christabel Pankhurst: Fundamentalism and Feminism in Coalition* (Woodbridge, Suffolk: The Boydell Press, 2002)

Hermione Lee, *Virginia Woolf* (London: Vintage, 1997)

'Life and Letters: O Bishops, Save Us!', *The Nation and Athenaeum*, 21 October 1922, pp. 114 – 116

Alison Light, *Forever England: Femininity, Literature and Conservatism Between the Wars* (London: Routledge, 1991)

Thomas Linehan, *British Fascism, 1918–1939: Parties, Ideology and Culture* (Manchester University Press, 2000)

David N. Livingstone, 'Preadamites: The History of an Idea from Heresy to Orthodoxy', *Scottish Journal of Theology*, 40, pp. 41 – 66

Kathryn Lofton, 'Queering Fundamentalism: John Balcom Shaw and the Sexuality of a Protestant Orthodoxy', *Journal of the History of Sexuality*, 17, No. 3 (September 2008) pp. 439 – 468

Peter Mandler, *The English National Character: The History of an Idea from Edmund Burke to Tony Blair* (New Haven and London: Yale University Press, 2006)

Flora Masson, *Victorians All* (London and Edinburgh: W. & R. Chambers, 1931)

(ed.) G. R. S. Mead, Pistis Sophia (London: John. M. Watkins, 1921)

Rosemary Mitchell, 'Mackonochie, Alexander Heriot (1825–1887)', *Oxford Dictionary of National Biography* (Oxford University Press, 2004) [http://www.oxforddnb.com/view/article/17627]

Frederic W. H. Myers, 'Automatic Writing or the Rationale of Planchette', *Contemporary Review*, 42 (1885)

Virginia Nicholson, *Singled Out: How Two Million Women Survived without Men After the First World War* (London: Viking, 2007)

Juliet Nicolson, *The Great Silence 1918–1920. Living in the Shadow of the Great War* (London: John Murray, 2009)

Octavia, *Healing for All: The Story of the Greatest Discovery of Any Age* (London: The Panacea Society, 1925)

Octavia, *Lifeboat to the Rescue of the Sinking Church* (Bedford: Panacea Society, 1923)

Octavia, *Octavia's Early Years* (published for private circulation by James H. Keys, Plymouth, no date)

Octavia, *Wrong at the Root, Or the Bishop's Chaplain* (Bedford: The Panacea Society, 1929)

Octavia, *The Rest House or The Bishop's Secret* (Bedford: The Panacea Society, 1934)

Octavia, *The Writings of the Holy Ghost*, volumes 1–16 (Bedford: The Panacea Society)

Janet Oppenheimer, *'Shattered Nerves': Doctors, Patients and Depression in Victorian England* (Oxford University Press, 1991)

Revd B. Ottley, Preface to *Theological Colleges: Their Aim and Spirit. Illustrated by Two Sermons . . . by the Rev. R. C. Moberly and Rev. E. S. Talbot* (Salisbury, 1881)

Richard Overy, *The Morbid Age: Britain Between the Wars* (London: Allen Lane, 2009)

Alex Owen, 'Borderland Forms: Arthur Conan Doyle, Albion's Daughters and the Politics of the Cottingley Fairies', *History Workshop Journal*, Issue 38, 1994, pp. 48–85

Alex Owen, *The Darkened Room: Women, Power and Spiritualism in Late Nineteenth-century England* (London: Virago Press, 1989)

The Panacea, volumes 1–11 (Bedford: The Panacea Society)

Tudor Parfitt, *The Lost Tribes of Israel: The History of a Myth* (London: Weidenfeld & Nicolson, 2002)

Judith Pettigrew, Rory W. Reynolds and Sandra Rouse, *A Place in the County: Three Counties Asylum* (Bedford: Bedfordshire Community Health Care, 1998)

Paul Peucker, 'Inspired by Flames of Love': Homosexuality, Mysticism, and Moravian Brothers around 1750', *Journal of the History of Sexuality*, 15, No. 1 (2006), pp. 30–64

William Poole, 'Seventeenth-century Preadamism, and an Anonymous English Preadamist', *The Seventeenth Century*, 19, No. 1 (Spring 2004), pp. 1–35

Harry Price, *Leaves from a Psychist's Case-Book* (London: Victor Gollancz, 1933)

Mark Proctor [Octavia], *The Impatience of the People: A Reply to 'The Impatience of a Parson'* (London: Cecil Palmer, 1928)

Martin Pugh, *Hurrah for the Blackshirts: Fascists and Fascism in Britain Between the Wars* (London: Jonathan Cape, 2005)

Martin Pugh, *We Danced All Night: A Social History of Britain between the Wars* (London: The Bodley Head, 2008)

Sheila Rowbotham, *Edward Carpenter: A Life of Liberty and Love* (London and New York: Verso, 2008)

Anne Saddlemyer, *Becoming George: The Life of Mrs W. B. Yeats* (Oxford University Press, 2002)

R. S. Sayers, *Gilletts in the London Money Market 1867–1967*, (Oxford: Clarendon Press 1968)

ed. Alice Seymour and Mary S. Robertson, *The Southcott Express* No. 4, December 1926

Alice Seymour, *The Voice in the Wilderness* (Ashford, Middlesex: Clockhouse Press, 1933)

H. R. L. Sheppard, *The Impatience of a Parson: A Plea for the Recovery of Vital Christianity* (London: Hodder & Stoughton, 1927)

G. G. Smith, 'Masson, David Mather (1822 – 1907)' revised by, Sondra Miley Clooney, *Oxford Dictionary of National Biography* (Oxford University Press, 2004)

Jeffrey Smith, *Where the Roots Meet for Water. A Personal and Natural History of Melancholia* (New York: North Point Press 2001)

Joanna Southcott, *An Explanation of the Parables* (1804)

Joanna Southcott, *Second Book of Visions* (1803)

Roger T. Stearn, 'Stanton, Arthur Henry (1839–1913)', *Oxford Dictionary of National Biography*, Oxford University Press, 2004 [http://www.oxford dnb.com/view/article/36254]

Audrey M. Taylor, *Gilletts, Bankers at Banbury and Oxford: A Study in Local Economic History* (Oxford: Clarendon Press, 1964)

Matthew Thomson, *Psychological Subjects. Identity, Culture and Health in Twentieth-Century Britain* (Oxford: Oxford University Press, 2006)

Gregory Tillett, *The Elder Brother: A Biography of Charles Webster Leadbeater* (London: Routledge & Kegan Paul, 1982)

John Tosh, *A Man's Place: Masculinity and the Middle-Class Home in Victorian England* (New Haven and London: Yale University Press, 1999)

Transactions of the Panacea Society with the Archbishops and Bishops of the Church of England (London: The Panacea Society, no date)

Aaron Spencer Vogleman, *Jesus is Female: Moravians and Radical Religion in Early America* (Philadelphia: University of Pennsylvania Press, 2008)

Judith R. Walkowitz, *City of Dreadful Delight: Narratives of Sexual Danger in Late-Victorian London* (Chicago: The University of Chicago Press, 1992)

A Watcher [Rachel Fox], *Rays of the Dawn: Fresh Teaching on New Testament Problems* (London: Kegan Paul, Trench, Trubner & Co., 1912)

Sara Weber Rea, *The Koreshan Story* (Estero, Florida: Guiding Star Publishing House, 1994)

Michael Woorboys, 'Bastian, (Henry) Charlton (1837 – 1915)' *Oxford Dictionary of National Biography* (Oxford University Press, 2004)'

Unpublished Sources

Case notes No. 6846 for Minnie Oppenheim, St Andrew's Hospital Archives

Case notes No. 7586 for Mabel Barltrop, St Andrew's Hospital Archives

Case notes No. 9972 for Mabel Barltrop, Three Counties Asylum (Bedfordshire County Archives)

Davidson Papers, Volume 485, f. 242, Lambeth Palace Archives

Philip J. Lockley, 'Millenarian Religion and Radical Politics in Britain 1815– 1835: A Study of Southcottians after Southcott' (D. Phil. thesis, University of Oxford, 2009)

Panacea Society Archives (PS)

Acknowledgements

First and foremost, my thanks go to the members of the Panacea Society for trusting me with their story. They were generous at every turn in allowing me full access to their archive. Very few historians have a chance to excavate an archive and write the history of a little known community: it is a rare privilege. I offer my sincere thanks to Ruth Klein and Gladys Powell for talking with me about their lives as Panaceans. Ruth Klein offered generous hospitality on numerous occasions at the Panacea Society and provided tea and sustenance during many long days in the archives. I am very grateful to the Society's administrator, David McLynn, who gave me advice and help throughout the researching and writing of this book, especially in the excavation of the archive, and shared my excitement about the discovery of the Panaceans' story. Gordon Allan, a Panacea Society Trustee, has an unparalleled knowledge of the various Southcottian groups, and has been exceptionally generous in sharing his knowledge with me, saving me from making various errors. He has been a delightful conversation partner, and kindly read a draft of the book and gave me invaluable feedback. I remember with profound gratitude the help given to me by the late John Coghill, who joined the Society in 1934 and was a faithful member until his death in 2008. My conversations with him gave me a sense of the Society and its ethos that could only be gained from someone who had been a Panacean for so long.

Several Panacea relatives were very helpful along the way. Rachel Fox's grandson, David Laity, and his wife Eileen, talked to me for several hours about Rachel; and her great grandson, Charles Fox, kindly gave me a tour of Glendurgan, her beautiful home near Falmouth. Anna Thomas has been a great support throughout: she offered all that she knew about her grandmother Mabel and the Barltop family, and she and Evan have been gracious hosts in Australia on several occasions. I am delighted to know them.

Several institutions have been very generous in their support of the writing of this book. New College, Oxford, where I was Dean of Divinity and Fellow, granted me three periods of sabbatical, and offered the most congenial atmosphere and interesting colleagues that anyone could wish for. I am exceptionally grateful for my nine years as a fellow there. It is a remarkable place. I began writing this book as a visiting scholar at Trinity College at the University of Melbourne, and I thank Don Markwell, Ross Fishburn and Andrew McGowan for their warm hospitality in 2005. A month's residence at the Rockefeller Center, on the shores of Lake Como in Bellagio, a place of incomparable beauty and great scholarly company, remains a wonderful memory of productive thinking and writing, and stimulating conversations. The Humanities Research Center at the Australian National University (ANU) gave me a generous fellowship in 2006 and it was there that I was able to work out what a biography of a community might look like. Surrounded by scholars working on life writing, I learnt much from them, especially the then director of the Center, and master biographer, Ian Donaldson. A return visit to ANU to run a conference on collective biography with Paul Pickering in 2008 enabled immensely useful conversations with an even larger circle of scholars engaged in this enterprise, and I am particularly grateful to Richard Holmes and Peter Rose for their time in discussing with me how to write certain sections of this book.

I have given papers and lectures on parts of the book at ANU, the University of Melbourne, UC Berkeley, the University of Oxford, New York University and the Center for Lesbian and Gay Studies in Berkeley. I am grateful to my hosts and audiences in all of those places for their responses, suggestions and constructive criticism, all of which have helped me shape the book.

Members of the Prophecy Project, a research project on Southcott and the Southcottian prophets, which I co-directed with my colleague Chris Rowland at the University of Oxford from 2003 to 2011, engaged in many wide-ranging and stimulating conversations about prophecy and millennarianism, and I am grateful to the researchers, graduate students and postdoctoral fellows of that Project for their comments on several chapters of this book. It has been a total joy to work with Chris Rowland, friend and colleague, who encouraged me in the writing of this book at every turn, and provided wisdom, advice and support on numerous occasions.

Several friends read drafts of the early chapters, giving me invaluable feedback at an early stage, and I offer them my thanks: Miranda Curtis, Carla Hesse, Tom Laqueur, Vincent Strudwick, Donna Tartt and Sandie Taylor. Many other friends and colleagues have helped me along the way, and I am grateful for their support. Hermione Lee, my colleague at New College, shared her insight and experience as a biographer, and asked me pertinent and perceptive questions over many cups of tea. Michael Burden visited the Panacea Society with me and offered valuable insights at an early stage in the project. Kate Shuttleworth did valuable work as my research assistant in the early days of my research for this book, especially in beginning to excavate the Panacea archives. Marilyn and Bob Adams engaged in numerous conversations about this book over many delicious meals. Their intellectual companionship and hospitality have been important and sustaining over many years. Ruth Harris, a fellow historian at New College, always asked at exactly the right moment how the project was going, and genuinely wanted to know. Tamson Pietsch offered frequent encouragement and brought her own interest in Greater Britain and transnational networks to bear on the 'Going Global' chapter. Carla Hesse and Tom Laqueur offered food, wine and much good conversation on many occasions, especially during the five months I spent as a visiting professor in the history department at U C Berkeley in 2009, when this project was drawing to a close. Phyllis Mack, as ever, asked the right questions about women and religion, and offered her wisdom. Fredrica Harris Thompsett's kindness and intellectual advice have been important throughout. Natalie Zemon Davis, with her customary generosity of spirit, engaged in several stimulating conversations about the Panaceans. Ann Pellegrini talked to me at length about the book, offering her shrewd insight and, in particular, giving me very helpful comments on Chapter 7. Martha Baer read the whole manuscript just as I was finishing it, and encouraged me greatly by liking it so much. Paul Fromberg, artist and priest, designed the book cover, conjuring up just the right sense of the extraordinary in the ordinary, for which many thanks. In the last stages of checking and sending off the proofs, my Grace Cathedral colleagues Bruce Bearden and Lori Coleman offered invaluable support.

Dan Franklin has been the finest of editors: he enthused about the project and then gave me the space and time to write the book, applying just the right amount of pressure to get me over the final hurdle. Gill Coleridge is the finest of agents: calm, kind, reassuring, encouraging and enthusiastic. I couldn't have wished for better support and guidance than that which I have received from both Dan and Gill. I feel enormously fortunate to have worked with them both on this project. Tom Avery, assistant editor at Jonathan Cape, has been consistently kind and patient and I am most grateful to him for his help.

Three people were absolutely essential to the writing of this book. Philip Lockley, my doctoral student, was my research assistant for several years. The organisation of the Panacea archives is largely his work: he employed physical labour in hauling cartons and boxes up from cellars, as well as intelligence and shrewdness in knowing how to catalogue the materials. On many occasions, he helped me to piece together the Panaceans' story and draw out connections between them. His generous spirit and fine abilities as an historian were invaluable. Sara Miles read not one but two drafts of this book, offering sound advice at every turn, discussing both the big picture and the smallest of details, quite beyond the demands of friendship. That she 'got' the book was enormously encouraging at a critical moment in its writing; that she applied her fine editing skills to two of its drafts has made it an infinitely better book. I offer my thanks for her kindness and friendship. Sarah Ogilvie has listened to me talk about this book since its inception. She read (multiple) drafts of chapters as I wrote them and helped me think through how to shape the book as a whole. She got to know the Panaceans almost as well as I did and has been my constant conversation partner, always asking the perfect question about them at the moment when I most needed it. Her emotional intelligence and intellectual curiosity helped me understand the Panaceans and their world more than she perhaps realises. It is to her that I dedicate this book.

Index